American Foreign Policy

American Foreign Policy

The Dynamics of Choice in the 21st Century

BRUCE W. JENTLESON

Duke University

W. W. NORTON & COMPANY
NEW YORK • LONDON

The text of this book is composed in Minion with the display set in Bauer Bodoni.
Composition by TSI Graphics
Manufacturing by Maple-Vail Book Manufacturing
Book design by Jack Meserole

ACKNOWLEDGMENTS

Copyright © July 11, 1983, *U.S. News & World Report:* Visit us at our Web site at
www.usnews.com for additional information.
Paterson, Thomas G., Clifford, Garry, and Hagan, Kenneth J., *American Foreign Relations.*
Copyright © 1995 by D.C. Heath and Company. Adapted with permission of Houghton Mifflin
Company.
Robert S. McNamara. From *In Retrospect* by Robert S. McNamara. Copyright © 1995 by Robert
S. McNamara. Reprinted by permission of Times Books, a division of Random House, Inc.
Copyright © 1998 by the New York Times Co. Reprinted by permission.
Copyright © 1996, the *Washington Post.* Reprinted with permission.
Reprinted with the permission of the Carnegie Commission on Preventing Deadly Conflict.
Copyright © 1996 by the New York Times Co. Reprinted by permission.
Copyright © 1996, the *Washington Post.* Reprinted with permission.
Copyright © 1996 by Stacy Sullivan. Originally printed in the *Washington Post.* Reprinted here
with permission from Stacy Sullivan.

Library of Congress Cataloging-in-Publication Data
Jentleson, Bruce W., 1951–
    American foreign policy : the dynamics of choice in the 21st century / Bruce W. Jentleson.
        p. cm.
    Includes bibliographical references and index.
    ISBN 0-393-97478-2 (pbk.)
    1. United States—Foreign relations—1989– 2. United States—Foreign relations—1989–
—Forecasting. I. Title.
E840.J46 1999
327.73—DC21   99-29686

W. W. Norton & Company, Inc., 500 Fifth Avenue, New York, N.Y. 10110
www.wwnorton.com
W. W. Norton & Company Ltd., 10 Coptic Street, London WCIA 1PU

2 3 4 5 6 7 8 9 0

To my students, and those of my colleagues,
with whom the choices soon will lie

Contents

PART **I**   *The Context of U.S. Foreign Policy: Theory and History*

1   *The Strategic Context: Foreign Policy Strategy and the Essence of Choice*

PART **II** *American Foreign Policy in
the Twenty-First Century:
Choices and Challenges*

6 *Foreign Policy Politics: Diplomacy Begins at Home*   186

7 *Peace: Building a Post–Cold War World Order?*   229

List of Maps and Boxed Features

Perspectives

Dynamics of Choice

Preface

The Cold War is over. A new era has begun. A new century awaits. Such are the opportunities and the challenges confronting American foreign policy, for those who make it—and for those who teach and study it.

American Foreign Policy: The Dynamics of Choice in the 21ˢᵗ Century is intended to help those of us who are professors and students take advantage of those opportunities and meet those challenges. The book is designed as a primary text for courses on American foreign policy. Its scope encompasses both key issues of *foreign policy strategy,* of what the U.S. national interest is and which policies serve it best, and key questions of *foreign policy politics,* of which institutions and actors within the American political system play what roles and have how much influence. Formulating foreign policy strategy is the "essence of choice," the means by which goals are established and the policies that are the optimal means of achieving them are forged. Foreign policy politics is the "process of choice," the making of foreign policy through the political institutions and amid the societal influences of the American political system.

Part I of this book provides the theory (Chapters 1 and 2) and history (Chapter 3 for 1789–1945, Chapters 4 and 5 on the Cold War) for establishing the framework of the dynamics of choice. The theory chapters draw on the international relations and American foreign policy literatures to introduce core concepts, pose debates over alternative explanations, and frame the analytic approach to foreign policy strategy and foreign policy politics. The history chapters help ensure that expressions like "break with the past" are not taken too literally. Not only must we still cope with the legacies of the Cold War, but many current issues are contemporary versions of long-standing "great debates" with lengthy histories in U.S. foreign policy.

Part II (Chapters 6–10) applies the framework to the post–Cold War foreign policy agenda and the major choices the United States faces as it enters the twenty-first century. What policies should the United States pursue in this post–Cold War era? What threats do we face, what interests do we have, where do our democratic values fit in? How well is the process for making our foreign policy working? The chapters are highly comprehensive, providing students with a broad survey of the post–Cold War foreign policy agenda. A wide range of issues is covered in a manner that both provides an initial understanding and lays the foundation for further reading and research.

Throughout the book a number of special pedagogical features are included: *Dynamics of Choice*, charts that illustrate and highlight key aspects of the analytic framework; *At the Source*, primary source materials such as major speeches and policy documents; *Perspectives*, providing insightful and often controversial views on major issues; plus a number of maps, tables, and other boxed elements.

Perspectives on American Foreign Policy: Readings and Cases, the supplemental volume, follows the same chapter structure as the main text. Each chapter includes either articles drawn from journals and books that delve deeper into theoretical, historical, and policy debates, or a case study (abridged from studies developed at Harvard University's Kennedy School of Government) that fleshes out and provides insights into policy and process. Icons in the margin of the main text call students' attention to related material in the *Perspectives* reader.

This book reflects my own belief in a "multi-integrative" approach to teaching about American foreign policy. By that I mean three things: an approach that breaks through the levels-of-analysis barriers and integrates international policy and domestic process; one that encompasses the full range of post–Cold War foreign policy issue areas (e.g., diplomacy, defense, international economic policy, global democratization, global environment); and one that "bridges the gap" between theory and practice by drawing on both perspectives. With regard to this last point, I have sought to incorporate the perspectives and experiences gained through my own work in the policy world (at the State Department on the Policy Planning Staff, in Congress as a Senate foreign policy aide, and in other capacities) as well as from more than fifteen years as a professor.

My interest in writing this book is a manifestation of my commitment to teaching. Throughout my university education I was fortunate to have some exceptional teachers. I was among the thousands of undergraduates at Cornell University over the past four decades who were first captivated by the study of foreign policy through Walter LaFeber's courses on diplomatic history. The late Bud Kenworthy, a superb and caring teacher in his own right, was instrumental in my realization as a senior that I wanted to pursue an academic career. When I went back to Cornell for my Ph.D., I was just as fortunate as a graduate student. Anyone who knows Theodore Lowi knows his intensity and passion for his work; these are especially evident in his teaching. Peter Katzenstein was my dissertation chair and a mentor in many ways, including in showing how commitments to superior scholarship and excellent teaching can be combined.

In my years as a professor my good fortune has continued. In both his approach and his persona, Alexander George has been a much-valued mentor and colleague. Thanks also to Larry Berman, Don Rothchild, Emily Goldman, Miko Nincic, Alex Groth, Ed Costantini, and other colleagues at the University of California at Davis who have been partners in trying to make our political science and international relations majors as rich and rewarding for our students as possible.

Rebecca Britton, Alexandra Pass, Kim Cole, and Sara Johnson were able research assistants. Librarians Jean Stratford at U.C. Davis and Jim Cornelius at the U.S. Institute of Peace helped greatly in accessing sources and checking citations. Melody Johnson, Lori Renard, Fatima Mohamud, and especially Barbara Taylor-Keil provided tremendous support by preparing the numerous drafts of the manuscript. I owe many thanks to them all. Thanks also to the U.C. Davis Academic Senate and Office of Research for research support and to the U.S. Institute of Peace, where I have been spending my sabbatical working on a new book while finishing this one.

At W. W. Norton, Roby Harrington has been there from the inception of the project and has provided the steady hand to see it through to completion. Authors know that we can count on Roby to be supportive and enthusiastic yet also committed to quality and focused on getting the book done. Thanks are due also to Sarah Caldwell, who helped in so many ways for much of the project, and Rob Whiteside, who came on to help bring it to completion. Traci Nagle's copy-editing was extremely helpful; the reader has her to thank for the book's reading as well as it does. Loch Johnson, Jim Lindsay, and other reviewers provided very helpful comments on an earlier draft.

Special thanks to my family: Katie, who embarks on her first study of foreign policy this year in high school; Adam, who is just setting out on his college years; Barbara, who once again has been consistently supportive and encouraging of a husband too often too long in his study; and my mother, Elaine, and the memory of my father, Ted, for their love and understanding.

B.W.J.
October 1999

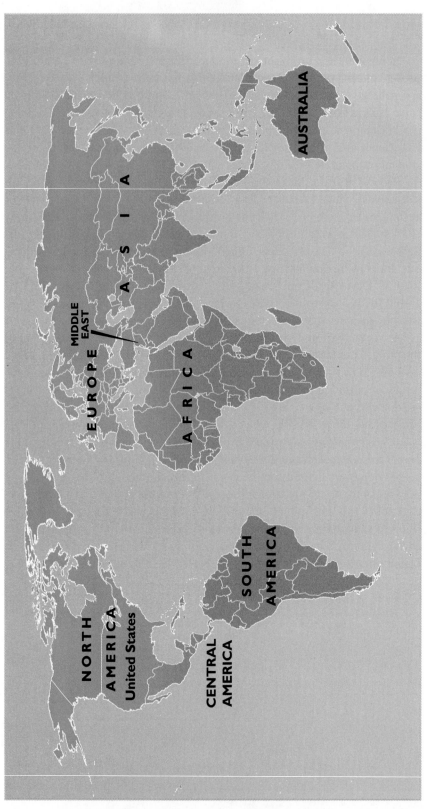

Africa, 1999

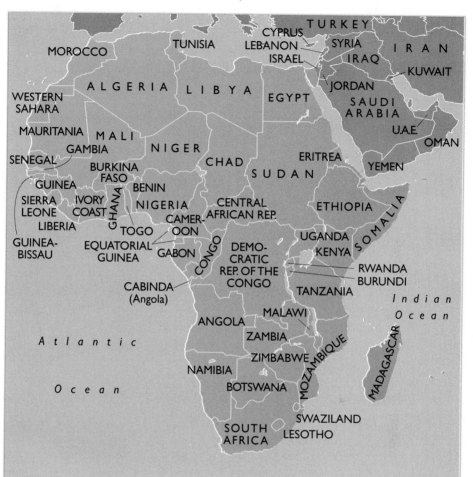

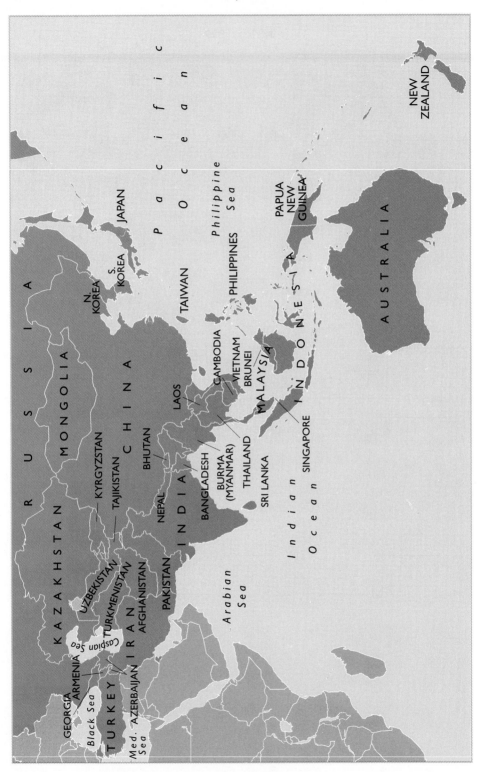

The Western Hemisphere, 1999

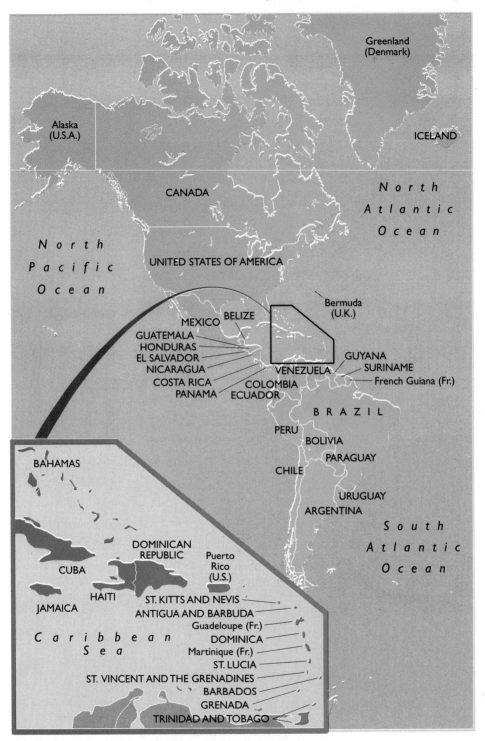

Greenland
(Denmark)

Alaska
(U.S.A.)

ICELAND

CANADA

North
Atlantic
Ocean

North
Pacific
Ocean

UNITED STATES OF AMERICA

Bermuda
(U.K.)

MEXICO   BELIZE
GUATEMALA
HONDURAS
EL SALVADOR
NICARAGUA
COSTA RICA
PANAMA   ECUADOR

GUYANA
SURINAME
French Guiana (Fr.)
VENEZUELA
COLOMBIA

B R A Z I L

PERU
BOLIVIA
PARAGUAY
CHILE

URUGUAY
ARGENTINA

South
Atlantic
Ocean

BAHAMAS

CUBA

DOMINICAN
REPUBLIC

Puerto
Rico
(U.S.)

HAITI

ST. KITTS AND NEVIS
ANTIGUA AND BARBUDA
Guadeloupe (Fr.)
DOMINICA
Martinique (Fr.)
ST. LUCIA
BARBADOS
GRENADA
TRINIDAD AND TOBAGO

JAMAICA

C a r i b b e a n
S e a

ST. VINCENT AND THE GRENADINES

The Middle East, 1999

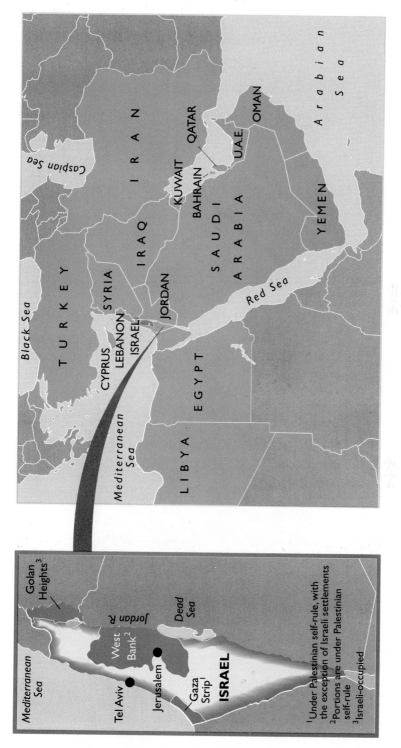

Mediterranean Sea

Golan Heights[3]

Jordan R.

West Bank[2]

Dead Sea

Tel Aviv

Jerusalem

Gaza Strip[1]

ISRAEL

[1] Under Palestinian self-rule, with the exception of Israeli settlements
[2] Portions are under Palestinian self-rule
[3] Israeli-occupied

Black Sea

Caspian Sea

TURKEY

CYPRUS

SYRIA

LEBANON

ISRAEL

JORDAN

IRAN

IRAQ

Mediterranean Sea

LIBYA

EGYPT

SAUDI ARABIA

Red Sea

KUWAIT

BAHRAIN

QATAR

U.A.E.

OMAN

YEMEN

Arabian Sea

The Former Communist Bloc

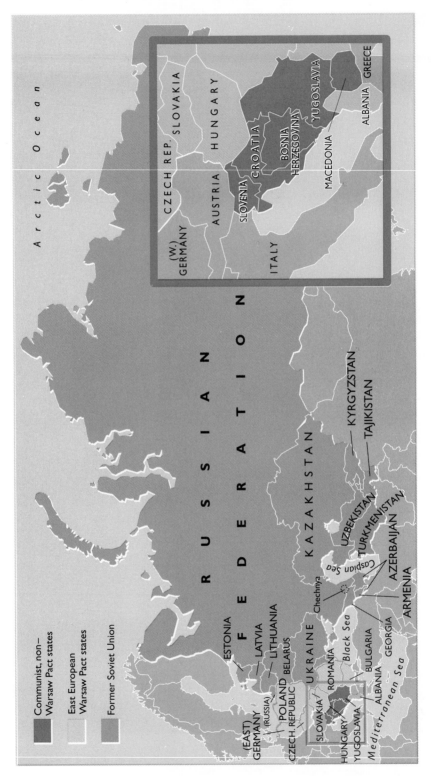

The Context of U.S. Foreign Policy: Theory and History

1

The Strategic Context: Foreign Policy Strategy and the Essence of Choice

Introduction: Foreign Policy in a Time of Transition

It was October 22, 1962, 7:00 P.M. A young boy sat on his living room floor watching television. President John F. Kennedy came on to warn the American public of an ominous crisis with the Soviet Union over nuclear missiles in Cuba. The boy's parents tried to look calm, but the fear in their eyes could not be masked. It seemed that the United States was on the brink of nuclear war.

The Cuban missile crisis ended up being settled peacefully, and the Cold War ultimately ended without nuclear war. Indeed, when the Berlin Wall came down in 1989, and then the Soviet Union fell apart in 1991, a sense of near euphoria enveloped the West. We won. They lost. President George Bush spoke of "a new world order . . . stronger in the pursuit of justice and more secure in the quest for peace . . . [in which all nations] can prosper and live in harmony."[1] Articles and books proclaimed "the end of history," the triumph of democracy, the "obsolescence" of war.

To be sure, the significance of families freed of the worry of an all-out nuclear war is not to be underestimated. In that sense the end of the Cold War has left the world more secure. The end of the Cold War, though, has not meant the end of war. The 1990s will be remembered for peace agreements and the advance of democracy—but also for ethnic "cleansings," civil wars, and terrorism. It was a decade of strides toward peace and order, but also stumbles toward anarchy and chaos. For American foreign policy, it was a decade of great successes, but also dismal failures.

Our times are times of historic transition to a new era and a new century. Like all transition periods, they provide hopeful opportunities and they pose dangerous challenges. No wonder they often seem so confusing and uncertain. We find many different views among scholars and analysts about the nature of this new world (see Perspectives on p. 4 for a sampling.) A Soviet official summed up the challenge of this new era for the West when he remarked toward the end of the Cold War, "We are about to do a terrible thing to you. We are going to deprive you of an enemy."[2] His remark was quite perceptive: for all the risks and burdens of the Cold War, politically and psychologically it was easier to focus attention and build support when there seemed to be a single, very threatening enemy. Without that one clear and present danger, some have even been questioning whether foreign policy is important anymore.

It would be wrong and quite dangerous, however, to equate the absence of an enemy with unimportance for foreign policy. For all their other differences, both President George Bush and President Bill Clinton have stressed the important role the United States needs to play in the post–Cold War world (see At the Source on p. 6). Five major reasons explain why this is the case.

First, the United States still faces significant potential threats to its national security. No great power threatens it today, but that doesn't mean an adversary will not emerge in the future. Relations with Russia and China are vastly improved but cannot be taken for granted, given both the policy differences that still exist and the political uncertainties and potential instabilities these giant countries face. Regions like the Middle East and East Asia, in which the United States has vital interests and long-standing commitments to allies, are still at significant risk of war. And while the specter of superpower nuclear war is behind us, the dangers of weapons of mass destruction—nuclear, chemical, and biological weapons—falling into the hands of rogue states or terrorists are even greater than before.

Second, the American economy is more internationalized than ever before. Whereas in 1970 foreign trade accounted for less than 15 percent of the U.S. gross domestic product (GDP), it now amounts to more than 30 percent. Exports fund a larger and larger number of American jobs. When the Federal Reserve Board sets interest rates, in addition to domestic factors like inflation, it increasingly also has to consider international ones, such as foreign-currency exchange rates and the likely reactions of foreign investors. Private financial markets also have become increasingly globalized. So when Asian stock markets plunged in late 1997, and when Russia's economy collapsed in

PERSPECTIVES
PERSPECTIVES
PERSPECTIVES

THE NATURE OF THE NEW ERA

What we may be witnessing is not just the end of the Cold War, or the passing of a particular period of postwar history, but the end of history as such: that is, the end point of mankind's ideological evolution and the universalization of Western liberal democracy as the final form of human government.

Francis Fukuyama, The End of History

The fundamental source of conflict in this new world will not be primarily ideological or primarily economic. The great divisions among humankind and the dominating source of conflict will be cultural. . . . The clash of civilizations will dominate global politics. The fault lines between civilizations will be the battle lines of the future. . . . The paramount axis of world politics will be the relations between "the West and the Rest."

Samuel Huntington, The Clash of Civilizations

The methods of commerce are displacing military methods—with disposable capital in lieu of firepower, civilian innovation in lieu of military-technical advancement, and market penetration in lieu of garrisons and bases. . . . Now, however, as the relevance of military threats and military alliances wanes, geo-economic priorities and modalities are becoming dominant in state action.

Edward Luttwak, Geo-Economics

Today, weapons of mass destruction (WMD) present more and different things to worry about than during the Cold War. For one, nuclear arms are no longer the only concern, as chemical and biological weapons have come to the fore. . . . If terrorists decide that they want to stun American policymakers by inflicting enormous damage, WMD become more attractive at the same time that they are becoming more accessible.

Richard Betts, The New Threat of Mass Destruction

(Continued on page 5)

(The Nature of the New Era   *Continued from page 4)*
In a world made smaller by global commerce and communication, cooperative engagement is more possible—and more necessary—than ever before.... "Social stewardship" is increasingly recognized as a component of national—and global—security. With the end of the Cold War, there is a growing understanding of nonmilitary threats to peace and security. International problems, such as resource scarcities and wide gaps between rich and poor, have the potential to destabilize nations and even precipitate military aggression. Successful social stewardship can address intranational problems before they metastasize into larger threats.

Rockefeller Brothers Fund Report

Sources: Francis Fukuyama, "The End of History?" *National Interest* 16 (Summer 1989), 4; Samuel P. Huntington, "The Clash of Civilizations?" *Foreign Affairs* 72:3 (Summer 1993), 22, 28; Edward Luttwak, "From Geo-Politics to Geo-Economics," *National Interest* 20 (Summer 1990), 17, 20; Richard K. Betts, "The New Threat of Mass Destruction," *Foreign Affairs* 77:1 (January/February 1998), 26, 29; Laurie Ann Mazur and Susan E. Sechler, *Global Interdependence and the Need for Social Stewardship* (New York: Rockefeller Brothers Fund, 1997), 9–10.

mid-1998, middle-class America felt the effects, as mutual funds, college savings, and retirement nest eggs plummeted in value.

Third, many other areas of policy that used to be considered "domestic" also have been internationalized. The environmental policy agenda has extended from the largely domestic issues of the 1960s and 1970s to international issues such as global warming and biodiversity. The "just say no" drug policy of the 1980s is insufficient as a policy when thousands of tons of drugs come into the United States every day from Latin America, Asia, and elsewhere. Whereas the Federal Bureau of Investigation's "Ten Most Wanted" fugitives list included mostly members of U.S.-based crime syndicates when it first started in 1950, by 1997 eight of the ten fugitives on the list were international criminals. Public-health problems like the spread of acquired immunodeficiency syndrome (AIDS) have to be combated globally. In these and other areas the distinctions between foreign and domestic policy have become increasingly blurred, as international forces impact in more and more ways on spheres of American life that used to be considered domestic.

At the Source

THE UNITED STATES IN THE POST–COLD WAR WORLD

As Seen by President George Bush

❝ The end of the Cold War . . . is a time of great promise. . . . But this does not mean that there is no specter of war, no threats to be reckoned with. And, already, we see disturbing signs of what this new world could become if we are passive and aloof. We would risk the emergence of a world characterized by violence, characterized by chaos, one in which dictators and tyrants threaten their neighbors, build arsenals brimming with weapons of mass destruction, and ignore the welfare of their own men, women and children. And we could see a horrible increase in terrorism with American citizens more at risk than ever before.

We cannot and we will not allow this to happen. Our objective must be to exploit the unparalleled opportunity presented by the Cold War's end to work toward transforming this new world into a new world order, one of governments that are democratic, tolerant and economically free at home and committed abroad to settling differences peacefully, without the threat or use of force. ❞

As Seen by President Bill Clinton

❝ As we approach the beginning of the 21st century, the United States remains the world's most powerful force for peace, prosperity and the universal values of democracy and freedom. Our nation's challenge— and responsibility—is to sustain that role by harnessing the forces of global integration for the benefit of our own people and people around the world. . . .

The security environment in which we live is dynamic and uncertain, replete with a host of threats and challenges that have the potential to grow more deadly, but also offering unprecedented opportunities to avert those threats and advance our interests. . . .

At this moment in history the United States is called upon to lead— to organize the forces of freedom and progress; to channel the unruly

(*Continued on page 7*)

> **(Post–Cold War World**   *Continued from page 6)*
> energies of the global economy into positive avenues; and to advance
> our prosperity, reinforce our democratic ideals and values, and enhance
> our security. "
>
> Sources: George Bush, "Remarks at the United States Military Academy in West Point, New
> York," January 5, 1993, *Public Papers of the Presidents: George Bush,* Vol. 2 (Washington,
> D.C.: Office of the Federal Register, National Archives and Records Administration, 1993),
> 2228–32; Bill Clinton, *A National Security Strategy for a New Century* (Washington, D.C.:
> U.S. Government Printing Office, 1998), iii, iv, 1.

Fourth, the increasing racial and ethnic diversity of the American people has produced a larger number and wider range of groups with personal bases for interest in foreign affairs. Some forms of "identity politics" can be traced all the way back to the nineteenth century, and some were quite common during the Cold War. But more and more Americans trace their ancestry and heritage to different countries and regions and are asserting their interests and seeking influence over foreign policy toward those countries and regions.

Fifth, it is hard for the United States to uphold its most basic values if it ignores grievous violations of those values that take place outside its national borders. It is not necessary to go so far as to take on the role of global missionary or world police. But it also is not possible to claim to stand for democracy, freedom, and justice, yet say "not my problem" to genocide, repression, torture, and other horrors.

Foreign policy thus continues to press upon us, as individuals and as a nation. The choices it poses are just as crucial for the twenty-first century as the Cold War choices were for the second half of the twentieth century.

This book has two principal purposes: (1) to provide a framework, grounded in international relations theory and U.S. diplomatic history, for foreign policy analysis; and (2) to apply that framework to the agenda for U.S. foreign policy in the post–Cold War world.

The analytic framework, as reflected in the book's subtitle, is *the dynamics of choice.* It is structured by two fundamental sets of questions that, whatever the specific foreign policy issues involved, and whatever the time period being discussed, have been at the center of debate:

- questions of *foreign policy strategy*—of what the national interest is and how best to achieve it; and
- questions of *foreign policy politics*—of which institutions and actors within the American political system play what roles and have how much influence.

Setting foreign policy strategy is the *essence of choice,* establishing the goals to be achieved and forging the policies that are the optimal means for achieving them. Foreign policy politics is the *process of choice,* the making of foreign policy through the political institutions and amid the societal influences of the American political system.

Part I of this book provides the theory (in this chapter and Chapter 2) and history (Chapters 3, 4, and 5) for establishing the framework of the dynamics of choice in U.S. foreign policy. Part II then applies the framework to the major foreign policy choices the United States faces as it enters the new era brought by the end of the Cold War and the start of a new century.

The Context of the International System

The United States, like all states, makes its choices of foreign policy strategy within the context of the international system. Although extensive study of international systems is taken up in international relations texts, three points are important to our focus on American foreign policy.

Quasi-anarchy

One of the fundamental differences between the international system and domestic political systems is the absence of a recognized central governing authority in the international system. This often is referred to as the *anarchic* view of international relations. Its roots go back to the seventeenth-century English political philosopher Thomas Hobbes and his classic treatise, *Leviathan.* Hobbes saw international affairs as a "war of all against all." Unlike in domestic affairs, where order was maintained by a king or other recognized authority figure, no such recognized authority existed in the international sphere, according to Hobbes. Others since have taken a more tempered view, pointing to ways in which international norms, laws, and institutions have provided some order and authority and stressing the potential for even greater progress in this regard. Yet even in our contemporary era, although we have progressed beyond the "nasty, brutish," unadulterated Hobbesian world by developing international institutions like the United Nations and the International Monetary Fund, as well as a growing body of international law, the world still has nothing at the international level as weighty and authoritative as a constitution, a legislature, a president, or a supreme court. The prevailing sense thus is that what makes international relations "unique and inherently different from relations within states" is that "no ultimate authority exists to govern the international system. . . . As a result the existence of a 'quasi-anarchy' at the international level conditions state-to-state relations."[3]

System Structure

System structure is based on the distribution of power among the major states in the international system. "Poles" refer to how many major powers there are—one in a unipolar system, two in a bipolar system, three or more in a multipolar system. Different patterns are said to characterize each of these system types, each with its own requisites for maintaining peace and stability—for example, primacy in a unipolar system, deterrence in a bipolar one, balance of power in a multipolar one. Here too, though, some tempering is needed to avoid too rigid a view of system requisites and too much of a sense of inevitabilities. Was the nearly half-century duration of the Cold War an inevitable consequence of the bipolar system structure, or could it have been either longer or shorter if not for the particular policy decisions made by leaders on both sides? Consider the Cuban missile crisis: the bipolar system structure raised the possibility of such a crisis, but did not make either its occurrence or its successful resolution inevitable. So too with many other situations and policies for which it is important to take system structure into account as a context for, but not a determinant of, choices of foreign policy strategy.

State Structural Position

Where a state ranks in the international system structure affects what it can do in foreign policy terms. Theorists such as Kenneth Waltz see system structure as very deterministic, making "[states'] behavior and the outcomes of their behavior predictable."[4] To know a state's structural position is thus to know its foreign policy strategy. Yet such claims also go too far, conveying a billiard ball–like image of states. The essence of billiards is the predictability of how a ball will move once it has been struck; hit the cue ball at a certain angle from a certain distance with a certain force, and you can predict exactly where on the table the target ball will go, regardless of whether it is solid or striped. In international systems theory the "hitting" is done by external threats and the "angles set" by the state's position in the structure of the international system, and the "path" the state's foreign policy takes is predictable regardless of the "stripes or solids" of its foreign policy priorities, domestic politics, or other characteristics. States are not like "crazy balls," bouncing wherever their domestic whims might take them. But they are not strictly reactive, either. Their foreign policy choices are constrained by the structure of the international system but are not determined by it.

The National Interest: The 4 Ps Framework

The national interest: all of us have heard it preached. Many of us may have done some of the preaching ourselves—that U.S. foreign policy must be made in the name of the national interest. No one would argue with the proposition that following the national interest is the essence of the choices to be made in a nation's foreign policy. But defining what the national interest is and then developing policies for achieving it have rarely been as easy or self-evident as such invocations would imply. Political scientists Alexander George and Robert Keohane capture this dilemma in a jointly authored article. They note the problems that have been encountered because the concept of the national interest has "become so elastic and ambiguous . . . that its role as a guide to foreign policy is problematical and controversial." Yet they also stress the importance that the national interest can have, and needs to have, to help "improve judgments regarding the proper ends and goals of foreign policy."[5]

Our approach in this book is to establish in general analytic terms the four core goals that go into defining the U.S. national interest: power, peace, prosperity, and principles. Dynamics of Choice on p. 11 depicts the "four Ps" framework and indicates the major "school" of international relations theory to which each is most closely linked.

Power

Power is the key requirement for the most basic goal of foreign policy, self-defense and the preservation of national independence and territory. It is also essential for deterring aggression and influencing other states on a range of is-

Core Goals of American Foreign Policy

National interest goal	Corresponding international relations theory
Power	Realism
Peace	Liberal Internationalism
Prosperity	International Political Economy
Principles	Democratic Idealism

sues. "Power enables an actor to shape his environment so as to reflect his interests," Professor Samuel Huntington states. "In particular it enables a state to protect its security and prevent, deflect or defeat threats to that security."[6] To the extent that a state is interested in asserting itself, advancing its own interests and itself being aggressive, it needs power. "The strong do what they have the power to do," the ancient Greek historian Thucydides wrote, "and the weak accept what they have to accept."[7]

Realism is the school of international relations theory that most emphasizes the objective of power. "International relations is a struggle for power," the noted Realist scholar Hans Morgenthau wrote; "statesmen think and act in terms of interest defined as power."[8] Morgenthau and other Realists view the international system in *balance-of-power* terms. They take a very Hobbesian view, seeing conflict and competition as the basic reality of international politics. The "grim picture" is painted by University of Chicago professor John Mearsheimer: "International relations is not a constant state of war, but it is a state of relentless security competition, with the possibility of war always in the background. . . . Cooperation among states has its limits, mainly because it is constrained by the dominating logic of security competition, which no amount of cooperation can eliminate. Genuine peace, or a world where states do not compete for power, is not likely."[9] States thus ultimately can rely only on themselves for security. It is a "self-help" system—and power is critical to the self-help states need to be secure.

Icons in the margin indicate that a related reading is to be found in *Perspectives on American Foreign Policy: Readings and Cases;* case studies are indicated by "CS."

Yet power is to international relations as love is to the human condition—everyone wants it, but no one can precisely define it. "Power is the ability to overcome obstacles and prevail in conflicts," one international relations textbook states; it is "the general capacity of a state to control the behavior of others," according to another.[10] The most important measure of power is military strength. But power also involves such intangibles as "credibility," or whether the state is perceived by others in the international system as having the will to use its capabilities.

The principal policies for achieving power-based foreign policy strategies are largely *coercive* ones. Most basic of all is maintaining a strong *defense* and a credible *deterrence*. The particular requirements to provide the United States with defense and deterrence have varied dramatically over time with changes in the identity of the potential aggressor—Great Britain in early U.S. history, Germany in the two world wars, the Soviet Union during the Cold War—and the nature of weaponry—from muskets and a few warships to nuclear weapons, submarines, and supersonic bombers. But the basic strategy always has been essentially the same: to deter aggression and, if deterrence fails, to ensure the defense of the nation.

Alliances against a mutual enemy are a key component of both defense and deterrence strategies. For most of American history, alliances were formed principally in wartime: for example, with France in 1778 when twelve thousand French troops came over to help the Americans fight for independence against the shared enemy, Britain; with Britain and France in World War I; with Britain and the Soviet Union in World War II; and with twenty-six other nations in the 1990–91 Persian Gulf War. During the Cold War (officially, peacetime), the United States set up a global network of alliances, including multilateral ones like the North Atlantic Treaty Organization (NATO), the Southeast Asia Treaty Organization (SEATO), and the Rio Treaty (with Latin American countries), as well as bilateral agreements with Japan, South Korea, Taiwan, Israel, Iran, and others. A related strategy is the provision of *military assistance,* such as weapons, advisers, financing, and other forms of aid, to a pro-American government or rebel group.

The ultimate power-based strategy, of course, is *war*—"the continuation of politics by other means," in the words of the great nineteenth-century Prussian strategist Karl von Clausewitz, "an act of violence intended to compel our opponent to fulfill our will." *Military interventions* are the "small wars," the uses of military force in a more limited fashion, as in the overthrow of governments considered hostile to U.S. interests and the protection or bringing to power of pro-U.S. leaders, of which there are numerous historical as well as contemporary examples.

Power can be exerted through more than just military force. Diplomacy also can be used coercively. *Coercive statecraft* takes a number of forms, from such low-level actions as the filing of an official protest or issuing a public condemnation, to withdrawing an ambassador and suspending diplomatic relations, to imposing *economic sanctions* and other, tougher measures. Then there is *covert action*, the secret operations of intelligence agencies conducted, as former secretary of state Henry Kissinger put it, to "defend the American national interest in the gray areas where military operations are not suitable and diplomacy cannot operate."[11] Although they were especially associated with the Cold War, covert actions go back to early U.S. history—as when Benjamin Franklin secretly bought arms from France during the Revolutionary War, or when President Thomas Jefferson secretly arranged the overthrow of the Pasha of Tripoli (in today's Libya).

Peace

In a certain sense, all four of the national interest objectives ultimately are about *peace.* But in this particular analytic category, we specifically have in mind theories of *Liberal Internationalism* and two types of foreign policy.

Liberal Internationalism views world politics as "a cultivable 'garden,'" in contrast to the Realist view of a global "'jungle.'"[12] Although they stop well short of world government, these theories emphasize both the possibility and the value of reducing the chances of war and of achieving common interests sufficiently for the international system to be one of *world order.* Liberal Internationalists recognize that tensions and conflicts among nations do exist, but see cooperation among nations as more possible and more beneficial than Realists do. Pursuing cooperation thus is neither naïve nor dangerous, but rather a rational way to reduce risks and make gains that even the most powerful state could not achieve solely on its own. To be sure, as Professor Inis Claude acknowledges, "the problem of power is here to stay; it is, realistically, not a problem to be eliminated, but"—the key point for Liberal Internationalists— "a problem to be managed."[13]

Consistent with this sense that peace is achievable but not automatic, theorists such as Keohane stress the importance of creating international institutions as the basis for "sustained cooperation." Anarchy cannot be eliminated totally, but it can be tempered or partially regulated. Indeed, it is precisely because the power and interests that Realists stress do generate conflicts that "international institutions . . . will be components of any lasting peace."[14] This also is true with regard to relations among allies. States may have friendly

1.2

relations and share common interests but still have problems of collective action or even just coordination. International institutions provide the structure and the commitments to facilitate, and in some instances require, the fulfillment of commitments to collective action and coordination.

International institutions may be formal bodies like the United Nations, but they also can be more informal, in what are often called "international regimes." Keohane defines international institutions both functionally and structurally, as "the rules that govern elements of world politics and the organizations that help implement those rules."[15] This definition encompasses norms and rules of behavior, procedures for managing and resolving conflicts, and the organizational bases for at least some degree of global governance, albeit well short of full global government.

We can identify five principal types of international institutions: (a) *global*, such as the League of Nations (an unsuccessful example) and the United Nations (a more successful one); (b) *regional*, such as the Cold War–era Conference on Security and Cooperation in Europe (CSCE), or the Pan American Conference of the late nineteenth century; (c) *international legal*, such as the Permanent Court of International Justice (World Court); (d) *arms control and nonproliferation*, such as the International Atomic Energy Agency and the Organization for the Prohibition of Chemical Weapons; and (e) *economic*, particularly global ones such as the International Monetary Fund, the World Bank, and the World Trade Organization, and also regional ones such as the Asia-Pacific Economic Cooperation forum. In none of these cases has the United States been the only state involved in establishing the institutions and organizations. But in most, if not all, the United States has played a key role.

The other type of foreign policy strategy that fits here is the *"peace broker"* role the United States has played in wars and conflicts to which it has not been a direct party. Familiar contemporary examples include the 1973–75 "shuttle diplomacy" in the Middle East by Henry Kissinger, the 1978 Camp David Accords between Egypt and Israel brokered by President Jimmy Carter, and the Clinton administration's role in the 1995 Dayton Accord ending the war in Bosnia. But this role, too, traces back historically, as with the peace treaty brokered by President Theodore Roosevelt ending the Russo-Japanese War, for which "TR" was awarded the 1906 Nobel peace prize.

Prosperity

Foreign policies motivated by the pursuit of *prosperity* are those which place the economic national interest above other concerns. They seek gains for the

American economy from policies that help provide reliable and low-cost imports, growing markets for American exports, profitable foreign investments,
and other international economic opportunities. Some of these involve policies that are specifically *foreign economic* ones, such as trade policy. Others involve general relations with countries whose significance to U.S. foreign
policy is largely economic, as with an oil-rich country like Saudi Arabia. Most
generally they involve efforts to strengthen global capitalism as the structure
of the international economy.

Theories that stress these kinds of interrelationships between political and
economic factors are called theories of *international political economy.* With
regard to U.S. foreign policy and its interests in prosperity, we can distinguish
between two main types of theories, one offering a benign view and the other
a critical view.

The benign one, dubbed *General Welfarism* (as in the clause of the U.S.
Constitution about promoting "the general welfare"), emphasizes the pursuit
through foreign policy of general economic benefits to the nation: a favorable
balance of trade, strong economic growth, a healthy macroeconomy.[16] The ultimate goal is collective prosperity, in which the interests served are those of
the American people in general. This was said to have been a major part of
U.S. foreign policy in the nineteenth century, when about 70 percent of the
treaties and other international agreements the United States signed were on
matters related to trade and international commerce.[17] It also has been evident in recent years, as in the 1995 statement by Secretary of State Warren
Christopher that whereas other secretaries of state put their main emphasis
on arms control, "I make no apologies for putting economics at the top of [the
U.S.] foreign policy agenda."[18]

More critical theories, such as *Imperialism,* see such policies as dominated
by and serving the interests of the capitalist class and other elites, such as
multinational corporations and major banks.[19] The prosperity that is sought
is more for the private benefit of special interests, and the ways in which it is
sought are highly exploitative of other countries. The basics of this theory go
back to the British economist John Hobson and his 1902 book *Imperialism.*
Because the unequal distribution of wealth leaves the lower classes with limited
purchasing power, capitalism creates for itself the twin problems of underconsumption and overproduction. It thus needs to find new markets for its
products if it is to avoid recession and depression. Although Hobson's own
Britain and its colonialism were his primary focus, his arguments also were
applicable to the United States and its more indirect "neocolonialism" in Latin
America and parts of Asia (see Chapter 3).

Vladimir Ilyich Lenin, while still in exile in Switzerland in 1916, the year before he would return to Russia to lead the Communist revolution, wrote his most famous book, *Imperialism: The Highest Stage of Capitalism.* Lenin's version of imperialist theory differed from Hobson's in rejecting the possibility that capitalism could reform itself.* One reason was that, in addition to the underconsumption/overproduction problem, Lenin emphasized the pursuit of inexpensive and abundant supplies of raw materials as another key motive for capitalist expansionism. Giving the working class more purchasing power would not do anything about the lust for the iron ore, foodstuffs, and later, oil that were so much more plentiful and so much cheaper in the colonial world (later called the Third World). Moreover, the essence of Lenin's theory was the belief that the capitalist class so dominated the political process and defined the limits of democracy that it never would allow the kinds of reforms Hobson advocated.

In sum, their differences notwithstanding, Imperialism and General Welfarism share an emphasis on economic goals as driving forces behind U.S. foreign policy. They differ over whose prosperity is being served, but they agree on the centrality of prosperity among the four Ps.

Principles

This fourth core goal involves the values, ideals, and beliefs that the United States has claimed to stand for in the world. As a more general theory, this emphasis on principles is rooted in *Democratic Idealism.*

Democratic Idealists hold to two central tenets about foreign policy. One is that when tradeoffs have to be made, "right" is to be chosen over "might." This is said to be particularly true for the United States because of the ostensibly special role bestowed on it—to stand up for the principles on which it was founded and not be just another player in global power politics. We find assertions of this notion of "American exceptionalism" throughout U.S. history. Thomas Jefferson, the country's first secretary of state and its third president, characterized the new United States of America as such: "the solitary republic of

---

*Hobson believed that liberal domestic reforms were possible, and would help capitalism break out of the underconsumption and overproduction cycle. Such reforms would create a more equitable distribution of wealth, bringing an increase in consumption, in the process both making the home society more equitable and alleviating the need for colonies, thus making foreign policy less imperialistic.

the world, the only monument of human rights . . . the sole depository of the sacred fire of freedom and self-government, from hence it is to be lighted up in other regions of the earth, if other regions shall ever become susceptible to its benign influence."[20] And then there was President Woodrow Wilson's famous declaration that U.S. entry into World War I was intended "to make the world safe for democracy": "We shall fight for the things which we have always carried nearest our hearts—for democracy, for the right of those who submit to authority to have a voice in their own government, for the rights and liberties of small nations, for a universal dominion of right by such a concert of free peoples as shall bring peace and safety to all nations and make the world in itself at last free." Idealism was also claimed by many a Cold War president, from Democrats such as John Kennedy with his call in his inaugural address to "bear any burden, pay any price" to defend democracy and fight communism, to Republicans such as Ronald Reagan and his crusade against "the evil empire."

The other key tenet of Democratic Idealism is that in the long run "right" makes for "might," that in the end interests like peace and power are well served by principles. One of the strongest statements of this view is the *democratic peace* theory, which asserts that by promoting democracy we promote peace because democracies do not go to war against each other. To put it another way, the world could be made safe *by* democracy. For all the attention the democratic peace theory has gotten in the post–Cold War era, its central argument and philosophical basis trace back to the eighteenth-century political philosopher Immanuel Kant and his book *Perpetual Peace*. "If . . . the consent of the citizenry is required in order to decide that war should be declared," Kant wrote, "nothing is more natural than that they would be very cautious in commencing such a poor game. . . . But, on the other hand, in a constitution which is not republican, and under which the subjects are not citizens, a declaration of war is the easiest thing to decide upon, because war does not require of the ruler . . . the least sacrifice of the pleasure of his table, the chase, his country houses, his court functions and the like."[21] As to serving the goal of power, Professor Joseph Nye of Harvard University coined the term "soft power" to refer to the ways in which the values for which a nation stands, its cultural attractiveness, and other aspects of its reputation can have quite practical value as sources of influence.[22] This is not just a matter of what American leaders claim in their rhetoric, but of whether other governments and peoples perceive for themselves a consistency between the principles espoused and the actual policies pursued by the United States. It also depends on how well America is deemed to be living up to its ideals within its own society on issues such as race relations, protection of the environment, and crime and violence.

Thus, on the one hand Democratic Idealism bears similarities to Liberal Internationalism, the former stressing the potency of adhering to ideals, the latter the embedding effects international institutions can have on such ideals. On the other hand, the implicit optimism about human nature espoused by Democratic Idealists contrasts sharply with both the power-based Realists and the more materialist view of either of the prosperity-based schools.

Dynamics of Choice, below, summarizes the 4 Ps of foreign policy strategy, highlighting how the categories differ among core national-interest goals, schools of international relations theory, principal conceptions of the international system, and principal types of policies pursued.

In later chapters we will apply this framework to foreign policy strategy historically, during the Cold War, and then as the basis for analyzing the post–Cold War era.

A Foreign Policy Strategy Typology

Core national interest goals	International relations theory	Conception of the international system	Main types of policies
Power	Realism	Balance of power	Coercive
Peace	Liberal Internationalism	World order	Diplomatic
Prosperity	International Political Economy	Global capitalism	Economic
Principles	Democratic Idealism	Global democracy	Political

Dilemmas of Foreign Policy Choice:
4 Ps Complementarity and Tradeoffs

4 Ps Complementarity: Optimal, but Infrequent

To the extent that all 4 Ps can be satisfied through the same strategy—i.e., they are complementary—the dilemmas of foreign policy choice are relatively easy. No major tradeoffs have to be made, no strict priorities set. This does happen sometimes, as the following two cases illustrate.

THE 1990–91 PERSIAN GULF WAR   The Gulf War was a great victory for American foreign policy in many respects. The invasion of Kuwait by Iraq, led by Saddam Hussein, was a blatant act of aggression—one of the most naked acts of aggression since World War II. Furthermore, the Iraqis were poised to keep going, straight into Saudi Arabia, an even more strategic country and a close U.S. ally.

But through U.S. leadership, the *peace* was restored. "This will not stand," President George Bush declared. Resolutions were sponsored in the United Nations (U.N.) Security Council, demanding an Iraqi withdrawal and then authorizing the use of military force to liberate Kuwait. A twenty-seven-nation diplomatic coalition was built, including most of western Europe, Japan, and much of the Arab world. A multinational military force went to war under the command of General Norman Schwarzkopf of the U.S. Army.

Operation Desert Storm, as it was named, was also a formidable demonstration of American *power*. It is important to recall how worried many military analysts were at the outset of Desert Storm about incurring high casualties, and even about the possibility that Saddam would resort to chemical or biological weapons. That the military victory came so quickly and with so few U.S. and allied casualties was testimony to the military superiority the United States had achieved. Striding tall from its Gulf War victory, American power was shown to be second to none.

Of course, this was not just about helping Kuwait. *Prosperity* also was at risk, in the form of oil. Twice before in recent decades war and instability in the Middle East had disrupted oil supplies and sent oil prices skyrocketing. The parents of today's college students still have memories of waiting in gasoline lines and watching prices escalate on a daily basis during the 1973 Arab-Israeli War and the 1979 Iranian Revolution. This time, though, because the

Gulf War victory came so swiftly, disruptions to the American and global economies were minimized.

Although Kuwait couldn't claim to be a democracy, other important *principles* were at issue. One was the right of all states to be free from aggression. Another was the moral imperative of standing up to a dictator as brutal as Saddam Hussein. Comparisons to Adolf Hitler went too far, but Saddam was a leader who left a trail of torture, repression, and mass killings.

THE MARSHALL PLAN, 1947   The Marshall Plan was the first major U.S. foreign aid program; it provided about $17 billion to Western Europe for economic reconstruction following World War II.* This was an enormous amount of money, equivalent to $60 billion today. Yet the Marshall Plan passed Congress by overwhelming majorities, 69 to 17 in the Senate and 329 to 74 in the House. Compare these figures to total U.S. foreign economic aid today, which is less than one-quarter as much and barely gets a congressional majority.

The key reason for such strong support was that the Marshall Plan was seen as serving the full range of U.S. foreign policy goals. The communist parties in France, Italy, and elsewhere in Western Europe were feeding off the continuing economic suffering and dislocation, making worrisome political gains. The Marshall Plan thus was a component of the broader strategy of containment of communism to keep the *peace* in Western Europe. It also asserted American *power*, for with the foreign aid came certain conditions, some explicit and some implicit. And in a more general sense, the United States was establishing its global predominance and leadership. The glorious nations of the Old World were now dependent on the New World former colony.

American *prosperity* was also well served. The rebuilding of European markets generated demand for American exports and created opportunities for American investments. Thus, although its motives were not strict altruism, the Marshall Plan was quite consistent with American *principles:* the stability of fellow Western democracies was at stake.

In both of these cases, peace, power, prosperity, and principles fit together quite effectively. But while optimal, such complementarity of core goals is infrequent. Much more common are cases in which one or more of the 4 Ps pull in competing directions, and choices have to be made among core national interest goals.

---

*The Marshall Plan is named for Secretary of State George Marshall, who made the initial public proposal in a commencement speech at Harvard University.

4 Ps Tradeoffs: More Frequent, More Problematic

Not only are cases with competing tensions more common, they require much tougher choices. Tradeoffs have to be made; priorities have to be set. The following two examples illustrate such choices.

TRADE WITH CHINA: POWER AND PROSPERITY VS. PRINCIPLES   In 1989, hundreds of Chinese students staged a massive prodemocracy sit-in in Tiananmen Square in Beijing, China's capital city. As one expression of their protest, they constructed a plaster replica of the American Statue of Liberty. The Communist government ordered the students to leave. They refused. The Chinese army then moved in with tanks and troops. An estimated 1,000 students were killed, and tens of thousands of students and other dissidents were arrested that night and in the ensuing months.

In reaction to the Chinese crackdown, many in the United States called for the imposition of economic sanctions. The focus of these efforts was on revoking China's most-favored-nation (MFN) status. Essentially MFN status limits tariffs on a country's exports to the United States to a standard, low level; without MFN status, a country's exports to the United States are much less competitive, and that country's international trade will be adversely affected.* The prosanctions argument, which came from a bipartisan coalition in Congress and from human-rights groups, was based on *principles:* How could the United States conduct business as usual with a government that massacred its own people? These prodemocracy Chinese protesters had turned to America for inspiration. How could the United States not now stand up for what it says are values and beliefs it holds dear?

The Bush administration, which was in office at the time, was willing to impose only limited economic sanctions; it would not revoke China's MFN status. Its main argument was based on *power*. The administration still considered the U.S.-Soviet rivalry to be the central issue in its foreign relations and thus gave priority to its geopolitical interests—namely, continued good relations with China. Among President Bush's critics was Democratic presidential candidate Bill Clinton, who castigated his opponent for coddling "the butchers of Beijing." Yet as president, Clinton also refused to revoke China's MFN status. His reasons, however, were based more on economic

---

*It is not that the country receiving MFN is favored over others, but rather that all countries receiving MFN get the same "most favored" tariff treatment.

considerations—*prosperity*—and the calculation of billions of dollars in potential trade and investment losses for the American economy.

Both Bush and Clinton claimed that they were not abandoning principles, that other steps were being taken to try to protect human rights and promote democracy in China. But although this justification was partly true, debate still raged over fundamentally competing definitions of the national interest. The requisites of power and prosperity pointed to one set of policies, principles to another. Tradeoffs were inevitable; choices had to be made.

GUATEMALA, 1954: PROSPERITY AND POWER VS. PRINCIPLES   In 1945, Guatemala, the Central American country just south of Mexico, had ended a long string of military dictatorships by holding free elections. A progressive new constitution was written, freedoms of the press and of speech were guaranteed, and workers and peasants were encouraged to organize. A number of military coups were attempted, but they were put down. In 1951, Colonel Jacobo Arbenz Guzman, a proreform military officer, was elected president.

One of Arbenz's highest priorities was land reform. Only 2 percent of the population owned 70 percent of the land in Guatemala. The largest of all landholders was the United Fruit Company (UFCO), a U.S.-owned banana exporter. In March 1953, Arbenz's government included about 230,000 acres of UFCO holdings in the land being expropriated for redistribution to the peasantry. Most of this land was uncultivated, but that didn't matter to the UFCO. The compensation offered to the company by the Guatemalan government was deemed inadequate, even though it was the same valuation rate (a low one) that the UFCO had been using to limit the taxes it had to pay.

This wasn't just a UFCO problem, its corporate president declared: "From here on out it's not a matter of the people of Guatemala against the United Fruit Company. The question is going to be communism against the right of property, the life and security of the Western Hemisphere."[23] It was true that Arbenz had members of the Guatemalan Communist Party in his government. He also was buying some weapons from Czechoslovakia, which was a Soviet satellite. Might this be the beginning of the feared Soviet "beachhead" in the Western Hemisphere?* In defending the anti-Arbenz coup d'état that it engineered in 1954 through covert CIA action, the Eisenhower administration

---

*Fidel Castro had not yet come to power in Cuba. That would happen in 1959.

stressed the *power* concerns raised by this perceived threat to containment. The evidence of links to Soviet communism was not that strong, but the standard that needed to be met was only what an earlier U.S. ambassador to Guatemala had called the "duck test": "Many times it is impossible to prove legally that a certain individual is a communist; but for cases of this sort I recommend a practical method of detection—the 'duck test.' The duck test works this way: suppose you see a bird walking around in a farmyard. The bird wears no label that says 'duck.' But the bird certainly looks like a duck. Also, he goes to the pond and you notice that he swims like a duck. Well, by this time you have probably reached the conclusion that the bird is a duck, whether he's wearing a label or not."[24]

An argument can be made that, given the Cold War, the duck test was sufficient from a power perspective. Even so, the anti-Arbenz coup was something of a "joint venture" strikingly consistent with Imperialist critiques of U.S. foreign policy (prosperity). The UFCO had close ties to the Eisenhower administration; the historical record shows evidence of collaboration between the company and the government; and one of the first acts of the new regime of General Carlos Castillo Armas, who was a graduate of the military-intelligence training school at Fort Leavenworth, Kansas, and whom the CIA installed in power after the coup, was to give land back to the UFCO.

The critical tension here was with *principles.* The Arbenz government had come to power through elections that, while not perfectly free and fair, were much more fair than those in most of Latin America. And the military governments that ruled Guatemala for the thirty-five years following the U.S.-engineered coup showed extreme brutality and wanton disregard for human rights, killing and persecuting tens of thousands of their own people. The U.S. role was hidden for decades but was pointedly revealed in 1999 in a shocking report by a Guatemalan historical commission, which estimated that two hundred thousand people had been killed by the U.S.-supported military regimes and provided strong evidence of U.S. complicity.[25]

These examples show the difficulties that ensue when choices need to be made among different core goals of the national interest. Other examples could be cited to show other lines of competing tensions; we will see many such situations in later chapters. And, as noted earlier, 4 Ps tradeoffs are much more common in American foreign policy than 4 Ps complementarity.

Summary

Whatever the issue at hand, and whether past, present, or future, American foreign policy has been, is, and will continue to be about the *dynamics of choice.*

One set of these choices is about *foreign policy strategy.* It is easy to preach about the national interest, but much harder to assess what that interest is in a particular situation. One or more of the four core goals—power, peace, prosperity, and principles—may be involved. Not only may basic analyses differ, but more often than not tradeoffs have to be made and priorities set among these four Ps. Views on this reflect different schools of international relations theory, carry with them alternative policy approaches, and can result in fundamentally different foreign policy strategies. This is the *essence of choice* that is inherent to every major foreign policy issue.

We will use this framework for analyzing U.S. foreign policy strategy historically (Chapter 3), during the Cold War (Chapters 4 and 5), and most especially in our current post–Cold War era (Part II, Chapters 6–10). First, though, we turn in Chapter 2 to foreign policy politics and lay out an analytic framework for this other key dimension of American foreign policy, the process of choice.

Notes

[1] George Bush, "Address before a Joint Session of Congress on the Persian Gulf Crisis and the Federal Budget Deficit," September 11, 1990, *Public Papers of the Presidents of the United States: George Bush,* Vol. 2 (Washington, D.C.: Office of the Federal Register, National Archives and Records Administration, 1991), 1218–22.

[2] Cited in Thomas McCormick, *America's Half-Century: United States Foreign Policy in the Cold War* (Baltimore: Johns Hopkins University Press, 1989), 232.

[3] Robert J. Lieber, *No Common Power: Understanding International Relations* (Boston: Scott, Foresman, 1988), 5.

[4] Kenneth N. Waltz, *Theory of International Politics* (Reading, Mass.: Addison-Wesley, 1979), 72.

[5] Alexander L. George and Robert O. Keohane, "The Concepts of National Interests: Uses and Limitations," in Alexander L. George, ed., *Presidential Decisionmaking in Foreign Policy: The Effective Use of Information and Advice* (Boulder, Colo.: Westview, 1980), 217–18.

[6] Samuel Huntington, "Why International Primacy Matters," *International Security* 17:4 (Spring 1993), 69–70.

[7] Thucydides, *History of the Peloponnesian War,* trans. R. Warner (New York: Penguin, 1972), 402.

[8] Hans J. Morgenthau, *Politics among Nations: The Struggle for Power and Peace* (New York: Knopf, 1948), 5.

[9] John J. Mearsheimer, "The False Promise of International Institutions," *International Security* 19:3 (Winter 1994/95), 9.

[10]Bruce Russett and Harvey Starr, *World Politics: The Menu for Choice* (New York: Freeman, 1996), 117; K. J. Holsti, *International Politics: A Framework for Analysis* (Englewood Cliffs, N.J.: Prentice-Hall, 1988), 141.

[11]Cited in Loch K. Johnson, *America as a World Power: Foreign Policy in a Constitutional Framework* (New York: McGraw-Hill, 1991), 239.

[12]Michael W. Doyle, *Ways of War and Peace* (New York: Norton, 1997), 19.

[13]Claude, cited in Mearsheimer, "False Promise of International Institutions," 26–27.

[14]Robert O. Keohane and Lisa L. Martin, "The Promise of Institutionalist Theory," *International Security* 20:1 (Summer 1995), 50.

[15]Robert O. Keohane, "International Institutions: Can Interdependence Work?" *Foreign Policy* 110 (Spring 1998), 82.

[16]See, for example, Joan E. Spero and Jeffrey A. Hart, *The Politics of International Economic Relations* (New York: St. Martin's, 1997); and Richard N. Gardner, *Sterling-Dollar Diplomacy: The Origins and Prospects of Our International Economic Order* (New York: Columbia University Press, 1980).

[17]James M. McCormick, *American Foreign Policy and Process* (Itasca, Ill.: F. E. Peacock, 1992), 15–16.

[18]Michael Hirsh and Karen Breslau, "Closing the Deal Diplomacy: In Clinton's Foreign Policy, the Business of America Is Business," *Newsweek,* March 6, 1995, 34.

[19]See, for example, V. I. Lenin, *Imperialism: The Highest Form of Capitalism* (New York: International Publishers, 1939); John A. Hobson, *Imperialism* (London: George Allen and Unwin, 1954); and Richard J. Barnet and Ronald E. Muller, *Global Reach: The Power of the Multinational Corporations* (New York: Simon and Schuster, 1974).

[20]Cited in Robert W. Tucker and David C. Hendrickson, "Thomas Jefferson and Foreign Policy," *Foreign Affairs* 69:2 (Spring 1990), 136.

[21]Immanuel Kant, "Perpetual Peace," cited in Michael W. Doyle, "Kant, Liberal Legacies and Foreign Affairs," in Michael E. Brown et al., eds., *Debating the Democratic Peace* (Cambridge, Mass.: MIT Press, 1997), 24–25.

[22]Joseph S. Nye, Jr., *Bound to Lead: The Changing Nature of American Power* (New York: Basic Books, 1990).

[23]Cited in James A. Nathan and James K. Oliver, *United States Foreign Policy and World Order* (Boston: Little, Brown, 1985), 176. See also Stephen Schlesinger and Stephen Kinzer, *Bitter Fruit: The Untold Story of the American Coup in Guatemala* (Garden City, N.Y.: Doubleday, 1982).

[24]Cited in Walter LaFeber, *Inevitable Revolutions: The United States in Central America,* 2d ed. (New York: Norton, 1993), 115–16.

[25]Mireya Navarro, "Guatemalan Army Waged 'Genocide', New Report Finds," *New York Times,* February 26, 1999, A1, A8. See also "Documents on U.S. Policy in Guatemala," at the Web site of the National Security Archive, http://www.seas.gwu.edu/nsarchive.

CHAPTER **2** *The Domestic Context:*
Foreign Policy Politics and
the Process of Choice

Introduction: Dispelling the "Water's Edge" Myth

When it comes to foreign policy, according to an old saying, "politics stops at the water's edge." In other words, partisan and other political differences that characterize domestic policy are to be left behind—"at the water's edge"—when entering the realm of foreign policy, so that the country can be united in confronting foreign threats.

The example most often cited by proponents of this ideal is the consensus of the early Cold War era, that "golden age of bipartisanship." Here is "a story of democracy at its finest," as one famous book portrayed it, "with the executive branch of the government operating far beyond the normal boundaries of timidity and politics, the Congress beyond usual partisanship, and the American people as a whole beyond selfishness and complacency. All three . . . worked together to accomplish a national acceptance of world responsibility."[1] That's how foreign policy politics is supposed to be, the "water's edge" thinking goes.

In three key respects, though, this notion of politics' stopping at the water's edge is a myth that needs to be dispelled. First, *historically, the domestic consensus that characterized the Cold War era was more the exception than the rule.* The common view is that divisive foreign policy politics started with the Vietnam War. But although Vietnam did shatter the Cold War consensus, it was hardly the first time that foreign policy politics hadn't stopped at the water's edge. In the years leading up to World War II, President Franklin

Roosevelt had his own intense political battles with an isolationist Congress. In the years following World War I, President Woodrow Wilson suffered one of the worst foreign policy politics defeats ever when the Senate refused to ratify the Treaty of Versailles. We can even go back to 1794 and President George Washington, the revered "father" of the country, and his battles with Congress over a treaty with Great Britain called the Jay Treaty. The bitter and vociferous attacks on the Jay Treaty for "tilting" toward Britain in its war with France were a rhetorical match for any of today's political battles. "Ruinous . . . detestable . . . contemptible," editorialized one major newspaper of the day, excoriating a treaty "signed with our inveterate enemy and the foe of human happiness." The Senate did ratify the treaty, but by a margin of only one vote. Indeed the whole Jay Treaty controversy was a key factor in President Washington's decision to retire to Mount Vernon instead of seeking a third term as president.

Second, *consensus has not always been a good thing.* It surely can be, in manifesting national solidarity behind the nation's foreign policy. But national solidarity is one thing, the delegitimization of dissent quite another. The most virulent example was the anticommunist witch-hunt spurred by the McCarthyism of the 1950s, during which accusations of disloyalty were hurled at government officials, playwrights, professors, scientists, and average citizens, often on the flimsiest of evidence. Dissent was also criminalized during both world wars, when domestic consensus was often crucial to meeting the wartime challenges; nevertheless, many Americans paid a severe price in civil liberties and individual rights during the wars. The Espionage and Sedition Acts passed during World War I permitted such repressive measures as banning postal delivery of any magazine that included views critical of the war effort—restrictions "as extreme as any legislation of the kind anywhere in the world."[2] During World War II the national security rationale was invoked to uproot 120,000 Japanese Americans and put them in internment camps, on the basis only of their ethnicity. During Vietnam, shouts of "America, love it or leave it" were aimed at antiwar critics and protesters. Consensus is not a particularly good thing when it equates dissent with disloyalty.

Third, *domestic political conflict is not necessarily always bad for foreign policy.* Debate and disagreement can facilitate a more thorough consideration of the issues. They can subject questionable assumptions to serious scrutiny. They can bring about constructive compromises around a policy that serves the national interest better than anything either side originally proposed. As former House Foreign Affairs Committee chair Lee Hamilton wrote, "debate, creative tension and review of policy can bring about decisions and actions that stand a better chance of serving the interests and values of the American people."[3] A good example of this was the outcome of the debate about the U.S. role in helping restore democracy in the Philippines in the mid-1980s. The policy preferred by President Ronald Reagan was to continue supporting the dictator Ferdinand Marcos, even after his forces had assassinated the democratic opposition leader, Benigno Aquino, and even amid mounting evidence of rampant corruption in the Marcos regime. But the U.S. Congress, led by a bipartisan coalition of Democrats and Republicans, refused to go along with a continued unconditional embrace of Marcos. It pushed for support for the prodemocracy forces led by Corazon Aquino, widow of the slain opposition leader. Democracy was restored, and an important U.S. ally was made more stable. This might not have been achieved, however, had it not been for the good that can sometimes come out of conflictual foreign policy politics.

Thus the realities of *foreign policy politics,* the process by which foreign policy choices are made, are more complex than the conventional wisdom holds. Our purpose in this chapter is to provide a framework for understanding the dynamics of foreign policy politics. We do so by focusing on five sets of domestic actors: the president and Congress, and the "Pennsylvania Avenue diplomacy" that marks (and often mars) their interbranch relationship; the policy- and decision-making processes within the executive branch; the pressures brought to bear by major interest groups; the impact of the news media; and the nature and influence of public opinion.

The President, Congress, and "Pennsylvania Avenue Diplomacy"

They stare at each other down the length of Pennsylvania Avenue. The White House and the Capitol: connected by the avenue, but also divided by it. The avenue: a path for cooperation, but also a line of conflict. The president and Congress: a relationship very much in need of its own "diplomacy."

Despite all the theories expounded, political positions taken, legal briefs filed, no one has come up with a definitive answer to the question of constitutional intent and design for presidential-congressional relations in the making of foreign policy. The Constitution left it, in one classic statement, "an invitation to struggle for the privilege of directing American foreign policy."[4] Indeed, although we usually are taught to think of the relationship between the president and Congress as a "separation of powers," it really is much more "separate institutions sharing powers."[5] A separation of powers would mean that the president has power *a*, Congress power *b*, the president power *c*, Congress power *d*, and so on. But the actual relationship is more one in which both the president and Congress have a share of power *a*, a share of power *b*, a share of power *c*, and so on—that is, the separate institutions *share powers*.

Politics, of course, also enters in, especially when there is "divided government," wherein one political party controls the White House and the other holds the majority in one or both houses of Congress. Fundamentally, though, the dynamic is a structural one; this basic structural relationship is evident in five key areas of foreign policy politics (see Dynamics of Choice, below).

Principal Foreign Policy Provisions of the Constitution

	Power Granted to:	
	President	**Congress**
War power	Commander in chief of armed forces	Provide for the common defense; declare war
Treaties	Negotiate treaties	Ratification of treaties, by two-thirds majority (Senate)
Appointments	Nominate high-level government officials	Confirm president's appointments (Senate)
Foreign commerce	No explicit powers, but treaty negotiation and appointment powers pertain	Explicit power "to regulate foreign commerce"
General powers	Executive power; veto	Legislative power; power of the purse; oversight and investigation

War Powers

No domain of foreign policy politics has been debated more hotly nor more recurringly than war powers. The Constitution designates the president as "commander in chief" but gives Congress the power to "declare war" and "provide for the common defense"—not separate powers, but each a share of the same power.

Both sides support their claims for the precedence of their share of the war power with citations from the country's founders. Presidentialists invoke the logic, developed by Alexander Hamilton in the Federalist Papers, that the need for an effective foreign policy was one of the main reasons the young nation needed an "energetic government" (Federalist no. 23); that "energy in the executive" was "a leading character in the definition of good govern- ment" (no. 70); and that "in the conduct of war . . . the energy of the executive is the bulwark of national security" (no. 75). Congressionalists, on the other hand, cite the proceedings of the Constitutional Convention. At James Madi- son's initiative, the original wording of the proposed constitution, which would have given Congress the power to "make war," was changed to "declare war." This is explained by congressionalists as intended to recognize that *how* to use military force ("make war") was appropriately a power for the com- mander in chief, whereas *whether* to use military force ("declare war") was for the Congress. Furthermore, as Madison stated in a letter to Thomas Jefferson, "the Constitution supposes what the history of all governments demonstrates, that the executive is the branch of power most interested in war, and most prone to it. It has accordingly with studied care vested the question of war in the legislature."[6]

Nor is the weight of historical precedent strictly on one side or the other. One of the favorite statistics of proponents of the presidency's war powers is that of the more than two hundred times that the United States has used mili- tary force, only five—the War of 1812, the Mexican War (1846–48), the Span- ish-American War (1898), World War I (1917–19), and World War II (1941–45)—have been through congressional declarations of war. Perhaps another eighty-five or ninety (e.g., the 1991 Persian Gulf War) have been through some other legislative authority. All the others have been by presi- dents acting on their own, which is taken as evidence of both the need for and the legitimacy of presidents' having such freedom of action.

This statistic, though, is somewhat deceptive. Many of the cases of presi- dents acting on their own involved minor military incidents generally re- garded as the business of a commander in chief. Besides that, defenders of

Congress's share of the war powers interpret this gross disproportion—many uses of military force yet few declarations of war—not as legitimizing the arrangement, but as emphasizing the problem. They put less emphasis on the overall numbers than on key cases like Vietnam, in which undeclared war had devastating consequences.

We will take war powers up again as a historical issue in Chapter 3, as an early Cold War–era issue in Chapter 4, as a Vietnam-era controversy over the 1973 War Powers Resolution in Chapter 5, and as a continuing debate in Chapters 6 and 8.

Treaties and Other International Commitments

The basic power-sharing arrangement for treaties vests negotiating power in the president, but requires that treaties be ratified by a two-thirds majority of the Senate. On the surface this appears to have worked pretty well: of the more than 1,700 treaties signed by presidents in U.S. history, only about 20 have been voted down by the Senate. But here, too, simple statistics can be misleading.

One reason is that although it may not happen often, Senate defeat of a treaty can have a huge impact—as with the 1919–20 defeat of the Treaty of Versailles and the 1999 defeat of the Comprehensive Test Ban Treaty. Another reason is that Congress has alternative ways to influence treaties other than by defeating them. For example, it can offer advice during negotiations through the official "observer groups" that often accompany State Department negotiators. It also can try to amend or attach a "reservation" to alter the terms of a treaty, which can be quite controversial, since it may require the reopening of negotiations with the other country or countries.

On the other hand, presidents also have an array of strategies at their disposal to circumvent Senate objections. In particular, they can resort to mechanisms other than treaties, such as *executive agreements,* for making international commitments. Executive agreements usually do not require congressional approval, let alone the two-thirds Senate majority that treaties do. Although in theory executive agreements are supposed to be used for minor government-to-government matters, leaving major aspects of relations to treaties, the line between the two has never been particularly clear. In addition, sometimes the most important foreign policy commitments do not come from treaties or executive agreements or any other written or legal form. Such *declaratory commitments* come from speeches and statements by presidents. This was the case, for example, with the Monroe Doctrine, which sprang from a speech by President James Monroe in 1823 to become the bedrock of U.S. foreign policy in the Western Hemisphere. So, too, with the Truman Doctrine (1947): its clarion call "to support free peoples who are resisting attempted subjugation by armed minorities or by outside pressures" became a basis for the containment strategy pursued in U.S. policy for the next 40–50 years.

Appointments of Foreign Policy Officials

The standard process as reflected in Dynamics of Choice on p. 29 is that the president nominates and the Senate confirms (by a simple majority) the appointments of Cabinet members, ambassadors, and other high-level foreign policy officials. In pure statistical terms the confirmation rate for presidential foreign policy nominees is higher than 90 percent. Yet here, too, we need to look past the numbers.

First of all, these numbers don't include nominations withdrawn before a formal Senate vote. When White House congressional-liaison aides come back from Capitol Hill reporting that "the vote count doesn't look good," a president often decides to avoid the embarrassment of a vote and instead withdraw the nomination. This happened to President Carter in 1977 when his original nominee as CIA director (Theodore Sorensen) was met with vocal opposition in Congress, and also to President Clinton in 1997 with his CIA director nominee (Anthony Lake). Second, precisely because it is often assumed that nominees will be confirmed, when they are not the political impact can be substantial. Thus, for example, in 1989 far less attention was given to all of the Bush administration's other foreign policy nominations combined than to the one case of former senator John Tower, Bush's nominee for secretary of defense, who ended up being voted down. The Senate also has left its mark on some nominees even in the process of confirming them. This was the fate of William Colby, confirmed as President Nixon's CIA director in 1973 amid controversies over Vietnam and covert action by the CIA, and of Paul Warnke, Carter's choice to head the Arms Control and Disarmament Agency, who was excoriated by conservatives as too "dovish": neither of these officials ever fully recovered from the wounds of their confirmation battles.

None of these legislative tactics, however, applies to foreign policy officials who do not require Senate confirmation. This in particular includes the assistant to the president for national security affairs (called the national security adviser, for short) and the staff of the National Security Council (NSC). Thus such major figures as Henry Kissinger and Zbigniew Brzezinski, who served as national security advisers to Presidents Nixon and Ford, and Carter, respectively, did not need Senate confirmation for that position. (When Kissinger was nominated by Nixon to be secretary of state, however, Senate approval was required.)

"Commerce with Foreign Nations"

In this area of foreign policy the Constitution is more explicit than in others. Congress is very clearly granted the power "to regulate commerce with foreign nations" and "to lay and collect . . . duties." Presidential authority over trade policy thus has been more dependent than in other areas on what and how much authority Congress chooses to delegate.[7] For about 150 years, Congress actually decided each tariff, item by item; one result of this was the infamous Smoot-Hawley Tariff Act of 1930, which set tariffs for more than 20,000 items—and moved almost all of them higher, the classic example of protectionism. The Reciprocal Trade Agreements Act of 1934, which arose from the Smoot-Hawley disaster, delegated to the president extensive authority to cut tariffs on his own by as much as 50 percent if he could negotiate reciprocal cuts with other countries. Both institutions were generally happy with this arrangement, especially under the international free trade system set up after World War II by the General Agreement on Tariffs and Trade (GATT). But beginning again in the mid-1970s, as trade became more politically controversial, the power-sharing pulls and tugs along Pennsylvania Avenue grew more frequent and more wrenching.

General Powers

The president and Congress both also bring to the foreign policy struggle their general constitutional powers.

EXECUTIVE POWER   The Constitution states that "the executive power shall be vested in the President," and roughly defines this power as to ensure "that the laws be faithfully executed." In itself this is a broad and vague mandate, which presidents have invoked as the basis for a wide range of actions taken in order to "execute" foreign policy, such as executive agreements, as already discussed, and executive orders, which are directives issued by the president for executive-branch actions not requiring legislative approval. Sometimes executive orders are issued just to fill in the blanks of legislation passed by Congress. But they also can be used by presidents as a way of getting around Congress. Thus, for example, President Truman integrated the armed forces by issuing Executive Order No. 9981 on July 26, 1948, because he knew the segregationists in Congress would block any integration legislation.

Then there is the veto, the most potent executive power the Constitution gives the president. The authority to block legislation unless Congress can pass it a second time, by a two-thirds majority in both chambers, is a formidable power. It is especially so in foreign policy, where the president can tap both patriotism and fear to intimidate potential veto overrides. Thus even amid the congressional activism and partisan battles of the 1970s and 1980s, presidential vetoes on foreign policy legislation were overridden only twice: Nixon's veto of the 1973 War Powers Resolution and Reagan's veto of the 1986 Anti-Apartheid Act.

In many respects even more important than a president's formal executive powers are the informal political powers of the office and the skills of being a practiced politician. Stories are legion of deal-making with members of Congress to get that one last vote to ratify a treaty or pass an important bill. President Lyndon Johnson was especially well known for this. So was President Reagan, who to get Senate approval of a major 1981 arms sale to Saudi Arabia doled out funds for a new hospital in the state of one senator, a coal-fired power plant for another, and a U.S. attorney appointment for a friend of another.[8]

The most significant political power a president has may well be what Teddy Roosevelt called the "bully pulpit." As Roosevelt once put it, "people used to say to me that I was an astonishingly good politician and divined what the people are going to think. . . . I did not 'divine' how the people were going to think, I simply made up my mind what they ought to think, and then did my best to get them to think it." And that was before television!

LEGISLATIVE POWER   Professor Louis Henkin of Columbia University goes so far as to claim that there is no part of foreign policy "that is not subject to legislation by Congress."[9] That may be an overstatement, as demonstrated by some of the examples of executive power just cited. But it is true that the legislative power gives Congress a great deal of influence over foreign policy.

The distinction made by James Lindsay between *substantive* and *procedural* legislation is a useful one for understanding that Congress has a number of ways of exerting its foreign policy influence.[10] Substantive legislation is policy-specific, spelling out what the details of foreign policy should or should not be. Disapproval of the 1919 Treaty of Versailles, approval of the 1947 Marshall Plan, ratification of the 1972 SALT arms-control treaty with the Soviet Union, approval of the 1993 North American Free Trade Agreement (NAFTA)—all are examples of substantive legislation.

Procedural legislation is a bit more subtle and requires more elaboration. It deals more with "the structures and procedures by which foreign policy is made. The underlying premise is that if Congress changes the decision-making process it will change the policy."[11] The War Powers Resolution is one example; it was an effort to restructure how decisions on the use of military force were made. The War Powers Resolution involved the use of the *legislative veto,* a procedure by which certain actions taken and policies set by the president can be overridden by Congress through a resolution rather than through a bill. The key difference is that whereas bills generally must be signed by the president to become law and thus give the president the opportunity to exercise a veto, congressional resolutions do not. For this very reason, the Supreme Court severely limited the use of the legislative veto in its 1983 decision in the case *INS v. Chadha,* to be discussed in the next section.

Among Congress's other powers are its oversight and investigative powers and, most especially, its *power of the purse:* "no money shall be drawn from the Treasury but in Consequence of Appropriation made by Law." This power gives Congress direct influence over decisions on how much to spend and what to spend it on. In addition to stipulating the total budget of, for example, the Defense Department, Congress can use its appropriations power directly to influence more basic policy decisions, such as by setting "conditionalities" as to how the money can or cannot be spent, or "earmarking" it for specific programs or countries.

The Supreme Court as Referee?

It is not that often that the Supreme Court gets involved in foreign policy politics. When the Court does become involved, it is usually because it has been turned to as a "referee" to resolve presidential-congressional conflicts over foreign policy power-sharing. But the Court generally has been unable and unwilling to take on this role.

It has been unable to do so in the sense that different Court rulings seem to lend support to each side. For example, a very strong statement of presidential prerogatives in foreign policy was made in the 1936 case *United States v. Curtiss-Wright Export Corp.* Although the specific case was over whether an embargo could be imposed against an American company's arms sales, the significance of the Court's ruling was in the general principle that the president could claim greater powers in foreign than in domestic policy because of "the law of nations" and not just the Constitution: "In this vast external realm, with its important, complicated, delicate and manifold problems, the President alone has the power to speak or listen as a representative of the nation. . . . The President is the sole organ of the nation in its external relations, and its sole

representative with foreign nations. . . . It is quite apparent that . . . in the maintenance of our international relations . . . [Congress] must often accord to the
President a degree of discretion and freedom from statutory restriction which
would not be admissible were domestic affairs alone involved."[12]

Yet the 1952 case *Youngstown Sheet and Tube Co. v. Sawyer* in many respects became the counterpart to *Curtiss-Wright*, establishing some limits on
executive power. In this case, involving a labor-union strike in the steel industry during the Korean War, the Court ruled against President Truman's claim
that he could break the strike in the name of national security. Going beyond
the specifics of the case, the Court focused on the problems of "zones of twi-
light," situations for which Congress had neither explicitly authorized the
president to take a certain action nor explicitly prohibited the president from
doing so. In these situations the president "and Congress may have concurrent
authority, or . . . its distribution is uncertain," and thus "any actual test of
power is likely to depend on the imperatives of events and contemporary im-
ponderables rather than on abstract theories of law." On these types of issues,
while stopping well short of asserting congressional preeminence, the Court
did not accept nearly as much presidential preeminence as it had in 1936 in its
Curtiss-Wright decision.[13]

In other instances the Supreme Court and other federal courts have been
unwilling even to attempt to adjudicate presidential-congressional foreign
policy disputes. In the 1970s and 1980s members of Congress took the president to court a number of times over issues of war and treaty powers.[14] In
most of these cases the courts refused to rule definitively one way or the other.
Although there were differences in the specifics of the rulings, the cases generally were deemed to fall under the "political question" doctrine, meaning that
they involved political differences between the executive and legislative
branches more than constitutional issues, and thus required a political resolution between the branches, rather than a judicial remedy. In other words, the
Supreme Court essentially told the president and Congress to work the issues
out themselves.

Another key case was the 1983 case *INS v. Chadha,* mentioned briefly earlier. In striking down the legislative veto as unconstitutional, the Court
stripped Congress of one of its levers of power. Even so, within a year and a
half of the *Chadha* decision, Congress had passed more than fifty new laws
that sought to accomplish the same goals as the legislative veto while avoiding
the objections raised by the Court. The constitutionality of some of these laws
remains untested, but they still cast a sufficient shadow for the president not
to be able to assume too much freedom of action.

Executive-Branch Politics

There was a time when books on foreign policy didn't include sections like this one. Foreign policy politics was largely seen as an *inter*-branch phenomenon, not an *intra*-branch one. The executive branch, after all, was the president's own branch. Its usual organizational diagram was a pyramid: the president sat atop it, the various executive-branch departments and agencies fell below. Major foreign policy decisions were made in a hierarchical, structured, and orderly manner. It was believed to be a highly *rational* process, often called a "rational actor" model.

Analytically speaking, five principal criteria need to be met for an executive-branch policy process to be considered rational: (1) adequate and timely *information* must be provided through intelligence and other channels, so that policy-makers are well informed of the nature of the issues on which they need to make decisions; (2) thorough and incisive *analysis* must be made of the nature of the threats posed, the interests at stake, and other key aspects of the issues; (3) the *range of policy options* must be identified, with an analysis of the relative pros and cons of each; (4) *implementation* strategies must be spelled out for how to proceed once the policy choice is made; and (5) a *feedback "loop"* must be established to evaluate how the policies are working in practice and to make adjustments over time.[15]

Yet, as we will see throughout this book, the executive branch's foreign policy process often has not met these criteria. The dynamics of decision-making and policy implementation tend to be less strictly hierarchical, less neatly structured, and much more disorderly than as portrayed in the rational-actor model. To put it more directly, the executive branch also has its own politics.

Presidents as Foreign Policy Leaders

For all the other executive-branch actors that play major foreign policy roles, the president remains the key decision-maker. How well the president fulfills that role depends on a number of factors.

One factor is the extent of foreign policy experience and expertise that a president brings to the office. Experience was an advantage for President George Bush, who had been CIA director, ambassador to the United Nations, and chief of the U.S. liaison office in China. Yet, surprisingly, it was much more common in the eighteenth and nineteenth centuries than in the twentieth for presidents to have had substantial prior foreign policy experience. Four of the first six presidents had served previously as secretary of state (Thomas Jefferson, James Madison, James Monroe, and John Quincy Adams). So had two other presidents in the nineteenth century (Martin Van Buren and James Buchanan). But no president since has had that experience. And of the seven war heroes who became president, only one (Dwight Eisenhower) was in this century; the others were in the eighteenth (George Washington) and nineteenth (Andrew Jackson, William Henry Harrison, Zachary Taylor, Ulysses Grant, and Benjamin Harrison). Many attribute some of the foreign policy problems that presidents like Ronald Reagan and Bill Clinton have had, especially initially, to their prior foreign policy inexperience.

A second set of factors influencing foreign policy decision-making are characteristics of the president as an individual. As with any individual in any walk of life, the president's personality affects how and how well the job gets done. Although personality is rarely the sole determinant of behavior, in some cases it does have a very strong bearing. Woodrow Wilson's unwillingness to compromise with Senate opponents on the Treaty of Versailles has been traced in part to his self-righteousness and other deep-seated personality traits. Richard Nixon's personality significantly affected his policy-making, particularly with regard to Vietnam. The consistent image of Nixon that comes through both in his own writing and that of biographers is of a pervasive suspiciousness: Nixon viewed opponents as enemies and political setbacks as personal humiliations, had an extreme penchant for secrecy, and seemed obsessed with concentrating and guarding power. These personality characteristics help explain the rigidity with which Nixon kept the Vietnam War effort going despite the evidence that it was failing, and the virtual paranoia he exhibited by putting antiwar figures on an "enemies list" and recruiting former CIA operatives to work in secret as "plumbers" to "plug" supposed leaks—actions that, like those of the self-destructive figures of ancient Greek tragedies, led to Nixon's own downfall through the Watergate scandal.

A more cognitive approach focuses on the president's worldview, or what a number of authors have called a *belief system*. No president comes to the job "tabula rasa," with a cognitive clean slate; quite to the contrary, as Robert Jervis states, "it is often impossible to explain crucial decisions and policies without reference to the decision-maker's beliefs about the world and their images of others."[16] Belief systems can be construed in terms of three core components:

1. the analytic component of the *conception of the international system:* What is the president's view of the basic structure of the international system? Who and what are seen as the principal threats to the United States?
2. the normative component of the *national interest hierarchy:* How are the core objectives of power, peace, prosperity, and principles prioritized?
3. the instrumental component of a basic *strategy:* Given both the conception of the international system and the national interest hierarchy, what is the optimal strategy to be pursued?

Dynamics of Choice, below, illustrates the importance of belief systems by contrasting those of Jimmy Carter and Ronald Reagan. The differences in their worldviews are quite pronounced, and the connections to their respective foreign policies are clear.

Presidents of course are also politicians, so another important factor affecting presidential foreign policy leadership is one of *political calculations.* This can work in different ways. Presidents in trouble at home may turn more to foreign policy to try to draw on the prestige of international leadership to bolster their domestic standing. At other times presidents feel pressured to give less emphasis to foreign policy to respond to criticisms about not paying

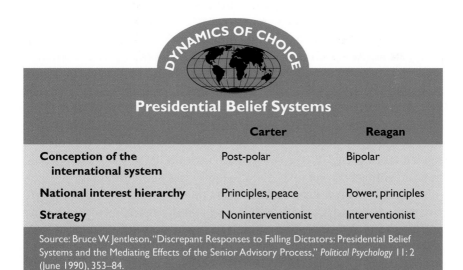

DYNAMICS OF CHOICE

Presidential Belief Systems

	Carter	Reagan
Conception of the international system	Post-polar	Bipolar
National interest hierarchy	Principles, peace	Power, principles
Strategy	Noninterventionist	Interventionist

Source: Bruce W. Jentleson, "Discrepant Responses to Falling Dictators: Presidential Belief Systems and the Mediating Effects of the Senior Advisory Process," *Political Psychology* 11:2 (June 1990), 353–84.

enough attention to the domestic front. The election cycle also enters in, with foreign policy tending to get more politicized during election years. And outside the election cycle there is the steady flow of public-opinion polls, which get factored in along with the intelligence analyses and other parts of the decision-making process.

Roles of Senior Foreign Policy Advisers

In looking at presidential advisers, we need to ask two sets of questions. The first concerns who among the "big four"—the national security adviser, the secretary of state, the secretary of defense, and the CIA director—has the most influential role? The answer depends on a number of factors, including respective relationships of these advisers with the president and their own prominence and bureaucratic skills. Henry Kissinger, who became so well known as to take on celebrity status, is everyone's major example. A Harvard professor, Kissinger served as national security adviser in Nixon's first term. When Nixon appointed him secretary of state in 1973, Kissinger also kept the national security adviser position, a highly unusual step that accorded him unprecedented influence. He continued to hold both positions under President Gerald Ford, until pressured in 1975 to give one up (national security adviser). All told, we find far more references in books on the foreign policy of that period to "Kissingerian" doctrines than to "Nixonian" or, especially, "Fordian" ones.

The other analytic question is whether *consensus or conflict* prevails among the senior advisers. Consensus does not necessarily mean perfect harmony, but it does mean a prevailing sense of teamwork and collegiality. President Bush's team of advisers was a good example of consensus. Secretary of State James Baker, National Security Adviser Brent Scowcroft, Secretary of Defense Dick Cheney, and Chair of the Joint Chiefs of Staff Colin Powell knew each other well and had worked together in previous administrations. We thus saw much less of the end runs, get-the-other-guy leaks to the press, and bureaucratic infighting than were evidenced in some other administrations.

A possible negative aspect of consensus, though, is that too much consensus among senior advisers can lead to *"groupthink,"* a social-psychology concept that refers to the pressures within small groups for unanimity that work against individual critical thinking.[17] Group cohesion is a good thing, but too much of it can be stifling. The result can be the kinds of decisions about which in retrospect the question gets asked, How did so many smart people make such a dumb decision? The Kennedy administration's decision-making on the disastrous 1961 Bay of Pigs invasion of Cuba is an oft-cited example, one we will discuss in Chapter 4.

As to conflict among senior advisers, we come back to Kissinger as a classic example. While Nixon's national security adviser, Kissinger clashed repeatedly with Secretary of State William Rogers, and while Ford's secretary of state, with Defense Secretary James Schlesinger. Kissinger won many of these battles, adding to his prominence. But the impact of these disagreements on foreign policy often was quite negative. Such high-level divisiveness made broader domestic consensus-building much more difficult. Moreover, with so much emphasis on winning the bureaucratic warfare, some ideas that were good on their merits, but that happened to be someone else's, were dismissed, buried, or otherwise condemned to bureaucratic purgatory.

Bureaucratic Politics and Organizational Dynamics

Politics in the executive branch do not occur only at the senior advisory level. Political battles go on daily at every level of the bureaucracy. "Where you stand depends on where you sit" is the basic dynamic of *bureaucratic politics*—i.e., the positions taken on an issue by different executive-branch departments and agencies depend on the interests of that particular department or agency. On economic sanctions, for example, the Commerce and Agriculture Departments, with their trade-promotion missions, often have opposed the Departments of State and Defense. This can be disaggregated even further to bureaus within the same department or agency, which may also "stand" differently depending on where they "sit." Within the State Department, the Bureau of Human Rights and the East Asia–Pacific Bureau disagreed over the linkage of MFN renewal with human rights progress in China in the early 1990s. And within the military, inter-service rivalry often breaks out as the Army, Navy, and Air Force compete for shares of the defense budget, higher profiles in military actions, and on other issues.

On top of these interest-based dynamics are the problems inherent in any large, complex bureaucracy: simply getting things done. The nineteenth-century German political philosopher Max Weber first focused on the problems inherent in large bureaucracies in government as well as other complex organizations. Often instead of using rational processes consistent with the criteria noted earlier, bureaucracies proceed according to their own standard operating procedures and in other cumbersome ways that remind us why the term "bureaucracy" has the negative connotations that it does.

As Figure 2.1 shows, the foreign affairs bureaucracy is vast and complex. We depict it here in five tiers:

- the departments and agencies with principal foreign affairs responsibility (National Security Council, State, Defense);
- those most involved in foreign economic policy (Commerce, Treasury, Agriculture, State's Bureau of Economic Affairs, U.S. Trade Representative, International Trade Commission;
- agencies that deal with political democratization and economic development (Agency for International Development, State's Bureau of Democracy, Human Rights, and Labor);
- intelligence agencies (the CIA, National Security Agency, Defense Intelligence Agency), and
- those agencies and offices that, while primarily focused on domestic policy, also have important foreign policy involvement: the Environmental Protection Agency on global environmental issues, the Office of National Drug Control Policy on international narcotics policy, the Department of Labor on international policies regarding employment practices.

Most of this discussion has been about normal foreign policy decision-making. When the situations faced are international crises, the challenges for meeting the criteria for a rational executive-branch decision-making process are even greater. The key characteristics of crises are a high level of threat against vital interests, a short time frame for decision-making, and usually a significant element of surprise that the situation arose. Such situations tend to give presidents more power, since they require fast, decisive action. They also often lead presidents to set up special decision-making teams, drawing most heavily on the most trusted advisers. The crisis most often cited as a model of effective decision-making is the Cuban missile crisis, which we will discuss further in Chapter 4.

In sum, a rational executive-branch policy-making process is desirable but difficult. The sources of executive-branch politics are many, and the dynamics can get quite intricate. We will see these played out in ways that show both striking similarities and sharp differences over time.

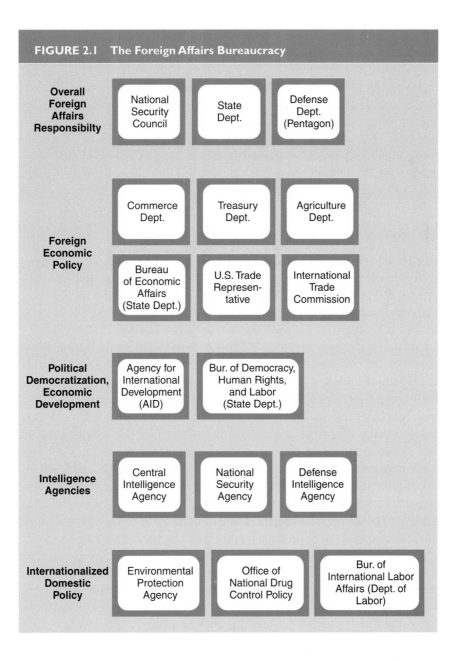

FIGURE 2.1   The Foreign Affairs Bureaucracy

Overall Foreign Affairs Responsibilty
- National Security Council
- State Dept.
- Defense Dept. (Pentagon)

Foreign Economic Policy
- Commerce Dept.
- Treasury Dept.
- Agriculture Dept.
- Bureau of Economic Affairs (State Dept.)
- U.S. Trade Representative
- International Trade Commission

Political Democratization, Economic Development
- Agency for International Development (AID)
- Bur. of Democracy, Human Rights, and Labor (State Dept.)

Intelligence Agencies
- Central Intelligence Agency
- National Security Agency
- Defense Intelligence Agency

Internationalized Domestic Policy
- Environmental Protection Agency
- Office of National Drug Control Policy
- Bur. of International Labor Affairs (Dept. of Labor)

Interest Groups and Their Influence

Interest groups are "formal organizations of people who share a common outlook or social circumstance and who band together in the hope of influencing government policy."[18] Three questions are central to understanding the foreign policy role of interest groups: (1) What are the principal types of foreign policy interest groups? (2) What are the main strategies and techniques of influence used by interest groups? (3) How much influence do interest groups have, and how much should they have?

A Typology of Foreign Policy Interest Groups

Distinctions can be made among five main types of foreign policy interest groups based on differences in the nature of the interests that motivate their activity and in their forms of organization. Dynamics of Choice on p. 45 presents the typology, with some general examples.

ECONOMIC INTEREST GROUPS   This category includes multinational corporations (MNCs) and other businesses, labor unions, consumers, and other groups whose lobbying is motivated principally by how foreign policy affects the economic interests of their members. These groups are especially active on trade and other international economic policy issues. Take the infamous 1930 Smoot-Hawley Act, which raised so many tariffs so high that it helped deepen and globalize the Great Depression. Some wondered how such a bill ever could have passed. Very easily, according to one senator who "brazenly admitted that the people who gave money to congressional campaigns had a right to expect it back in tariffs."[19] In the South Africa case many American businesses actively opposed the anti-apartheid sanctions as threatening their economic interests by damaging trade, endangering investments, and hurting profits.

IDENTITY GROUPS   These groups are motivated less by economic interests than by ethnic or religious identity. Irish Americans, Polish Americans, African Americans, Greek Americans, Cuban Americans, Vietnamese Americans—these and other ethnic identity groups have sought to influence U.S. relations with the country or region to which they trace their ancestry or heritage. The group most often pointed to as the most powerful ethnic lobby is Jewish Americans and their principal organization, the American-Israel Public Affairs Committee (AIPAC); indeed, one book on AIPAC was titled *The*

A Typology of Foreign Policy Interest Groups

Type	General examples
Economic groups	AFL-CIO (organization of trade unions) National Association of Manufacturers Consumer Federation of America Major multinational corporations (MNCs)
Identity groups	Jewish Americans Cuban Americans Greek Americans African Americans
Political issue groups	Anti–Vietnam War movement Committee on the Present Danger Amnesty International World Wildlife Fund Refugees International
State and local governments	Local Elected Officials for Social Responsibility California World Trade Commission
Foreign governments	Washington law firms, lobbyists, public-relations companies (hired to promote interests of foreign governments in Washington)

Lobby. But while the Jewish lobby unquestionably has been quite influential, it is not nearly as all-powerful or always-winning as it is often portrayed. It has lost, for example, on some Arab-Israeli issues in part because major oil companies and arms exporters with key interests in the Arab world (i.e., economic interest groups) have pressured more strongly for the opposite policy. The Jewish-American community itself at times has been split, reflecting Israel's own deep political splits on issues like the Arab-Israeli peace process. Moreover, the Jewish-American lobby is not solely responsible for pro-Israel U.S. policy; both power (the geostrategic benefits of a reliable ally in a region known for its anti-Americanism) and principles (Israel is the only democracy in the entire Middle East region) have also been served.

POLITICAL ISSUE GROUPS   This third category includes groups that are organized around support for opposition to a political issue that is not principally a matter of their economic interests or group identity. Among these are antiwar groups and movements, such as the anti–Vietnam War movement; the America First Committee, which tried to keep the United States out of World War II; and the Anti-Imperialist League, which opposed the Spanish-American War of 1898. During the Cold War, groups such as the Council for a Livable World and the Nuclear Freeze Movement pushed for ratcheting down the levels of armaments and greater efforts at U.S.-Soviet accommodation. On the other hand, quite a few groups have been strong advocates of more assertive foreign policies, such as the American Legion, the Veterans of Foreign Wars, and the tellingly named Committee on the Present Danger.

Other sub-areas of foreign policy also have their sets of political issue groups. There are environmental groups (the World Wildlife Federation, the Sierra Club), human rights groups (Amnesty International, Human Rights Watch), women's rights groups, advocates of the rights of refugees (InterAction, Refugees International), and many others. Groups such as these are most commonly called *nongovernmental organizations* (NGOs) and have been playing increasingly important roles in influencing American foreign policy.

STATE AND LOCAL GOVERNMENTS   Although they do not fit the term "interest groups" in the same way, state and local governments increasingly seek to influence foreign policy as it affects their interests.[20] In the early 1980s, for example, they pressured the federal government to end the arms race through groups such as the Local Elected Officials for Social Responsibility and by proclamations and referendums by more than 150 cities and counties declaring themselves "nuclear-free zones" or otherwise opposing the nuclear arms race. Conversely, states and cities with large defense industries have pressured the federal government not to cut defense spending. Local activism has been even greater on trade issues. The California World Trade Commission, part of the state government, sent its own representative to the GATT trade talks in Geneva, Switzerland. Many state and local governments actually led the effort to combat apartheid in South Africa. In fact the pressure on Congress to pass national sanctions legislation was strengthened because so many state and local governments, including California and New York City, already had imposed their own sanctions by prohibiting purchases and divesting pension-fund holdings from companies still doing business with South Africa.

FOREIGN GOVERNMENTS   It is of course normal diplomacy for governments to have embassies in each others' capitals. The reference here is to the American law firms, lobbyists, and public relations companies hired by foreign governments to lobby for them. These foreign lobbyists often are former members of Congress (both Republican and Democratic), former Cabinet members, other former top executive-branch officials, and other "big guns." Indeed by the early 1990s there were well over one thousand lobbyists in Washington who were representing foreign countries. Major controversies have arisen over foreign lobbying; one high-profile case involved Japan and, as claimed in a book provocatively titled *Agents of Influence,* its "manipulation" of U.S. policy through lobbyists to the point where "it threatens our national sovereignty."[21] Another striking case was that of Angola in the mid-1980s, in which American lobbyists were hired both by the Angolan guerrillas, to try to improve their image and otherwise win support for military aid, and by the Angolan government, to try to block the aid to the guerrillas. More than $2 million was paid out by the rebels and almost $1 million by the government in just one year—a hefty sum for a country so poor.

Not all issues have all five types of interest groups involved. But all have at least some of these groups seeking to exert their influence.

Strategies and Techniques of Influence

Interest groups seek to influence foreign policy according to many different strategies aimed at the various foreign policy actors.

INFLUENCING CONGRESS   Foreign policy legislation generally needs to pass through five principal stages within Congress: the writing of a bill, hearings and mark-up by the relevant committees, votes on the floors of the House of Representatives and the Senate, reconciliation of any differences between the House and Senate bills in a conference committee, and the appropriations process, in which the actual amounts of money are set for defense spending, foreign aid, and other items. Lobbyists will seek to influence legislation at each of these stages. Much, of course, also goes on behind the scenes. Lobbyists regularly meet privately with senators and representatives who are allies to set strategy, count votes, and in some cases even to help write the legislation. Indeed, influence in Congress often seems like an MCI "friends and family" circle: who you know and who your political friends are does matter.

Interest groups also try to go even more to the source by influencing who wins elections. Defense industry political action committees (PACs), for example, are major campaign contributors, especially for members of Congress who serve on defense-related committees. A 1982 study showed that almost half of the PAC contributions made by the nation's twelve largest defense contractors went to members of Congress's armed services committees and defense and military-construction subcommittees.

INFLUENCING THE EXECUTIVE BRANCH   Interest groups also try to directly influence executive-branch departments and agencies as they formulate and implement foreign policy on a day-to-day basis. In the 1980s, AIPAC broadened its efforts from being heavily focused on Capitol Hill to also work with mid-level officials in the State and Defense Departments who were working on U.S.-Israeli relations. In trade policy there is a whole system of advisory committees through which the private sector can channel its influence to executive-branch officials who negotiate trade treaties.

Another strategy is to try to influence who gets appointed to important foreign policy positions. One case in which interest groups were able to have significant influence over an executive appointment involved the ability of the conservative Cuban-American National Foundation (CANF) in 1992–93 to block the nomination of Mario Baeza, a Cuban American whose views on how to deal with Fidel Castro were seen as too moderate, as assistant secretary of state for Inter-American affairs. In another case Ernest Lefever, President Reagan's nominee for assistant secretary of state for human rights, was not confirmed because of opposition by pro–human rights groups who viewed him as more a critic than an advocate of their cause.

INFLUENCING PUBLIC OPINION   Groups also take their efforts to influence foreign policy outside the halls of Congress and the executive branch, mobilizing protests and demonstrations to show "shoulder-to-shoulder" support for their causes. This is an old tradition, going back to peace movements in the early twentieth century, as well as to such nineteenth-century events as the Civil War veterans' march on Washington demanding payment of their pensions. The anti–Vietnam War movement was particularly known for its demonstrations on college campuses as well as in Washington. In the spring of 1970, for example, college campuses around the country were shut down (and final exams were even canceled on many campuses) and almost half a million protesters descended on Washington. An even larger demonstration was staged in 1990 on the twentieth anniversary of "Earth Day" to pressure the government for stronger and more forward-looking policies on global environmental issues.

Especially in recent years, foreign policy interest groups have become quite astute at using the media as a magnifying glass to enlarge their exposure and as a megaphone to amplify their voice. For all the econometric models that were run and other studies that were conducted to show the damage done to the American auto industry by Japanese auto imports in the 1970s and 1980s, for example, none had nearly the impact of the televised image of two members of Congress smashing a Toyota with a sledgehammer in front of the Capitol. Members of the anti-apartheid movement dramatized their cause by handcuffing themselves to the fence around the South African embassy in Washington, D.C., and staging other civil disobedience protests, a major objective of which was to get on the nightly television news.

CORRUPTION   Popular images of suitcases stuffed with $100 bills, exorbitant junkets, and other corruption at times get grossly exaggerated. Nevertheless, there have been sufficient instances of corrupt efforts to influence foreign policy that to not include it as a technique of influence would be a glaring omission. For example, Koreagate was a 1976 scandal over alleged South Korean influence-peddling in Congress. Another example was the 1980s Pentagon defense-contract scandals involving bribes, cover-ups, and cost overruns that led to the purchase of "specially designed" $600 toilet seats and $1,000 coffee machines.

The Extent of Interest-Group Influence: Analytic and Normative Considerations

"The friend of popular governments never finds himself so much alarmed for their character and fate," James Madison warned back in Federalist no. 10, "as when he contemplates their propensity to . . . the violence of faction." Madison defined a "faction" not just as a group with a particular set of interests but as one whose interests, or "common impulse of passion," were "adverse to the rights of other citizens, or to the permanent and aggregate interests of the community."

Madison's concern with what we now call the extent of interest-group influence bears particularly on foreign policy, for three principal reasons. First, if there is even the slightest sense that the nation is asking its citizens to make the ultimate sacrifice of war for interests that are more group-specific than collectively national, the consequences on national morale and purpose can be devastating. Even in more ongoing, less dramatic areas of policy the effects of such an impression on the overall state of democracy and conceptions of public authority can be deeply corrosive.

Second, this "capturing" by interest groups of areas of policy makes change much more difficult because of the many vested interests that get ensconced.[22] This is especially a problem in foreign policy, given the many threats and challenges to which the United States must respond, including the rigors of staying competitive in the international economy. The work of political scientist Mancur Olson asserts that throughout history it has been the sapping of capacity for change and adaptation brought on by too many vested interests that has brought down one empire and major power after another—and into which, he warned in 1982, the United States was sinking.[23]

Third is the highly emotionally charged nature of so many foreign policy issues. The "impulses of passion" Madison warned about can be quite intense. The stakes tend to be seen not as just winning or losing, but as tests of morality and even of patriotism.

One of the examples most often cited of excessive interest-group influence is the *military-industrial complex.** Consider the warning sounded in a famous speech in 1961 (see At the Source on p. 51). Sound like something that might have come from Nikita Khrushchev? Fidel Castro? Or maybe Abbie Hoffman or some other 1960s radical? None of the above. It is from the farewell address of President (and former general) Dwight D. Eisenhower.

Some of the statistics on the Cold War military-industrial complex really are staggering. By 1970 the Pentagon owned 29 million acres of land (almost the size of New York State) valued at $47.7 billion, and had "true wealth" of $300 to $400 billion, or about six to eight times greater than the annual after-tax profits of all U.S. corporations.[24] During the Reagan defense buildup in the mid-1980s, "the Pentagon was spending an average of $28 million *an hour.*" One out of every sixteen American workers as well as 47 percent of all aeronautical engineers, more than 30 percent of mathematicians, and 25 percent of physicists either worked directly for or drew grants from the defense sector.[25]

One of the best examples of how the military-industrial complex was set up involved the B-1 bomber, a highly capable but expensive new strategic

---

*The formal political science definition of the military-industrial complex is a social and political subsystem that integrates the armament industry, the military-oriented science community, the defense-related parts of the political system, and the military bureaucracies. David Skidmore and Valerie M. Hudson, eds., *The Limits of State Autonomy: Societal Groups and Foreign Policy Formation* (Boulder, Colo.: Westview, 1992), 36.

> ### ▶ At the Source ◀
>
> ## BEWARE THE MILITARY-INDUSTRIAL COMPLEX
>
> " The conjunction of an immense military establishment and a large arms industry is new in the American experience. The total influence—economic, political, even spiritual—is felt in every city, every statehouse, every office of the federal government. . . . We must not fail to comprehend its grave implications. Our toil, our resources and livelihood all are involved; so is the very structure of our society.
>
> In the councils of government, we must guard against the acquisition of unwarranted influence, whether sought or unsought, by the *military-industrial complex* [emphasis added]. The potential for the disastrous rise of misplaced power exists and will persist.
>
> We must never let the weight of this combination endanger our liberties or democratic processes. "
>
> Source: Dwight D. Eisenhower, "Farewell Address," January 1961, *Public Papers of the Presidents of the United States, Dwight D. Eisenhower,* Vol. 8 (Washington, D.C.: U.S. Government Printing Office, 1962), 1035–41.

bomber whose production President Carter sought to cancel but was unable to, largely because of the "gerrymandered subcontracting" depicted in Figure 2.2. The main contractor for the B-1 was Rockwell International, based in California. In subcontracting out the various parts of the plane, Rockwell astutely ensured that contracts would go to companies in forty-eight states: the defensive avionics to a firm in New York, the offensive avionics to one in Nebraska, the tires and wheels to Ohio, the tail to Maryland, the wings to Tennessee, etc. To make sure they knew the score, Rockwell spent $110,000 on a study delineating the B-1's economic benefits on a state-by-state, district-by-district basis. Thus when President Carter did not include funding for the B-1 in his version of the annual defense budget, he was threatening jobs in the states and districts of a majority of the members of both the House and the Senate. Voting records show that even many liberal Democrats who otherwise were opposed to high levels of defense spending and in favor of arms control voted against Carter and added enough funding to keep the B-1 alive.[26] When Ronald Reagan became president in 1981, the B-1 production spigot was turned on full force.

FIGURE 2.2   The Political Building of a Bomber

Parts for the B-1 bomber are made in every state except Alaska and Hawaii. Some of the larger components and their sources—

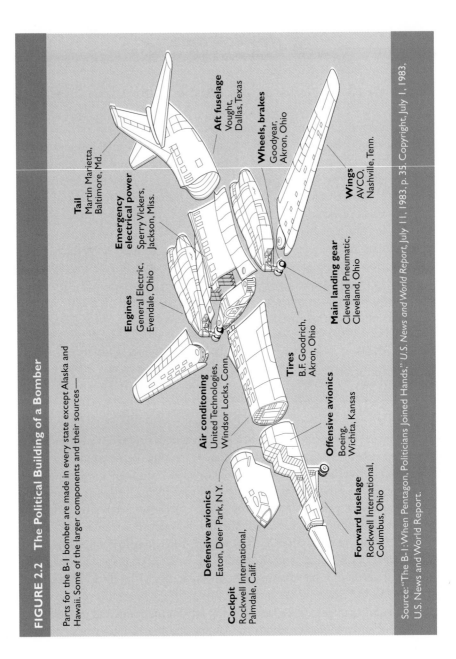

Tail
Martin Marietta,
Baltimore, Md.

Aft fuselage
Vought,
Dallas, Texas

Wheels, brakes
Goodyear,
Akron, Ohio

Wings
AVCO,
Nashville, Tenn.

**Emergency
electrical power**
Sperry Vickers,
Jackson, Miss.

Engines
General Electric,
Evendale, Ohio

Main landing gear
Cleveland Pneumatic,
Cleveland, Ohio

Tires
B.F. Goodrich,
Akron, Ohio

Air conditioning
United Technologies,
Windsor Locks, Conn.

Offensive avionics
Boeing,
Wichita, Kansas

Defensive avionics
Eaton, Deer Park, N.Y.

Cockpit
Rockwell International,
Palmdale, Calif.

Forward fuselage
Rockwell International,
Columbus, Ohio

Source: "The B-1: When Pentagon, Politicians Joined Hands," *U.S. News and World Report*, July 11, 1983, p. 35. Copyright, July 1, 1983, U.S. News and World Report.

Yet there is significant debate over how extensive interest-group influence is. In their review of the literature on the military-industrial complex, professors David Skidmore and Valerie Hudson conclude that the record is mixed, that while there are numerous cases of significant influence, especially in weapons development and procurement, the more sweeping claims of dominance are not borne out by the empirical research.[27] Moreover, and more generally, we also have to go back to Madison for a note of caution about efforts to somehow ban or otherwise "remove the causes" of interest groups: "It could never be more truly said than of [this] remedy that it was worse than the disease. Liberty is to faction what air is to fire, an aliment without which it instantly expires. But it could not be a less folly to abolish liberty, which is essential to political life, because it nourishes faction than it would be to wish the annihilation of air, which is essential to animal life, because it imparts to fire its destructive agency."[28]

Madison is more positive on efforts to "control the effects" of factions, efforts that today would include such initiatives as campaign-finance reform, reforms of the defense-procurement process, tighter oversight of covert action, and broad general efforts to educate and engage the public.

Experience, though, teaches that this is a problem for which there is no full or enduring solution. Reform measures such as the ones noted above can help correct some of the worst excesses of interest-group influence. But this is one of those dilemmas for which, as American government scholars Theodore Lowi and Benjamin Ginsberg write, "there is no ideal answer. . . . Those who believe that there are simple solutions to the issues of political life would do well to ponder this problem."[29]

The Impact of the News Media

It was just a few hours short of prime time, on the evening of January 16, 1991, when American bombers started attacking Iraq, live on CNN. A war was starting, and Americans and much of the world could see it (at least some of it) right there on their living-room TVs. The Persian Gulf War made the foreign policy role of the news media more graphic and more evident than ever before. Here, too, though, as with much of what we have discussed in this chapter, the key questions debated were not totally new: (1) What role should the news media play? (2) How much influence do they actually have? (3) How is the balance to be struck between freedom of the press and national security?

Role of the Media: Cheerleader or Critic?

In 1916, in an effort to ensure support for a just-launched military intervention into Mexico, President Woodrow Wilson stated, "I have asked the several news services to be good enough to assist the Administration in keeping this view of the expedition constantly before both the people of this country and the distressed and sensitive people of Mexico."[30] The president was asking newspapers to be his "cheerleaders." The matter-of-fact tone of his statement, made in a public speech, not just leaked from some secret memo, conveys the expectation that although the press could muckrake all it wanted in domestic policy, in foreign policy, especially during wars or other crises, it was to be less free and more friendly.

Grandparents can tell you about World War II and how strongly the media supported the war effort. Foreign correspondents filled the newspapers, and newsreels played in the movie theaters, with stories and pictures of American and allied heroism, and Nazi and Japanese evil and atrocities. This was "the good war," and there generally was a basis for positive reporting. It did get intentionally manipulative, however. A book called *Hollywood Goes to War* tells the story of how "officials of the Office of War Information, the government's propaganda agency, issued a constantly updated manual instructing the studios in how to assist the war effort, sat in on story conferences with Hollywood's top brass, . . . pressured the movie makers to change scripts and even scrap pictures when they found objectionable material, and sometimes wrote dialogue for key speeches."[31]

Even in the early days of U.S. involvement in Vietnam, the media were largely supportive. But as the war went on, and went bad, the media sent back reports that were much more critical of the conduct of the war and that contradicted the official versions being put out by the Johnson and Nixon administrations. In one telling incident a reporter who had written critical stories was dressed down by a military commander for "not getting on the team." Similar questions were raised during the Persian Gulf War, when some journalists who wrote stories about "collateral damage" to Iraqi civilians from the bombing attacks were viewed even by some sections of the public as unpatriotic.

Cheerleader or critic? Which role have the media played? And which role should they play? These are crucial questions to bear in mind.

Modes of Influence

Three main distinctions are made as to the modes of influence the media have on foreign policy politics. First is *agenda setting*. "The mass media may not be successful in telling people what to think," one classic study put it, "but the media are stunningly successful in telling their audience what to think about."[32] Or, to put it more colloquially, if a tree falls in the woods and CNN doesn't cover it, did it really fall? The media play a crucial role in determining which issues get focused on and which do not. Some issues do force their way onto the agenda, and the media are largely reactive and mirroring. But there are many other issues that would get much less policy attention if it were not for major media coverage. Conversely, there are foreign policy issues that despite their importance don't get media coverage and thus don't get on the agenda—whole "forests" may fall down with no CNN cameras in sight.

As to *shaping public opinion,* in terms of its substantive content, the main impact of the media is in what researchers call "framing" and "priming" effects.[33] The stakes involved in a particular foreign policy issue are not necessarily self-evident or part of a strictly objective reality. How an issue is cast ("framed") affects the substantive judgments people make—and the media play a key role in this framing. The media also influence ("prime") the relative priority the public gives to one issue over another, as well as the criteria by which the public makes its judgments about success and failure.

To the extent that the media's substantive impact goes beyond these framing and priming effects, it tends to be on two kinds of foreign policy issues. One set comprises those for which the public has little prior information and few sources other than the media. The other set includes those issues that have strong symbolic significance and are heavily emotionally charged, such as the 1979–81 Iranian hostage crisis. The intense media coverage of the hostage crisis made sure this issue stayed front-and-center on the agenda, which, given the nature of the issue, also influenced the substance of public opinion.* A more indirect way the shaping effect works is by influencing "opinion leaders"—i.e., business, community, educational, and other leaders—to whom the public often looks for cues, in part because opinion leaders follow the news most closely.

A third type of influence is directly on *policy-makers.* "What will the press think?" is a common question inside the White House and the State Department. It is asked in an anticipatory manner and thus can impact policy as it is formulated. The concern with how a policy will be perceived comes into play

---

*Ted Koppel's *Nightline,* which went on to become one of the top-rated news shows ever, started out as nightly coverage of just the hostage crisis. Every show would be introduced as "Day 1 of the Hostage Crisis," "Day 2 . . . ," "Day 50 . . . ," "Day 100 . . . ," all the way through "Day 444," when on January 20, 1981, the last hostages were finally released.

as part of the plans for pursuing a policy, with strategies for press conferences, special briefings, and "political spin" at times almost as detailed as military battle plans. Also, in a more informational sense, smart policy-makers draw on dispatches and analyses by the more prominent foreign-affairs journalists as additional and independent sources of information to supplement even their own intelligence sources.

Freedom of the Press vs. National Security

How to strike the balance between freedom of the press and national security has been a recurring issue in American politics. The First Amendment guarantees freedom of the press. Yet situations can arise when the nation's security would be endangered if certain information became public. This national-security rationale can be, and has been, very real; it also can be, and has been, abused.

Historical precedents cut both ways. For example, in 1961 the *New York Times* had uncovered information on the secret Bay of Pigs invasion of Cuba being planned by the Kennedy administration. Under some pressure from the White House, but primarily as their own self-censorship based on the national-security rationale, the *Times*'s publisher and editors decided not to print the information. The Bay of Pigs invasion went ahead, and it failed disastrously—leaving many to question whether national security would have been better served had the story been run and the plan unmasked.[34] On the other hand, in 1962, during the Cuban missile crisis, the press again restrained some of its reporting. An ABC correspondent even served as a secret intermediary for some tense negotiations between President Kennedy and Soviet leader Nikita Khrushchev. This time the outcome was more positive: the crisis was resolved, and many concluded that the restraint on full freedom of the press was justified.

The Vietnam War "get on the team" view noted earlier in this chapter came to a head as a freedom of the press issue in the "Pentagon Papers" case. In mid-1967, at a point when the war was going very badly, Defense Secretary Robert McNamara set up a comprehensive internal review of U.S. policy. By the end of the Johnson administration the forty-seven-volume *History of the United States Decision-Making Process on Vietnam Policy,* which came to be called the "Pentagon Papers," had been completed. It was given highly classified status, to be kept secret and for high-level government use only. But in March 1971, Daniel Ellsberg, who had been one of the researchers and authors of the Pentagon Papers but now was a critic and opponent of the war, leaked a copy to a *New York Times* reporter. On June 13, 1971, the *Times* began publishing excerpts. The Nixon administration immediately sued to stop publication, claiming potential damage to national security. (The administration also had a political agenda, fearing that already-eroding public support for the war would crumble even more.) On June 30 the Supreme Court ruled 6 to 3 against the Nixon administration. The Court did not totally disregard the national-security justification but ruled that the standard had not been met in this case, and that therefore First Amendment freedom of the press rights took precedence.[35] The *Times* continued its stories on the Pentagon Papers, as did other newspapers.* Freedom of the press and national-security issues also grew heated during the 1990–91 Persian Gulf War, as we will see in Chapter 6.

The Nature and Influence of Public Opinion

With respect to public opinion and foreign policy, our concern is with two principal questions: (1) What is its nature? (2) How much influence does it have?

Ignorant or Sensible? The Nature of Public Opinion about Foreign Policy

To read some of the commentaries on American public opinion and foreign policy, one would think that Americans believe much more in government *for* the people than in government *by* and *of* the people. Walter Lippmann, the leading U.S. foreign-affairs journalist of the first half of the twentieth century, disparaged public opinion as "destructively wrong at critical junctures . . . a dangerous master of decision when the stakes are life and death."[36] Nor was the traditional view taken by leading scholars any more positive. "The rational

---

*It was in reaction to the Pentagon Papers leak that Nixon set up the special White House unit known as the "plumbers" to "plug" any further leaks. Among the operations carried out by the "plumbers" was an illegal break-in to the offices of Daniel Ellsberg's psychiatrist, seeking information with which to discredit Ellsberg; and the 1972 June break-in at the headquarters of the Democratic National Committee in the Watergate building. These events and actions, and others later uncovered, ultimately led to an impeachment investigation against Nixon and on August 9, 1974, his resignation as president.

requirements of good foreign policy," wrote the eminent Realist Hans Morgenthau, "cannot from the outset count upon the support of a public whose preferences are emotional rather than rational."[37] Gabriel Almond, in his *The American People and Foreign Policy,* a 1950 study long considered the classic in the field, stressed the "inattentiveness" of the vast majority of the public to foreign policy, an inattentiveness he attributed to the lack of "intellectual structure and factual content." [38] Others took this even further, positing a historical pattern of reflexively alternating "moods" of introversion and extroversion, sort of a societal biorhythm by which every two decades or so the public shifted between internationalism and isolationism.[39]

These criticisms are built around a basic distinction between the "mass public," prone to all of the above and more, and the better-informed, more thoughtful, and more sophisticated "elites." The general public consistently has shown very little knowledge about foreign affairs. The following facts illustrate general public ignorance:

- Only 58 percent of the public in 1964 knew that the United States was a member of NATO, and 38 percent thought the Soviet Union was.
- In 1986, despite the extreme attention being given to the conflict in Nicaragua by the Reagan administration, only 38 percent of Americans could correctly identify whether the United States was supporting the contras or the Sandinistas.
- Only four months after the dramatic ceremony held on September 13, 1993, on the White House lawn with President Clinton, Israeli Prime Minister Yitzhak Rabin, and Palestine Liberation Organization leader Yasir Arafat, 56 percent of Americans could not identify the group that Arafat headed.[40]

Other critics point to overreactive tendencies in the mass public. Take the "rally 'round the flag" pattern in times of crisis. On the one hand this can be quite positive in helping build consensus and national solidarity when the nation faces a serious threat. It also can be politically helpful to presidents whose popularity gets boosted as part of the rallying effect. But often it becomes blind "followership," and in extremes can pose dangers to democracy by equating dissent with disloyalty (as we saw earlier in this chapter).

An alternative view of the public sees it as much more sensible about foreign policy than it gets credit for. Elmo Roper, who founded a trailblazing public-opinion-polling firm, observed back in 1942 that "during my eight years of asking the common man questions about what he thinks and what he wants ... I have often been surprised and elated to discover that, despite his lack of information, the common man's native intelligence generally brings him to a sound conclusion."[41]

Two key points are made by those who share the "sensible public" view. One is that rather than being wildly and whimsically fluctuating, public opinion has been quite stable over time. Take, for example, basic attitudes toward isolationism ("stay out of world affairs") vs. internationalism ("play an active role"). For the entire 1945–95 period, as illustrated in Figure 2.3, despite some ups and downs the overall pro-internationalism pattern holds. We can see a definite narrowing of the gap from the mid-1960s (Vietnam War) on, but even then the pattern holds.

The second point made by those who view public opinion positively is that to the extent that public views on foreign policy have changed over time, it has been less a matter of moodiness and much more a rational process. A study of the fifty-year period 1935–85 concludes that "virtually all the rapid

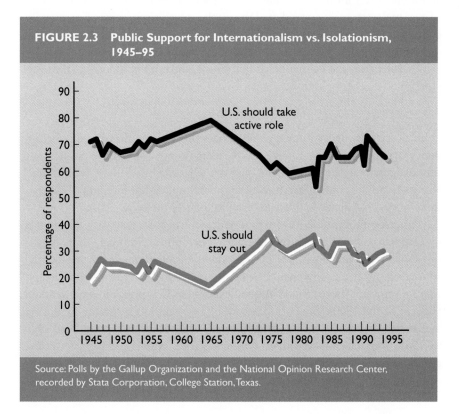

FIGURE 2.3   Public Support for Internationalism vs. Isolationism, 1945–95

U.S. should take active role

U.S. should stay out

Percentage of respondents

Source: Polls by the Gallup Organization and the National Opinion Research Center, recorded by Stata Corporation, College Station, Texas.

shifts [in public opinion] . . . were related to political and economic circumstances or to significant events which sensible citizens would take into account. In particular, most abrupt foreign policy changes took place in connection with wars, confrontations or crises in which major policy changes in the actions of the United States or other nations quite naturally affect preference about what policies to pursue."[42] This is termed an "event-driven" process; that is to say, when the threats facing the United States or other aspects of the international situation have changed, in an altogether rational way so too has public opinion.

What, for example, was so feckless about the public turning against the Vietnam War when many people believed at the time, and now former defense secretary Robert McNamara's memoirs have confirmed, that even those at the highest levels did not believe the war could be won? "It is difficult to fault the American people," writes Army Major Andrew F. Krepinevich, Jr., "when, after that long a period of active engagement, the Joint Chiefs of Staff could only offer more of the same for an indefinite period with no assurance of eventual success."[43] Indeed, had the public stayed supportive of such an ill-conceived war effort, we might *then* really have wondered about its rationality.

We thus get two very different views of the nature of public opinion. The analytic challenge is that neither holds all the time, and both hold some of the time.

The Influence of Public Opinion on Foreign Policy

Political scientist Bruce Russett characterizes the basic public opinion–foreign policy dynamic as an *interactive* one. Leaders do not control the public; they cannot "persuade the populace to support whatever the leaders wish to do." Nor is the public controlling, having so much impact that foreign policy basically "obeys [its] dictates." Instead "each influences the other."[44]

Public opinion influences foreign policy in five principal ways. The first is by *parameter setting*, which means that public opinion imposes limits on the range of the president's policy options via assessments made by presidential advisers of what has any chance of being made "to fly" with the public and what options are "nonstarters." A good example is U.S. policy toward Saddam Hussein in the 1980s, the period before he became Public Enemy #1 during the Persian Gulf War. During Saddam's war with Iran, which lasted from 1980 to 1988, the Reagan administration gave Iraq extensive support on the grounds that "the enemy of my enemy is my friend." Once the Iran-Iraq War was over, and Saddam then attacked the Iraqi Kurds with chemical weapons and showed other signs of aggression in the region, the State Department began to question whether the United States should continue aiding Iraq. But with the Iran-contra affair still in the political air, the Reagan administration flatly ruled out any shift from the pro-Saddam policy as risking being seen by the public as "soft on Iran." Consequently, when the internal State Department study proposing such a shift in policy was leaked to the press, Secretary of State George Shultz "called a meeting in his office, angrily demanding to know who was responsible for the paper. . . . [The paper] was dismissed less by any analytic refutation of its strategic logic than on political grounds. . . . On the cover page, in big letters, [Shultz] had written 'NO.'"[45]

A second way that public opinion influences policy is through *centripetal pull* toward the center on presidents who need to build supportive coalitions. This centering pull has worked both on presidents whose tendencies were too far to the left and on those too far to the right to gain sufficient political support. With Jimmy Carter, whose foreign policy reputation generally raised doubts as to whether he was "tough" enough, the public sought to balance this concern by expressing low levels of approval of Carter's Soviet policy when it was in its conciliatory phases (1977–78, most of 1979), and higher levels of support when Carter got tough (mid-1978, 1979–80). Ronald Reagan's foreign policy reputation, in contrast, was plenty tough but raised concerns among a substantial segment of the public as to whether it was reckless and risked war. Thus public approval of Reagan's Soviet policy fell when it was most strident and confrontational (1981–83), and then increased only in late 1985 once it started to become more genuinely open to cooperation, peaking at 65 percent following Reagan's first summit with Soviet leader Mikhail Gorbachev in November 1985.[46]

The third influence of public opinion is its *impact on Congress.* Congress is very sensitive, arguably too sensitive, to public opinion on foreign policy. It responds both to polls on specific issues and to more general assessments of whether the public really cares much about foreign policy at all. Often this translates into Congress's paying the most attention to the groups that are the most vocal and are the most politically potent, and caring less about broader opinion-poll trends. Former senator Hubert H. Humphrey, a leading figure from the late 1940s to his death in 1978, excoriated many of his colleagues for being "POPPs," or what he called "public opinion poll politicians," on foreign policy.[47]

Fourth, public opinion can *affect diplomatic negotiations.* Public opinion does not just come into play once a treaty or other diplomatic agreement is reached; it also can affect the actual diplomatic negotiations themselves, because U.S. diplomats need to know while still at the table what terms of agreement are politically viable back home.[48] This kind of influence is not necessarily a bad thing. It can be, to the extent that it ties the negotiators' hands in ways that are politically popular but unsound in policy terms. But public opinion also can strengthen negotiators' hands, as part of a "good cop–bad cop" dynamic. "I'd be more than willing to consider your proposal," a U.S. negotiator might say to his Japanese or Russian counterpart, "but the American public would never accept it."

The fifth avenue for public opinion's influence is *through presidential elections.* Voting analysts identify three factors as key to attributing significant electoral impact to a foreign policy issue: the issue must be demonstrated through survey questions to be highly salient; there must be significant differences between the positions of the Republican and Democratic candidates; and the public's awareness of these differences must be evident.[49] Recent examples of the strong impact of foreign policy issues in elections were in the 1952 (Dwight Eisenhower vs. Adlai Stevenson), 1972 (Richard Nixon vs. George McGovern), and 1980 (Jimmy Carter vs. Ronald Reagan) presidential contests.[50] In other instances the public has focused less on a specific issue than on a general sense of which candidate generally seems to be a strong leader, or which seems too "soft" to stand up to foreign enemies and otherwise be entrusted with the nation's security. Admittedly these are highly subjective assessments, and harder for pollsters and political scientists to measure precisely. But experience has shown that these difficulties don't make the opinions any less important.

Summary

Foreign policy politics is the process by which the choices of foreign policy strategy are made. It is much more complex than the conventional wisdom depicts; as we have seen in this chapter, politics' stopping "at the water's edge" has been more the exception than the rule. The basic patterns are of both consensus and conflict, with positive and negative variations of each in terms of their effects on policy.

The basic framework this chapter has laid out for foreign policy politics is a structural one, focusing on the roles of the principal political institutions involved in the making of foreign policy (the president, Congress, and the executive branch) and the major societal influences (interest groups, the news media, and public opinion).

In the next few chapters we will see how the dynamics of foreign policy politics have played out historically.

Notes

[1] Joseph Marion Jones, *The Fifteen Weeks (February 21–June 5, 1947)* (New York: Harcourt Brace and World, 1955), 8.

[2] James M. McCormick, *American Foreign Policy and Process* (Itasca, Ill.: F. E. Peacock, 1992), 478.

[3] Quoted in Bruce W. Jentleson, "American Diplomacy: Around the World and Along Pennsylvania Avenue," in Thomas E. Mann, ed., *A Question of Balance: The President, the Congress and Foreign Policy* (Washington, D.C.: Brookings Institution Press, 1990), 184.

[4] Edward S. Corwin, *The President: Office and Powers, 1787–1957,* 4th rev. ed. (New York: New York University Press, 1957), 171.

[5] Richard E. Neustadt, *Presidential Power: The Politics of Leadership* (New York: Wiley, 1976), 101.

[6] Cited in Arthur M. Schlesinger, Jr., *The Imperial Presidency* (New York: Atlantic Monthly Press, 1974), 17.

[7] Excellent books on the executive-legislative politics of trade policy are I. M. Destler, *American Trade Politics,* 3d ed. (Washington, D.C.: Institute of International Economics, 1995); and Robert A. Pastor, *Congress and the Politics of Foreign Economic Policy, 1929–1976* (Berkeley: University of California Press, 1980).

[8] James M. Lindsay, *Congress and the Politics of U.S. Foreign Policy* (Baltimore: Johns Hopkins University Press, 1994), 90.

[9] Cited in McCormick, *American Foreign Policy and Process,* 268.

[10] Lindsay, *Congress and the Politics of U.S. Foreign Policy,* chaps. 4 and 5.

[11] Lindsay, *Congress and the Politics of U.S. Foreign Policy,* 99.

[12] *United States v. Curtiss-Wright Export Corp.* (1936), quoted in Thomas M. Franck and Michael J. Glennon, eds., *Foreign Relations and National Security Law: Cases, Materials and Simulations* (St. Paul, Minn.: West Publishing, 1987), 32–37.

[13] *Youngstown Sheet and Tube Co. v. Sawyer* [the *Steel Seizure* case] (1952), quoted in Franck and Glennon, eds., *Foreign Relations and National Security Law,* 5–28.

[14] One of these cases was *Goldwater et al. v. Carter* (1979), in which Republican Senator Barry Goldwater led a suit challenging the constitutionality of President Carter's decision to terminate the Mutual Defense Treaty with Taiwan as part of his policy of normalizing relations with the People's Republic of China. The others were four suits brought by Democratic members of Congress in the Reagan and Bush administrations on war powers issues: *Crockett v. Reagan* (1984), on U.S. military aid and advisers in El Salvador; *Conyers v. Reagan* (1985), over the 1983 invasion of Grenada; *Lowry v. Reagan* (1987), over the reflagging and naval operations in the Persian Gulf during the Iran-Iraq War; and *Dellums v. Bush* (1990), over the initial Operation Desert Shield deployment following the Iraqi invasion of Kuwait.

[15] Alexander L. George, *Presidential Decisionmaking in Foreign Policy: The Effective Use of Information and Advice* (Boulder, Colo.: Westview, 1980), 10.

[16] Robert Jervis, *Perception and Misperception in International Politics* (Princeton: Princeton University Press, 1976), 28.

[17]See Irving L. Janis, *Groupthink: Psychological Studies of Policy Decisions and Fiascos* (Boston: Houghton Mifflin, 1982).

[18]Larry Berman and Bruce Murphy, *Approaching Democracy* (Englewood Cliffs, N.J.: Prentice-Hall, 1996), 408.

[19]Quoted in Pastor, *Congress and the Politics of Foreign Economic Policy*, 79.

[20]Earl H. Fry, *The Expanding Role of State and Local Governments in U.S. Foreign Policy* (New York: Council on Foreign Relations Press, 1998); also Chadwick Alger, "The World Relations of Cities: Closing the Gap between Social Science Paradigms and Everyday Human Experience," *International Studies Quarterly* 34:4 (1990), 493–518; and Michael H. Shuman, "Dateline Main Street: Local Foreign Policies," *Foreign Policy* 65 (1986/87), 154–74.

[21]Pat Choate, *Agents of Influence: How Japan's Lobbyists in the United States Manipulate America's Political and Economic System* (New York: Knopf, 1990), xiv.

[22]Theodore J. Lowi, *The End of Liberalism: Ideology, Policy, and the Crisis in Public Authority* (New York: Norton, 1969).

[23]Mancur Olson, *The Rise and Decline of Nations: Economic Growth, Stagflation, and Social Rigidities* (New Haven: Yale University Press, 1982).

[24]Sidney Lens, *The Military-Industrial Complex* (Philadelphia: Pilgrim, 1970), 12.

[25]Charles W. Kegley, Jr., and Eugene R. Wittkopf, *American Foreign Policy: Pattern and Process*, 5th ed. (New York: St. Martin's, 1996), 302.

[26]"The B-1: When Pentagon, Politicians Join Hands," *U.S. News and World Report*, July 1, 1983, 34. See also Nick Kotz, *Wild Blue Yonder: Money, Politics and the B-1 Bomber* (New York: Pantheon, 1988).

[27]David Skidmore and Valerie M. Hudson, eds., *The Limits of State Authority: Societal Groups and Foreign Policy Formation* (Boulder, Colo.: Westview, 1992), 36–38.

[28]James Madison, "Federalist no. 10," in Clinton Rossiter, ed., *The Federalist Papers* (New York: New American Library, 1961), 78.

[29]Theodore J. Lowi and Benjamin Ginsberg, *American Government: Freedom and Power*, 3d ed. (New York: Norton, 1993), 540.

[30]Quoted in Will Friedman, "Presidential Rhetoric, the News Media and the Use of Force in the Post–Cold War Era," paper presented to the Annual Conference of the American Political Science Association, New York, September 1994, 9.

[31]Clayton R. Koppes and Gregory D. Black, *Hollywood Goes to War: How Politics, Profits and Propaganda Shaped World War II Movies* (New York: Free Press, 1987), vii.

[32]Bernard C. Cohen, *The Press and Foreign Policy* (Princeton: Princeton University Press, 1963), cited in Kegley and Wittkopf, *American Foreign Policy*, 310.

[33]See Shanto Iyengar, *Is Anyone Responsible? How Television Frames Political Issues* (Chicago: University of Chicago Press, 1991); and Shanto Iyengar and Donald R. Kinder, *News That Matters: Television and American Opinion* (Chicago: University of Chicago Press, 1987).

[34]James Aronson, *The Press and the Cold War* (New York: Bobbs Merrill, 1970), chap. 11.

[35]*New York Times Co. v. United States* (1971), cited in Franck and Glennon, *Foreign Relations and National Security Law*, 863–78.

[36]Walter Lippmann, *Essays in the Public Philosophy* (Boston: Little, Brown, 1955), 20.

[37]Hans J. Morgenthau, *Politics among Nations: The Struggle for Power and Peace* (New York: Knopf, 1955), 20.

[38]Gabriel Almond, *The American People and Foreign Policy* (New York: Harcourt, Brace, 1950), 69.

[39] Frank L. Klingberg, "The Historical Alternation of Moods in American Foreign Policy," *World Politics* 4:2 (January 1952), 239–73.

[40] Lloyd A. Free and Hadley Cantril, *The Political Beliefs of Americans* (New York: Simon and Schuster, 1968), 60; Kegley and Wittkopf, *American Foreign Policy: Pattern and Process,* 265.

[41] Cited in Miroslav Nincic, *Democracy and Foreign Policy: The Fallacy of Political Realism* (New York: Columbia University Press, 1992), 48.

[42] Benjamin I. Page and Robert Y. Shapiro, "Changes in Americans' Policy Preferences, 1935–1979," *Public Opinion Quarterly* 46:1 (1982), 34.

[43] Andrew F. Krepinevich, Jr., *The Army and Vietnam* (Baltimore: John Hopkins University Press, 1986), 270.

[44] Bruce M. Russett, *Controlling the Sword* (Cambridge, Mass.: Harvard University Press, 1990), chap. 4.

[45] Bruce W. Jentleson, *With Friends Like These: Reagan, Bush and Saddam, 1982–1990* (New York: Norton, 1994), 90–91.

[46] Miroslav Nincic, "The United States, the Soviet Union and the Politics of Opposites," *World Politics* 40:4 (July 1988), 452–75.

[47] Interview by author, July 20 and 22, 1977, published in Bruce W. Jentleson, ed., *Perspectives 1979* (Washington, D.C.: Close Up Foundation, 1979), 273–79.

[48] Robert Putnam, "Diplomacy and Domestic Politics: The Logic of Two-Level Games," *International Organization* 42:3 (Summer 1988), 427–60.

[49] John H. Aldrich, John L. Sullivan, and Eugene Borgida, "Foreign Affairs and Issue Voting: Do Presidential Candidates 'Waltz Before a Blind Audience'?" *American Political Science Review* 83 (March 1989), 123–42.

[50] In the 1952 election, with the Korean War mired in stalemate, the public had much more confidence in the Republican candidate, General Dwight D. Eisenhower, the triumphant World War II commander of U.S. forces in Europe, than in the Democratic candidate, Illinois governor Adlai Stevenson. In the 1972 election, foreign policy was crucial in the Democratic presidential nomination process; Senator George McGovern (D–S.D.) won the nomination largely on the basis of being the candidate the most strongly opposed to the Vietnam War. But McGovern lost to President Richard Nixon in the general election. Although the Vietnam War was highly unpopular, McGovern was seen as too "dovish," whereas Nixon countered some of the sense of his responsibility for the war with announcements in the month before the election that "peace [was] at hand." In the 1980 election, data show that whereas only 38.3 percent of the public could articulate the differences between Jimmy Carter and Ronald Reagan on inflation and unemployment, 63.5 percent could on defense spending and 58.8 percent could on relations with the Soviet Union. Moreover, the taking of American hostages in Iran was for many Americans "a powerful symbol of American weakness and humiliation," and, whether fairly or unfairly, the dominant view was "that an inability to bring the hostages home reflected directly on [Carter's] competence." Samuel L. Popkin, *The Reasoning Voter* (Chicago: University of Chicago Press, 1991), 111.

3 *The Historical Context:*
Great Debates in American
Foreign Policy, 1789–1945

Introduction: "The Past Is Prologue"

The words "The past is prologue" are inscribed on the base of the National Archives in Washington, D.C. For all the ways that today's world is new and different, there is much to be learned from history. The particular choices debated for U.S. foreign policy in the twenty-first century clearly differ in many ways from past agendas. But for all the changes, we still wrestle with many of the same core questions of foreign policy strategy and foreign policy politics that have been debated for more than two hundred years of American history.

To provide part of this important historical context, this chapter examines the "great debates" from pre–Cold War history (1789–1945) that are most relevant to U.S. foreign policy in the post–Cold War era. Six of these "great debates" deal with foreign policy strategy:

- the overarching debate over isolationism vs. internationalism, encompassing considerations of power, peace, principles, and posterity;
- power and peace debates over how big a military the United States should have and how much to spend on defense;
- how true U.S. foreign policy has been to its democratic principles;
- whether U.S. foreign policy has been imperialistic (prosperity);
- relations with Latin America as a key case exemplifying the competing tensions among the 4 Ps; and
- U.S. emergence as a Pacific power and its relations with the countries of Asia as another key case.

The National Archives building in Washington, D.C., bears the inscription "The past is pro- logue" at its base (*courtesy the National Archives*).

Three others deal with foreign policy politics:

■ recurring struggles between the president and Congress over going to war;
■ tensions between considerations of national security and the constitu- tional guarantees of civil liberties; and
■ interest-group pressures and other political battles over free trade vs. protectionism.

Great Debates over Foreign Policy Strategy

Isolationism vs. Internationalism

Should the United States seek to minimize its involvement in world affairs, to "isolate" itself from the rest of the world? Or should it take an active, "interna- tionalist" role? Which strategy would best serve the national interest in all of its 4 Ps components?

This debate traces back to President George Washington's 1796 farewell address, in which he urged the young nation to "steer clear of permanent al- liances with any portion of the foreign world" (see At the Source on p. 68 for extended excerpts). Temporary alliances were fine—Washington knew how important the alliance with France had been to winning the Revolutionary War against Britain. French loans had kept the new nation solvent and French

At the Source

GEORGE WASHINGTON'S FAREWELL ADDRESS

❝. . . History and experience prove that foreign influence is one of the most baneful foes of republican government. . . . Excessive partiality for one foreign nation and excessive dislike of another cause those whom they actuate to see danger only on one side and serve to veil and even second the arts of influence on the other. . . .

The great rule of conduct for us in regard to foreign nations is, in extending our commercial relations to have as little political connection as possible. So far as we have already formed engagements let them be fulfilled with perfect good faith. Here let us stop.

Europe has a set of primary interests which to us have none or a very remote relation. Hence she must be engaged in frequent controversies, the causes of which are essentially foreign to our concerns. Hence, therefore, it must be unwise for us to implicate ourselves by artificial ties in the ordinary vicissitudes of her politics or the ordinary combinations and collisions of her friendships or enmities.

Our detached and distant situation invites and enables us to pursue a different course. . . . Why forego the advantages of so peculiar a situation? . . . Why, by interweaving our destiny with that of any part of Europe, estrange our peace and prosperity in the toils of European ambition, rivalship, interest, humor or caprice?

It is our true policy to steer clear of permanent alliances with any portion of the foreign world, so far, I mean, as we are at liberty to do it. . . .

Taking care always to keep ourselves to suitable establishments on a respectable defensive posture, we may safely trust to temporary alliances for extraordinary emergencies. . . .

There can be no greater error than to expect or calculate upon real favors from nation to nation. It is an illusion which experience must cure, which a just pride ought to discard. . . . ❞

Source: George Washington, "Farewell Address," September 17, 1796, reprinted in *Congressional Record*, 106th Cong., 1st sess., February 22, 1999, p. S1673.

military support was so extensive that at the decisive Battle of Yorktown there actually were more French soldiers than Americans fighting against the British. But the best way for the young, New World nation to preserve its own peace, according to its first president, was to avoid getting "entangled" in the affairs of Europe. "Europe has a set of primary interests which to us have none or a very remote relation," Washington stated. Those interests lead its nations to "be engaged in frequent controversies, the causes of which are essentially foreign to our concerns." Moreover, "foreign influence is one of the most baneful foes of republican government," Washington cautioned with regard to the impact on the principles of the nascent American democracy. So the United States should take advantage of its "detached and distant situation" in the New World, which made it physically possible to avoid such entanglements.

Washington's dictum sometimes has been mistakenly interpreted as advocating total isolation from the affairs of the world. But even in 1796, foreign trade was necessary; Washington's advice was to try to develop commercial relations with as little political connection as possible. In his first inaugural address in 1801, President Thomas Jefferson reaffirmed "entangling alliances with none" while also calling for "peace, commerce and honest friendship with all nations." The goal was to extend commercial relations (prosperity) more than political ones. About 70 percent of the treaties and other international agreements the United States signed in the nineteenth century were on matters related to trade and commerce.[1] Nor did isolationism preclude assertions of U.S. power and interests in its own hemisphere, as through the Monroe Doctrine. What it did mean most essentially, and what the United States did do, was to stay out of the various wars Europe fought in the nineteenth century.

Many view the Spanish-American War of 1898 as marking the beginning of the emergence of the United States as a world power. The Americans won the war, defeating a European power, and for the first time gained a far-flung colony of their own: the Philippines. Theodore Roosevelt, as a "Rough Rider" during the Spanish-American War and as president from 1901 to 1908, embodied the new and more muscular spirit of internationalism. Isolationism was no longer in the national interest, as Roosevelt saw it. "The increasing interdependence and complexity of international political and economic relations," he explained, "render it incumbent on all civilized and orderly powers to insist on the proper policing of the world."[2]

President Woodrow Wilson also was inclined to internationalism, although his emphasis was more on principles than on power. Yet the old tradition of noninvolvement in Europe's wars was still strong enough that when

World War I broke out in Europe, the Wilson administration tried to stay out. Even the usually sober *New York Times* editorialized as to how the nations of Europe had "reverted to the condition of savage tribes roaming the forests and falling upon each other in a fury of blood and carnage to achieve the ambitious designs of chieftains clad in skins and drunk with mead."[3] It was only after the threat to U.S. interests became undeniably direct that the futility of trying to stay isolated became evident. When the "Zimmermann telegram," a secret German message in early 1917 proposing an alliance with Mexico against the United States, was intercepted, the United States learned that the Germans were offering to help Mexico "reconquer the lost [Mexican] territory in Texas, New Mexico and Arizona." And German U-boats had opened up unrestricted submarine warfare and sank three U.S. merchant ships. Isolation no longer was possible; the world's war had come home for the United States.

However, immediately after the war, isolationism reasserted itself over what role the United States should play in building the peace. The League of Nations would create a "community of power" and provide a structure of peace, the internationalist President Wilson argued, with the collective security commitment embodied in Article X of the League Covenant destroying "the war-breeding alliance system and the bad old balance of power."[4] No, his isolationist opponents argued, it was precisely this kind of commitment that would obligate the United States to go to war to defend other League members and that would entangle Americans in other countries' problems. This was a time not "to make the world safe for democracy," as Wilson aspired, but for a "return to normalcy," back to the way things were before the war. The isolationists prevailed as the Senate refused to ratify U.S. membership in the League of Nations.

For the next two decades, Congress refused to budge from a strongly isolationist foreign policy. Interestingly, although their specific reasons for being isolationist differed, both the left and the right political wings feared the reverberations at home if the United States went to war again. As World War II brewed in Europe, conservatives such as Robert E. Wood, chairman of Sears, Roebuck and Co. and head of the America First Committee, argued that entry into the war against Hitler would give President Franklin Roosevelt the opportunity to "turn the New Deal into a permanent socialist dictatorship." At the other end of the political spectrum, socialists like Norman Thomas feared that war would provide justification for repression that "would bring fascist dictatorship to America."[5] Congress even came very close to passing the "Ludlow amendment," a proposed constitutional amendment that would have required a national referendum before any decision to go to war.

FDR tried taking his case directly to the American people, as with his 1937 "quarantine of aggressor nations" speech:

> The very foundations of civilization are seriously threatened. . . . If those things come to pass in other parts of the world, let no one imagine that America will escape, that it will continue tranquilly and peacefully to carry on. . . . When an epidemic of physical disease starts to spread, the community approves and joins in a quarantine of the patients in order to protect the health of the community against the spread of the disease. . . . The peace-loving nations must make a concerted effort in opposition to those violations of treaties and those ignorings of humane instincts which today are creating a state of international anarchy and instability from which there is no escape through mere isolation or neutrality.

His appeal, however, fell flat. The public still did not see the connection between what was happening "over there" and American interests and security. A public-opinion poll taken the week *after* Hitler invaded Poland in September 1939 showed 94 percent of Americans opposed to declaring war.

In 1940, with FDR running for re-election to an unprecedented third term, even the fall of France to Hitler's armies was not enough to break through the isolationist American politics. With Britain also about to fall, and Prime Minister Winston Churchill urging the United States to provide support, FDR resorted to an "end run" around Congress to provide some support through the famous "destroyers-for-bases deal."*[6]

It wasn't until December 7, 1941, when the Japanese launched a surprise attack on Pearl Harbor, that the politics changed and the United States joined the effort to restore world peace. The full national mobilization that ultimately transpired during World War II stands as a monumental example of what the United States is capable of achieving. Even then, however, FDR worried during the closing months of the war that "anybody who thinks isolationism is dead in this country is crazy. As soon as this war is over, it may well be stronger than ever."[7] Indeed, once victory was achieved there was a rapid demobilization, another yearning to "bring the boys home" and get back to normal—only to be confronted by the threats of the Cold War.

---

*Under this agreement, the U.S. Navy provided the British navy with fifty destroyer warships in exchange for the rights to British military bases in the Western Hemisphere. The "end run" came from the deal being made as an executive agreement, not requiring any congressional approval.

Power, Peace: How Big a Military, How Much for Defense?

For the United States to maximize its power and to pursue peace, how big a military is required? How much needs to be spent on defense? These issues, which we know very well from recent debates, have been hotly contested throughout American history.

This is evident even in the Constitution. On the one hand the Constitution provides for the creation of an army and a navy. On the other, it dedicates both the Second Amendment, the right of states to have their own militias, and the Third Amendment, the prohibition on "quartering" of troops in private homes without the owner's permission, to checks on the national military. Nor was much done initially with the constitutional provisions authorizing a standing army and navy. Building more than a few naval frigates was too expensive for the young country. And when in 1790 President Washington proposed a permanent peacetime draft, Congress rejected it.

But the risks of a weak military were quickly made evident. By 1798 the United States was on the verge of war with its former ally and patron, France. President John Adams got Congress to authorize increases in the Army and the Navy, and General George Washington came out of retirement to take command. War was avoided through a combination of successful diplomacy and displays of naval strength. Still, though, the British navy utilized its superiority over the next decade to continually harass American merchant ships with blockades and impressment (seizing) of sailors. Tensions escalated in the 1807 *Chesapeake* affair to an attack on an American naval ship. The sense of vulnerability in these years was expressed by Secretary of the Treasury Albert Gallatin, who warned that the British "could land at Annapolis, march to the city [Washington, D.C.], and re-embark before the militia could be collected to repel [them]."[8] Gallatin's warning proved all too prophetic when, during the War of 1812, the British did march on Washington and burned down much of the capital city, the White House included. To fight the War of 1812 the U.S. Army had to be more than tripled in size from its standing level of about 12,000 troops (see Dynamics of Choice on p. 73). Once the war was over, the Army was rapidly demobilized.

The same pattern of small troop levels, massive mobilization, and rapid demobilization was played out even more dramatically during the Civil War. When the war broke out the Union Army had only about 16,000 troops. President Abraham Lincoln mobilized the state militias and took unilateral action without prior budget approved from Congress to rapidly enlarge both the Army and the Navy. He also instituted the first military draft in U.S. history.

DYNAMICS OF CHOICE

Wartime Mobilization, Peacetime Demobilization

	Prewar troop levels	Wartime mobilization	Postwar demobilization
War of 1812	12,000	36,000	n/a
Civil War, 1861–65	16,000	1,000,000	25,000
World War I, 1917–19	130,000	2,000,000	265,000
World War II, 1941–45	175,000	8,500,000	550,000

Note: Figures are for the Army only, and are approximate.

Through these and other measures the Union forces grew to almost one million. Then, in the decade following the end of the Civil War in 1865, the Army went back down to 25,000 troops.

In the late nineteenth century the main debate was over building up a larger and more modern Navy. There was general consensus that the Army could be kept small; another direct attack on the United States by Britain or another European power now seemed highly unlikely. The real competition with the Europeans was on the high seas. The greatness of a nation, argued Navy Captain Alfred Thayer Mahan in his seminal book *The Influence of Sea Power upon History* (1890), depends on a strong navy capable not just of its own coastal defense but of command of the seas. Congress was sufficiently persuaded by Mahan and others to fund enough naval construction to make the U.S. Navy the seventh largest in the world by 1893. Yet there also were critics. Some objected to Mahan's naval buildup as draining resources from domestic priorities. Others warned that the new sense of power would make the pull toward the pursuit of empire irresistible.

When World War I came, because of the new Navy buildup, the United States was better prepared on the seas than on land. The United States entered the war with only 130,000 soldiers in its Army. One of the first actions Congress took was passage of the Selective Service Act of 1917, reviving the military draft. At its World War I peak the Army reached over two million soldiers.

Yet President Wilson also realized that "it is not [just] an army that we must shape and train for war, it is a nation—including its economy. Indeed, during World War I Wilson requested and Congress approved powers over the economy that, in the view of noted historians Samuel Eliot Morison and Henry Steele Commager, were "more extensive than those possessed by any other ruler in the Western world."[9] The president was empowered to seize and operate factories, to operate all systems of transportation and communication, to allocate food and fuel, to set industrial production schedules, and to fix prices. To exercise these vast economic regulatory powers for which there was no precedent, Wilson set up a host of new executive-branch agencies. The War Shipping Board was charged with keeping merchant shipping going and with building two ships for each one sunk by German U-boats. The Food Board supervised both food production and consumption, setting rules for "Wheatless Mondays" and "Meatless Tuesdays" to ensure enough food surplus to help feed the allies. The War Industries Board regulated virtually every production and investment decision made by private companies, from the number of automobiles rolling off Henry Ford's assembly lines, to the number of colors on typewriter ribbons (reduced from 150 to 5 to free up carbon and other chemicals for the war effort), to cutting down the length of the upper parts of shoes (to save leather for uniforms and supplies). Wilson was even able to impose new taxes on consumption and to increase existing income, inheritance, and corporate taxes, all with relatively little political opposition.

Yet once the war ended, this vast governmental economic bureaucracy was disbanded, as was the military. The Army came down to 265,000 troops by 1920. As part of the naval arms-control treaties signed at the 1921–22 Washington Naval Conference with the four other major naval powers (Britain, France, Italy, and Japan), the U.S. Navy scrapped, sank, or decommissioned about two million tons of ships, including thirty-one major warships.

The mobilization-demobilization pattern recurred yet again with World War II. The Army started at about 175,000 troops and grew to almost 8,500,000 by 1945. The Navy amassed another 3,400,000 sailors in a fleet of 2,500 warships. President Roosevelt's wartime powers over the economy were even more extensive than his New Deal ones. He created the War Production Board (WPB), which mobilized and allocated industrial facilities and plants; the War Manpower Commission, which had sweeping authority to mobilize labor to meet the WPB's production goals; and the Office of Price Administration, which set prices and rationed goods even for such staples as meat, sugar, tires, and gasoline. The fiats these and other agencies could issue went so far as prohibiting the pleasure driving of automobiles, cutting the production of consumer durable goods by almost 30 percent, imposing wage and price controls, passing major tax increases, and taking other measures deemed necessary for "forging a war economy."[10]

The overall scope of the economic effort involved in World War II dwarfed that of any previous period in American history. The number of civilian employees of the federal government climbed from 1 million to 3.8 million. Annual budget expenditures soared from $9 billion to $98.4 billion. All told, the federal government spent nearly twice as much between 1940 and 1945 as it had in the preceding 150 years. The Manhattan Project, the program that developed the atomic bomb, itself involved expenditures of more than $2 billion, the employment of more than 150,000 people, and the building of new cities in Los Alamos, New Mexico; Oak Ridge, Tennessee; and Hanford, Washington—all with the utmost secrecy, so much so that little was known even by Vice President Harry Truman, let alone Congress.

Once Hitler was defeated and Japan had surrendered, however, the recalculation of how big a military and how much for defense was made anew. By 1948 most of the wartime economic agencies had been dismantled. The Army was down to 550,000 troops. The Navy also was being scaled back. But then the Cold War raised yet again the how big, how much questions for assuring the peace and maintaining U.S. power.

Principles: True to American Democratic Ideals?

The United States often has claimed to be the defender of democracy, a country that defines its national interest very much in terms of principles. But has it been as true to these values historically as it has claimed?

The concept of "American exceptionalism" mentioned in Chapter 1, that the United States has a special role to play in the world, was evoked early on in a poem by David Humphreys, a protégé of George Washington:

> All former empires rose, the work of guilt,
> On conquest, blood or usurpation built;
> But we, taught wisdom by their woes and crimes,
> Fraught with their lore, and born to better times;
> Our constitutions form'd on freedom's base,
> Which all the blessings of all lands embrace;
> Embrace humanity's extended cause,
> A world of our empire, for a world of our laws ...[11]

Yes, ours was to be an empire, but it would not be built like the Old World ones on "guilt, . . . conquest, blood or usurpation." It instead would serve "humanity's extended cause."

The same themes were developed further in the mid-nineteenth century in the concept of "manifest destiny." As the term was originally coined in 1845, it referred to the "right" claimed for the United States "to overspread and to possess the whole continent which Providence has given us for the development of the great experiment of liberty and federated self government."[12] The immediate reference was to continental expansion and specific territorial disputes, including the immediate one with Mexico that resulted in the 1846–48 war.

Again, though, this was said not to be just typical self-interested expansionism, but rather based on principles and thus also in the interest of those over whom the United States was expanding, such as Native Americans and Mexicans. Toward the end of the nineteenth century, by which time the United States pretty much had finished its continental territorial expansion, manifest destiny was invoked in a similar spirit as part of the justification for the Spanish-American War and the acquisition of colonies and quasi-colonies in the Pacific and the Caribbean.

For Woodrow Wilson the main reason for fighting World War I was "to make the world safe for democracy." His message to Congress requesting a declaration of war was heavily laden with appeals to principles (see At the Source on p. 77). "Our motive will not be revenge or the victorious assertion of the physical might of the nation," Wilson proclaimed, "but only the vindication of right." And so too was the postwar order to be built on democratic principles and ideals.[13] Many of Wilson's Fourteen Points dealt with self-determination for various central and eastern European peoples and nations that had been subjugated in the Austro-Hungarian and Ottoman (Turkish) empires. Despite some compromises with Britain and France, which had little interest in dismantling their own empires, a "mandate" system was established under the League of Nations that was supposed to begin the process of decolonization in Africa, the Middle East, and Asia.

The case for the values at stake in the war against Hitler and Nazism was about as incontrovertible as is possible. Underlying the political and strategic issues were what FDR called the "Four Freedoms": freedom of religion, freedom of speech, freedom from fear, and freedom from want. The Atlantic Charter, a joint statement by FDR and Churchill even before the United States entered the war (August 1941), pledged to "respect the right of all peoples to choose the form of government under which they will live; and . . . to see

> ### ► At the Source ◄

MAKING THE WORLD SAFE FOR DEMOCRACY

❝. . . It is a war against all nations. American ships have been sunk, American lives have been taken, in ways which it has stirred us very deeply to learn of, but the ships and people of other neutral nations have been sunk and overwhelmed in the waters in the same way. There has been no discrimination. The challenge is to all mankind. Each nation must decide for itself how it will meet it. The choice we make for ourselves must be made with a moderation of counsel and a temperateness of judgment befitting our character and our motives as a nation. We must put excited feeling away. Our motive will not be revenge or the physical might of the nation, but only the vindication of right, of human right, of which we are only a single champion. . . .

With a profound sense of the solemn and even tragical character of the step I am taking and of the grave responsibilities which it involves, but in unhesitating obedience to what I deem my constitutional duty, I advise the Congress to declare the recent course of the Imperial German Government to be in fact nothing less than war against the government and people of the United States. . . .

We are accepting this challenge of hostile purpose because we know that in such a government, following such methods, we can never have a friend; and that in the presence of its organized power, always lying in wait to accomplish we know not what purpose, there can be no assured security for the democratic governments of the world. . . . *The world must be made safe for democracy* [emphasis added]. . . .

It is a distressing and oppressive duty, Gentlemen of the Congress, which I have performed in thus addressing you. There are, it may be, many months of fiery trial and sacrifice ahead of us. . . . But the right is more precious than the peace, and we shall fight for the things we have always carried nearest our hearts—for democracy, for the rights and liberties of small nations, for a universal dominion of right by such a concert of free peoples as shall bring peace and safety to all nations and make the world itself at last free. To such a task we can dedicate our lives and our fortunes, everything that we are and everything that we have,

(*Continued on page 78*)

> **(Making the World Safe for Democracy** *Continued from page 77)*
> with the pride of those who know that the day has come when America
> is privileged to spend her blood and her might for the principles that
> gave her birth and happiness and the peace which she has treasured.
> God helping her, she can do no other."
>
> Source: Woodrow Wilson, "Address to Joint Session of Congress," April 2, 1917, reprint-
> ed in Arthur S. Link, ed., *Papers of Woodrow Wilson*, Vol. 41 (Princeton: Princeton Uni-
> versity Press, 1966), pp. 519–27.

sovereign rights and self-government restored to those who have been forcibly
deprived of them."[14] The latter was a reference to those countries in Europe
overrun by Hitler's Germany. The former was ostensibly about the colonial
world and was something from which Churchill soon backed off, and on
which, although FDR was sincere at the time, with the onset of the Cold War
the United States also did not fully or speedily follow through.

The basis for debate on how true to its principles the United States historically has been is threefold: questions of consistency, of contradictions, and of
cover stories. The question of consistency allows for acknowledgment that
there has been some practicing of what is preached, but less than has been
claimed. Quite often the United States has opposed, not supported, social and
political revolutions against undemocratic and colonial governments. We will
see this, for example, in the discussion later in this chapter of U.S. relations
with Latin America. We can also see it in the case of the Philippines, where
after gaining colonial control 125,000 American troops fought to put down
the pro-independence Filipino forces in what has been called "one of the ugli-
est wars in American history," in battles that took a death toll of more than
5,000 Americans and 200,000 Filipinos.[15]

Elements of racism found in a number of aspects of U.S. foreign policy also
stand in contradiction of the ideals Americans espoused. This racism goes back
to the African slave trade and the foreign policy importance given to protecting
those trade routes. It also goes to the core of manifest destiny. "White Americans had not inherited the fabled empty continent," historian Michael Hunt
writes with reference to what happened to Native Americans. "Rather, by their
presence and policies, they had emptied it."[16] Similarly, the Mexican War was
"fought with clear racial overtones."[17] These racial attitudes were captured by
the poet James Russell Lowell: "Mexicans wor'nt human beans," just "the sort

o'folks a chap could kill an' never dream on't after."[18] In another example, even if one were to concede a degree of benevolence in the paternalism, a sense of racial superiority was undeniable in President William McKinley's justification for making the Philippines a U.S. colony because "we could not leave [the Filipinos] to themselves—they were unfit for self-government, and they would soon have anarchy over there worse than Spain's was . . . [so] there was nothing left for us to do but take them all, and to educate the Filipinos and uplift and civilize them as our fellow-men."[19]

In addition, there have been times when principles have been less a genuine driving force than something of a cover story for other objectives. This was the case, for example, with Panama and the Panama Canal in the early years of the twentieth century. Up until then Panama had been a rebellious province of Colombia. And up until then U.S. efforts to acquire the rights to build a canal across the Panamanian isthmus had been stymied by the unwillingness of the Colombian government to agree to the terms the United States demanded. So although President Theodore Roosevelt could cite the historical basis for Panama's claim to independence, the landing of U.S. troops to support the revolt had far more to do with the willingness of the Panamanian leaders to make a deal for a canal. Less than a month after Panama had declared its independence, Teddy Roosevelt had a treaty with terms even more favorable to the United States than the one the Colombian legislature had rejected the year before.

Prosperity: U.S. Imperialism?

Those who see U.S. foreign policy as historically imperialistic focus particularly on the late nineteenth and early twentieth centuries. An 1898 editorial from the *Washington Post* evoked—indeed, lauded—the temper of the times:

> A new consciousness seems to have come upon us—the consciousness of strength—and with it a new appetite, the yearning to show our strength. . . . Ambition, interest, land hunger, pride, the mere joy of fighting, whatever it may be, we are animated by a new sensation. . . . The taste of Empire is in the mouth of the people. . . . It means an Imperial policy, the Republic, renascent, taking her place with the armed nations.[20]

One gets a different view, however, from Mark Twain's parody of the "Battle Hymn of the Republic":

Mine eyes have seen the orgy of the launching of the sword;
He is searching out the hoardings where the strangers' wealth is stored;
He has loosed his fateful lightning, and with woe and death has scored;
His lust is marching on.[21]

Consistent with theories of Imperialism as examined in Chapter 1, the growing U.S. interest in foreign markets was in part a consequence of the severe economic crises of this period (there were depressions in 1873–78 and 1893–97) setting off the problems of underconsumption and overproduction. "We have advanced in manufactures, as in agriculture," Secretary of State William M. Evans stated in 1880, "until we are being forced outward by the irresistible pressure of our internal development." The United States needed new markets or, as an economist of the day warned, "we are certain to be smothered in our own grease."[22]

Those new markets were sought out principally in Latin America. U.S. exports to Latin America increased more than 150 percent between 1900 and 1914. Investments in plantations, mining, manufacturing, banking, and other industries shot up at an even faster pace. And the flag seemed to be following the dollar. As shown by the map on p. 81, during this era the United States launched numerous military interventions in Latin America. In many instances these actions clearly were taken in defense of the foreign investments and other economic interests of American corporations and financiers. By 1913, for example, the United Fruit Company (UFCO) owned more than 130,000 acres of plantations (bananas and other fruits) in Central America— and it was in significant part to defend the economic interests of the UFCO that the U.S. Marines went into Nicaragua (1909–10, 1912–25) and Honduras (1924–25). So too with other American corporations and the military interventions in Haiti (1915–34) and the Dominican Republic (1916–24).

In Cuba, "liberated" from Spain in the Spanish-American War only to be put under U.S. neocolonial domination, the pattern was even more pronounced. While formally allowing Cuba independence, the United States insisted that the "Platt Amendment" be attached to the Cuban constitution, granting the United States the right to intervene to, among other things, protect the property of U.S. corporations.* And so the Marines did on a number

---

*This amendment was named for its principal congressional sponsor, U.S. Senator Orville Platt. This was not, however, a case of Congress imposing something the executive branch didn't want. Secretary of War Elihu Root worked closely with Senator Platt in writing the amendment. Thomas G. Paterson, J. Gary Clifford, and Kenneth J. Hagan, *American Foreign Relations: A History to 1920*, Vol. 1 (Lexington, Mass.: D. C. Heath, 1995), 254–55.

U.S. Military Interventions in Latin America, Early Twentieth Century

Texas

Gulf of Mexico

Florida

Cuba
1898–1902
1906–9
1912
1917–1922

Dominican Republic
1916–24

Atlantic Ocean

Mexico
1914
1916–17

Belize

Guatemala
El Salvador

Caribbean Sea

Haiti
1915–34

Honduras
1924–25

Costa Rica

Venezuela

Guyana
Suriname

Nicaragua
1909–10
1912–25
1926–33

Panama
1903 (Canal
Zone acquired)

Colombia

Brazil

Ecuador

Pacific Ocean

Peru

Source: Adapted from Thomas G. Paterson, J. Gary Clifford, and Kenneth J. Hagan, *American Foreign Relations: A History since 1895*, Volume II, 4th ed. (Lexington, Mass.: D.C. Heath, 1995), p. 55.

of occasions. The Platt Amendment also gave the United States the power to veto treaties between Cuba and other governments, as another way of giving U.S. interests special status. These measures made conditions as conducive as possible for American business: U.S. investments in Cuba increased from $50 million in 1896 to $220 million in 1913, and Cuban exports to the United States grew from $31 million in 1900 to $722 million in 1920.[23]

The other side of the debate, questioning the Imperialist analysis, makes two principal arguments. One is based on counterexamples that are said to show that U.S. foreign policy has not consistently been geared to the defense of American capitalist interests. One such example is from early in the Mexican Revolution, when Woodrow Wilson refused to recognize the military government of General Victoriano Huerta despite pressures from U.S. corporations with some $1.5 billion in Mexican investments. "I . . . am not the servant of those who wish to enhance the value of their Mexican investments," Wilson declared.[24]

The other argument is based on alternative explanations. This argument doesn't deny that American foreign policy has had its expansionist dimension but attributes it less to prosperity than to other factors, such as power and principles. For example, a power-based alternative explanation of the U.S. military interventions in Latin America accepts that capitalist interests were well served, but emphasizes political and military factors as the driving forces. Similarly, although no question is raised that the Panama Canal had economic value, some would argue that what really was motivating Teddy Roosevelt was linking up the Atlantic and Pacific fleets of the U.S. Navy, and the confirmation of U.S. status as an emerging global power.

Key Case: U.S. Relations with Latin America—Good Neighbor or Regional Hegemon?

U.S. relations with Latin America, mentioned a number of times already, warrant special focus as a historical case providing numerous examples of the competing tensions among the 4 Ps. As the richest and most powerful country in the Western Hemisphere, was the United States to be the regional hegemon—the dominant country lording over its sphere of influence—exerting its power largely as it saw fit, managing hemispheric peace but on its own terms, and dominating economically for the sake of its own prosperity? Or was the United States to be the good neighbor, true to its principles, a benefactor for those in its hemispheric neighborhood who had less and were less powerful, promoting democracy and acting respectfully of their equal rights and privileges as sovereign nations?

For the most part the United States has played the role of regional hegemon. This role goes back to the Monroe Doctrine (1823) and its warning to the European powers not to seek to recolonize or in other ways to "extend their system to any position of this hemisphere" (see At the Source on p. 83). Initially, some Latin American countries saw this very positively, as a U.S. pledge to help them maintain their independence, and even proposed "that the Doctrine be transformed into a binding inter-American alliance." But "[Secretary of State John Quincy] Adams said no. He emphasized that the Doctrine was a unilateral American statement and that any action taken under it would be for the United States alone to decide."[25] There was little

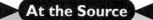

At the Source

THE MONROE DOCTRINE (1823) AND
THE ROOSEVELT COROLLARY (1904)

Monroe Doctrine

66 ... The American continents, by the free and independent condition which they have assumed and maintained, are henceforth not to be considered as subjects for future colonization by any European powers. ...

In the wars of the European powers in matters relating to themselves, we have never taken any part, not does it comport with our policy so to do. It is only when our rights are invaded or seriously menaced that we resent injuries or make preparations for our defense. With the movements in this hemisphere, we are of necessity more immediately connected, and by causes which must be obvious to all enlightened and impartial observers. ...

We should consider any attempt on [the Europeans'] part to extend their system to any portion of this hemisphere as dangerous to our peace and safety. With the existing colonies or dependencies of any European power, we have not interfered and shall not interfere. But with the Governments who have declared their independence and maintained it, and whose independence we have, on great consideration and on just principles acknowledged, we could not view any interposition for the purpose of oppressing them, or controlling in any other manner their destiny, by any European power in any other light than as the manifestations of an unfriendly disposition toward the United States. 99

Roosevelt Corollary

66 It is not true that the United States feels any land hunger or entertains any projects as regards the other nations of the Western Hemisphere save such as are for their welfare. All that this country desires is to see the neighboring countries stable, orderly and prosperous. Any country whose people conduct themselves well can count upon our hearty friendship. If a nation shows that it knows how to act with reasonable sufficiency and decency in social and political matters, if it keeps order

(*Continued on page 84*)

(The Monroe Doctrine   *Continued from page 83)*
and pays its obligations, it need fear no interference from the United States. Chronic wrongdoing, or an impotence which results in the general loosening of the ties of civilized society, may in America, as elsewhere, ultimately require intervention by some civilized nation, and in the Western Hemisphere the adherence of the United States to the Monroe Doctrine may force the United States, however reluctantly, in flagrant cases of such wrongdoing or impotence, to the exercise of an international police power. . . .

It is a mere truism to say that every nation, whether in America or anywhere else, which desires to maintain its freedom, its independence, must ultimately realize that the right of such independence can not be separated from the responsibility of making good use of it. . . . "

Sources: James Monroe, "Seventh Annual Message," December 2, 1823, *The Writings of James Monroe*, Vol. 6, ed. Stanislaus Murray Hamilton (New York: G. P. Putnam, 1912), 325–42; Theodore Roosevelt, "Fourth Annual Message," December 16, 1904, *A Compilation of the Messages and Papers of the Presidents*, Vol. 14 (New York: Bureau of National Literature, 1923), 6894–930.

altruism in this policy, or even straightforward good neighborliness; it represented much more the self-interest of a regional power seeking to preserve its dominant position against outside challenges.

For the rest of the nineteenth century there were quite a few outside challenges from the European powers. Britain and the United States contested in the 1840s and 1850s for rights to build a transisthmian canal across Central America. In a particularly bold episode, amid the American Civil War, France sought to install its own handpicked nobleman, Archduke Ferdinand Maximilian, as Napoleon III, emperor of Mexico. The Spanish-American War was in significant part about getting Spain not only out of Cuba but totally out of the hemisphere. Yet the U.S. support for Cuba's effort to end Spain's colonial rule was one thing, support for genuine Cuban independence quite another. U.S. troops stayed in Cuba for four years after the war (1898–1902) and then, as noted earlier, reintervened repeatedly in 1906–9, 1912, and 1917–22. And then there was the Platt Amendment—what clearer manifestation of hegemony could there be than writing oneself into another country's constitution?

In 1904 President Theodore Roosevelt pronounced his "corollary" to the Monroe Doctrine (see At the Source on p. 83). The "Roosevelt Corollary" claimed for the United States the "international police power" to intervene when instability within a Latin American country risked creating the pretext (e.g., to collect debts or protect property) for an Old World power to intervene. This policy became the basis for a bevy of interventions and extended military occupations in Cuba, the Dominican Republic, Haiti, Mexico, and Nicaragua. U.S. troops stayed in Haiti for almost twenty years, and in Cuba and Nicaragua on and off for twenty-five.

President Franklin Roosevelt sought to pursue a much different approach to Latin America than had his cousin Theodore and most of his other predecessors. A few years before becoming president, FDR had written an article in *Foreign Affairs* quite critical of U.S. interventionism in Latin America. "Never before in our history," he wrote, "have we had fewer friends in the Western Hemisphere than we have today. . . . The time has come when we must accept not only certain facts but many new principles of a higher law, a newer and better standard in international relations. . . . [N]either from the argument of financial gain, nor from the sound reasoning of the Golden Rule, can our policy, or lack of policy, be approved."[26] We want to be "the good neighbor," FDR proclaimed once elected, "the neighbor who resolutely respects himself and because he does so, respects the rights of others—the neighbor who respects the sanctity of his agreements in and with a world of neighbors."[27] As part of this new approach FDR repealed the Platt Amendment, withdrew the Marines from Nicaragua and Haiti, settled a long-standing oil dispute with Mexico, signed bilateral trade treaties as well as treaties of nonaggression and conciliation with a number of Latin American countries, and became the first U.S. president to visit South America. As World War II approached FDR also struck a number of mutual security deals, including affirming a Monroe Doctrine–like commitment at the 1938 Pan-American Conference to resist any foreign intervention in the hemisphere.

Regional hegemon or good neighbor? Not only did the historical record feed this debate, but as we will see in the next chapter, the onset of the Cold War made it even more controversial.

Key Case: The United States as a Pacific Power

Trade and commerce first took the United States across the Pacific to Asia. In the 1840s American ships were sailing to China with cotton and returning with tea. The Treaty of Wangxia, the first trade treaty with China, was signed in 1844. Close to a decade later (1853) Commodore Matthew C. Perry sailed into Tokyo Harbor and "opened up" Japan. "Our steamships can go from California to Japan in eighteen days," President Millard Fillmore stated in the letter delivered to Japanese rulers by Commodore Perry. "I am delighted that our two countries should trade with each other, for the benefit both of Japan and the United States."[28]

But it was never really just trade and commerce (prosperity) that the United States was after. America's sense of moral mission (principles) also was at work. Interestingly, it cut both ways. On the one hand was the U.S. desire to liberalize and democratize these societies. "The thirty millions of Japan," wrote one author at the time of Commodore Perry's expedition, "await the key of the western Democrat to open their prison to the sun-light of social interchange."[29] On the other hand was fear and animosity toward the Orient and its culture, the view that "there were in conflict two great types of civilization, ... Eastern and Western, inferior and superior."[30]

The power motivation was also at work. Historian Thomas Paterson and his colleagues describe it thus: "Perry saw his Japanese expedition as but one step toward a U.S. empire in the Pacific. . . . Eventually, the commodore prophesied, the American people would 'extend their dominion and their power, until they shall have brought within their mighty embrace the Islands of the great Pacific, and place the Saxon race upon the eastern shores of Asia.'"[31] Asia was yet another region for competition with the Europeans, who had the advantage of colonies and experience but who lacked the U.S. geographic advantage of being a Pacific as well as an Atlantic country. Hawaii, Samoa, and other Pacific island territories were acquired by the United States in an effort to further develop that advantage, as later was the Philippines. The United States also began maintaining a military presence in the region, thanks to Captain Mahan's "new Navy." The Open Door policy of the 1890s, contrary to self-justifying claims of being intended to help China against the encroachments of European colonialism, actually was a self-interested demand made on the major European powers that the United States not be closed out of spheres of trade and influence in China.

At the same time that the United States was extending its influence in Asia and the Pacific, so too was Japan. As but one example of the emerging rivalry, Japan initially refused to recognize the U.S. annexation of Hawaii, asserting its own claim based on the larger number of immigrants to Hawaii from Japan than from any other country. The antagonisms subsided somewhat when, in 1904 at the invitation of the Japanese government, President Theodore Roosevelt successfully mediated an end to the Russo-Japanese

War.* Yet when the Japanese didn't get everything they wanted and for reasons of domestic politics and national honor blamed Roosevelt, the first anti-American demonstrations in Japanese history broke out. Relations improved sufficiently by 1908 for the Root-Takahira Agreement to be signed, mutually recognizing the status quo in the Asia-Pacific region.

By World War I suspicions and tensions over commercial competition and naval rivalry again were running high. The wartime alliance against Germany superseded these tensions for a while, and the Washington Naval Conference of 1921–22 worked out naval arms-control agreements (also involving the European powers). But political forces at home were making Japan increasingly militaristic and expansionist. In 1931 it took the bold and provocative step of invading Manchuria, against which neither the United States nor the League of Nations responded effectively. U.S.-Japanese tensions mounted over the rest of the 1930s, culminating on December 7, 1941, in the attack on Pearl Harbor.

U.S. relations with China went through even more extreme fluctuations as China began what would become more than a half-century of revolution. The Chinese revolution in its various stages would be antiforeigner, prodemocracy, anti–indigenous warlords, anti–Japanese occupation, and Marxist. The United States had to grapple with how best to defend American interests and stand up for American ideals as its relationship with China shifted from friendship and even emulation to antipathy. In 1921 Nationalist prorepublic revolutionary leader Sun Yat-sen appealed for assistance to the United States as "the champion of liberalism and righteousness, whose disinterested friendship and support of China in her hour of distress has been demonstrated to us more than once." Three years later, though, Sun expressed his disappointment not only in how little support had come, but in the United States's having joined with other foreign powers in yet another intervention in China over an economic dispute. "We might well have expected that an American Lafayette would fight on our side in this good cause. In the twelfth year of our struggle towards liberty there comes not a Lafayette but an American Admiral with more ships of war than any other nation in our waters."[32] The Nationalists soon thereafter struck their alliance with the Communists of Mao Zedong. This alliance was short-lived and gave way to renewed civil war. But although the United States resumed its friendship with the Nationalists in 1928, the

---

*For his efforts Roosevelt was awarded the 1905 Nobel peace prize; he was the first American president to win that esteemed recognition.

1931 invasion of Manchuria by Japan made the limits of this support abundantly clear.

Thus by the time World War II broke out, American interests in Asia and the Pacific had been developing for close to a century.

Great Debates in Foreign Policy Politics

Going to War

Americans have a tendency to think that it has only been since the trauma of the Vietnam War that political controversy and uncertainty have existed on whether to go to war. Yet as we discussed in Chapter 2, no domain better fits the "invitation to struggle" characterization of the foreign policy provisions of the Constitution than war powers. A closer look at the historical record shows that decisions on going to war rarely have come easily or readily; time and again they have been the subject of intense political debate.

In the War of 1812, for example, it took almost three weeks after President James Madison's request for a declaration of war for Congress to approve it. Even then the votes were far from unanimous—79 to 49 in the House, 19 to 13 in the Senate—and closely followed party and regional lines. Opposition in the New England states was so strong that state leaders initially withheld both money and troops. Although myths later developed about the war being "a glorious triumph," the historian Donald Hickey takes the view that "Mr. Madison's war" was "a futile and costly struggle in which the United States had barely escaped dismemberment and disunion." Hickey also quotes Thomas Jefferson that the War of 1812 "arrested the course of the most remarkable tide of prosperity any nation ever experienced."[33]

Controversy and interbranch maneuvering characterized the politics that led up to the Mexican War of 1846–48. The key issue in this war was the annexation of Texas, the "lone star republic," which in 1836 had declared its independence from Mexico. In the 1840s, knowing that Congress was divided on the issue and thus was not likely to authorize a troop commitment to defend the annexation against the Mexicans, President John Tyler sought to make war secretly. Word leaked, however, prompting Senator Thomas Hart Benton, a leading politician of the day, to denounce President Tyler's actions as "a crime against God and man and our own Constitution . . . a piece of business which belonged to Congress and should have been referred to them."

President Tyler next tried the treaty route, proposing a treaty of annexation to the Senate. But the ratification vote in the Senate fell short of the two-thirds margin needed. Tyler then pulled a deft legislative maneuver by which he re-introduced the annexation proposal in the form of a joint resolution. A joint resolution must be approved by both the House and the Senate but requires only a majority vote in each house. Although denounced as "an undisguised usurpation of power and violation of the Constitution," it worked—Texas was annexed as the twenty-eighth state.[34]

Mexico responded by breaking off diplomatic relations with the United States. New president James K. Polk, Jr., who had defeated Tyler in the 1844 elections, "stampeded Congress" into a declaration of war by sending Ameri-can troops into an area of disputed land where "Mexican units who, operating no doubt on their own theory of defensive war, supposed themselves repelling an invasion of Mexico." Many in Congress "had the uneasy feeling that the President had put something over on them."[35] But political considerations then were no different than today: when forced to vote one way or the other, elected representatives were reluctant to go on record against declaring war on a country whose troops, however provoked, had fired on American troops.

Among those who had that uneasy feeling was a first-term representative from Illinois named Abraham Lincoln. "Allow the President to invade a neigh-boring nation, whenever he shall deem it necessary," Representative Lincoln wrote at the time, "and you allow him to make war at [his] pleasure. Study to see if you fix *any limit* to his power in this respect."[36] Many a member of Con-gress would invoke Lincoln's views a century and a quarter later in the context of the Vietnam War.

The Spanish-American War of 1898 did begin with quite a bit of fervor, especially among expansionists in Congress and as whipped up by the "yellow journalism" of newspaper tycoon William Randolph Hearst. The main precip-itating incident was the bombing of the battleship U.S.S. *Maine,* allegedly by Spain, killing 266 Americans in Havana Harbor. Spurred by rallying cries like "Remember the *Maine,* To Hell with Spain," Congress declared war and thou-sands of young men enlisted in what was dubbed "a splendid little war." But although it took only four months of fighting before Spain sued for peace, the death toll was much heavier than expected. For many this was no more "splendid" than other wars, as movingly conveyed in the letter to the editor of the *San Francisco Examiner* from the widow of a fallen soldier, excerpted in Perspectives on p. 90.

As we saw earlier in this chapter, U.S. entry into World War I came almost three years after the war had started, and only after German U-boats and

PERSPECTIVES
PERSPECTIVES
PERSPECTIVES

ANTIWAR SENTIMENT IN THE SPANISH-AMERICAN WAR

Among those killed in the Spanish-American War was Captain William "Bucky" O'Neill, the mayor of Prescott in the then-territory of Arizona. Mayor O'Neill had been hailed in a newspaper of the day as "the most many-sided man Arizona had produced." He had left to join Teddy Roosevelt's fabled "Rough Riders" and was killed in the battle for Kettle Hill, outside Santiago, Cuba. The sentiments expressed by his wife, Pauline O'Neill, reflected the deep disillusionment shared by many from what turned out to be not so "splendid" a war:

You men who clamored for war, did you know what it would mean to the women of our country, when strife and bloodshed should sweep o'er the land; when the shouts of victory would but ineffectually drown the moans of the women who mourned for the lives of those that were given to make that victory possible? . . .

To you who will celebrate our nation's success, when your spirits are raised in triumph and your songs of thanksgiving are the loudest, remember that we, who sit and weep in our closed and darkened homes, have given our best gifts to our country and our flag.

Patriotism, how many hearts are broken in thy cause?

Source: Pauline O'Neill, letter published in the *San Francisco Examiner*, August 7, 1898, in the collection of the Sharlott Hall Museum, Prescott, Arizona.

other direct threats to U.S. security drove home the point that isolationism no longer was possible. Germany, as President Wilson made the case, had "thrust" war upon the United States. In this context of a clear and present danger the vote in Congress for approval of a declaration of war was by wide margins, 82 to 6 in the Senate and 373 to 50 in the House. The country pulled together, enlisting in droves under the rallying cry "Johnny Get Your Gun" and doing whatever was necessary for the war effort. Yet what was supposed to be "the war to end all wars" proved not to be so. More people died in this war than had in all the wars of all the world over the preceding century. The American death toll was 116,516, with more than twice that many wounded.

No wonder the pattern of going to war reluctantly repeated itself in World War II. It was only after the direct attack by Japan on Pearl Harbor—a day of "infamy," as FDR called it—that the United States entered a war that already had been raging for more than two years in Europe and even longer than that in Asia. Some historians, noting that the initial declaration of war passed by Congress was only against Japan, still wonder whether the United States would have gone to war against Germany had not Hitler declared war against it a few days later.

Americans came to know World War II as "the Good War," in author Studs Terkel's phrase. But the "Good War" took a heavy toll, including more than one million American soldiers killed or wounded. The belief in the justness and righteousness of the cause against Hitler and Nazism and against Japanese aggression—of peace, power, principles, and prosperity all being at stake—kept public support solid despite such high casualties. This was, however, compared with earlier wars and with later wars, very much the historical exception.

National Security vs. the Bill of Rights

Another major recurring foreign policy politics debate has been over the tension between the demands and exigencies of safeguarding the nation's security, and the guarantees of individual rights and civil liberties ensconced in the Bill of Rights. "Perhaps it is a universal truth," James Madison wrote in a letter to Thomas Jefferson in 1798, "that the loss of liberty at home is to be charged to provisions against danger, real or pretended, from abroad."[37] How far can the justification of national security be taken, even with respect to what Madison meant by "real" danger from abroad, let alone as a rationale for "pretended" ones?

Madison himself fought bitterly against the repressive Alien and Sedition Acts passed by Congress and signed by President John Adams in 1798. On their face these laws were protection against subversive activities by the French and their sympathizers at a time when the United States and France were on the verge of war. But in reality they were intended to silence the opponents of war—the leaders of whom were none other than Madison and Jefferson—by limiting their freedom of speech and of the press. The acts represented a "loss of liberty" in the name of a "danger from abroad" which, while not fully "pretended," also was not as real as it was made out to be.

In the name of saving the Union, over the course of the Civil War, President Lincoln took a number of actions that infringed on the Bill of Rights and other civil liberties. He suspended *habeas corpus* and claimed authority to arrest without warrant persons suspected of "disloyal" practices. He banned "treasonable" correspondence from being delivered by the U.S. Postal Service. He censored newspapers. He seized property. He proclaimed martial law. To those who criticized such actions as going too far, Lincoln responded that "measures otherwise unconstitutional might become lawful by becoming indispensable to the preservation of the Constitution through the preservation of the Nation." Yet he also stressed that these must be temporary powers. "The Executive power itself would be greatly diminished," he stated in 1864, "by the cessation of actual war."[38]

The Espionage and Sedition Acts of 1917–18, passed during World War I, were "as extreme as any legislation of the kind anywhere in the world." They made it illegal to "willfully utter, print, write or publish any disloyal, profane, scurrilous or abusive language about the United States, its form of government, the Constitution, soldiers and sailors, the flag or uniform of the armed forces . . . or by word or act oppose the cause of the United States."[39] Quite the broad prohibition! Ads were placed in the *Saturday Evening Post* and other mass-circulation magazines urging readers to report to the government "the man who spreads pessimistic stories . . . cries for peace or belittles our effort to win the war."[40] The postmaster general refused to deliver any magazine that included critical views. Schools dropped German from their curricula. German books were taken off the shelves of public libraries. Some cities banned dachshunds from their streets. Restaurants and snack bars stopped serving sauerkraut and started calling hamburgers "liberty steaks." All told, about 2,000 people were prosecuted and 800 convicted of violations of the Espionage and Sedition Acts. The most prominent was Eugene V. Debs, leader of the Socialist Party, who as a candidate for president in 1912 had received about 6 percent of the vote. Debs was given a twenty-year prison sentence for giving a speech against the war—and while still in prison during the 1920 presidential election received nearly one million votes!

World War I ended and the German enemy was defeated, but a new enemy had arisen with the 1917 Communist revolution in Russia. The "Red Scare" of 1919–20 was a period in which the Wilson administration, led by Attorney General A. Mitchell Palmer, grossly overreacted to fears of internal subversion linked to "world communism" with heavy-handed repression and blatant disregard for civil liberties. "The blaze of revolution," Palmer propounded, was "eating its way into the home of the American workman, its sharp tongues of revolutionary heat . . . licking the altars of churches, leaping into the belfry of the school bell, crawling into the sacred corners of American homes, burning up the foundations of society."[41] Claiming the wartime Sedition Act as authority, on the night of January 2, 1920, Palmer sent his agents sweeping into meeting halls, offices, and homes all over the country, arresting about 4,000 people as alleged communists, many even without warrants. The "Palmer raids" were so extreme that Congress almost impeached the attorney general. But it didn't, and he kept up his anticommunist attacks.

Perhaps the most profound violation of civil liberties in the name of national security came during World War II with the internment of 120,000 Japanese Americans in prison camps. On February 19, 1942, about three months after the Japanese attack on Pearl Harbor, President Franklin Roosevelt issued Executive Order 9066, uprooting people of Japanese ethnicity from their homes, jobs, and communities and banishing them to fenced-in prison camps, in the name of the war effort. "A Jap's a Jap!" proclaimed one general. "It makes no difference whether he's an American or not." In reality, though, not only were the vast majority of Japanese Americans loyal and patriotic citizens of the United States, once they were allowed in 1943 to join the military more than 17,000 Japanese Americans volunteered. "Even though my older brother was living in Japan," one Japanese American stated, "I told my parents that I was going to enlist because America was my country."[42] One unit, the Japanese-American 442nd Regimental Combat Team, fought with such valor as to amass more than 18,000 individual decorations, more than any other unit of its size and duration.[43]

At the time of the Japanese-American internments, but a few voices were raised in protest in government, the media, or society at large. The Supreme Court even ruled that FDR's executive order was constitutional.[44] Not until more than thirty years later was a law passed as an official apology, providing monetary compensation to those Japanese Americans who had been interned and to their families. Although this was an important act of repentance and retribution, it hardly made up for the thousands of lives damaged and destroyed. The Bill of Rights was trampled insofar as it pertained to Japanese Americans, in the name of national security.

Thus, repeatedly, tensions have arisen between considerations of national security and fundamental guarantees provided in the Bill of Rights. Repeatedly, the latter have been overtaken by the former. And, repeatedly, the criticisms and outrage that later followed were quite severe. Yet, as we will see in the next chapter, the pattern was repeated during the Cold War.

Free Trade vs. Protectionism

A member of Congress from Detroit smashing a Toyota with a sledgehammer in a photo opportunity in front of the Capitol dome; Ross Perot warning of the "giant sucking sound" that passage of NAFTA (the North American Free Trade Agreement) would set off: recent years have been full of controversies over trade and other international economic policies. But although it is true that this recent discord contrasts with the prevailing pro–free trade consensus of 1945–71, most of the rest of American history has had extensive interest-group pressure and other political conflict over free trade vs. protectionism.

In the first half of the nineteenth century, divisions over the tariff issue largely followed regional lines. Northern industrialists seeking protection from foreign competition for their "infant industries" and Northern and Western farmers who produced primarily for the domestic market favored high tariffs on imported goods. Northeastern merchants, whose economic interests lay in import and export businesses, and Southern plantation owners, whose cotton and tobacco crops were in high demand in Europe, favored low tariffs in order to facilitate international trade. Indeed, while slavery clearly was the most contentious issue, the Civil War also was fed by these fundamental differences over trade policy.

In the late nineteenth century not only was the tariff the primary foreign policy issue of the day, tariff policies were one of the defining differences between the Democratic and Republican parties. In those days the Democrats were predominately in support of free trade, and the Republicans were so protectionist as to proclaim high tariffs as one of the "plain and natural rights of Americans."[45] When President Grover Cleveland, a Democrat, managed to get a tariff reduction bill through the House, the Republican-controlled Senate killed it. The Republicans rode their protectionist position to a major victory in the 1888 elections, with Benjamin Harrison defeating Cleveland for president and Republicans winning majorities in both the House and the Senate.

Yet the Republican-controlled Congress and the new Republican president also fought over trade issues. They did agree on higher tariffs and passed these in the McKinley Tariff Act (named for William McKinley, then-chair of the House Ways and Means Committee). The most significant battle centered on the Harrison administration's proposal for authority to negotiate reciprocity treaties. A reciprocity treaty involves an agreement with another country for mutual reductions in tariffs. The Senate was willing to go along with this since it still would be a player through its treaty-ratification authority. But the House, which has no constitutional authority over treaties, was concerned about being left out of the ball game. It took extensive negotiations—seven days of Republican party caucuses, according to the leading historian of the period—to get the House to agree even to a compromise version.[46]

Politics in these days was extremely volatile. Democrats took control of both the House and the Senate in the 1890 midterm elections, and Grover Cleveland won back the White House in 1892, becoming the only president ever to win two nonconsecutive terms. Since Democratic victories were in large part attributable to the political pendulum having swung back toward antitariff sentiment, President Cleveland made major tariff reductions one of his highest priorities. But with special interests exerting extensive pressure, by the time his antitariff bill passed the Senate it had 634 amendments. It still reduced tariffs, but by much less than the president had wanted.

In 1896, in yet another swing of the political pendulum, Republican William McKinley was elected president and the Republicans regained control of Congress. Ironically, President McKinley now pushed for an even greater congressional delegation of authority to negotiate trade treaties than that which Representative McKinley had opposed as inimical to the Constitution. McKinley won the authority, but although he and his successors would use this authority to negotiate eleven trade treaties over the next decade, not a single one was ever ratified.[47] In 1909 Congress took back the reciprocal trade treaty authority and did not regrant it to the president for another quarter-century, until after the 1930 Smoot-Hawley protectionist tariff had worked its disastrous effects, including contributing to the Great Depression.

Like the reformed alcoholic acknowledging his need to steer clear of the temptations of the liquor store, Congress ceded much of its authority to set tariffs to the president in the Reciprocal Trade Agreements Act (RTAA) of 1934. The RTAA, called "a revolution in tariff making" by one historian,[48] delegated to the president authority to cut tariffs on his own by as much as 50 percent if he could negotiate reciprocal cuts with other countries. This laid the basis for a fundamental shift away from protectionism and toward free trade, a shift that was further manifested following World War II, when the United States played a key role in setting up the General Agreement on Tariffs and Trade as the basis for an international system of free trade.

Summary

In studying history, change often is more readily apparent than continuity. In so many ways the twenty-first century and its foreign policy challenges are vastly different from those of even the recent past, let alone those of the eighteenth, nineteenth, and early twentieth centuries. Yet many of the foreign policy choices we debate today, at their core, are about the same fundamental questions that have been debated over two centuries of U.S. history.

Can the United States best fulfill its national interest in all its components through isolationism or internationalism? How big a military and how much defense spending are needed to ensure U.S. power and assure the peace? How true to its democratic principles does U.S. foreign policy need to be? Are those who criticize U.S. foreign policy as imperialistic right? How is the record of relations in such major regions as Latin America and Asia to be assessed? Every one of these questions of foreign policy strategy has a long history that provides important context for current foreign policy choices.

The same is true with regard to the three historical debates over foreign policy politics examined in this chapter. Struggles between the president and Congress over decisions to go to war are hardly just a post-Vietnam matter; they go back a long way in U.S. history. The profoundly difficult tradeoffs between the demands of national security and the constitutional guarantees of civil liberties have been demonstrated all too many times in U.S. history. The interest-group pressures over free trade vs. protectionism were at least as intense in the late nineteenth century as in the late twentieth century.

It is therefore crucial that as we consider the foreign policy challenges today, we not only seek to understand what is new about our world, but also seek to learn from the prologue that is the past.

In the next chapter we will look at the Cold War and the contemporary historical context it provides to our analysis of today's challenges.

Notes

1. James M. McCormick, *American Foreign Policy and Process* (Itasca, Ill.: F. E. Peacock, 1992), 15–16.
2. Cited in John Gerard Ruggie, "The Past as Prologue? Interests, Identity and American Foreign Policy," *International Security* 21:4 (Spring 1997), 89–90.
3. Richard J. Barnet, *The Rockets' Red Glare: War, Politics and the American Presidency* (New York: Simon and Schuster, 1990), 142.
4. President Woodrow Wilson, "An Address to a Joint Session of Congress," in Ray Stannard Baker and William E. Dodd, eds., *The Public Papers of Woodrow Wilson*, Vol. 5 (New York: Harper and Brothers, 1927), 6–16.
5. Both cited in Barnet, *Rockets' Red Glare*, 200.
6. Robert Shogan, *Hard Bargain: How FDR Twisted Churchill's Arm, Evaded the Law, and Changed the Role of the American Presidency* (New York: Scribner's, 1995).
7. Arthur M. Schlesinger, Jr., "Back to the Womb? Isolationism's Renewed Threat," *Foreign Affairs* 74:4 (July/August 1995), 4.
8. Quoted in Paul A. Varg, *Foreign Policies of the Founding Fathers* (Baltimore: Penguin, 1970), 192.

[9]Samuel Eliot Morison and Henry Steele Commager, *The Growth of the American Republic,* Vol. 2 (New York: Oxford University Press, 1940), 471.

[10]Richard Polenberg, *War and Society: The United States, 1941–1945* (New York: J. B. Lippincott, 1972), 5.

[11]Cited in Anders Stephanson, *Manifest Destiny: American Expansionism and the Empire of Right* (New York: Hill and Wang, 1995), 19.

[12]The term was first used by John L. O'Sullivan, editor of the *Democratic Review.* O'Sullivan was an interesting character, the descendant of "a long line of Irish adventurers and mercenaries," known among other things for being involved in failed plots to annex Cuba, and said by his friend, the writer Nathaniel Hawthorne, to be a "bizarre" fellow. Stephanson, *Manifest Destiny,* xi–xii.

[13]Woodrow Wilson, "Address to Joint Session of Congress," April 2, 1917, reprinted in Arthur S. Link, ed., *Papers of Woodrow Wilson* (Princeton: Princeton University Press, 1966), 519–27.

[14]"Atlantic Charter," joint statement by President Roosevelt and Prime Minister Churchill, August 14, 1941, in U.S. Department of State. *Foreign Relations of the United States: 1941, Volume 1: General, the Soviet Union* (Washington, D.C.: U.S. Government Printing Office, 1958), 367–69.

[15]Thomas G. Paterson, J. Gary Clifford, and Kenneth J. Hagan, *American Foreign Relations: A History to 1920* (Lexington, Mass.: D. C. Heath, 1995), 233.

[16]Michael Hunt, *Ideology and U.S. Foreign Policy* (New Haven: Yale University Press, 1987), 53.

[17]Thomas Bortelsmann, "Race and Racism," in Bruce W. Jentleson and Thomas G. Paterson, eds., *Encyclopedia of U.S. Foreign Relations* (New York: Oxford University Press, 1997), Vol. 3, 451–52.

[18]Cited in Alexander DeConde, "Ethnic Groups," in Jentleson and Paterson, eds., *Encyclopedia of U.S. Foreign Relations,* Vol. 2, 111.

[19]Cited in Walter LaFeber, *The American Age: United States Foreign Policy at Home and Abroad,* 2d ed. (New York: Norton, 1994), 213.

[20]Cited in Morison and Commager, *Growth of the American Republic,* 324.

[21]Cited in Paterson, Clifford, and Hagan, *American Foreign Relations,* 229, from Hugh Deane, *Good Deeds and Gunboats* (San Francisco: China Books and Periodicals, 1990), 65.

[22]Both cited in Paterson, Clifford, and Hagan, *American Foreign Relations,* 175.

[23]Paterson, Clifford, and Hagan, *American Foreign Relations,* 254–57.

[24]Quoted in Paterson, Clifford, and Hagan, *American Foreign Relations,* 262–63.

[25]Gaddis Smith, "Monroe Doctrine," in Jentleson and Paterson, eds., *Encyclopedia of U.S. Foreign Relations,* Vol. 3, 159–67.

[26]Franklin D. Roosevelt, "Our Foreign Policy: A Democratic View," *Foreign Affairs* 6:4 (July 1928), 584.

[27]Cited in Peter W. Rodman, *More Precious Than Peace: The Cold War and the Struggle for the Third World* (New York: Scribner's 1994), 38.

[28]Quoted in Paterson, Clifford, and Hagan, *American Foreign Relations,* 133.

[29]Quoted in Akira Iriye, *Across the Pacific: An Inner History of American-East Asian Relations* (New York: Harcourt, Brace, 1967), 23.

[30]Iriye, *Across the Pacific,* 60.

[31]·Paterson, Clifford, and Hagan, *American Foreign Relations,* 135.

[32]Both quotes given in Iriye, *Across the Pacific,* 147–48.

[33]Donald R. Hickey, *The War of 1812: A Forgotten Conflict* (Urbana, Ill.: University of Illinois Press, 1989), 305, 309.

[34]Arthur M. Schlesinger, Jr., *The Imperial Presidency* (New York: Atlantic Monthly Press, 1974), 51–52.

[35]Schlesinger, *The Imperial Presidency,* 53.

[36]Schlesinger, *The Imperial Presidency,* 54, emphasis in original.

[37]S. Padover, ed., *The Complete Madison* (New York: Harper, 1953), 258.

[38]Quoted in Schlesinger, *The Imperial Presidency,* 71, 75.

[39]Morison and Commager, *Growth of the American Republic,* 478.

[40]Cited in Barnet, *Rockets' Red Glare,* 158.

[41]Paterson, Clifford, and Hagan, *American Foreign Relations,* 324.

[42]Both quoted in Jerel A. Rosati, *The Politics of United States Foreign Policy* (New York: Harcourt, Brace, 1993), 476–78.

[43]Ronald Smothers, "Japanese-Americans Recall War Service," *New York Times,* June 19, 1995, A8.

[44]*Korematsu v. United States* (1944), cited in Thomas M. Franck and Michael J. Glennon, eds., *Foreign Relations and National Security Law: Cases, Materials and Simulations* (St. Paul, Minn.: West, 1987), 43–53.

[45]Tom E. Terrill, *The Tariff, Politics and American Foreign Policy, 1874–1901* (Westport, Conn.: Greenwood, 1973), 199.

[46]Terrill, *The Tariff,* 172.

[47]Robert A. Pastor, *Congress and the Politics of Foreign Economic Policy, 1929–1976* (Berkeley: University of California Press, 1980), 75.

[48]Sidney Ratner, cited in Pastor, *Congress and the Politics of Foreign Economic Policy,* 92.

4 *The Cold War Context: Origins and First Stages*

Introduction: "Present at the Creation"

"Present at the Creation" is how Dean Acheson, secretary of state in the early days of the Cold War, titled his memoirs. At the outset of the Cold War, Americans felt they were facing threats as dangerous and challenges as profound as any ever before faced in American history. Moreover, the United States was no longer pursuing just its own foreign policy; it was being looked to as a world leader, a "superpower." It had been a leader in World War II, but only after overcoming isolationism, and even then only for a period that, as dire as it was, lasted less than four years. The Cold War, though, would go on for more than four decades. And so it was, when years later Acheson wrote his memoirs, he chose a title that reflected his generation's sense of having created their own new era.[1]

During World War II the United States and the Soviet Union had been allies. President Franklin D. Roosevelt, British prime minister Winston Churchill, and Soviet leader Josef Stalin were known as the "Big Three." The Soviets were second only to the British as beneficiaries of American Lend-Lease economic assistance during the war, receiving more than $9 billion worth of food, equipment, and other aid. Even Stalin's image as a ruthless dictator who viciously purged his own people in the 1930s was "spun" more favorably, to the more amiable "Uncle Joe." Yet, fundamentally, the American-Soviet wartime alliance was based on the age-old maxim that *the enemy of my enemy is my friend.* "I can't take communism," was how FDR put it, "but to cross this bridge I'd hold hands with the Devil."[2] After the war was over and the shared common enemy of Nazi Germany had been vanquished, would the alliance continue? Should it?

Different views on these questions are reflected in the debate over the origins of the Cold War. In the *orthodox* view principal responsibility is put squarely on the shoulders of Josef Stalin and the Soviet Union.[3] This view has been strengthened by revelations in recent years from Soviet and other archives. "We now know," historian John Lewis Gaddis contends, that "as long as Stalin was running the Soviet Union, a cold war was unavoidable." The Soviets used the Red Army to make Eastern Europe their own sphere of influence. They sought to subvert governments in Western Europe. They blockaded West Berlin in an effort to force the United States, France, and Britain out. In Asia they supported the Chinese communists and helped start the Korean War. They supported communist parties in Southeast Asia, Latin America, and within African anticolonial movements; indeed, one of the fundamental tenets of Soviet communist ideology was to aid revolution everywhere. And in the United States they ran a major spy ring trying, among other things, to steal the secret of the atomic bomb.

In the *revisionist* view of the origins of the Cold War the United States bears its own significant share of the responsibility.[4] Some revisionists see the United States as seeking its own empire, for reasons of both power and prosperity. Its methods may have been less direct and more subtle, but its objectives nevertheless were for domination to serve American grand ambitions. In citing evidence for U.S. neo-imperialist ambitions, these critics point as far back as the 1918–19 U.S. "expeditionary force" that, along with European forces, intervened in Russia to try to reverse the Russian Revolution. Other revisionists see the problem more as one of U.S. miscalculation. They maintain that the Soviets were seeking little more than to assure their own security by preserving Poland and Eastern Europe as a *cordon sanitaire* to prevent future invasions of Soviet soil. What transpired in those early post–World War II years, these revisionists argue, was akin to the classic "security dilemma," often present in international politics, in which both sides are motivated less by aggression than by the fear that the other side cannot be trusted, and thus see their own actions as defensive while the other side sees them as offensive. Had U.S. policy been more one of reassurance and cooperation, rather than deterrence and containment, there might not have been a Cold War.

With this debate in mind, in this chapter and the next we analyze the dynamics of foreign policy choice for the United States as played out during the Cold War, with regard to both foreign policy strategy and foreign policy politics.

In so doing we will gain a deeper understanding of the Cold War itself and provide the contemporary context to go with the historical one (from Chapter 3) for the challenges and choices that face the United States in the post–Cold War era.

Peace: Liberal Internationalism and the United Nations

Work on the United Nations (U.N.) was begun well before World War II was over. One of the primary reasons that World War I had not turned out to be "the war to end all wars," as Woodrow Wilson and other leaders had hoped, was the weakness of the League of Nations. Franklin Roosevelt and other world leaders felt they had learned from that experience, and this time intended to create a stronger global body as the basis for a stable peace.

The Original Vision of the United Nations

The grand hope for the United Nations, as articulated by FDR's secretary of state, Cordell Hull, was that "there would no longer be need for spheres of influence, for alliances, for balance of power, or any other special arrangements through which, in the unhappy past, nations strove to safeguard their security or promote their interests." Their vision was of "one world," and a peace that was broad and enduring.

This was quintessential Liberal Internationalism, a vision of international relations in which the national interest of the United States, as well as the national interests of other nations, would best be served by multilateral cooperation through international institutions—a world that could be, in the metaphors cited back in Chapter 1, the "cultivable garden" of peace, not necessarily the "global jungle" of power. It was the United States, more than any other country, that saw the world in these terms and pushed for the creation of the U.N. It was in San Francisco on June 26, 1945, that the U.N. Charter was signed (with 51 original signatories), and New York City was chosen as the location for U.N. headquarters.

The lesson drawn from the failure of the League of Nations was not that the Liberal Internationalist strategy was inherently flawed, but that there were two crucial errors in the post–World War I version of it. One was U.S. nonmembership. FDR knew that American membership was key to the U.N. and that the U.N. was necessary in order that the United States not revert to isolationism. U.S. membership in the U.N. thus was "an institutional tripwire," as John Ruggie calls it, "that would force American policymakers to take positions on potential threats to international peace and security . . . not simply to look the other way, as they had done in the 1930s."[5] FDR was determined not to make the same political mistakes that Woodrow Wilson had made. Roosevelt worked closely with Congress, including giving a major role in the U.S. delegation to the San Francisco Conference to senior Republicans such as Senator Arthur Vandenberg of Michigan. He also used his "fireside chats" and other political techniques to ensure that public opinion supported the U.N. All this work paid off: the Senate vote on U.S. membership in the U.N. was 89 to 2, and public-opinion polls showed that 66 percent of Americans favored U.S. membership and only 3 percent were opposed (31 percent were uncertain).

Following the second lesson drawn from the interwar years, world leaders strove to ensure that the U.N. would be a stronger institution than the League had been. Having the United States as a member was part of this plan, but so was institutional design. The League had allocated roughly equal powers to its Assembly, comprising all member nations, and to its Council, made up of permanent seats for the four "great powers" who were League members (Britain, France, Italy, and Japan) and four seats to be rotated among other member nations; all seats on the Council were equally powerful. In contrast, the U.N. gave its Security Council much greater authority than its General Assembly. The U.N. Security Council could authorize the use of military force, order the severance of diplomatic relations, impose economic sanctions, and take other actions and make them binding on member states. And the five permanent members of the Security Council—the United States, the Soviet Union, Britain, France, and China—were made particularly powerful, as they were given the power to veto any Security Council action.

The U.N. Charter even envisioned a standing U.N. military force. Article 43 of the charter had called on "all Members . . . to make available to the Security Council, on its call and with special agreement or agreements . . . [to be] negotiated as soon as possible . . . armed force, assistance and facilities . . . necessary for the purpose of maintaining international peace and security." This standing force was to be directed by a Military Staff Committee, consisting of the chiefs of staff of the armed forces of the permanent members of the Security Council. The Military Staff Committee would directly advise the Security Council and be in operational charge of the military forces. No Article 43 agreements were ever concluded, however. Over the years the U.N. has raised temporary military forces for particular missions such as peacekeeping, but has never had a permanent standing military of its own. In this and other re-spects, the U.N. did not prove able to provide the institutional infrastructure for a "one world" peace.

The Scaled-Back Reality

One reason the U.N. was unable to ensure peace was the political ambivalence of a number of countries, including the United States, who wanted an inter-national institution strong enough to help keep the peace but not so strong as to threaten nation-state supremacy or sovereignty. Although Roosevelt and Truman administration officials had helped write the Article 43 provision into the U.N. Charter, many in Congress saw it as a step too far toward "world government." They supported the U.N., but not that much, and had the power of the purse and other legislative authority to ensure that no American troops would be put under any sort of permanent U.N. command. Congress demon-strated similar reticence with two U.N. treaties signed in 1948, the Genocide Convention and the Universal Declaration of Human Rights. The goals of preventing genocide and promoting human rights obviously were nonobjec-tionable. But the U.S. Senate refused for years to ratify either treaty because they ostensibly risked giving the U.N. and international courts jurisdiction over American domestic affairs in a manner that threatened American sover-eignty. We will come back to this issue of international institutions/national sovereignty in Part II of this book; it has resurfaced as a major debate in post–Cold War foreign policy. The point here is that this issue was there even amid the original grand vision of the U.N.

The other, more important reason that the U.N. fell short of its original vi-sion was the onset of the Cold War and the resultant priority given to consid-erations of power. Even before the U.N. Charter was signed, U.S.-Soviet tensions had flared over the future of Poland and other states of Eastern Eu-rope. It also was only weeks after the signing of the U.N. Charter that the United States dropped the world's first atomic bombs on Japan. President Harry Truman defended his A-bomb decision as the only alternative to a major and risky invasion, but some critics believed it was less about getting Japan to surrender and establishing peace than about demonstrating Ameri-can military might so as to intimidate the Soviet Union.[6] Whichever interpre-tation one took, the tensions that arose during this time demonstrated the limits of the U.N. for managing key international events and actions. This weakness was confirmed by the controversy in 1946 over the Baruch Plan. Named for Truman adviser Bernard Baruch, the plan was a U.S. proposal to the U.N. Atomic Energy Commission for establishing international control of nuclear weapons. The Soviet Union rejected the Baruch Plan. Some cited this as evidence of Stalin's nonpeaceful intentions. Others assessed the Baruch Plan as one-sided and actually intended to spur a rejection.[7]

In other ways as well, instead of a unifying institution the U.N. became yet another forum for the competition between the United States and the Soviet Union and their respective allies. They differed over who should be secretary-general. They disagreed on which countries would be admitted to the General Assembly. Each used its veto so much that the Security Council was effectively paralyzed. At one point, following the October 1949 communist triumph in the Chinese civil war, the Soviets boycotted the Security Council in protest against its decision to allow Chiang Kai-shek and his anticommunist Nationalist government, which had fled to the island of Taiwan, to continue to hold China's U.N. seat. In fact, one of the few times the Security Council did act decisively in these early years was in June 1950, when communist North Korea invaded South Korea, setting off the Korean War: the United States took advantage of the Soviet boycott of the Security Council to get a resolution passed creating a U.N.-sponsored military force to defend South Korea.

Thus, although for most of this period the U.N. was more pro-U.S. than pro-Soviet, as an international institution it was not strong enough to end the global game of "spheres of influence . . . alliances . . . balance of power" and make the break with that "unhappy past" as envisioned by Secretary of State Hull and other U.N. founders. This was not the peace that was supposed to be.

Power: Nuclear Deterrence and Containment

A "one world" peace had its attractiveness, but was unrealistic—power had to be met with power. Some argued that this should have been foreseen even before World War II was over, and that FDR had conceded too much at the Yalta summit on issues such as the future of Poland. Now more than ever, in the classic Realist dictum presented back in Chapter 1, American foreign policy had to be based on interests defined in terms of power.

For all the other differences that emerged over the course of the Cold War, two basic doctrines of power developed in these early years remained the core of U.S. foreign policy. One was *nuclear deterrence*. As devastating as the 1941 Japanese attack on Pearl Harbor had been, the United States managed to absorb it and recover from it. But nuclear weapons, so much more destructive than anything the world had ever seen, changed the world's security landscape. The single atomic bomb dropped on Hiroshima killed instantly 130,000 people, one-third of the city's population; another 70,000 died later of radiation poisoning and other injuries. As the United States thought about its own national security in the nuclear age, its leaders realized that a strong and resilient defense, while still necessary, no longer was sufficient. Any attack with nuclear weapons or that could lead to the use of nuclear weapons had to be deterred before it began. This capacity for deterrence required a strong military, and especially nuclear weapons superiority, so that the Soviet Union or any other potential attacker would have to fear American retaliation at least as devastating. The requisites for nuclear deterrence changed over time, but the basic strategy of preventing attack through fear of retaliation stayed the same.

Containment was the other basic doctrine that developed in the early Cold War. In February 1946, George F. Kennan, then a high-ranking U.S. diplomat in Moscow, sent a "long telegram" back to Washington, in which he sounded the alarm about the Soviet Union. A version of the long telegram later appeared in the prestigious journal *Foreign Affairs* as "The Sources of Soviet Conduct," with authorship attributed to an anonymous "X." Kennan's analysis of Stalin and his Soviet Union was that "there can never be on Moscow's side any sincere assumption of a community of interests between the Soviet Union and powers which are regarded as capitalist." American strategy therefore had to seek the "patient but firm and vigilant containment of Russian expansive tendencies." The Soviet Union was seeking "to make sure that it has filled every nook and cranny available to it in the basin of world power." Kennan recommended a policy of "containment," whereby the United States would counter any attempt by the Soviets to expand their sphere of influence or to spread communism beyond their own borders. Only sustained containment had a chance of bringing about "the gradual mellowing of Soviet power," Kennan argued; it might even reveal the internal contradictions of their system to the point that the Soviet Union would "break up."[8]

4.4

Formative Period, 1947–50

Both these doctrines were evident in Truman administration foreign policies. The Truman Doctrine, proclaimed in March 1947, was essentially a U.S. commitment to aid Greece and Turkey against Soviet and Soviet-assisted threats. The U.S. aid was economic, not military, and it totaled only about $400 million. But the significance, as President Truman stressed in his historic speech to Congress and the nation, was much more sweeping (see At the Source on p. 106). This was not just another foreign policy issue involving a couple of important but minor countries. It was a defining moment in history with

At the Source

THE TRUMAN DOCTRINE AND THE MARSHALL PLAN

Truman Doctrine

❝ At the present moment in world history nearly every nation must choose between alternative ways of life. The choice too often is not a free one.

One way of life is based upon the will of the majority, and is distinguished by free institutions, representative government, free elections, guaranties of individual liberty, freedom of speech and religion, and freedom from political oppression.

The second way of life is based upon the will of a minority forcibly imposed upon the majority. It relies upon terror and oppression, a controlled press and radio, fixed elections, and the suppression of personal freedoms.

I believe that it must be the policy of the United States to support free peoples who are resisting attempted subjugation by armed minorities or by outside pressures. . . .

Should we fail to aid Greece and Turkey in this fateful hour, the effect will be far-reaching to the West as well as to the East. . . . ❞

Marshall Plan

❝ In considering the requirements for the rehabilitation of Europe, the physical loss of life, the visible destruction of cities, factories, mines and railroads was correctly estimated, but it has become obvious during recent months that this visible destruction was probably less serious than the dislocation of the entire fabric of European economy.

The truth of the matter is that Europe's requirements for the next three or four years of foreign food and other essential products—principally from America—are so much greater than her present ability to pay that she must have substantial additional help or face economic, social, and political deterioration of a very grave character. The remedy lies in breaking the vicious circle and restoring the confidence of the European people in the economic future of their own countries and of Europe as a whole. . . .

(*Continued on page 107*)

(The Truman Doctrine and the Marshall Plan *Continued from page 106)*

It is logical that the United States should do whatever it is able to do to assist in the return of normal economic health in the world, without which there can be no political stability and no assured peace. Our policy is directed not against any country or doctrine but against hunger, poverty, desperation, and chaos. Its purpose should be the revival of a working economy in the world so as to permit the emergence of political and social conditions in which free institutions can exist. ""

Sources: Harry Truman, "Special Message to the Congress on Greece and Turkey: The Truman Doctrine," March 12, 1947, in *Documents on American Foreign Relations*, Vol. 9 (Princeton, N.J.: Princeton University Press for the World Peace Foundation, 1947), 6–7; George Marshall, "European Initiative Essential to Economic Recovery," speech made June 5, 1947, at Harvard University, reprinted in *Department of State Bulletin* 16 (June 15, 1947), 1159.

significance for the fate of the entire post–World War II world. And the United States was the only country that could provide the necessary leadership.

A few months later the Marshall Plan was announced in a commencement speech at Harvard University by Secretary of State George Marshall (see also At the Source on p. 106). Most of Western Europe still had not recovered economically from the devastation of World War II. In France, Italy, and elsewhere communist parties were gaining support by capitalizing on the economic discontent. To meet this threat to containment the Marshall Plan pledged enormous amounts of money, the equivalent of $60 billion today, as U.S. economic assistance to the countries of Western Europe. Thus began the first major U.S. Cold War foreign-aid program.

The creation of the North Atlantic Treaty Organization (NATO) in 1949 marked the first peacetime military alliance in American history. To the Truman Doctrine's political-diplomatic commitments and the Marshall Plan's economic assistance, NATO added the military commitment to keep U.S. troops in Europe and the *collective security* pledge that the United States would defend its European allies if they were attacked. Article 5 of the NATO treaty affirmed this pledge of collective security: "The Parties agree that an armed attack against one or more of them in Europe or North America shall be considered an attack against them all" (see At the Source on p. 108). This included the commitment to use nuclear weapons against the Soviet Union, even if

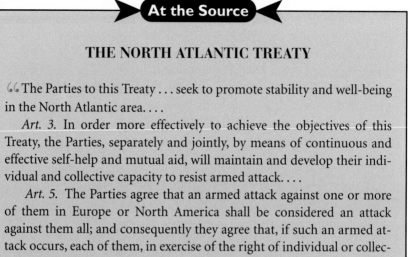

At the Source

THE NORTH ATLANTIC TREATY

❝ The Parties to this Treaty . . . seek to promote stability and well-being in the North Atlantic area. . . .

Art. 3. In order more effectively to achieve the objectives of this Treaty, the Parties, separately and jointly, by means of continuous and effective self-help and mutual aid, will maintain and develop their individual and collective capacity to resist armed attack. . . .

Art. 5. The Parties agree that an armed attack against one or more of them in Europe or North America shall be considered an attack against them all; and consequently they agree that, if such an armed attack occurs, each of them, in exercise of the right of individual or collective self-defense recognized by Article 51 of the Charter of the United Nations, will assist the Party or Parties, [using] such actions as it deems necessary, including the use of armed force, to restore and maintain the security of the North Atlantic area. . . . ❞

Signed in 1949 by twelve founding members: Belgium, Canada, Denmark, France, Iceland, Italy, Luxembourg, the Netherlands, Norway, Portugal, the United Kingdom, and the United States.

Source: *Department of State Bulletin* 20:507 (March 20, 1949).

their attack was on Europe but not directly on the United States. All this was quite a change from earlier American foreign policy, such as George Washington's "beware entangling alliances" and 1930s isolationism. The 82-to-13 Senate vote ratifying the NATO treaty made clear that it was a consensual change.

Yet within months the Soviet threat became even more formidable. Reports emerged in August 1949 that the Soviet Union now also had nuclear weapons. This came as a surprise to the American public and even to the Truman administration. Could the Soviets really have achieved this on their own? Were spies at work stealing America's nuclear secrets? Although the answers to these questions were unclear at the time, what was certain was that the U.S. nuclear monopoly was broken, and thus the requirements of nuclear deterrence were going to have to be recalculated.

At virtually the same time the threat to containment grew worse as the Cold War was extended from Europe to Asia. On October 1, 1949, the People's Republic of China was proclaimed by the Chinese communists, led by Mao Zedong and Zhou Enlai, who had won China's civil war. Now China, the world's most populous country, joined the Soviet Union, the world's largest, as communism's giant powers. "Red China," for many Americans, seemed an even more ominous enemy than the Soviet Union.

These developments prompted a reassessment of U.S. strategy. NSC-68, a seminal security-planning paper developed in early 1950 by President Truman's National Security Council, called for three important shifts in U.S. strategy (see At the Source on p. 110). First, there needed to be a *globalization* of containment. The threat was not just in Europe and Asia, but everywhere: "the assault on free institutions is world-wide now."[9] This meant that U.S. commitments had to be extended to span the globe. Allies needed to be defended, vital sea lanes protected, and access to strategic raw materials maintained. Part of the rationale was also psychological: the concern that a communist gain anywhere would be perceived more generally as the tide turning in their favor and thus would hurt American credibility.

Second, NSC-68 proposed a *militarization* of containment. The Truman Doctrine and the Marshall Plan were largely economic measures. What was needed now was a broad and extensive military buildup: a global ring of overseas military bases, military alliances beyond NATO, and a substantial increase in defense spending. The latter had to be pursued, the NSC-68 strategists stressed, even if it meant federal budget deficits and higher taxes.

The third step called for by NSC-68 was the development of the *hydrogen bomb*. As destructive as the atomic bomb was, a hydrogen bomb (or H-bomb) would be vastly more destructive. Now that the Soviets had developed the A-bomb much sooner than anticipated, the development of the H-bomb was deemed necessary to maintain American nuclear superiority. Some policymakers believed that the United States should pursue nuclear arms-control agreements with the Soviet Union before crossing this next threshold of a nuclear arms race. But NSC-68 dismissed the prospect of the Soviets being serious about arms-control negotiations.

NSC-68 was never formally approved. Its recommendations were tough, both strategically and politically, and thus stirred debate within the Truman administration. All that debate became largely moot, though, when a few months later the Korean War broke out. There now could be little doubt that, as President Truman stated it, "communism was acting in Korea just as Hitler, Mussolini, and the Japanese had acted 10, 15, and 20 years earlier."[10] The

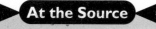

NSC-68

    The fundamental design of those who control the Soviet Union and the international communist movement . . . calls for the complete subversion or forcible destruction of the machinery of government and structure of society in the countries of the non-Soviet world and their replacement by an apparatus and structure subservient to and controlled from the Kremlin. To that end Soviet efforts are now directed toward the domination of the Eurasian land mass. The United States, as the principal center of power in the non-Soviet world and bulwark of opposition to Soviet expansion, is the principal enemy whose integrity and vitality must be subverted or destroyed by one means or another if the Kremlin is to achieve its fundamental design.

    The Soviet Union is developing the military capacity to support its design for world domination. . . .

    A more rapid build-up of political, economic, and military strength and thereby of confidence in the free world than is now contemplated is the only course which is consistent with progress toward achieving our fundamental purpose. The frustration of the Kremlin design requires the free world to develop a successfully functioning political and economic system and a vigorous political offensive against the Soviet Union. These, in turn, require an adequate military shield under which they can develop. It is necessary to have the military power to deter, if possible, Soviet expansion, and to defeat, if necessary, aggressive Soviet or Soviet-directed actions of a limited or total character. . . . Unless our combined strength is rapidly increased, our allies will tend to become increasingly reluctant to support a firm foreign policy on our part and increasingly anxious to seek other solutions, even though they are aware that appeasement means defeat. . . .

    The whole success of the proposed program hangs ultimately on recognition by this Government, the American people, and all free peoples, that the cold war is in fact a real war in which the survival of the free world is at stake.

Source: Text of memorandum no. NSC-68, from U.S. Department of State, *Foreign Relations of the United States 1950*, Vol. 1, 237–39.

Korean War lasted three years and ended largely in stalemate. Its lessons were mixed, on the one hand reinforcing the view of the communist threat as globalized, while on the other showing the difficulties of land wars in Asia. It was also during this time that the United States first began getting involved in another part of Asia, Vietnam, sending aid to the French as they sought to maintain their colonial control against nationalist-communist independence forces led by Ho Chi Minh.

Intensification, 1950s to the Early 1960s

Over the rest of the 1950s and into the 1960s the Cold War intensified in virtually every global region. In Europe, West Germany was brought into NATO, not only to strengthen the NATO alliance, but also to address concerns rooted deeply in European historical memories about Germany rising again. In addition to "keeping the Americans in" and "the Soviets out," by integrating Germany into the U.S.-dominated alliance, NATO also was intended to "keep the Germans down."[11] The Soviet response, though, was to formalize their military alliance in Eastern Europe through the Warsaw Pact. The Soviets also demonstrated their determination to maintain their bloc when in 1956 they invaded Hungary to put down a political revolution that threatened communist control. The Soviet invasion left thousands dead and even more imprisoned. NATO and the United States, despite much rhetoric from Secretary of State John Foster Dulles about not just the containment but the "rollback" of communism, did nothing significant to aid the Hungarian freedom fighters.

As mentioned in the preceding section, during the 1950s and 1960s the United States became involved in an ongoing conflict in Asia: Vietnam. The United States provided some aid to the French, for whom Vietnam was still a colony, and then stepped up its involvement following the French defeat in 1954. The American concern was not only Vietnam itself: Vietnam was the original case on which the domino theory was based. "You have a row of dominoes set up," as President Eisenhower stated at a 1954 press conference. "You knock over the first one, and what will happen to the last one is the certainty that it will go over very quickly. So you could have a beginning of a disintegration that would have the most profound influences."[12] Throughout this period the United States got more and more involved in Vietnam. Also in Asia, the United States and its allies created the Southeast Asia Treaty Organization (SEATO), somewhat modeled after NATO, to be the Asian link in the chain of alliances with which Eisenhower and Dulles sought to ring the globe.

In the Middle East, the Baghdad Pact was set up in 1955; within a year it included Iran, Iraq, Pakistan, Turkey, and Great Britain, with the United States as a de facto but not formal member. Iraq withdrew from the group in 1958 following a radical coup against its monarchy; the rest of the alliance continued, albeit weakened, under the title Central Treaty Organization (CENTO). Containment was also manifested in Iran in 1953 in the U.S.-led covert action to bring the shah of Iran back to power and depose the anti-Western prime minister, Mohammed Mossadegh, and in Lebanon in 1958 with the intervention of U.S. Marines in support of the pro-American government against its more radical domestic foes. The Lebanon case was made into a more general precedent, under the rubric of the Eisenhower Doctrine, of U.S. willingness to provide military support to any state in the Middle East against "overt armed aggression from any nation controlled by international communism."[13]

In Latin America, Cold War opposition to Soviet influence was cast as the contemporary follow-on to the Monroe Doctrine. The major challenge came in Cuba in 1958–59 with the revolution led by Fidel Castro. As in Vietnam and elsewhere, the Cuban revolution was a mix of nationalism, anti-imperialism, and communism. Historians continue to debate whether the absolute antagonism that developed between Castro's Cuba and the United States was inevitable, or whether some modus vivendi could have been worked out. Whatever chance there may have been for something other than adversarial relations was gone after the disastrous 1961 Bay of Pigs invasion. The Eisenhower administration planned and the Kennedy administration launched this covert project, in which the United States trained, supplied, and assisted Cuban exiles in an attempted invasion of Cuba aimed at overthrowing Castro. The invasion failed miserably, embarrassing the United States, leaving Castro in power, and intensifying hatreds and fears on both sides.*

As to nuclear-deterrence doctrine, this period saw a number of developments. For a while the Eisenhower administration pursued the doctrine of "massive retaliation," by which it threatened to resort to nuclear weapons to counter any Soviet challenge anywhere of any kind. This doctrine was not very credible, though, along the lines of the boy who cried wolf. It also was quite risky, especially as the Soviets kept pace with and even seemed poised to overtake the U.S. nuclear program. The Soviets beat the Americans into space in 1957 with the launching of the *Sputnik* satellite. That same year they also

---

*Later in this chapter we will discuss the Bay of Pigs as an example of "groupthink" in executive-branch decision-making.

tested their first intercontinental ballistic missile (ICBM), which meant that they now had the capacity to overcome the large distances and reach U.S. territory with a nuclear attack. This led to great fears of a "missile gap," a Soviet advantage in nuclear weapons, and prompted a massive U.S. nuclear buildup during the Kennedy administration.

In October 1962 the Cuban missile crisis brought the United States and the Soviet Union to the brink of nuclear war.[14] The Soviet decision to base nuclear missiles in Cuba was a daring and by most accounts a reckless move. The Soviets defended it as an attempt to equalize the imbalance caused by the massive U.S. nuclear buildup under Kennedy and by the stationing of U.S. nuclear forces close to Soviet borders at bases in Turkey and other NATO countries in Europe. For its part, Cuba saw this new Soviet commitment as a way to insure itself against another Bay of Pigs invasion. Whatever the claims, the effect was to take the world to the brink of nuclear war.

In the end the crisis ended up being effectively managed.* Nuclear war was averted. And by most assessments, especially at the time, it was the Soviets who were seen as having backed down, the United States as having "won." But the world had come so close, too close, to nuclear war. Thus, while many saw in the Cuban and Soviet actions that started the crisis confirmation for U.S. global-containment and nuclear-deterrence doctrines, the dangerous dynamics of a crisis that could have had catastrophic consequences drove home, like never before, the risks of the Cold War.

Principles: Ideological Bipolarity and the Third World "ABC" Approach

One of the primary differences between the Cold War and other historical great-power struggles was that the Cold War was about principles, not just power. The competition was not just between rival nations but also between opposing ideologies. This "ideological bipolarity" can be seen in the Truman Doctrine, the Marshall Plan, and many other official pronouncements. There was not much doubt then, and even less now, about the evils of communism. Almost immediately after World War II, the Soviets had shown in Poland and

---

*See p. 126 for a further discussion of the Cuban missile crisis as an example of successful crisis decision-making.

elsewhere in Eastern Europe that they had little interest in allowing democracy. In this respect containment was consistent with American principles. The controversy, though, was less about what the United States opposed than whom it supported, and how it did so.

This wasn't so much a problem in Western Europe, where genuinely democratic leaders and political parties emerged (although in countries like Italy, where the Communist Party had major electoral strength, the CIA did covertly seek to manipulate elections). But quite a few Third World dictators were garbed in the rhetoric of freedom and democracy, but really fit only an "ABC" definition of democracy—"anything but communism." One doesn't have to be so naive as to expect the United States to support only regimes good of heart and pure in practice. But the ABC rationale was used repeatedly as if there could be only two options, the communists or the other guy, whoever he might be and whatever his political practices. Moreover, the criteria by which leaders, parties, and movements were deemed communist were often quite subjective, if not manipulative.

Support for "ABC Democrats"

Vietnam is a good example of the U.S. support for an "ABC" leadership. There is much historical debate over whether a relationship could have been worked out with Ho Chi Minh, the Vietnamese leader who was both nationalist and communist. Ho had worked with the Allies during World War II against the Japanese occupation of Vietnam, even receiving arms and aid from the United States. After the war he made appeals to Washington for help, based on America's professed anticolonialism, against France's effort to re-establish its own colonial rule. He even cited the American Declaration of Independence in proclaiming Vietnam's independence in 1945. There was no question that Ho was a communist; he believed in social revolution at home and received support from the Soviet Union and the Chinese communists. Yet when it was suggested that as a nationalist, and like Tito in Yugoslavia,* it was not inevitable that Ho would make his country a mere communist satellite, such thinking was patently rejected. It wasn't so much that there was evidence to the con-

---

*Josip Broz, more famously known as Tito, was a communist who led the Yugoslav Partisans in resistance against Nazi Germany and who became Yugoslavia's dictator after the war. In 1948, however, Tito broke with Stalin and the other members of the Warsaw Pact, and began to develop independent ties to the West.

trary as that, as put in a 1949 State Department cable to the U.S. consulate in Hanoi, the "question of whether Ho was as much nationalist as Commie was irrelevant."[15] His communism was all that mattered.

Thus the United States threw its support to one Vietnamese "ABC democrat" after another. In 1949, as their alternative to Ho Chi Minh, the French reinstalled Emperor Bao Dai. He was neither a democrat—he bore the title "emperor"—nor a nationalist—having sat on the throne during the Japanese occupation, he had little credibility with his own people. Internal State Department documents showed that Bao Dai was recognized as a French colonial puppet, but U.S. support for him was rationalized as the only alternative to "Commie domination."[16]

In 1954 the Vietnamese had won their war for independence and the French were forced to withdraw. Two nations, North and South Vietnam, were established, with Ho and the communists in control of the North and the anti-communists in control of the South. This partition was supposed to be temporary, with unification and general elections to be held within a few years. In searching for someone who could be built up as a nationalist alternative to Ho, the Eisenhower administration came up with Ngo Dinh Diem. Diem was not communist, but his "nationalist" credentials were more made in America than earned in the Vietnamese colonial struggles. He also was a Catholic in a largely Buddhist country. Diem's rule was highly authoritarian—opposing political parties were abolished, press censorship strictly enforced, Buddhists brutally repressed. He gave extensive power to his brother Ngo Dinh Nhu, a shadowy and sinister figure by most accounts. When a seventy-three-year-old Buddhist monk set himself aflame to protest the regime's repression, Nhu's wife made a sneering remark about Buddhist "barbecues."[17] Indeed, by 1963 Diem was so unpopular that the Kennedy administration had a hand in the coup that brought him down and killed him. Thus the cycle of contradicting principles ran its course in this case—support an ally in the name of democracy who is at best an ABC democrat, but kill him off when he clearly is not the solution, and may even be part of the problem.

In Latin America generally, U.S. policy in the early Cold War was summed up in the comment about support for Nicaraguan dictator Anastasio Somoza: "He may be an S.O.B., but he's our S.O.B."[18] The Alliance for Progress, established in 1961 by the Kennedy administration, initially was heralded as a shift away from this approach and toward promotion of democracy. "Our Alliance for Progress is an alliance of free governments," President Kennedy proclaimed, "and it must work to eliminate tyranny from a hemisphere in which it has no rightful place."[19] While JFK was pointing his rhetorical finger at

Cuba and Fidel Castro, the social and economic elites and the militaries in much of the rest of Latin America, seeing their own oligarchic interests threatened by political and economic reforms, undermined "la Alianza." Military coups ousted reformist governments in the early 1960s in Argentina, Brazil, Ecuador, Honduras, and elsewhere. While the coup makers invoked anticommunism and containment, in most cases this was a transparent rationalization. Yet the United States largely bought it. In fact, in the case of Brazil, U.S. "enthusiasm" for the coup "was so palpable that Washington sent its congratulations even before the new regime could be installed."[20] That these regimes were pro-American (power) was a higher priority than their being nondemocratic (principles).

To be sure, there were those who genuinely believed that communism was so bad that support for "anybody but a communist" and "anything but communism" was consistent with American principles, at least in relative terms and given an imperfect world. One of the problems with this defense, however, was the inclusion of more-moderate socialists and nationalists in the "irredeemable communists" category. This attitude no doubt was due in part to the intolerance of ideological biopolarity: it recognized no third way. The ABC attitude also reflected a power calculation that, in the event of conflicts between power and principles in the U.S. national interest, principles were to give way.

CIA Covert Action

Questions about consistency with principles also were raised by CIA covert action seeking the overthrow of anti-American governments, including democratically chosen ones. A commission established by President Eisenhower provided the following recommendation: "Another important requirement is an aggressive covert psychological, political and paramilitary organization more effective, more unique, and if necessary, more ruthless than that employed by the enemy. No one should be permitted to stand in the way of the prompt, efficient and secure accomplishment of this mission. It is now clear that we are facing an implacable enemy.... There are no rules in such a game. Hitherto acceptable norms of human conduct do not apply."[21]

One of the cases in which this strategy was applied, in Guatemala in 1954, was discussed in Chapter 1 as an example of 4 Ps tensions and tradeoffs. Another case was that of Iran in 1953. In this case, as we saw earlier in this chapter, the target was Iranian prime minister Mohammed Mossadegh, who had begun to both nationalize foreign-owned oil companies (prosperity) and develop closer relations with the Soviet Union (power). The United States supported the exiled shah, and the CIA assisted royalist forces in a plot to return the shah to power. The plot succeeded, albeit with a "wave of repression" and "a purge of the armed forces and government bureaucracy" that "continued for more than a year, silencing all sources of opposition to the new regime." In the years following the coup the CIA helped establish and train the shah's new secret police, known as SAVAK. Over the next 20–25 years, SAVAK "became not just an externally directed intelligence agency but also a powerful, feared and hated instrument of domestic repression"—not exactly a practitioner of democratic principles.[22]

Prosperity: Creation of the Liberal International Economic Order

Along with the dangers of isolationism and appeasement, one of the other lessons that U.S. leaders had learned from the 1920s and 1930s concerned the dangers of trade protectionism and other "beggar-thy-neighbor" economic policies. These policies hurt prosperity globally as well as in the United States. They also contributed to the political instabilities that ultimately led to World War II. Thus one of the other major components of postwar U.S. policy was the creation of the *liberal international economic order* (LIEO). The term "liberal" as used in this context means a relatively open, market-based free-trade system with a minimum of tariffs and other government-initiated trade barriers, and with international economic relations worked out through negotiations. The opposite of liberalism in this context is not conservatism, as in the domestic-policy context, but protectionism.

The Major International Economic Institutions

As set up in the 1940s, the LIEO had three principal components: (1) a free trade system under the rubric of the *General Agreement on Tariffs and Trade* (GATT); (2) an international monetary system, based on fixed exchange rates and the gold standard, and overseen by the International Monetary Fund (IMF); and (3) an international lending and aid system under the International Bank for Reconstruction and Development, also known as the World Bank.

The establishment of GATT did not bring about instantaneous free trade. Exceptions were made—e.g., for agriculture, which for political and other reasons was much harder to open up to free trade. There were loopholes, as for labor-intensive industries such as shoes and textiles, which were allowed some, albeit not total, protection. And trade disputes continued. The success of GATT was in keeping the arrow pointed in the direction of free trade, in providing a mechanism for managing trade disputes so as to prevent their escalation to trade wars, and in moving the world gradually toward freer trade through periodic "rounds" of negotiations.

Protectionism had generated another insidious practice: the competitive manipulations of currencies. The fixed exchange rates of the IMF system sought to eliminate this form of destructive economic competition and help provide the monetary stability essential for global economic growth. The basic gold-standard exchange rate was set at $36 per ounce of gold. Countries whose international payments were not in balance (i.e., who imported more than they exported) could get some assistance from the IMF, but also had to meet stringent IMF guidelines called "conditionalities" for economic and other reforms in order to get that assistance.

The World Bank later would grow into a major source of development aid for Third World countries, but initially it was focused more on European reconstruction. As of 1955, even though the U.S. Marshall Plan had ceased, about half of World Bank loans were going to industrialized countries; by 1965 this was down to one-fourth, and by 1967 virtually all lending was going to Third World development projects. The World Bank itself was chartered to lend only to governments, but over time it added an affiliate, the International Finance Corporation, that made loans to private enterprises involved in development projects.

Critiques: Hegemony? Neo-Imperialism?

While in these and other respects the LIEO did provide broad economic benefits internationally, critics point out that it largely reinforced American economic dominance, or *economic hegemony*. Voting rights in both the IMF and the World Bank were proportional to capital contributions, which meant that, as the largest contributor of funds, the United States had a correspondingly large voting share. In the GATT negotiations American positions prevailed more often than not. Indeed the whole emphasis on free markets, open trade, and minimal government intervention in the economy also fit American laissez-faire economic ideology. And with Europe and Japan still recovering and rebuilding from World War II, the United States dominated the world economy. Thus, even though other countries benefited from the LIEO, it did also help maintain American economic hegemony to go with American diplomatic dominance and military superiority.

Another critique points to corporate interests as driving U.S. policy. This point is often stressed by revisionists in the debate over the origins of the Cold War. Critics cite cases like Guatemala, where U.S. policy followed the interests of the United Fruit Company, and Iran, where big oil companies were eager to see the shah restored to power, knowing he would return property to them that had been nationalized under Mossadegh. Even in the case of Vietnam, where the intrinsic economic interests were more limited, the fear was said to be of a succession of communist "dominoes" that would undermine global capitalism. So, too, the Marshall Plan is explained as an effort to rebuild European markets in order to generate demand for American exports and investments, thereby overcoming the underconsumption-overproduction dilemma and averting a depression. The deciding factor in the formation of U.S. foreign policy, in this view, was the private interests of multinational corporations, big banks, and the other captains of global capitalism.

Foreign Policy Politics and the Cold War Consensus

The main pattern in U.S. foreign policy politics during this period was the "Cold War consensus." This consensus was marked by three fundamental components: presidential dominance over Congress, a vast expansion of the executive-branch foreign and defense policy bureaucracy, and a fervent anticommunism pervading public opinion, culminating in the scourge of McCarthyism.

Pennsylvania Avenue Diplomacy: A One-Way Street

The term "spirit of bipartisanship" was coined during this period to describe the strong support for the foreign policies of President Truman, a Democrat, from the Republican-majority Congress, led by Senate Foreign Relations Committee Chair Arthur Vandenberg. What made this support especially striking was the extent of the foreign commitments being made—declaring U.S. willingness "to support free peoples everywhere" (the Truman Doctrine), spending billions of dollars in foreign aid (the Marshall Plan), joining a military alliance during peacetime for the first time in U.S. history (NATO)—all as a matter of consensus and presidential-congressional cooperation.

Before crumbling over the Vietnam War in the Johnson and Nixon administrations, this foreign policy bipartisanship lasted through almost every conceivable Pennsylvania Avenue combination: a Democratic president supported by a Republican Congress (Truman, 1947–48), a Republican president supported by a Democratic Congress (Eisenhower, 1955–60), a Republican president and a Republican Congress (Eisenhower, 1953–54), and Democratic presidents and Democratic Congresses (Truman 1949–52, Kennedy 1961–63, and Johnson 1963 to about 1966). One prominent theory of the day spoke of "one President but two presidencies": the domestic policy one, in which the president succeeded in getting his proposals through Congress only 40 percent of the time, and the foreign policy one, in which the president's success rate was 70 percent.[23]

One of the reasons for this presidential dominance was that, although the Cold War was not a war per se, the fearsome nature of the Soviet threat and the overhanging danger of nuclear war were seen as the functional and moral equivalent of war. Given these exigencies, the presidency had the greater institutional capacity to conduct foreign affairs. Only the presidency possessed the information and expertise necessary for understanding the world, could move with the necessary speed and decisiveness in making key decisions, and had the will and the capacity to guard secrecy. Almost everywhere the president went, the "button" (i.e., the code box for ordering a nuclear attack) went with him—and it was conceivable that he would have less time to make a decision about whether to press it than it typically takes Congress just to have a quorum call. For its part, Congress was seen as too parochial to pay sufficient attention to world affairs, too amateur to understand them, and too slow and unwieldy in its procedures to respond with the necessary dispatch. Even its own foreign policy leaders had expressed strong doubts about its foreign policy competence. Congress "has served us well in our internal life," wrote Senator J. William Fulbright, the longest-serving chair of the Senate Foreign Relations Committee in American history, but "the source of an effective foreign policy under our system is Presidential power." Fulbright went on to propose that the president be given "a measure of power in the conduct of our foreign affairs that we [i.e., the Congress] have hitherto jealously withheld."[24] Fulbright's counterpart, House Foreign Affairs Committee Chair Thomas (Doc) Morgan, went even further, saying that he had a "blanket, all-purpose decision rule: support all executive branch proposals."[25]

Three areas of foreign policy show how the basic relationship of separate institutions sharing powers now had the presidency with the much larger share.

WAR POWERS   In the Korean War, Truman never asked Congress for a declaration of war. He claimed that the resolution passed by the U.N. Security Council for "urgent military measures . . . to repel the attack" provided him with sufficient authority to commit U.S. troops. Moreover, this wasn't really a war, Truman asserted, just "a police action." There is little doubt that Congress would have supported the president with a declaration of war if it had been asked. But in not asking, Truman set a new precedent for presidential assertion of war powers. This "police action" lasted three years, involved a full-scale military mobilization, incurred more than 50,000 American casualties, and ended in stalemate.

In January 1951 Truman announced his intention to send the first divisions of U.S. ground troops to be stationed in Europe as part of NATO. Here he argued that he was merely fulfilling international responsibilities that Congress had previously approved (in this instance by Senate ratification in 1949 of the NATO treaty) and thus did not need any further congressional approval. Congressional opposition to the NATO deployment was greater than in the Korean War case, but still was not strong enough to pass anything more than a nonbinding resolution urging, but not requiring, the president to obtain congressional approval for future NATO deployments.

The trend continued under President Eisenhower, although with some interesting twists. In 1955 a crisis was brewing over threats by China against Taiwan. Unlike Truman, Eisenhower did go to Congress for formal legislative authorization, but he did so with a very open-ended and highly discretionary resolution authorizing him to use military force if and when he deemed it necessary as the situation developed. This kind of anticipatory authorization was very different from declaring war or taking other military action against a specific country. Yet Eisenhower's request was approved by overwhelming margins, 83 to 3 in the Senate and 410 to 3 in the House. House Speaker Sam Rayburn (D-Texas) even remarked, "If the President had done what is proposed here without consulting Congress, he would have had no criticism from me."[26]

In 1957 Eisenhower requested and got a very similar anticipatory authorization for a potential crisis in the Middle East. Here the concern was Soviet gains of influence amid increasing radicalism and instability in a number of Arab countries. Yet once again by lopsided votes, Congress authorized the president "to employ the armed forces of the United States as he deems necessary . . . [against] international communism."[27]

COVERT ACTION   One finds scattered examples of covert action throughout U.S. history. In 1819, for example, President James Monroe took covert action aimed against Spain in the Spanish territory of Florida, and kept it secret from Congress. In World War II the Office of Strategic Services (OSS) played a key role in the war effort. But it was only with the onset of the Cold War that the CIA was created as the first permanent intelligence agency in U.S. history and that covert action was undertaken on a sustained, systematic basis.

Here we see another pattern of disproportionate power-sharing, and again as much because of congressional abdication as presidential usurpation. It was Congress that created the CIA as part of the National Security Act of 1947 and the Central Intelligence Agency Act of 1949. The latter legislation included a provision authorizing the CIA to "perform such other functions and duties related to intelligence affecting the national security"—i.e., covert operations. The members of congressional oversight committees were charged with responsibility for keeping an eye on these covert operations. But most senators and representatives who served on these committees during the early Cold War saw their roles more as boosters and protectors than as checkers and balancers. The "black budget" procedure, whereby funds are appropriated to the CIA without its having to provide virtually any details of its programs and its accounts, was set up with a congressional wink and nod.

INTERNATIONAL COMMITMENTS   Another manifestation of presidential dominance was the much greater use of executive agreements rather than treaties for making significant international commitments.[28] Consider the statistics in Dynamics of Choice on p. 123 comparing treaties and executive agreements for the Cold War era with the full span of earlier U.S. foreign policy. One obvious trend is the huge overall increase in U.S. international commitments during the Cold War. The skyrocketing number of treaties and executive agreements in the three decades after World War II in itself demonstrates how much more extensive U.S. international involvements had become. But it is the increase in the proportion of U.S. commitments represented by executive agreements—from 64 percent to 94 percent—that shows how much presidents were trying to reduce Congress's role in the making of foreign policy.[29]

It does need to be noted that many executive agreements dealt with technicalities and details of relations and were pursuant to statutes passed by Congress, and thus some of the statistical difference is accounted for simply by the sheer increase in technicalities and details that had to be worked out. But some of the pattern is due to the fact that, the greater the policy significance of the

DYNAMICS OF CHOICE

Executive Agreements vs. Treaties

	Treaties	Executive agreements	Total	Annual average total	Percentage of total represented by executive agreements
1789–1945	843	1,492	2,335	15	64%
1945–1976	437	6,983	7,420	239	94%

Data derived from Michael Nelson, ed., *Congressional Quarterly's Guide to the Presidency* (Washington, D.C.: Congressional Quarterly Press, 1989), 1104.

issue, the more likely were Cold War–era presidents to use executive agreements rather than treaties. Military and diplomatic matters, for example, were more than 50 percent more likely to take the form of executive agreements than were economic, transportation, communications, or cultural-technical matters. Among the significant political-military commitments made by executive agreements were the placement of U.S. troops in Guatemala (1947) and in mainland China in support of Chiang Kai-shek (1948), the establishment of U.S. bases in the Philippines (1947), the sending of military missions to Honduras (1950) and El Salvador (1957), security pledges to Turkey, Pakistan, and Iran (1959), and an expanded security commitment to Thailand (1962).[30]

In sum, Pennsylvania Avenue had pretty much become a one-way street in terms of foreign policy politics during the first half of the Cold War. The arrow pointed down the avenue, away from Capitol Hill and toward the White House.

Executive-Branch Politics and the Creation of the "National Security State"

To exercise his expanded powers the president needed larger, stronger, and more numerous executive-branch departments and agencies. Again, we can draw a parallel with the expansions of the executive branch during World

Wars I and II, only this time the expansion was even more far-reaching and longer-lasting; it created the "national security state."[31]

One of the first steps in this process was the formation in 1947 of the National Security Council (NSC). The original purpose of the NSC was to provide a formal mechanism for bringing together the president's principal foreign policy advisers.* The NSC originally had only a small staff, and the national security adviser was a low-profile position. Few people can even name Truman's or Eisenhower's national security advisers. But beginning in the Kennedy administration, and peaking with Henry Kissinger in the Nixon administration, the national security adviser became even more powerful and prominent than the secretary of state in the making of U.S. foreign policy.

The Department of Defense (DOD) was created in 1949 to combine the formerly separate Departments of War (created in 1789) and the Navy (separated from the Department of War in 1798). During World War II the Joint Chiefs of Staff had been set up to coordinate the military services. In 1947 the position of secretary of defense was created, but each military service still had its own Cabinet-level secretary. But even this proved to be inadequate coordination and consolidation, and DOD was established with the Army, Navy, and Air Force and a newly created chair of the Joint Chiefs of Staff all reporting to the secretary of defense, who by law had to be a civilian. Measured in terms of both personnel and budget, DOD was and is the largest Cabinet department. And its building, the Pentagon, is the largest government office building.

The Central Intelligence Agency (CIA) was also created in this period, as noted earlier in this chapter. In addition, a number of other intelligence agencies were created, including the National Security Agency (1952) and the Defense Intelligence Agency (1961).

The State Department itself was vastly expanded. It grew from pre–World War II levels of about 1,000 employees in Washington and 2,000 overseas to about 7,000 and 23,000, respectively. It also added new bureaus and functions, notably the Policy Planning Staff established in 1949 with George Kennan (Mr. "X") as its first director, charged with strategic planning.

---

*The standing members of the NSC are the president, the vice president, the secretary of state, and the secretary of defense. The national security adviser, the CIA director, and the chair of the Joint Chiefs of Staff are technically defined as advisers. Depending upon the issue at hand, other Cabinet officials such as the attorney general and the secretary of the treasury may also be included in NSC meetings. The same is true for political officials such as the White House chief of staff.

A number of other foreign-policy-related agencies were also created during this time: the Economic Cooperation Administration to administer the Marshall Plan; the Agency for International Development (AID), in charge of distributing foreign aid; the Arms Control and Disarmament Agency (ACDA) to monitor and negotiate arms-control agreements; the U.S. Information Agency (USIA) to represent U.S. policies abroad; the U.S. Trade Representative (USTR) to conduct international trade negotiations; and others.

It again is important to stress that this vast expansion of the executive branch was done largely with the consent of Congress. Some presidents did exploit, manipulate, and go beyond the intended congressional mandates. But to appreciate fully the politics of the Cold War era, we need to take into account both seizings by presidential usurpation and cedings by congressional abdication.

FLAWED EXECUTIVE-BRANCH DECISION-MAKING: THE BAY OF PIGS, 1961   The 1961 Bay of Pigs debacle is one of the most often cited cases of flawed executive-branch decision-making.[32] It involved a U.S.-engineered invasion of Cuba by exiled forces seeking to overthrow Fidel Castro (the Bay of Pigs was where they landed on the Cuban coast). Not only did the invasion fail miserably, but major questions were raised about how the Kennedy administration could have believed that it had any chance of succeeding. Many of the assumptions on which the plan was based were exceedingly weak: for example, the cover story that the United States played no role in the invasion had already been contradicted by press reports that anti-Castro rebels were being trained by the CIA; and the planners asserted that the Cuban people were ready to rise up, even though it was less than two years since Castro had come to power and he was still widely seen by his people as a great liberator. Despite these obvious warning signs, the groupthink dynamic dominated the policy-making process. Arthur Schlesinger, Jr., a noted historian and at the time a special assistant to President Kennedy, later explained that he felt that "a course of objection would have accomplished little save to gain me a name as a nuisance."[33]

CIA intelligence failures also contributed to the Bay of Pigs fiasco. A report by the CIA's own inspector general, written in the immediate aftermath but declassified only in 1998, stressed the agency's "failure to subject the project, especially in its latter frenzied stages, to a cold and objective appraisal.... Timely and objective appraisal of the operation in the months before the invasion, including study of all available intelligence, would have demonstrated to agency officials that the clandestine paramilitary operation had almost totally failed." The report also criticized the "failure to advise the President, at an appropriate time, that success had become dubious and to recommend that the operation be therefore cancelled."[34]

SUCCESSFUL CRISIS DECISION-MAKING: THE CUBAN MISSILE CRISIS, 1962

On the other hand, the case most often cited as a model of effective decision-making is the 1962 Cuban missile crisis.[35] Having learned from the Bay of Pigs, President Kennedy set up a process and structure that were more deliberate in their pace and deliberative in their consideration of options. He went outside normal bureaucratic channels and established a special crisis decision-making team, called ExCom, with members drawn from his own Cabinet and from former high-ranking foreign policy officials of previous administrations, such as Dean Acheson, secretary of state under Truman. Robert Kennedy also was a key player, an unusual foreign policy crisis role for an attorney general, but a logical one for the brother of the president.

In one sense the reason why the decision-making process worked so well in this case was that formal structures were adapted and modified. The ExCom process ensured a deliberative approach that gets much of the credit for bringing the superpowers back from the brink of nuclear war and for the successful resolution of the crisis. President Kennedy himself also gets an important share of the credit: no structure like ExCom can be established, no decision-making process function effectively, unless the president provides the mandate and the leadership.

It also was out of the Cuban missile crisis that bureaucratic politics and other important theories of intrabranch politics were developed. Much of what transpired during the Cuban missile crisis was quite inconsistent with the traditional rational-actor model (described in Chapter 2) of hierarchical, orderly, and structured decision-making and policy implementation. For example, at one point during the crisis, seeking to delay a possible direct confrontation with Soviet ships headed to Cuba, Defense Secretary Robert McNamara ordered the Navy to move its blockade from 500 miles off the Cuban coast to 300 miles off the coast. But the Navy, following its own "standard operating procedures" of staying far enough offshore to be outside the range of enemy weapons, never followed the order. The original study of the Cuban missile crisis by Harvard professor Graham Allison, as well as studies of other issues, called attention to this phenomenon of bureaucratic politics.[36]

Although bureaucratic politics was a positive influence in this case, it would prove to be more of a problem in other cases, as we will see in Chapter 6.

Interest Groups, the Media, and Public Opinion: Benefits and Dangers of Consensus

On the one hand there clearly are benefits to presidents being able to count on public, interest-group, and even media support for their foreign policies. But consensus, when taken too far, also poses dangers and has downsides.

THE MEDIA AS CHEERLEADER   The news media largely carried over its role as uncritical supporter, even cheerleader, for official policy from World War II to the Cold War. To the extent that there was media criticism and pressure, it was for the president to take a tougher stand. Indeed, the news media played a significant role in the shaping of Cold War attitudes. Many give the credit for coining the term "Cold War" to Walter Lippmann, the leading newspaper columnist of the day. Henry Luce, owner and publisher of *Time* and *Life*, the two leading newsmagazines, personally championed South Vietnamese president Diem and ensured favorable, even laudatory coverage for him. Even the *New York Times* followed suit, as in a 1957 editorial titled "Diem on Democracy" in which the editors hailed Diem for being so true to democracy that "Thomas Jefferson would have no quarrel."[37]

In the Bay of Pigs case, the media actually had prior information about the planned invasion but for the most part refrained from publishing it. Most of what appeared in the media about the plan was "designed not to alert the American public to the potentially disastrous course of its own government, but to advance the universally accepted propaganda line that Cuba under Castro was courting disaster."[38] Although some of the postmortems were self-critical, others were more "expressions of sadness that the job was 'bungled,' that it did not 'succeed'—and that a well-meaning President *got caught* and got a 'bloody nose.'"[39] A few weeks after the Bay of Pigs, and despite his other acknowledgements of responsibility, President Kennedy delivered a very strong speech to the American Newspaper Publishers Association broadly construing the national security rationale as a constraint on freedom of the press (see At the Source on p. 128).

INTEREST GROUPS   Foreign policy interest groups were few in number and mostly supportive during the early Cold War. There were some protest movements, such as in the late 1950s in favor of nuclear disarmament. But more common, and more influential, were groups in favor of Cold War policies.

If anything, some of these groups were more assertive and more anticommunist than official policy. The "China lobby" strongly sided with Chiang

At the Source

"IS IT NEWS?" OR "IS IT IN THE INTEREST OF NATIONAL SECURITY?"

A Speech by President John F. Kennedy

I do ask every publisher, every editor, and every newsman in the nation to reexamine his own standards, and to recognize the nature of our country's peril. In time of war, the Government and the press have customarily joined in an effort, based largely on self-discipline, to prevent unauthorized disclosure to the enemy. In times of clear and present danger, the courts have held that even the privileged rights of the First Amendment must yield to the public's need for national security.

Today no war has been declared—and however fierce the struggle may be, it may never be declared in the traditional fashion. Our way of life is under attack. . . .

If the press is awaiting a declaration of war before it imposes the self-discipline of combat conditions, then I can only say that no war has ever imposed a greater threat to our security. If you are awaiting a finding of 'clear and present danger,' then I can only say that the danger has never been more clear and its presence has never been more imminent. . . .

It requires a change in outlook, a change in tactics, a change in mission by the Government, by the people, by every businessman and labor leader, and by every newspaper. For we are opposed around the world by a monolithic and ruthless conspiracy that relies primarily on covert means for expanding its sphere of influence—on infiltration instead of invasion, on subversion instead of elections, on intimidation instead of free choice, on guerrillas by night instead of armies by day. . . .

The facts of the matter are that this nation's foes have openly boasted of acquiring through our newspapers information they would otherwise hire agents to acquire through theft, bribery or espionage; that details of this nation's covert preparations to counter the enemy's covert operations have been available to every newspaper reader, friend and foe alike; that the size, the strength, the location, and the nature of our forces and weapons, and our plans and strategy for their use, have

(*Continued on page 129*)

("Is It News?" . . . *Continued from page 128*)

all been pinpointed in the press and other news media to a degree suffi-cient enough to satisfy any foreign power. . . .

The newspapers which printed these stories were loyal, patriotic, re-sponsible and well-meaning. Had we been engaged in open warfare, they undoubtedly would not have published such items. But in the ab-sence of open warfare, they recognized only the tests of journalism and not the tests of national security. And my question tonight is whether additional tests should not now be adopted. . . .

I am asking the members of the newspaper profession and the in-dustry in this country to reexamine their own responsibilities—to con-sider the degree and nature of the present danger—and to heed the duty of self-restraint which that danger imposes upon all of us.

Every newspaper now asks itself with respect to every story: 'Is it news?' All I suggest is that you add the question: 'Is it in the interest of national security?'"

Source: John F. Kennedy, speech to the American Newspaper Publishers Association, April 27, 1961, from *Public Papers of the Presidents, John F. Kennedy, 1961* (Washington, D.C.: U.S. Government Printing Office, 1962), 334–38.

Kai-shek and Taiwan, criticizing various administrations for not "unleashing" Chiang to retake mainland China. Another example hails from the early 1960s when, in the wake of the Cuban missile crisis, Kennedy explored a "mini-détente" with the Soviets. He was attacked quite stridently when he gave a June 1963 commencement speech at American University proposing that the United States "re-examine our attitude" toward the Soviet Union. He continued that the United States should "not be blind to our differences—but let us also direct our attention to our common interests and to the means by which those differences can be resolved."[40] When later that year Kennedy announced a $250 million sale of grain to the Soviet Union, even agricultural interest groups were unwilling to breach their anticommunism. "We oppose this action," ten Republican mem-bers of the House Agriculture Committee stated, "because we believe the vast majority of American farmers, like the vast majority of all Americans, are un-willing to sell out a high moral principle, even for solid gold."[41] At the same time a group called the Committee to Warn of the Arrival of Communist Merchandise on the Local Business Scene was operating in forty-seven states, harassing merchants who dared to sell Polish hams or other "commie" products.[42]

PUBLIC OPINION   Public opinion was grounded firmly in the Cold War consensus. Internationalism prevailed over isolationism—65 percent to 8 percent in a typical poll. Eighty percent of Americans expressed support for NATO. Containment was ranked second by the public among all national objectives, domestic policy included.[43]

Consensus, though, when taken too far, can breed intolerance, suspicion, and repression. This is what happened in the late 1940s and early 1950s. First, the revealingly named House Un-American Activities Committee (HUAC) launched a series of investigations claiming that communists had infiltrated American government and society. It would be discovered much later, after the fall of the Soviet Union and the opening of Soviet archives, that some of these allegations in fact were true. Soviet spies did steal secrets for building the atomic bomb. They also operated within the State Department and other U.S. government agencies.[44] But the manner in which early Cold War anticommunism was pursued took a profound toll on civil liberties and created an environment inimical to the openness of a democratic society. This was especially the case with McCarthyism.

Senator Joseph McCarthy, until then a relatively unknown junior Republican senator from Wisconsin, became the most rabid spokesperson and instigator in the hunt for "reds under the beds." The essence of the appeal of McCarthyism comes through in a speech the senator gave in Wheeling, West Virginia, in February 1950 (see At the Source on p. 131). "The chips are down," McCarthy warned, not because communists were superior in any way, but because of "traitorous actions" by Americans. He pointed his finger right at the State Department—"the bright young men who are born with silver spoons in their mouths," this heart of America's foreign policy "thoroughly infested with Communists." Nor did McCarthy and his cohort stop there. One member of Congress even charged Secretary of State Dean Acheson with being "on Stalin's payroll." No less a figure than George Marshall—General Marshall, the World War II hero, former secretary of state, former secretary of defense—was accused by one reckless senator of being "a front man for traitors, a living lie."[45]

Nor was it just government that was being purged. Accusations were hurled all over American society. Hollywood blacklisted writers, actors, and directors accused of being communists even though they had not been convicted. Universities fired professors. Scientists who held jobs requiring security clearances lost their jobs. The whole country was consumed with paranoia. Ironically, many of the accusations that were true were discredited by the broader sense of injustice and illegitimacy. And from a foreign policy perspective, McCarthyism's equation of dissent with disloyalty had a chilling

At the Source

MCCARTHYISM

A Speech by Senator Joseph McCarthy

Today we are engaged in a final, all-out battle between Communistic atheism and Christianity. The modern champions of Communism have selected this as the time. And, ladies and gentlemen, the chips are down—they are truly down. . . .

Ladies and gentlemen, can there be anyone here tonight who is so blind as to say that the war is not on? Can there be anyone who fails to realize that the Communist world has said, 'The time is now'—that this is the time for the show-down between the democratic Christian world and the Communistic atheistic world?

The reason why we find ourselves in a position of impotency is not because our only powerful potential enemy has sent men to invade our shores, but rather because of the traitorous actions of those who have been treated so well by this Nation. It has not been the less fortunate or members of minority groups who have been selling this Nation out, but rather those who have had all the benefits that the wealthiest nation on earth has had to offer—the finest homes, the finest college education, and the finest jobs in Government we can give. This is glaringly true in the State Department. There the bright young men who are born with silver spoons in their mouths are the ones who have been worst. . . .

In my opinion the State Department, which is one of the most important government departments, is thoroughly infested with Communists.

I have in my hand 57 cases of individuals who would appear to be either card carrying members or certainly loyal to the Communist Party, but who nevertheless are still helping to shape our foreign policy. . . .

However the morals of our people have not been destroyed. They still exist. This cloak of numbness and apathy has only needed a spark to rekindle them. Happily, this spark has finally been supplied.

Source: Senator Joseph McCarthy, speech given February 9, 1950, in Wheeling, W.V., from *Congressional Record*, 81st Cong., 2nd sess., February 20, 1954, 58–61.

effect on those both within government and outside it who might have provided constructive criticisms, alternative policy ideas, and the like. The kind of self-examination that is essential for any successful policy process thus was closed off.

Summary

The early Cold War years were a period of crucial choices for American foreign policy. The policies pursued in these years not only addressed the immediate issues, they became the foundations and framework for the decades that followed. Containment and nuclear deterrence were the central foreign policy doctrines by which American power was exercised. The United Nations was the main political-diplomatic institutional structure for the pursuit of peace. The LIEO was the main institutional structure for the international economy and the pursuit of prosperity. Anticommunism was the dominant set of beliefs by which American principles were said to be manifested. And foreign policy politics was marked by a strong consensus, even as American political institutions underwent major changes in their structure and interrelationship.

A number of questions were raised, however, both at the time and in retrospect. Although Cold War strategy proponents stressed the complementarity among the four core national-interest objectives, critics pointed out tensions and tradeoffs that pitted one objective against another: e.g., strengthening the United Nations vs. maximizing American power; pursuing containment vs. being true to principles. Concerns also were raised about the domestic political consensus, which, for all its benefits, also had a downside in the expansion of presidential power and violation of civil liberties.

These and other issues would become more difficult and more controversial beginning in the late 1960s and continuing through the 1980s.

Notes

[1] Dean G. Acheson, *Present at the Creation: My Years at the State Department* (New York: Norton, 1969).

[2] Winston Churchill put it in very similar terms: "If Hitler invaded hell, I should at least make a favorable reference to the Devil in the House of Commons." Both quotes cited in Stephen M. Walt, *The Origins of Alliances* (Ithaca, N.Y.: Cornell University Press, 1987), 38.

[3] See, for example, Adam B. Ulam, *The Rivals: America and Russia since World War II* (New York: Viking, 1971); Arthur M. Schlesinger, Jr., "Origins of the Cold War," *Foreign Affairs* 46:1 (October 1967); John Spanier, *American Foreign Policy since World War II* (New York: Praeger, 1968).

[4]See, for example, Walter LaFeber, *America in the Cold War* (New York: Wiley, 1969); Thomas G. Paterson, *Meeting the Communist Threat: From Truman to Reagan* (New York: Oxford University Press, 1988); Melvyn P. Leffler, *A Preponderance of Power: National Security, the Truman Administration, and the Cold War* (Stanford: Stanford University Press, 1992).

[5]John Gerard Ruggie, "The Past as Prologue? Interests, Identity and American Foreign Policy," *International Security* 21:4 (Spring 1997), 100.

[6]Gar Alperovitz, *Atomic Diplomacy: Hiroshima and Potsdam* (New York: Simon and Schuster, 1965); Martin J. Sherwin, "The Atomic Bomb and the Origins of the Cold War: U.S. Atomic Energy Policy and Diplomacy," *American Historical Review* 78:4 (October 1973), 945–68.

[7]Martin J. Sherwin, "Baruch, Bernard Mannes," in Bruce W. Jentleson and Thomas G. Paterson, eds., *Encyclopedia of U.S. Foreign Relations* (New York: Oxford University Press, 1997), Vol. 1, 135–36.

[8]X [George F. Kennan], "The Sources of Soviet Conduct," *Foreign Affairs* 25: 4 (July 1947), 572, 575, 582.

[9]"NSC-68, A Report to the President Pursuant to the President's Directive of January 31, 1950," in U.S. Department of State, *Foreign Relations of the United States: 1950,* Vol. 1, 240.

[10]Cited in Thomas G. Paterson, "Korean War," in Jentleson and Paterson, eds., *Encyclopedia of U.S. Foreign Relations,* Vol. 3, 30.

[11]Quote from Lord Ismay, cited in David S. Yost, *NATO Transformed: The Alliance's New Role in International Security* (Washington, D.C.: U.S. Institute of Peace Press, 1998), 52.

[12]Jonathan Nashel, "Domino Theory," in Jentleson and Paterson, eds., *Encyclopedia of U.S. Foreign Relations,* Vol. 2, 32–33.

[13]Text of the legislation as passed by Congress, cited in Seyom Brown, *The Faces of Power: Constancy and Change in United States Foreign Policy from Truman to Reagan* (New York: Columbia University Press, 1983), 124.

[14]Graham Allison, *The Essence of Decision: Explaining the Cuban Missile Crisis* (Boston: Little, Brown, 1971); Robert F. Kennedy, *Thirteen Days: A Memoir of the Cuban Missile Crisis* (New York: Norton, 1969); James Blight and David Welch, eds., *On the Brink: Americans and Soviets Re-examine the Cuban Missile Crisis* (New York: Hill and Wang, 1989).

[15]"Telegram, Secretary of State to the Consulate at Hanoi, May 20, 1949," in U.S. Department of State, *Foreign Relations of the United States: 1949,* Vol. 7 (Washington, D.C.: U.S. Government Printing Office, 1973), 29–30.

[16]Secretary of State Dean Acheson, cited in Thomas G. Paterson, J. Gary Clifford, and Kenneth J. Hagan, *American Foreign Relations: A History since 1895* (Lexington, Mass.: D. C. Heath, 1995), 369.

[17]Cited in Paterson, Clifford, and Hagan, *American Foreign Relations,* 405.

[18]Many attribute this quotation to President Franklin Roosevelt. Although there are doubts as to whether he actually said it, few doubt that the statement captures the essence of U.S. policy. See Robert A. Pastor, *Condemned to Repetition: The United States and Nicaragua* (Princeton: Princeton University Press, 1987), 3.

[19]"Address at a White House Reception for Members of Congress and for the Diplomatic Corps of the Latin American Republics, March 13, 1961," in *Public Papers of the Presidents: John F. Kennedy, 1961* (Washington, D. C.: U.S. Government Printing Office, 1962), 170–75.

[20]Abraham F. Lowenthal, *Partners in Conflict: The United States and Latin America* (Baltimore: Johns Hopkins University Press, 1987), 30.

[21]Report of the Hoover Commission, cited in "Get Personal," *New Republic,* September 14 and 21, 1998, 11.

[22]Mark J. Gasiorowski, "Iran," in Jentleson and Paterson, eds., *Encyclopedia of U.S. Foreign Relations,* Vol. 2, 415–16. See also James A. Bill, *The Eagle and the Lion: The Tragedy of American-Iranian Relations* (New Haven: Yale University Press, 1988); Bruce R. Kuniholm, *The Origins of the Cold War in the Near East* (Princeton: Princeton University Press, 1980); and Kermit Roosevelt, *Countercoup: The Struggle for the Control of Iran* (New York: McGraw-Hill, 1979).

[23]Aaron Wildavsky, "The Two Presidencies," *Trans-action* 3 (December 1966), 8.

[24]Senator Fulbright titled the article quoted here "American Foreign Policy in the 20th Century under an 18th-Century Constitution" (*Cornell Law Quarterly* 47 [Fall 1961], 2). He wrote further, "The question we face is whether our basic constitutional machinery, admirably suited to the needs of a remote agrarian republic in the eighteenth century, is adequate for the formulation and conduct of the foreign policy of a twentieth-century nation, pre-eminent in political and military power and burdened with all the enormous responsibilities that accompany such power. . . . My question, then, is whether we have any choice but to modify, and perhaps overhaul, the eighteenth-century procedures that govern the formulation and conduct of American foreign policy" (1–2).

[25]Richard F. Fenno, Jr., *Congressmen in Committees* (Boston: Little, Brown, 1973), 71.

[26]Cited in James M. Lindsay, *Congress and the Politics of U.S. Foreign Policy* (Baltimore: Johns Hopkins University Press, 1994), 22.

[27]Text of the legislation as passed by Congress, cited in Brown, *Faces of Power,* 124.

[28]The main precedent for the use of executive agreements rather than treaties as a way of getting around Congress had actually been set by Franklin Roosevelt in 1940 with the "destroyers for bases" deal with Britain (discussed in Chapter 3). Even among those who agreed with Roosevelt's objectives, there was some concern at the time about the precedent being set. This also was the view taken in a 1969 report by the Senate Foreign Relations Committee: "Had the president publicly acknowledged his incursion on the Senate's treaty power and explained it as an emergency measure, a damaging constitutional precedent would have been averted. Instead, a spurious claim of constitutionality was made, compounding the incursion on the Senate's authority into a precedent for future incursions." Cited in Loch K. Johnson, *America as a World Power: Foreign Policy in a Constitutional Framework* (New York: McGraw-Hill, 1991), 108–9.

[29]There actually was one major effort in the early 1950s to rein in executive agreements. This was the Bricker Amendment, named for its principal sponsor, Senator John W. Bricker (R-Ohio), which would have amended the Constitution to require congressional approval of all executive agreements. Support for the Bricker Amendment was in part a reflection of McCarthyite distrust of the executive branch, and it too faded with the overall discrediting of McCarthyism. Indeed, until the late 1960s little was heard even about the executive's taking full advantage of the lack of any deadline in the requirement that executive agreements be reported to Congress, reporting very few of these agreements—and even those in a not particularly timely manner.

[30]Loch K. Johnson and James M. McCormick, "Foreign Policy by Executive Fiat," *Foreign Policy* 28 (Fall 1977), 121.

[31]Daniel Yergin, *Shattered Peace: The Origins of the Cold War and the National Security State* (Boston: Houghton Mifflin, 1977).

[32]See, for example, James G. Blight and Peter Kornbluh, eds., *Politics of Illusion: The Bay of Pigs Invasion Re-examined* (Boulder, Colo.: Lynne Rienner, 1997); "A Perfect Failure: The Bay of Pigs," in Irving L. Janis, *Groupthink: Psychological Studies of Policy Decisions and Fiascoes,* 2d ed. (Boston: Houghton Mifflin, 1982), 14–47; Peter Wyden, *Bay of Pigs: The Untold Story* (New York: Simon and Schuster, 1979).

[33]Cited in Janis, *Groupthink,* 39.

[34]Peter Kornbluh, ed., *Bay of Pigs Declassified: The Secret CIA Report on the Invasion of Cuba* (New York: Norton, 1998).

[35]Allison, *Essence of Decision;* Blight and Welch, *On the Brink.*

[36]Allison, *Essence of Decision;* Morton H. Halperin, *Bureaucratic Politics and Foreign Policy* (Washington, D.C.: Brookings Institution Press, 1974); Morton H. Halperin and Arnold Kanter, eds., *Readings in American Foreign Policy: A Bureaucratic Perspective* (Boston: Little, Brown, 1973); David C. Kozak and James M. Keagle, *Bureaucratic Politics and National Security: Theory and Practice* (Boulder, Colo.: Lynne Rienner, 1988).

[37]James Aronson, *The Press and the Cold War* (New York: Bobbs Merrill, 1970), 186.

[38]Aronson, *The Press and the Cold War,* 159.

[39]Aronson, *The Press and the Cold War,* 159–60.

[40]"Commencement Address at American University in Washington," June 10, 1963, in *Public Papers of the Presidents: John F. Kennedy, 1963* (Washington, D.C.: U.S. Government Printing Office, 1964), 459–64.

[41]Quoted in Bruce W. Jentleson, *Pipeline Politics: The Complex Political Economy of East-West Energy Trade* (Ithaca, N.Y.: Cornell University Press, 1986), 129.

[42]Jentleson, *Pipeline Politics,* 100.

[43]See Dynamics of Choice on p. 146.

[44]Harvey Klehr, John Earl Haynes, and Kyrill M. Anderson, *The Soviet World of American Communism* (New Haven: Yale University Press, 1998); Ronald Radosh and Joyce Milton, *The Rosenberg File* (New Haven: Yale University Press, 1997).

[45]Cited in Jerel A. Rosati, *The Politics of United States Foreign Policy* (New York: Harcourt, Brace, 1993), 285.

The Cold War Context: Lessons and Legacies

Introduction: Turbulent Decades

The 1960s, 1970s, and 1980s were turbulent decades for the United States. Foreign policy was not the only reason—the civil rights movement, the counterculture, economic change, and other forces and factors also were at work. But the setbacks, shifts, and shocks endured by American foreign policy clearly were major factors.

The Vietnam War was the most profound setback American foreign policy had suffered since the beginning of the Cold War, if not in its entire history. Many saw it as the first war the United States had ever lost. The reasons why were hotly debated—and still are. But the profundity of the loss as it affected both foreign policy strategy and foreign policy politics was undeniable.

The fate of détente with the Soviet Union—first its rise and then its fall—marked major shifts. The rise of détente challenged the dominant belief of the first quarter-century of the Cold War that minimal U.S.-Soviet cooperation was possible. This was especially true since the switch to détente was led by President Richard Nixon, who had built his political career on staunch anticommunist credentials. Yet although détente had some successes, its hopes and promises went largely unfulfilled. It engendered major political controversy at home. And when the Soviets invaded Afghanistan in December 1979, détente was pronounced dead.

The United States also endured tremendous economic shocks in the 1970s. Although not as bad as the Great Depression, these shocks were historically unique, for they came from the international economy. In 1971, for the first time since 1893, the American merchandise trade balance was in deficit. Then came the oil embargo and price hikes by the Organization of Petroleum Exporting Countries (OPEC), first in 1973 and again in 1979. The assumption of cheap and reliable supplies of oil, in some respects no less a bedrock of the post–World War II order than anticommunism, was being called into question. Third World countries tried to capitalize on the OPEC success in bringing the industrialized West to its knees by trying to shift the defining axis of the international system from East-West to North-South. Another major economic blow came as Japan, the country defeated in and occupied after World War II, became the United States' main economic competitor.

The 1980s thus began amid great foreign policy uncertainty, and they, too, proved a turbulent decade. Initially, following the demise of détente and the election of Ronald Reagan, the Cold War resurged. Policies on both sides grew increasingly confrontational, the rhetoric highly antagonistic. Fears of war, even nuclear war, were rising. In 1985 the Soviets selected a leader, Mikhail Gorbachev, who made dramatic changes in Soviet foreign policy. By the end of the decade the Cold War was over. How much credit for the end of the Cold War goes to Gorbachev, and how much to Reagan, has been and continues to be debated. The Cold War did end, though, and it ended peacefully.

In this chapter we examine these and other developments in U.S. foreign policy in the second half of the Cold War, with an eye to the lessons and legacies of the Cold War.

The Vietnam War: America's Most Profound Foreign Policy Setback

In 1995 Robert McNamara, secretary of defense under Presidents Kennedy and Johnson and the official most closely associated with the Vietnam War, published his startling mea culpa memoirs, *In Retrospect: The Tragedy and Lessons of Vietnam*. For almost thirty years McNamara had refused to talk about Vietnam. He had left government and had gone on to be president of the World Bank and to work in the 1980s for nuclear arms control, but stayed mum on Vietnam. Now, though, he laid out his view of the causes for our failure in Vietnam (see Perspectives on p. 138). Some were political, such as the failure to maintain congressional and public support. Some were strategic, such as misjudging the geopolitical intentions of U.S. adversaries and

PERSPECTIVES
PERSPECTIVES
PERSPECTIVES

WHY THE UNITED STATES LOST THE VIETNAM WAR
According to former secretary of defense Robert McNamara

- We misjudged . . . the geopolitical intentions of our adversaries . . . and we exaggerated the dangers to the United States of their actions.

- We viewed the people and leaders of South Vietnam in terms of our own experience. We saw in them a thirst for—and a determination to fight for—freedom and democracy. We totally misjudged the political forces within the country.

- We underestimated the power of nationalism to motivate a people (in this case, the North Vietnamese and Vietcong) to fight and die for their beliefs and values. . . .

- Our misjudgments of friend and foe alike reflected our profound ignorance of the history, culture, and politics of the people in the area and the personalities and habits of their leaders.

- We failed then—as we have since—to recognize the limitations of modern, high-technology military equipment, forces, and doctrine in confronting unconventional, highly motivated people's movements.

- We failed to draw Congress and the American people into a full and frank discussion and debate of the pros and cons of a large-scale U.S. military involvement in Southeast Asia before we initiated the action.

- We did not recognize that neither our people nor our leaders are omniscient. . . .

- We did not hold to the principle that U.S. military action—other than in response to direct threats to our own security—should be carried out only in conjunction with multinational forces supported fully (and not merely cosmetically) by the international community.

- We failed to recognize that in international affairs, as in other aspects of life, there may be problems for which there are no immediate solutions.

- Underlying many of these errors lay our failure to organize the top echelons of the executive branch to deal effectively with the

(*Continued on page 139*)

> **(Why the United States Lost . . .**   *Continued from page 138)*
> extraordinarily complex range of political and military issues, in-
> volving the great risks and costs—including, above all else, loss of
> life—associated with the application of military force under sub-
> stantial constraints over a long period of time.
>
> From *In Retrospect*, pp. 321–33, by Robert S. McNamara. Copyright © 1995 by Robert S.
> McNamara. Reprinted by permission of Times Books, a division of Random House, Inc.

exaggerating the actual threats to American interests. Some were diplomatic.
Some were military.

McNamara was not the only former high-level government official to
have expressed such doubts and criticisms about Vietnam. Former secretary
of state Dean Acheson later acknowledged receiving advice that there was
"real danger that our efforts would fail," but nevertheless deciding that "having put our hand to the plow, we would not look back."[1] Dwight Eisenhower
wrote of being "convinced that the French could not win" the 1945–54 colonial war, but that nevertheless "the decision to give this aid was almost com-
pulsory. The United States had no real alternative."[2] John Kennedy was said
to be "skeptical of the extent of our involvement in Vietnam but unwilling to
abandon his predecessor's pledge."[3] And during Lyndon Johnson's "Americanization" of the war, Vice President Hubert Humphrey, Undersecretary of
State George Ball, Senator J. William Fulbright, journalist Walter Lippmann,
and all other proponents of alternative options were closed out of the decision-
making process because of their misgivings. Henry Kissinger himself later
described "Vietnamization," the centerpiece of his own policy, as "the operation, conceived in doubt and assailed by skepticism [which] proceeded in
confusion"—but proceeded nevertheless.[4]

Some critics argued that Vietnam was a war that should not have been
fought, could not have been won, and could and should have been halted at
several key junctures. Others vehemently contended that it was right to
have fought it, and that it could have been won through tougher policies
and more commitment by U.S. policy-makers. The one point on which
there has been consensus is that Vietnam was the most profound foreign policy setback the United States suffered during the Cold War era. For
American foreign policy strategy, it amounted to failure on all counts:
peace was not served, power was eroded, principles were violated, prosperity
was damaged. In American foreign policy politics, the Cold War consensus

was shattered, in terms of both its institutional structures and its societal underpinnings.

Foreign Policy Strategy: Failure on All Counts

PEACE   American casualities in Vietnam numbered more than two hundred thousand, including almost sixty thousand deaths. Vietnamese casualties numbered in the hundreds of thousands, as well. And rather than keeping the dominoes from falling, communism came to Vietnam, got stronger in Laos, and spread to Cambodia.

Whether peace was achievable through the war effort is one of the main debates between the contending schools noted above. Secretary McNamara believed not, in part because of the inherent "limitations" of modern high-technology warfare when pitted against "the power of nationalism to motivate a people to fight and die for their beliefs and values."[5] Others faulted what was not done more than what was; one general wrote that American strategy violated two of the "time-honored principles of war. . . . We lacked a clear objective and an attainable strategy of a decisive nature."[6]

The sense of the war's unwinnability was not just retrospective. Even while he was intensifying American bombing of the Vietnamese, President Nixon privately acknowledged that "there's no way to win the war. But we can't say that, of course. In fact, we have to seem to say the opposite, just to keep some bargaining leverage." At the peace negotiations with the North Vietnamese in Paris, the ultimate objective was not to win but, as Kissinger stated it, to be able "to withdraw as an expression of policy and not as a collapse."[7] This approach continued after the Treaty of Paris had been signed in 1973. The Ford administration pushed for retaliation against North Vietnamese treaty violations. But it did so less to ensure a peace than to gain a "decent interval" that might convince the global audience that the United States had not lost.[8]

POWER   All along the main factor driving U.S. involvement in Vietnam was the belief that the credibility of American power was being tested there. A 1952 State Department memorandum delineated three reasons for "the strategic importance of Indochina": "its geographic position as key to the defense of mainland Southeast Asia," a somewhat dubious proposition; "its economic importance as a potential large-scale exporter of rice," an interest much closer to trivial than vital; and *"as an example of Western resistance to Communist expansion"* (emphasis added).[9] In 1965, when the decision finally was made to send in American troops, President Johnson quite explicitly articulated the need to demonstrate American credibility, as it pertained to both global allies and adversaries alike: "Around the globe, from Berlin to Thailand, are people whose well-being rests, in part, on the belief that they can count on us if they are attacked. To leave Vietnam to its fate would shake the confidence of all these people in the value of an American commitment and in the value of America's word."[10]

This same precept carried over into the Nixon and Ford administrations. Kissinger stated uncategorically that "the commitment of 500,000 Americans has settled the issue of the importance of Vietnam. For what is involved now is confidence in American promises."[11] If the United States failed this test, President Nixon claimed, it would be perceived as "a pitiful, helpless giant" and "the forces of totalitarianism and anarchy will threaten free nations around the world."[12] On the eve of the American evacuation of Saigon in 1975, President Ford beseeched Congress in similar terms not to cut off aid, arguing that to do so "would draw into question the reliability of the United States and encourage the belief that aggression pays."[13]

Ironically, though, nothing damaged the perception of American power more than these very policies that were supposed to preserve it. No less a figure than Hans Morgenthau, whose books were cited in our original discussion of the Realist paradigm in Chapter 1, had opposed the Vietnam War as early as 1967, precisely because he believed it would be damaging to American power. The interests at stake were not worth the commitments needed. To the contrary, as Morgenthau himself argued, U.S. power could best be served by developing a relationship with Ho Chi Minh that, even without converting him from communism, would "prevent such a communist revolution from turning against the interests of the United States."[14]

PRINCIPLES   In the late 1950s, then-senator John Kennedy tried to make the moral case for American responsibility: "If we are not the parents of little Vietnam, then surely we are the godparents."[15] When American troops were first sent to these distant jungles, LBJ described the action as necessary because "we remain fixed on the pursuit of freedom as a deep and moral obligation that will not let us go."[16] President Nixon turned the principles argument inward with his rebuttal to the antiwar movement: if we withdrew from Vietnam, Nixon claimed, "we would lose confidence in ourselves. . . . North Vietnam cannot defeat or humiliate the United States. Only Americans can do that."[17]

Yet nowhere did Americans feel their foreign policy more violated their principles than in Vietnam. It needs to be acknowledged that among much of the antiwar movement there was a great deal of naiveté, wishful thinking, and rationalization. Ho Chi Minh and the Vietcong hardly were strictly freedom fighters, Jeffersonians, or the like. The horrors that the communist Khmer Rouge inflicted against their own people when they came to power in Cambodia shocked the world. But only according to the Cold War "ABC" definition did the likes of Presidents Ngo Dinh Diem and Nguyen Van Thieu in Vietnam, and Prime Minister Lon Nol in Cambodia, each of whom received staunch U.S. support, qualify as democrats. Moreover, the scenes of peasant villagers fleeing American aircraft spreading napalm, and of incidents like the 1968 My Lai massacre, in which U.S. soldiers killed more than 500 innocent Vietnamese villagers, were deeply disturbing to the American national conscience.

PROSPERITY   Theorists of the military-industrial complex claim that the raging appetite of an economy in which defense industries were so central was a key factor leading to Vietnam. Whether or not that analysis is true, from the more general perspective of the overall American economy, the effects of the war were quite damaging to prosperity. LBJ calculated that cutting domestic spending to finance the war would only further weaken political support, but his "guns and butter" strategy of trying to keep spending up in both areas backfired. The federal budget deficit grew. "Stagflation," meaning simultaneous high unemployment and high inflation, set in. For the first time since 1893, the trade balance went into deficit. The economic situation got so bad that Nixon, a Republican, imposed wage and price controls and other stringent measures typically identified with liberal, Democratic politicians. But these moves only made the economic situation worse.

Foreign Policy Politics: Shattering the Cold War Consensus

As for politics, here too the effects were paradoxical. "If I did not go into Vietnam," LBJ reflected, "there would follow in this country an endless national debate—a mean and destructive debate—that would shatter my Presidency, kill my administration, and damage our democracy. I knew that Harry Truman and Dean Acheson had lost their effectiveness from the day that the Communists took over China. I believed that the loss of China had played a large role in the rise of Joe McCarthy. And I knew that all these problems, taken together, were chickenshit compared with what might happen if we lost Vietnam."[18] The last part of this statement at least was right, but because LBJ went in, not because he stayed out.

PRESIDENTIAL-CONGRESSIONAL RELATIONS   Recall Senator Fulbright's 1961 statement cited in Chapter 4 about the need to give the president more power. It was the same Senator Fulbright who, as chairman of the Senate Foreign Relations Committee, became one of the leading opponents of the war. More sweepingly he now warned of "presidential dictatorship in foreign affairs. . . . I believe that the presidency has become a dangerously powerful office, more urgently in need of reform than any other institution in government."[19] Similarly, historian and former Kennedy aide Arthur Schlesinger, Jr., attacked "the imperial presidency . . . out of control and badly in need of new definition and restraint."[20]

Now Congress was urged to be more assertive and less deferential. Some of its most ardent supporters even proclaimed the 1970s to be an age of "foreign policy *by* Congress."[21] Many of its members were now less parochial and more worldly, some having served earlier in their careers as State or Defense Department officials or Peace Corps members or even as political science and international relations professors. Greater expertise also was available from the expanded and more-professional staffs of congressional committees. For example, between 1960 and 1975, the staff of the Senate Foreign Relations Committee increased from 25 to 62 members, and the House Foreign Affairs Committee staff grew from 14 to 54.[22] Moreover, as Senator Fulbright wrote, only partially in jest, "whatever may be said against Congress . . . there is one thing to be said for it: It poses no threat to the liberties of the American people."[23]

Congress relied heavily on procedural legislation (defined in Chapter 2) in seeking to redress the imbalance of foreign policy powers. The *War Powers Resolution (WPR) of 1973* was among the most central and controversial of these procedural initiatives. No declaration of war had ever been passed for the military action in Vietnam. Johnson and Nixon both justified their actions on the basis of the 1964 Tonkin Gulf Resolution, which Congress did pass by overwhelming margins, with an open-ended authorization to use military force.* For Vietnam itself Congress tried a number of ways to end the war, eventually using the power of the purse to cut off funds. The WPR was intended to increase Congress's share of the war powers for the next Vietnam. Nixon vetoed the WPR, claiming it was unconstitutional as an infringement of his presidential powers as commander in chief. But with Republicans

---

*It later was revealed that at least one of the two alleged incidents of North Vietnamese attacks on U.S. naval ships, which were the ostensible bases for the Tonkin Gulf Resolution, never actually occurred.

joining Democrats in a show of bipartisanship, the necessary two-thirds margin was reached in both the House and Senate to override his veto.

The WPR limited presidential power through two sets of provisions. One set sought to tighten up requirements for the president to consult with Congress before, or at least soon after, committing U.S. troops in any situation other than a genuine national emergency. This stipulation was intended to give Congress more say in whether initial troop commitments were made. The other established the "sixty-day clock," by which the president would have to withdraw U.S. forces unless Congress explicitly allowed an extension. As things have turned out in practice, the WPR has not worked very well (see Chapter 6). But at the time it seemed like a significant rebalancing of the war powers.

Congress also tried to stake its claims to a larger share of other aspects of shared foreign policy powers. With respect to treaties and other international commitments, it passed legislation trying to clamp down on the excessive use of executive agreements. It used its investigative and oversight powers to tighten the reins on executive-branch departments and agencies, most notably on the CIA. It made frequent use of the legislative veto in policy areas such as arms sales, nuclear nonproliferation, foreign aid, and trade. All told, it was a period in which Congress was trying to make Pennsylvania Avenue more of a two-way street.

EXECUTIVE-BRANCH POLITICS   It was from Vietnam that the "credibility gap" arose. The Johnson and Nixon administrations kept trying to put the best face on the war by holding back from the public some information and distorting other information, and by outright lying. The public was left doubting the credibility of its leaders. Not only did this sense of skepticism, if not cynicism, cause the public to lose faith in the truthfulness of its leaders about Vietnam, it was applied increasingly to all high-level officials in all arenas of government, and thus became the more generalized problem of the credibility gap.

SHATTERING THE COLD WAR CONSENSUS   During the Cold War a few protest movements had emerged, but none that had any significant impact. The anti–Vietnam War movement marked a major change in this pattern. Hundreds of thousands of demonstrators marched on Washington, not just once but repeatedly. "Teach-ins" spread on college campuses, as did sit-ins and in some instances more violent demonstrations. In one particularly tragic incident in the spring of 1970, National Guard troops fired on antiwar protesters at Kent State University in Ohio, killing four students. Although some of its excesses worked against its very goals, overall the antiwar movement was an important influence on U.S. policy in Vietnam.

As for the news media, the old "cheerleader" role that had prevailed for much of the early Cold War was supplanted by the media as "critic." This, too, was born in Vietnam, where it was the media that first brought home to Americans news of how badly the war was going and how much of a credibility gap there was between official accounts and the reality on the ground. In one telling encounter a reporter posed a tough question to an American official at a press conference. The official asked the reporter his name. "Malcolm Browne of the Associated Press," he said. "So you're Browne," the official responded, revealing a knowledge of Browne's critical reporting. "Why don't you get on the team?"[24]

The Watergate scandal took media-government antagonism further. President Johnson and his administration had done quite a bit of shading of the truth, but Watergate revealed that Nixon and his cronies had lied, covered up, and even committed crimes. Had it not been for the media, none of this may have been known. Moreover, even though Watergate wasn't a foreign policy scandal per se, among its revelations was Nixon's "enemies list," which included some journalists as well as leaders of the antiwar movement.

Dynamics of Choice on p. 146 shows the sharp contrasts in public opinion between the Cold War consensus and the new mindset of "the Vietnam trauma." Whereas only 24 percent considered the Vietnam War a mistake when the United States first sent troops in 1965, by 1971 61 percent did. More generally, the public had become much less internationalist and much more isolationist, as can be seen in its low ranking of the importance of containment as a national objective, and its reduced willingness to use American troops to defend non-American territory, even in Western Europe.

These shifts reflected the differences between the "Munich–Pearl Harbor generation," which came of age during World War II, and the "Vietnam generation," which came of age during the Vietnam War. The lessons of Munich and Pearl Harbor were about the folly of isolationism, the dangers of appeasement, the risks of being unprepared—mistakes that led to World War II and that then became the core lessons for U.S. Cold War strategy. In sending the first U.S. troops to Vietnam in 1965, Defense Secretary McNamara cited a speech by a Vietnamese communist leader as "a speech that ranks with Hitler's *Mein Kampf*"; a Senate supporter flat out stated that "the situation in Vietnam today bears many resemblances to the situation just before Munich."[25]

Public Opinion from Cold War Consensus to Vietnam Trauma

	Cold war consensus	Vietnam trauma
a. Percentage who support internationalism	65%	41%
b. Percentage who support isolationism	8%	21%
c. Rank of containment as a national objective	2nd	7th
d. Percentage supporting troops to defend Western Europe	80%	39%
e. Percentage supporting troops to defend the Western Hemisphere	73%	31%
f. Percentage responding yes to, "Was the Vietnam War a mistake?"	24%	61%

Sources: (a, b) William Watts and Potomac Associates, presented in Charles W. Kegley, Jr., and Eugene R. Wittkopf, *American Foreign Policy: Pattern and Process,* 3d ed. (New York: St. Martin's, 1987), 292; (c) Lloyd A. Free and Hadley Cantril, *The Political Beliefs of Americans* (New York: Simon and Schuster, 1968), 52; Michael Mandelbaum and William Schneider, "The New Internationalisms: Public Opinion and American Foreign Policy," in *Eagle Entangled: U.S. Foreign Policy in a Complex World,* ed. Kenneth A. Oye, Donald Rothchild, and Robert J. Lieber (New York: Longman, 1979), 41–42; (d) Eugene R. Wittkopf, "Elites and Masses: Another Look at Attitudes toward America's World Role," *International Studies Quarterly* 31:7 (June 1987), 131–59; Mandelbaum and Schneider, "New Internationalisms," 82; (e) Wittkopf, "Elites and Masses"; (f) Barry B. Hughes, *The Domestic Context of American Foreign Policy* (San Francisco: Freeman, 1978), 38–40.

The experience of the Vietnam War, however, left the next generation with what Graham Allison has called a "militant disbelief in the older axioms."[26] Whatever lessons had been drawn from Munich and Pearl Harbor about what should have been done in the 1930s and early 1940s was seen by this new generation as having been misapplied in or inapplicable to the Vietnam War. The Vietnam experience was a searing one; it destroyed the Cold War consensus and left the country deeply divided and for years opposed to almost any use of military force.

Clearly, a lot had changed. The shift wasn't just because of Vietnam; there were other issues as well on which questions were increasingly being asked about foreign policy strategy and in foreign policy politics. But Vietnam in particular stood as a profound setback for American Cold War strategy and shattered the political patterns of the Cold War.

The Rise and Fall of Détente: Major Foreign Policy Shifts

Détente literally means a "relaxation of tensions." It was the principal term used to characterize efforts in the 1970s to break out of the Cold War and improve relations between the United States and the Soviet Union. But whereas at the beginning of the decade détente was heralded as the dawn of a new era, by the end of the decade these hopes had been dashed and the Cold War had resumed.

Nixon, Kissinger, and the Rise of Détente

What made the rise of détente possible were shifts in all 4 Ps, as well as in foreign policy politics.

Peace was a driving force behind détente for both the Americans and the Soviets. Both sides shared interests in stabilizing Europe, which is where the Cold War had originated and where it had been waged for nearly a quarter-century. It thus was important both substantively and symbolically that one of the first détente agreements achieved (1971) was on Berlin, the divided German city that had been the locus of recurring Cold War crises. Berlin's status as a divided city was not ended, but new agreements did allow increased contact between West and East Berlin, and West and East Germany more generally.

Other important agreements created the Conference on Security and Cooperation in Europe (CSCE) and adopted the Helsinki Accords of 1975. The CSCE was the first major international organization other than the U.N. to include countries of both Eastern and Western Europe, both NATO allies (including the United States and Canada) and Warsaw Pact members; it also included neutral countries like Sweden and Switzerland. The Helsinki Accords were something of a tradeoff. On the one hand they gave the Soviets the recognition they long had wanted of territorial borders in central and Eastern Europe as drawn after World War II. On the other hand they established human rights and other democratic values as basic tenets that CSCE members agreed to respect. Although this provision was not fully binding on Moscow or other communist governments, it provided a degree of legitimization and protection for dissidents that, as we will see later, nurtured the seeds of what would become the great anticommunist revolutions of 1989.

The United States and the Soviet Union also increasingly had come to recognize, especially in the wake of the Cuban missile crisis, their shared interest in working together to reduce the risks of nuclear war. This interest was clearly stated in the "Basic Principles of Relations," a charter-like document signed by Nixon and Soviet leader Leonid Brezhnev at their 1972 summit (see At the Source on p. 149). Underlying this recognition was an important shift in nuclear deterrence doctrine (power). One of the reasons noted in Chapter 4 that the Soviets put nuclear missiles in Cuba was to pose a threat close to American territory as a counterweight to the overall American nuclear superiority. Even though this didn't succeed, or, arguably, precisely because it didn't succeed, the Soviets came out of the Cuban missile crisis determined to close the nuclear-weapons gap. The nuclear arms race thus got another kick upward. On the U.S. side the rising costs of maintaining nuclear superiority, especially on top of the costs of the Vietnam War, were becoming more burdensome. Moreover, even if nuclear superiority were maintained, the Soviets had increased their own nuclear firepower sufficiently that security would not be assured. The dilemma was laid out in a 1967 speech by Defense Secretary McNamara: "In the larger equation of security, our 'superiority' is of limited significance. . . . Even with our current superiority, or indeed with any numerical superiority realistically attainable, the blunt inescapable fact remains that the Soviet Union could still—with its present forces—effectively destroy the United States, even after absorbing the full weight of an American first strike."[27]

The strategic situation he was describing was one of *"mutually assured destruction,"* or MAD, as it became known in a fitting acronym. Yet as paradoxical as it might sound, MAD was seen as potentially stabilizing. Since neither side could launch a "first strike" without risking getting devastated itself in a "second strike"—i.e., with destruction assured to be mutual—the chances were slim that either side would resort to nuclear weapons. Trying to break out of this situation could make the arms race endless. Both sides thus had an interest in nuclear arms control.

Prior to the détente era there had been only a few U.S.-Soviet nuclear arms-control agreements.[28] Thus the signing in 1972 of the first *Strategic Arms Limitation Treaty* (SALT I) was highly significant as recognition that peace and stability were not achievable only through arms but also required arms control.

At the Source

U.S.-SOVIET DÉTENTE

The United States of America and the Union of Soviet Socialist Republics . . . Have agreed as follows:

First. They will proceed from the common determination that in the nuclear age there is no alternative to conducting their mutual relations on the basis of peaceful coexistence. Differences in ideology and in the social systems of the USA and the USSR are not obstacles to the bilateral development of normal relations based on the principles of sovereignty, equality, non-interference in internal affairs and mutual advantage.

Second. The USA and the USSR attach major importance to preventing the development of situations capable of causing a dangerous exacerbation of their relations. Therefore, they will do their utmost to avoid military confrontations and to prevent the outbreak of nuclear war. They will always exercise restraint in their mutual relations, and will be prepared to negotiate and settle differences by peaceful means. Discussions and negotiations on outstanding issues will be conducted in a spirit of reciprocity, mutual accommodation and mutual benefit.

Both sides recognize that efforts to obtain unilateral advantage at the expense of the other, directly or indirectly, are inconsistent with these objectives. The prerequisites for maintaining and strengthening peaceful relations between the USA and the USSR are the recognition of the security interests of the Parties based on the principle of equality and the renunciation of the use or threat of force. . . .

Sixth. The Parties will continue their efforts to limit armaments on a bilateral as well as on a multilateral basis. They will continue to make special efforts to limit strategic armaments. Whenever possible, they will conclude concrete agreements aimed at achieving these purposes.

The USA and the USSR regard as the ultimate objective of their efforts the achievement of general and complete disarmament and the establishment of an effective system of international security in accordance with the purposes and principles of the United Nations.

Seventh. The USA and the USSR regard commercial and economic ties as an important and necessary element in the strengthening of their

(*Continued on page 150*)

(U.S.-Soviet Détente   *Continued from page 149)*
bilateral relations and thus will actively promote the growth of such ties. ...

Ninth. The two sides reaffirm their intention to deepen cultural ties with one another and to encourage fuller familiarization with each other's cultural values. They will promote improved conditions for cultural exchanges and tourism. "

Source: "Basic Principles of Relations," signed by the United States and the Soviet Union, May 1972, in *American Foreign Relations, 1972: A Documentary Record* (New York: New York University Press for the Council on Foreign Relations, 1976), 75–78.

SALT I set limits on strategic nuclear weapons according to a formula known as "essential equivalence," whereby the Soviets were allowed a larger quantity of missiles because the United States had technological advantages that allowed it to put more bombs on each missile.* The idea was that if the Soviets had a quantitative edge and the United States a qualitative one, both would be assured of deterrence. SALT I also severely limited anti–ballistic missile (ABM) defense systems, on the grounds that such defensive systems were destabilizing: if one side knew it could defend itself against nuclear attack, then mutual destruction no longer would be assured and that side might be more likely to launch a first strike.

Trade was also a major component of détente, both for economic reasons (prosperity) and because of its utility for peace and power objectives. With respect to the latter two, as stated in one Nixon administration report, "our purpose is to build in both countries a vested economic interest in the maintenance of a harmonious and enduring relationship. ... If we can create a situation in which the use of military force would jeopardize a mutually profitable relationship, I think it can be argued that security will have been enhanced."[29] The linkages between prosperity and peace and power were evident both in the grain deal the United States offered the Soviets in 1971 at cut-rate prices, in part to induce them to agree to SALT I, and in the pressure

---

*The technical term is MIRVs, or multiple independently targeted re-entry vehicles. Think of missiles as delivery vehicles on which nuclear bombs are put. A MIRVed missile is one that can hold multiple bombs, each aimed at its own target.

the Soviets put on North Vietnam in late 1972 to sign the Paris Peace treaty in order to keep U.S. trade flowing.*

In terms of economic benefits for the United States, interests were strongest in two sectors. One was agriculture. Up until the 1970s the Soviets had been largely self-sufficient in grain. The only prior major grain deal with the United States was in 1963. But for reasons both of bad weather and bad planning, Soviet grain harvests now were falling far short of their needs. Ironically, their first purchases of American grain were so huge and transacted through such clever manipulation of the markets that they garnered low prices for themselves while leaving U.S. domestic grain markets with short supplies and high inflation. The Nixon and Ford administrations worked out trade agreements for future purchases that tried to lock in the export benefits from the grain sales while insulating American markets from further inflationary effects. By 1980, American exporters supplied 80 percent of Soviet grain imports.

The other key sector was energy. The Soviet Union was second only to Saudi Arabia in the size of its oil reserves, and it was first in the world in natural-gas reserves. Even before the OPEC shocks hit in late 1973, the Nixon administration assessed that "with the tremendous increases that are projected in our energy requirements by the end of this century, it may be very much in our interest to explore seriously the possibility of gaining access to, and in fact to aid in the development of energy fields as rich as those possessed by the Soviet Union."[30] After the OPEC shocks there was even more basis for this economic calculus, not least because while supporting the OPEC embargo against the United States and the Netherlands in their rhetoric, the Soviets had undercut it by quietly providing both countries with some additional oil.

The role of principles in promoting détente was mixed. The Nixon-Kissinger approach was to give limited emphasis in their "high politics" to Soviet dissidents and other such issues. "The domestic practices of the Soviet Union are not necessarily related to détente," which was primarily related to foreign policy, Kissinger stated in testimony to Congress. Such a position was not "moral callousness" but rather a recognition of the "limits on our ability

---

*According to the *Wall Street Journal,* when President Nixon announced stepped-up bombing of North Vietnam and mining of its harbors, Soviet trade minister Nikolai Patolichev was meeting with U.S. commerce secretary Peter G. Peterson. "After hearing Mr. Nixon's tough words, he [Patolichev] turned to his host [Peterson] and said: 'Well, let's get back to business.' And a couple of days later he posed happily with the President, a clear signal to Hanoi that Moscow put its own interests first." Cited in Bruce W. Jentleson, "The Political Basis for Trade in U.S.-Soviet Relations," *Millennium: Journal of International Studies* 15 (Spring 1986), p. 31.

to produce internal change in foreign countries."[31] A particularly contentious issue in this regard was the linkage between most-favored-nation (MFN) status and other trade benefits for the Soviet Union and U.S. pressures for increased emigration rights for Soviet Jews. In keeping with his view of détente as more about Soviet foreign policy than its domestic policy, Kissinger preferred to leave the Soviet Jewry issue to "quiet diplomacy." Congress, however, saw it differently, and in 1974 passed the Jackson-Vanik Amendment linking MFN status to a prescribed increase in emigration visas for Soviet Jews.

The Carter administration put much more emphasis on human rights in its détente strategy, in two respects. One was directly vis-à-vis the Soviet Union, as when President Carter personally met with Aleksandr Solzhenitsyn, the renowned Soviet dissident who had been exiled in 1974 after decades in prison camps (gulags), and with whom Ford and Kissinger had refused to meet. Also in a radical departure from the policies of his predecessors, Carter championed human rights with respect to the Third World. Declaring in his 1977 inaugural address that "our commitment to human rights must be absolute," Carter cut or withdrew support from such traditional "ABC" allies as the Somozas in Nicaragua and the shah of Iran.[32]

As for foreign policy politics, initially it seemed that détente might provide the basis for a new consensus. It may have seemed ironic that Richard Nixon, who had launched his political career as a staunch anticommunist, was now the one both to pursue détente with the Soviet Union and to visit "Red" China. But there was a political logic to this seeming reversal, as someone with impeccable anticommunist credentials could be insulated from charges of being soft on communism. In any case, the public was captivated by images of Nixon in China sharing champagne toasts with Mao Zedong, and of Soviet leader Brezhnev donning a cowboy hat and giving a bear hug to the star of a popular American television series.

Even so, détente encountered some opposition from both ends of the political spectrum. Liberals supported its overall thrust but were critical on issues like the Nixon-Kissinger de-emphasis of human rights. Conservatives, while Nixon's longtime political comrades, were not yet ready to admit that anything other than confrontation was possible with the Soviets. They were skeptical of arms control in general and of SALT I in particular. Their main criticism of SALT I was that it gave the Soviets a potential advantage once they developed the MIRV technology, breaking out of essential equivalence and gaining true superiority. And on China, Mao was still the subversive who wrote that "little red book," and conservatives' real passion was to stop the "abandonment" of Taiwan.

Executive-branch politics was marked more by the personality of Henry Kissinger than by the policy of détente. Kissinger's biographers paint a picture of a man whose ego often got in the way of his brilliance.[33] Many examples can be drawn from Kissinger's penchant for bureaucratic warfare. As Nixon's national security adviser, he tried to confine Secretary of State William Rogers to minor issues only. When Nixon in his second term made Kissinger secretary of state, he allowed him to keep the national security adviser title as well. When Kissinger did give up the NSC post once Gerald Ford became president, he ensured that the position went to his former deputy Brent Scowcroft. Kissinger also fought major bureaucratic battles with Defense Secretary James Schlesinger, who tended to be more hawkish on arms control and defense issues. To be sure, Kissinger won more rounds of executive-branch politics than he lost. And there is something to be said for a take-charge approach that avoids bureaucratic bogs. But some of the flaws in his policies were due to his resistance to input from other top officials, and some of the enemies he made engendered political problems that in turn hampered his effectiveness.

Executive-branch politics during this period was also marked by a number of scandals. The CIA was especially hard hit, both in congressional hearings and in the media, with revelations and allegations ranging from assassination plots concocted against Fidel Castro and other foreign leaders, to illegal spying on U.S. citizens at home, including monitoring and intercepting the mail of members of Congress. Covert actions, in the words of the Senate Select Committee on Intelligence Activities (known as the Church Committee, after its chair, Senator Frank Church, a Democrat from Idaho), had been intended only as "exceptional instruments used only in rare instances," but "presidents and administrations have made excessive, and at times self-defeating, use of covert action."[34]

No doubt the greatest political scandal during these years was Watergate. The Watergate break-in occurred in June 1972, only a little more than a month after Nixon's first major summit in Moscow. As it built up over the next two years, the Watergate scandal dominated the media and public opinion, crowding out most other news stories. And it precluded any chance Nixon had of converting his 1972 landslide re-election victory into a mandate for foreign or domestic policy. Ultimately, on August 9, 1974, it led to Nixon's resignation. Although Nixon didn't take détente down with him, his political self-destruction surely added to the political problems détente faced.

Reasons for the Fall of Détente

The December 1979 Soviet invasion of Afghanistan is the event most often cited as marking the end of détente. President Carter called it "a clear threat to peace" and warned the Soviets that unless they withdrew "this will inevitably jeopardize the course of United States–Soviet relations throughout the world."[35] Even more than the Soviet presence in Afghanistan, the U.S. government's main concern was that the Soviets would not stop in Afghanistan but would continue on into the oil-rich Persian Gulf region. The Carter Doctrine, proclaimed in January 1980, echoed the Truman Doctrine and other cornerstones of the early Cold War: "Let our position be clear," Carter declared. "An attempt by any outside force to gain control of the Persian Gulf region will be regarded as an assault on the vital interests of the United States of America, and such an assault will be repelled by any means necessary, including military force."[36] This was much tougher talk and a more centrist policy than President Carter originally articulated and pursued.

Yet Afghanistan wasn't solely responsible for détente's fall. There were two deeper reasons. One was that all along, and for both sides, the relaxation of tensions and increased cooperation of détente did not put an end to continued competition and rivalry. The 1972 Basic Principles of Relations agreement cited earlier (see At the Source on p. 149) may have stated that "both sides recognize that efforts to obtain unilateral advantage at the expense of the other, directly or indirectly, are inconsistent" with the objectives of détente. This statement, though, was an example of papering over rather than resolving fundamental differences. The differences are well stated by Raymond Garthoff, a scholar and former State Department official:

> The U.S. conception of détente . . . called for U.S. manipulation of incentives and penalties in bilateral relations in order to serve other policy interests . . . a strategy for managing the emergence of Soviet power by drawing the Soviet Union into the existing world order through acceptance of a code of conduct for competition that favored the United States.
>
> The Soviet conception of détente was one of peaceful coexistence, which would set aside direct conflict between the two superpowers, in order to allow socialist and anti-imperialist forces a free hand. The Soviet leadership thus saw their task as maneuvering the United States into a world no longer marked by U.S. predominance.
>
> This discrepancy led to increasing friction.[37]

For both sides the main objective still was power much more than peace. This fact was evident in the different ways each side tried to use its relations with

China as leverage in great-power politics. The Soviets were trying to get U.S. support in their split with China. The Soviet-Chinese split long had been much worse than generally was realized in the United States. In 1969 military skirmishes took place along the Soviet-Chinese border. The Soviets even tried to find out what the U.S. reaction would be if they went to war with China. Not only was this inquiry rebuffed, but one of the strategic calculations for Nixon and Kissinger in their surprise opening to China (see At the Source, p. 156) was to use this new relationship as leverage in U.S.-Soviet relations. It thus was no coincidence that the Nixon-Kissinger trip to China came a few months earlier in 1972 than the trip to Moscow.

The clashing conceptions of the purposes of détente also were evident in the limits of what was achieved through arms control. The best that could be said for SALT I and SALT II (the follow-on agreement) was that they somewhat limited the growth of nuclear arsenals. No cuts were made by either side, just limits on future growth, and there was plenty of room within those limits for new and more destructive weapons. In addition, the Soviets were discovered to have cheated in certain areas. It took seven years after SALT I was signed until Carter and Brezhnez signed SALT II. American conservatives were strongly opposed to the new treaty, and they raised the specter of the Soviets' gaining nuclear superiority and the United States' facing a "window of vulnerability." Liberals were more supportive, although some only begrudgingly so, as they did not think the treaty went far enough. SALT II never was ratified by the Senate, because Carter withdrew it in response to the Soviet invasion of Afghanistan.

Nor was it just in Afghanistan that U.S.-Soviet Third World rivalries intensified and expanded. The U.S. expectation had been that détente amounted to Soviet acceptance of containment, that the Soviets would step back from spreading Marxist-Leninist revolution. The Soviets, though, as Garthoff indicated, saw détente mainly as a way to avoid escalation to superpower conflict while global geopolitical competition went on. Thus in Vietnam the Soviets helped pressure North Vietnam to sign the 1973 Paris peace treaty, but then aided the North's military victory and takeover in 1975. They also became much more active in Africa, supporting Marxist coups and guerrilla wars in places like Angola and Ethiopia.

U.S. Third World policy was still mired in confusion and contradiction. On the one hand, the Nixon and Ford administrations were still intent on containment. In Chile, for example, the CIA was heavily involved in 1970–73 efforts to overthrow socialist (but freely elected) president Salvador Allende. In Angola, CIA and military aid were started for the pro-American faction battling the pro-Soviet one, but then Congress passed legislation prohibiting further aid. On these and other issues, the essence of the debate was over

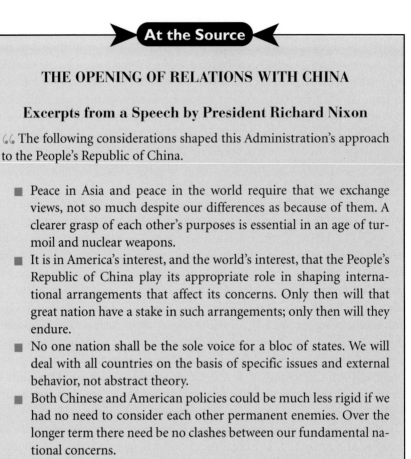

At the Source

THE OPENING OF RELATIONS WITH CHINA

Excerpts from a Speech by President Richard Nixon

“ The following considerations shaped this Administration's approach to the People's Republic of China.

- Peace in Asia and peace in the world require that we exchange views, not so much despite our differences as because of them. A clearer grasp of each other's purposes is essential in an age of turmoil and nuclear weapons.
- It is in America's interest, and the world's interest, that the People's Republic of China play its appropriate role in shaping international arrangements that affect its concerns. Only then will that great nation have a stake in such arrangements; only then will they endure.
- No one nation shall be the sole voice for a bloc of states. We will deal with all countries on the basis of specific issues and external behavior, not abstract theory.
- Both Chinese and American policies could be much less rigid if we had no need to consider each other permanent enemies. Over the longer term there need be no clashes between our fundamental national concerns.
- China and the United States share many parallel interests and can do much together to enrich the lives of our peoples. It is no accident that the Chinese and American peoples have such a long history of friendship.

On this basis we decided that a careful search for a new relationship should be undertaken. ”

Source: President Richard M. Nixon, "U.S. Foreign Policy for the 1970s: The Emerging Structure of Peace," report to Congress, February 9, 1972, reprinted in *Department of State Bulletin* 66:1707 (March 13, 1972), 327.

which "lessons of Vietnam" were the right ones—that communism really did have to be contained, or that such efforts ended up as costly quagmires.

Another, related part of the debate was over Carter's emphasis on human rights. In Nicaragua, where the dictatorship of the Somoza family had a long record of human rights violations, the Carter administration cut back support and brought pressure for reform. Although this had some positive effects, the ensuing revolution that deposed Anastasio Somoza brought to power the Sandinistas, who initially were a mix of nationalists, socialists, Marxist-Leninists, and anti-Americans. Even though the history of U.S. imperialist domination was more the cause of the revolution than was the Carter human rights policy, the Carter policy got much of the blame. The same dynamic played out in Iran, with the fall of the shah to the virulently anti-American Islamic fundamentalist revolution led by the Ayatollah Ruhollah Khomeini. Not only did the United States lose a strategically located ally when the shah fell, but the whole American psyche was deeply shaken by the November 1979 seizure of the U.S. embassy in Teheran and the taking of more than seventy Americans as hostages. The Ayatollah Khomeini justified the hostage-taking as action against "this great Satan—America" (see At the Source, p. 158). These developments were quite traumatic for Americans, unaccustomed to the sense of vulnerability that the Iranian hostage crisis evoked. Those shock waves were still being felt—strategically, politically, and psychologically—when barely a month later the Soviets launched their invasion of Afghanistan.

Amid all this, the divisiveness of domestic politics grew worse and worse. Carter had a Democratic Congress, but that mattered only marginally in getting congressional support. His executive branch was stricken by bitter internal politics, with National Security Adviser Zbigniew Brzezinski and Secretary of State Cyrus Vance waging their own bureaucratic warfare. Conservatives, now led by an organization called the Committee on the Present Danger, became increasingly active in opposition to détente. Carter also felt pressure from agricultural interest groups when he imposed grain sanctions as part of his response to the Soviet invasion of Afghanistan. General public opinion was deeply split, and increasingly confused.

Disparagements of "the decade of so-called détente" were staples of candidate Ronald Reagan's speeches. "We are blind to reality," he said on the campaign trail, "if we refuse to recognize that détente's usefulness to the Soviets is only as a cover for their traditional and basic strategy for aggression.[38] In November 1980 Ronald Reagan was elected president. The Cold War would be renewed, and then ultimately start to end, during the Reagan presidency.

AMERICA HELD HOSTAGE

A Speech by the Ayatollah Khomeini

❝ In this revolution, the big Satan is America, which is clamoring to gather other Satans around it; this includes both the Satans inside and outside Iran. You know that during the rule of these two devils [presumably the shah and his father], whose rule was in contravention of the law, Iran was in turn enslaved by Britain and then America. This great Satan—America—is clamoring and gathering around it other Satans because its hand has been cut off from our resources. It is afraid this amputation may become permanent. Therefore, it is plotting.

As for that center [the U.S. embassy in Teheran] occupied by our young men, I have been informed that it has been a lair of espionage and plotting. America expects to take the shah there, engage in plots, create a base in Iran for these plots, and our young people are expected simply to remain idle and witness all these things.

The rotten roots have become active, hoping we would mediate and tell the young people to leave this place. Our young people resorted to this action because they saw that the shah was allowed in America.

America expects our nation, our young people, our university and our young religious people to sit idle and see the blood of the nearly 100,000 martyrs shed in vain. Obviously, had it not been for the plots, sabotage and all those corrupt acts, everyone could have remained here in freedom. However, when we face plots, our young people cannot wait and see their country return to the past and everything go with the wind. Our young people must foil all these plots with all their might. Today we cannot simply remain idle and watch things; today we are facing underground treason, treason devised in these same embassies, mainly by the great Satan, America. They must bear in mind that Iran is still in a state of revolution; a revolution greater than the first one. They must be put in their place and return this criminal to us as soon as possible. ❞

Source: Ayatollah Khomeini, speech broadcast in Persian on Tehran Domestic Service, November 5, 1979, reported in "Khomeini on Occupation," Foreign Broadcast Information Service: Middle East/North Africa, November 6, 1979, pp. R2–R3.

1970s Economic Shocks

The 1970s was the decade that the myth of assured prosperity was shattered. The American economy, and the economic psyche of the American people, endured a series of shocks that recast the international economy and the U.S. position in it as less hegemonic and more uncertain than it had been in generations. Some of the fundamental sources of these new economic problems actually were rooted in U.S. domestic and economic policies: such as Johnson's "guns and butter" and the stagflation that ensued, and Nixon's overstimulation of the economy as part of his 1972 re-election strategy. But the focus was more on external (foreign) sources.

The Nixon Shock, 1971

On August 15, 1971, with the value of the dollar at its lowest point since World War II, President Nixon announced that the United States was unilaterally devaluing the dollar, suspending its convertibility to gold, and imposing a 10 percent special tariff on imports. These moves, which came to be known as the "Nixon shock," were targeted principally at Europe and Japan, who were still strategic allies, but increasingly had also become economic competitors. "Foreigners are out to screw us," Treasury Secretary John Connally rather indelicately put it, "and it's our job to screw them first."[39]

In more analytical terms the principal significance was threefold. First, whereas for the previous quarter-century the United States had been willing to grant economic concessions to its allies to help them with their economic reconstruction and ensure their political stability as part of containment, now it was projecting onto them responsibility for its own economic problems. The United States was coming close, as Kissinger and others warned, to economic war with its own allies.

Second, one of the key pillars of the liberal international order (LIEO), the international monetary system based on fixed exchange rates and the gold standard, had crumbled with the U.S. abandonment of the gold standard. The world risked descending back into competitive devaluations and other monetary manipulations. Some efforts were made to prevent such moves, first with a system of "floating" exchange rates and then "flexible" ones, but the new reality fell well short of the stability and multilateralism of the old system.

Third, the free trade vs. protectionism debate was reopened in U.S. domestic politics. Labor unions such as the AFL-CIO had been generally supportive of free trade in the 1950s and 1960s. They had lobbied for loop-holes for industries facing the toughest competition from imports (textiles, for instance) but had supported most free-trade bills. As long as the United States was running a trade surplus, more jobs were being created by exports than were being lost to imports. But with the United States running a mer-chandise trade balance for the first time since 1893, labor unions shifted their politics accordingly, becoming much more protectionist.

The OPEC Shocks, 1973 and 1979

The American automobile culture was built on a steady and inexpensive sup-ply of oil. American suburban families and college students alike took for granted driving to a nearby gas station and filling up at prices of about thirty-three cents per gallon. That all changed in October 1973 when Americans had to learn a new acronym: OPEC.

OPEC had been founded back in 1960. It had tried oil embargoes and oil price hikes before, but they hadn't succeeded. In 1967, during the Arab-Israeli Six Day War, two factors undermined the embargo that OPEC instituted to weaken international support for Israel. One was that some of OPEC's non-Arab members, such as Iran (a Muslim but non-Arab country) and Venezuela, didn't go along, and even stepped up their oil production. The other was that the United States at that time was still the world's largest oil producer and was able to compensate by increasing its own production by a million barrels per day. In 1973, though, the cartel held together, with all OPEC members agree-ing to 25 percent production cuts, full oil embargoes targeted at the United States and the Netherlands for their support of Israel in the Yom Kippur War, and a worldwide price increase of 325 percent. U.S. oil production had been falling since 1970, and this time only a meager increase of one hundred thou-sand barrels per day could be mustered.

Economically the OPEC embargo was, as they say, like pouring fuel onto a fire. The stagflation, the trade imbalance, and other economic problems plaguing the American economy were made much worse. No commodity was as central to industry as oil, and no commodity was as essential to the con-sumer culture. Moreover, beyond the material impact, the psychological shocks were highly disorienting. The easy-in/easy-out of gas stations gave way to gas lines miles long. For a while gas was rationed, with fill-ups alternated daily for even-numbered and odd-numbered license plates. The ultimate in-sult was that it wasn't even the Soviet Union or a European great power that was revealing American vulnerabilities—it was weaker, less-developed, not even "modern" countries of sheiks and shahs. That type of thinking may be condemned as arrogant, but it is important to any understanding of the trauma of the OPEC oil shock.

In case there were doubts or hopes that this may have been a one-time thing, the second OPEC oil shock hit in 1979 with the Iranian Revolution. Oil supplies again were disrupted. Prices were hiked. Gas lines returned, unemployment was fed, inflation skyrocketed, interest rates hit double digits, trade deficits shot up. By the mid-1980s, oil prices actually started to come down in real terms, but the marks left by the OPEC shocks were permanent.

The North-South Conflict and Demands for an "NIEO"

Despite having 74 percent of the world's population, as of the early 1970s Third World countries accounted for only 17 percent of the global gross national product (GNP). So when OPEC was so successful in bringing the industrialized world to heel, many Third World countries saw an opportunity to redefine international economic relations toward greater equity and justice for the developing-world "South" against the industrialized "North." They criticized the LIEO for giving inadequate attention to issues of development and for perpetuating inequalities in the global distribution of wealth. GATT may have been opening markets, but the terms of trade tended to favor the industrial exports of the developed countries over the raw materials and foodstuffs exported by the developing world. The IMF and the "conditionalities" it attached to its loans were under so much fire as to be the target of protests and riots in Third World cities. So, too, with foreign aid, criticized as too little and not the right kind of development assistance.

In May 1974, at a special session of the U.N. General Assembly, the South put forward a "Declaration of New International Economic Order" (see At the Source, p. 162). This NIEO was intended to replace the LIEO. For the United States, this proposal threatened both its economic interests and its free-market ideology. The American economy depended on cheap commodities and raw materials, yet the NIEO demanded higher prices for raw materials and commodities in the name of "justice and equity." American multinational corporations had substantial investments in the Third World, yet the NIEO called for some form of international "regulation and supervision." The NIEO even demanded that modern science and technology be "given" to developing countries. Among proposals for "special measures in favor of the least developed" and the "full and equal participation" of developing countries in setting international economic policy were direct and indirect accusations that the

At the Source

THE DECLARATION OF A NEW INTERNATIONAL ECONOMIC ORDER

❝ *We, the Members of the United Nations,*
Having convened a special session of the General Assembly to study for the first time the problems of raw materials and development, devoted to the consideration of the most important economic problems facing the world community. . .

Solemnly proclaim our united determination to work urgently for the establishment of a new international economic order based on equity, sovereign equality, interdependence, common interest and co-operation among all States, irrespective of their economic and social systems which shall correct inequalities and redress existing injustices, make it possible to eliminate the widening gap between the developed and the developing countries and ensure steadily accelerating economic and social development and peace and justice for present and future generations, and to that end declare . . .

It has proved impossible to achieve an even and balanced development of the international community under the existing international economic order. The gap between the developed and the developing countries continues to widen in a system which was established at a time when most of the developing countries did not even exist as independent States and which perpetuates inequality. . . .

The developing world has become a powerful factor felt in all fields of international activity. These irreversible changes in the relationship of forces in the world necessitate the active, full and equal participation of the developing countries in the formulation and application of all decisions that concern the international community. . . .

The prosperity of the international community as a whole depends upon the prosperity of its constituent parts. International co-operation for development is the shared goal and common duty of all countries. Thus the political, economic and social well-being of present and future generations depends more than ever on co-operation between all members of the international community on the basis of sovereign equality

(*Continued on page 163*)

(New International Economic Order   *Continued from page 162)*
and the removal of the disequilibrium that exists between them.

The new international economic order should be founded on full respect for the following principles: . . .

The broadest co-operation of all the State members of the international community, based on equity, whereby the prevailing disparities in the world may be banished and prosperity secured for all; . . .

The necessity to ensure the accelerated development of all the developing countries, while devoting particular attention to the adoption of special measures in favour of the least developed. . . .

The right [of] every country to adopt the economic and social system that it deems to be the most appropriate for its own development and not to be subjected to discrimination of any kind as a result; . . .

Regulation and supervision of the activities of transnational corporations by taking measures in the interest of the national economies of the countries where such transnational corporations operate on the basis of the full sovereignty of those countries; . . .

Just and equitable relationship between the prices of raw materials, primary products, manufactured and semi-manufactured goods exported by developing countries and the prices of raw materials, primary commodities, manufactures, capital goods and equipment imported by them with the aim of bringing about sustained improvement in their unsatisfactory terms of trade and the expansion of the world economy; . . .

Giving to the developing countries access to the achievements of modern science and technology, and promoting the transfer of technology and the creation of indigenous technology for the benefit of the developing countries in forms and in accordance with procedures which are suited to their economies. "

Source: "Declaration on Establishment of a New International Economic Order," *Annual Review of UN Affairs 1974* (New York: Oceana Publications, 1976), 208–12.

United States was the source of much that was wrong with the international economy.

The NIEO declaration was formally adopted by the U.N. General Assembly, and some of its measures were initiated. However, it was mostly a symbolic vote. Actual economic changes were limited, and many Third World countries fell even further behind economically. For the United States, though, here was yet another external source of disruption and challenge. Anti–U.N., anti–foreign aid, and anti–Third World sentiments grew ever stronger in the U.S. Congress and among the American public.

Trade with Japan

In the 1950s and 1960s, an American child whose parent came back from a business trip might be told, "I got you just a little something as a present; it's a toy made in Japan." By the 1970s and 1980s, though, any child told that a present had come from Japan would think it was a stereo, or television, or VCR— not exactly a "little" something. And his or her parents might be thinking "automobile."

In 1960 Japan's per capita income was only 30 percent of the U.S. level, about equal to that of Mexico. But between 1960 and 1970 its real GNP grew at an average of more than 10 percent per year. Its merchandise exports grew even faster, and its share of world exports doubled between the mid-1960s and the mid-1980s. U.S. trade with Japan went from surplus to deficit. Indeed, the deficit with Japan was the single largest component of the overall U.S. trade deficit.

The United States had had trade disputes with allies before. In the 1960s, for example, it fought "chicken wars" and "pasta wars" with the Europeans. But the trade tensions with Japan threatened to rise to an even more intense level. Some of the criticism of Japan was little more than protectionism. Some was more legitimate, as Japan did have higher trade barriers and more unfair trade practices than the United States did. The two sets of issues that these discrepancies generated, closing U.S. import markets to Japanese exports and opening Japanese markets to U.S. exports, were distinct but interconnected, especially in their politics.

Things started to come to a head in the late 1970s over the issue of Japanese auto imports. Toyota, Nissan, and other Japanese car companies were beating Ford, General Motors, and Chrysler on both price and reputation for quality. Chrysler was losing so much money that the Carter administration and Congress put together a bail-out package for the company. However, when the American auto companies and unions took their case to the International Trade Commission (ITC), the main U.S. regulatory agency on import-relief cases, the ITC ruled that the main problem was of the Big Three's own creation and denied the requests to restrict Japanese auto imports. Pressure nevertheless continued in Congress. Numerous protectionist and retaliatory bills were introduced. Some members of Congress even took to smashing a Toyota with a sledgehammer in front of the Capitol. In 1981 the Reagan administration negotiated a "voluntary" agreement with Japan for some limits on Japanese auto imports. Voluntary is in quotes because in reality, Japan had little choice.

Reagan, Gorbachev, and the End of the Cold War

The 4Ps under Reagan

Ronald Reagan came into office firmly believing that American foreign policy had to be reasserted along all four dimensions of the national interest.

PEACE   Détente not only had failed to bring about peace, but as far as Reagan and his supporters were concerned it had been used by the Soviets "as a cover for their traditional and basic strategy of aggression." Reagan pulled few rhetorical punches: the Soviets "lie and cheat"; they had been "unrelenting" in their military buildup; indeed, "the Soviet Union underlies all the unrest that is going on. If they weren't engaged in this game of dominoes, there wouldn't be any hot spots in the world."[40] The reference to the early Cold War domino theory was intentional, and it was telling. The Soviets hadn't changed one iota as far as Reagan was concerned. Democrats like Carter, and even Republicans like Nixon, Ford, and Kissinger, had been deluding themselves, and endangering the country, to think the Soviets had changed.

With Reagan, then, peace was not going to be achieved through negotiations. It could be achieved only through strength. "Peace through strength" was the Reagan motto.

POWER   American power had to be reasserted, in a big way, and in all its aspects. The Reagan Doctrine developed as the basis not only for taking a harder line on global containment, but going further than every before toward rollback—i.e., ousting communists who had come to power. Whereas John Foster Dulles failed to deliver on rollback against the 1956 Soviet invasion of Hungary, the Reagan administration provided extensive military aid, weapons, and covert action for the Afghan mujahideen fighting against the Soviets and the puppet government they set up in the Afghan capital, Kabul. The struggle was a protracted one, as Afghanistan became the Soviets' Vietnam. They suffered their own decade of defeat and demoralization, and in 1989 were forced to withdraw from Afghanistan.

Another Reagan Doctrine target was Nicaragua, where the communist-nationalist Sandinistas had triumphed. They were being opposed by the Nicaraguan contras (in Spanish, "those against"), to whom the Reagan administration supplied extensive military aid, CIA assistance, and other support. For the Reagan administration the Nicaragua issue embodied all that was wrong with the Vietnam syndrome and Carterite moralism. The Sandinistas professed Marxism-Leninism as their ideology. They were Soviet and Cuban allies. They were running guns to comrades in El Salvador and other neighboring countries. Their heritage as a movement was rooted in anti-American songs, slogans, and versions of history. But even more than that, their very existence was deemed a challenge to the credibility of American power. "If the United States cannot respond to a threat near our own borders," Reagan asked, "why should Europeans or Asians believe that we are seriously concerned about threats to them? . . . Our credibility would collapse, our alliances would crumble."[41]

Opponents of the Reagan Nicaragua policy also invoked analogies to Vietnam, but as a quagmire to be avoided, not a syndrome to be overcome. They did not necessarily embrace the Sandinistas or deny that the United States had vital interests in the region; instead they stressed the possibilities for a negotiated settlement establishing viable terms for coexistence. As to the credibility issue, they saw this as a matter of judgment more than resolve; what would truly be impressive would be a demonstration that the United States could distinguish a test from a trap.

Power considerations also were the basis for the Reagan nuclear buildup. That "window of vulnerability" that the Reaganites believed had opened up because of the combined effects of the Soviet nuclear buildup and the Carter "defense neglect" needed to be closed, and quickly. Overall defense spending went up 16 percent in 1981, and another 14 percent in 1982. Major new nuclear-weapons systems, such as the B-1 bomber, the Trident submarine, and the MX missile, whose development had been shelved and slowed by Carter, were revived and accelerated. The go-ahead was given for deployment in Europe of the Pershing and cruise missiles, modern and more capable intermediate-range nuclear missiles. And with great fanfare the Strategic Defense Initiative (SDI), also known as "Star Wars," was announced as an effort to build a nationwide defense umbrella against nuclear attack.

Guiding the Reagan nuclear buildup were two main shifts in deterrence doctrine. First, the Reagan administration was much more skeptical of arms control than the Nixon, Ford, or Carter administrations. Security had to be guaranteed principally by one's own defense capabilities. They did not write off arms-control prospects totally, but at minimum they wanted more bargaining chips to bring to the table. Second, they doubted the security and stability of the MAD doctrine. Thus they advocated replacing MAD with NUTS(!), which stood for "nuclear utilization targeting strategy" and which constituted a nuclear war-fighting capability. Only by having the capacity to fight a "limited" nuclear war would deterrence be strengthened—and would the United States be in a position to "win" should it come to that. Their defensive strategy involved SDI, which reopened the question, presumably settled with the SALT I–ABM treaty, of the desirability and feasibility of building a defensive shield against nuclear attacks.

However, just as a president who was perceived as pursuing peace at the expense of power (Carter) was pulled from the left toward the center, now a president perceived as excessively risking peace in pursuit of power (Reagan) was pulled from the right back toward the center.[42] In the early 1980s the "nuclear freeze" movement gathered strength. A rally in New York City attracted some seven hundred thousand people. Large demonstrations also were held in Western Europe, protesting the Pershing and cruise missile deployments. *The Day After,* a made-for-television movie about a nuclear war actually occurring, was both indicative of and a further contributor to a widespread fear that the buildup was going too far and that things might be careening out of control. These developments slowed the Reagan nuclear buildup, but they did not stop it.

PRINCIPLES   They were "the focus of evil in the modern world," headed for "the ash bin of history." President Reagan didn't mince words in how he saw the Soviet Union (see At the Source, p. 168). In one of the television debates during his 1984 re-election campaign, he accused his Democratic opponent, Walter Mondale, of being so misguided as to believe that the "Soviets were just people like ourselves." Reagan matched this demonic view of the enemy with classic American exceptionalism. America was "a shining city on a hill," the "nation of destiny," the "last best hope of mankind." Even the Vietnam War (especially the Vietnam War) had been "a noble cause."[43]

In Nicaragua and elsewhere, the ostensibly principled human rights policies of the Carter administration came in for scathing attacks as having their own "double standards." Jeane Kirkpatrick, then a political science professor, wrote an article in 1979 strongly making this argument, which led to her appointment as Reagan's U.N. ambassador. How morally defensible was it, she

At the Source

FREEDOM VS. "TOTALITARIAN EVIL"

Excerpts from a 1982 Speech by President Ronald Reagan

❝ We're approaching the end of a bloody century plagued by a terrible political invention—totalitarianism. Optimism comes less easily today, not because democracy is less vigorous, but because democracy's enemies have refined their instruments of repression. Yet optimism is in order, because day by day democracy is proving itself to be a not-at-all fragile flower. From Stettin on the Baltic to Varna on the Black Sea, the regimes planted by totalitarianism have had more than 30 years to establish their legitimacy. But none—not one regime—has yet been able to risk free elections. . . .

The decay of the Soviet experiment should come as no surprise to us. Wherever the comparisons have been made between free and closed societies—West Germany and East Germany, Austria and Czechoslovakia, Malaysia and Vietnam—it is the democratic countries that are prosperous and responsive to the needs of their people. And one of the simple but overwhelming facts of our time is this: Of all the millions of refugees we've seen in the modern world, their flight is always away from, not toward the Communist world. Today on the NATO front line our forces face east to prevent a possible invasion. On the other side of the line, the Soviet forces also face east to prevent their people from leaving. . . .

The objective I propose is quite simple to state: to foster the infrastructure of democracy, the system of a free press, unions, political parties, universities, which allows a people to choose their own way to develop their own culture, to reconcile their differences through peaceful means. . . .

No, democracy is not a fragile flower. Still it needs cultivating. If the rest of this century is to witness the gradual growth of freedom and democratic ideals, we must take action to assist the campaign for democracy. . . .

This is not cultural imperialism, it is providing the means for genuine self-determination and protection for diversity. Democracy already flourishes in countries with very different cultures and historical experi-

(*Continued on page 169*)

(Freedom vs. "Totalitarian Evil" *Continued from page 168)*
ences. It would be cultural condescension, or worse, to say that any people prefer dictatorship to democracy. Who would voluntarily choose not
to have the right to vote, decide to purchase government propaganda
handouts instead of independent newspapers, prefer government to
worker-controlled unions, opt for land to be owned by the state instead
of those who till it, want government repression of religious liberty, a
single political party instead of a free choice, a rigid cultural orthodoxy
instead of democratic tolerance and diversity? "

Source: Ronald Reagan, "Address to Members of the British Parliament," June 8, 1982,
Public Papers of the Presidents: Ronald Reagan, 1982 (Washington, D.C.: U.S. Government
Printing Office, 1983), 742–48.

questioned, to have cut support for Somoza in Nicaragua and the shah in Iran
when the regimes that came to power in their wake (the Marxist-Leninist Sandinistas, the Ayatollah Khomeini and Islamic fundamentalists) were not just
authoritarian but totalitarian? While authoritarians weren't democratic, at least
they largely limited their repression to the political sphere; totalitarian regimes
sought "total" domination of the personal as well as the political spheres of life.
Therefore, Kirkpatrick contended, there *was* a moral basis to the "ABC" rule, as
communists often were far more repressive than other leaders, however imperfect those others may be. This argument resquared the circle, casting principles
and power as complementary once again. The contras were freedom fighters,
nothing less than the "moral equal of our Founding Fathers."[44]

This view was hard to reconcile, though, with the U.S. support for the military regime in El Salvador, which tacitly supported the mass murder of its citizens. The Salvadoran "death squads" were brutal in their tactics and sweeping
in whom they defined as a communist—as but one example, they assassinated
Roman Catholic archbishop Oscar Romero in his cathedral while he was saying Mass. It was Congress, over Reagan administration objections, that attached human rights conditions to U.S. aid to El Salvador. A few years later the
Salvadoran defense minister conceded that Congress's insistence on these
human rights conditions made the Salvadoran military realize that "in order
to receive U.S. aid, we had to do certain things."[45] Among those "certain
things" was cracking down on the death squads.

PROSPERITY   It often is forgotten that in the early 1980s the American economy was so mired in the deepest recession since the Great Depression that Ronald Reagan's popularity fell as low as 35 percent. So, too, is the fact often forgotten that for all the attacks on Democrats for deficit spending, the Reagan administration ran up greater budget deficits during its eight years than the total deficits of every previous president from George Washington to Jimmy Carter combined. And the U.S. trade deficit, which had caused alarm in the 1970s when it was running around $30 billion, went over $100 billion in 1984, and over $150 billion in 1986.

Nevertheless the Reagan years were prosperous ones. Inflation was tamed, brought down from more than 20 percent in 1979 to less than 10 percent in 1982. The economy boomed at growth rates of over 7 percent per year. The increases in defense spending were in part responsible for this prosperity. One of candidate Reagan's most effective lines in the 1980 presidential campaign was the question posed in his closing statement in one of the debates with Carter: "Are you better off now than you were four years ago?" With inflation and unemployment both running so high then, most Americans answered "no." In 1984, with the economic recovery racing along, voters seemed to answer "we are now," as the revived prosperity contributed significantly to Reagan's landslide re-election victory.

Confrontational Foreign Policy Politics

Pennsylvania Avenue diplomacy really broke down during the Reagan years. The dominant pattern of presidential-congressional relations was confrontational.

The politics of aid to the contras and other aspects of the Nicaragua issue were the most glaring example. The debate was extremely bitter. The National Conservative Political Action Committee circulated a letter to all senators before one crucial vote on aid to the contras, threatening that "should you vote against Contra aid, we intend to see that a permanent record is made—a roll of dishonor, a list of shame, for all to see—of your failure of resolve and vision at this crucial hour."[46] For their part, liberal groups had no less harsh words for contra supporters, making for a virulent and vitriolic debate.

The contra-aid issue also got caught in "backward" institutional power-sharing arrangements. Each branch coveted the policy instruments of the other. The policy instrument the executive branch needed most—money—was controlled by Congress. The Reagan administration did get Congress to appropriate contra aid in 1983. But the aid was defeated in 1984, then passed again in 1985 but with restrictions, increased and de-restricted in

1986, cut back and re-restricted in 1987, and cut back and restricted further in 1988.

On the other side, for its preferred policy objective of a negotiated regional peace plan, Congress needed diplomatic authority and negotiating instruments of its own. But that remained the nearly exclusive authority of the executive branch, and the Reagan administration preferred to merely appear to support peace negotiations than to seriously pursue them. At one point House Speaker Jim Wright actually launched his own "alternative-track diplomacy," meeting with Nicaraguan president Daniel Ortega. Irrespective of the ends being pursued, this was a serious breach, for the costs and risks are substantial when any member of Congress tries to become an alternative negotiating partner for a foreign leader to circumvent the president.

The greatest breach of all was the Iran-contra scandal, which combined the potent Nicaragua issue with U.S. Middle East policy, particularly the problem of the American hostages taken by Iranian-supported fundamentalist terrorists in Lebanon. The basic deal, as worked out by National Security Council aide Colonel Oliver North and other Reagan administration officials, was that the United States would provide arms to Iran in exchange for Iran's help in getting the American hostages in Lebanon released; the profits from the arms sales would be used to fund the Nicaraguan contras, thereby circumventing congressional prohibitions on funding for the contras. The scheme fell apart for a number of reasons, not the least of which was that at its core it was an illegal and unconstitutional effort to get around Congress. When the cover was broken and the scheme was revealed, Congress launched its most significant investigation since Watergate. "Secrecy, deception and disdain for the law," were among the findings of the congressional investigative committees. "The United States Constitution specifies the processes by which laws and policies are to be made and executed. Constitutional process is the essence of our democracy and our democratic form of Government is the basis of our strength. . . . The Committees find that the scheme, taken as a whole . . . violated cardinal principles of the Constitution. . . . Administration officials holding no elected office repeatedly evidenced disrespect for Congress' efforts to perform its constitutional oversight role in foreign policy."[47]

We save for Part II of the book a full look back at the War Powers Resolution (WPR) and why it has failed to resolve the presidential-congressional war powers issue. During the Reagan years members of Congress resorted to lawsuits as a means of trying to rein the president in. In 1982 eleven House members filed suit claiming that the commitment of U.S. military advisers to El Salvador without congressional consent violated the Constitution. A similar claim was made about the October 1983 sending of U.S. troops to Grenada, which the Reagan administration defended as a "rescue mission" to protect endangered American medical students, but which congressional critics claimed was an invasion undertaken without their consent. A third suit involved the 1987–88 naval "reflagging" operations in the Persian Gulf during the Iran-Iraq War, which also involved military action taken by the Reagan administration without congressional authorization.

Yet in all three cases the courts refused to rule and dismissed the suits. These were some of the cases referred to in Chapter 2 as falling under the "political question" doctrine and therefore to be "nonjusticiable," meaning that they involved political differences between the executive and legislative branches more than constitutional issues, and thus required a political resolution directly between those two branches rather than a judicial remedy. In other words, the courts were telling the president and Congress to go work the issues out themselves.

There were other issues on which Reagan and Congress had less conflict, and some on which they even cooperated. The number of these common-ground issues increased in the second Reagan term, especially as the Cold War began to thaw.

The End of the Cold War: Why Did the Cold War End, and End Peacefully?

Just as we couldn't say precisely when the Cold War began, no specific date can be pinpointed for its end. The year 1989 was truly revolutionary, as one East European Soviet-satellite regime after another fell (see Table 5.1). Some point to November 9, 1989, the day the Berlin Wall came down, as the Cold War's end. Others cite December 25, 1991, the day the Soviet Union officially was disbanded. Others place it on other dates.

But whatever the precise dating, few if any academics, policy-makers, intelligence analysts, journalists, or other "experts" predicted that the Cold War would end when it did, or as peacefully as it did. As with the origins of the Cold War, different theories have been put forward to explain the end of the Cold War. Here we group them into two principal categories.[48]

U.S. TRIUMPHALISM   This theory gives the United States, and particularly Ronald Reagan, the credit for having pursued a tough and assertive foreign policy that pushed the Soviets into collapse. The domestic and foreign policy changes undertaken by Mikhail Gorbachev, who became the leader of the So-

TABLE 5.1 1989: Eastern Europe's Year of Revolution

Date	Event
January 11	Hungarian parliament permits independent political parties for the first time under communist rule
April 5	Ban repealed on Solidarity movement in Poland
May 2	Hungary takes major steps to further open its borders with Austria, providing a route for thousands of East Germans to emigrate to West Germany
June 3	Solidarity candidates for parliament win by huge margin in Poland
July 21	General Wojciech Jaruzelski, who had led the imposition of martial law in Poland in 1981, has no choice but to invite Solidarity to form a coalition government
October 18	Hungary adopts a new constitution for multiparty democracy
October 18	Longtime East German Communist leader Erich Honecker is forced to resign, and is replaced by another, much weaker, Communist
November 3	Czechoslovakia opens border for East Germans seeking to go to the West
November 9	Amid mounting protests, East Germany opens the Berlin Wall and promises free elections in 1990
November 10	Unrest in Bulgaria forces resignation of Communist Party leader, Todor Zhivkov
November 24	Peaceful mass protests, dubbed the "velvet revolution" and led by former political prisoner Vaclav Havel, overthrow the communist government of Czechoslovakia
December 6	East German government resigns
December 22–25	Protests turn violent in Romania, leading to execution of Communist leader Nicolae Ceausescu

viet Union in 1985, were more reactions to the limited options the Reagan policies left him than bold new peace initiatives of his own.

The Soviets simply couldn't match American power, as it had been rebuilt and reasserted by Reagan. SDI was a good example. For all the questioning by critics within the United States whether it was technologically feasible, SDI sure worried the Soviets. The Kremlin feared that their economy couldn't finance the huge expenditures necessary to keep up and doubted their scientists could master the new technologies needed. So when Gorbachev showed new interest in arms control, it was less because of his heralded "new thinking" than because he finally had to admit that his country couldn't win an arms race with the United States. So too with the Intermediate Nuclear Forces treaty in 1987, eliminating major arsenals of nuclear weapons stationed in Europe.[49] This was the first U.S.-Soviet arms control treaty ever to actually reduce nuclear weapons, not just limit their future growth (as with the SALT treaties). Yet in the triumphalist view, the INF treaty never would have happened if the Reagan administration had not withstood the political pressures of the nuclear freeze movement at home and the peace movements in Western Europe and gone ahead with the Pershing and cruise missile deployments.

The Reagan Doctrine, with its rollback as well as containment components, stopped the tide of Soviet geopolitical gains in the Third World. In Nicaragua the Sandinistas were forced to agree to elections as part of a peace agreement; sure enough, when elections were held in 1990 they lost. In El Salvador a peace accord was reached that included elections, and the pro-American side also won these elections. Most of all, the Red Army was forced to beat a retreat out of Afghanistan, with politically wrenching and demoralizing consequences back in the Soviet Union.

The triumph also was of American principles. The fall of communism in Eastern Europe was a revolution from below, brought about by masses of people who wanted freedom and democracy. When Vaclav Havel, a playwright who had been a human rights activist and political prisoner under the communists in Czechoslovakia, became the new democratically elected president, he quoted Thomas Jefferson in his inaugural speech. Lech Walesa, the courageous Polish shipyard worker and leader of the Solidarity movement who was arrested when martial law was imposed in 1981 at Moscow's behest, now was elected president of Poland. Throughout most of the former Soviet bloc, and ultimately in most of the former Soviet Union itself, new constitutions were written, free elections held, an independent and free press established, and civil societies fostered. The "campaign for democracy" that Reagan had heralded in his 1982 speech (see At the Source, p. 168) had been successful; "man's instinctive drive for freedom and self-determination" that throughout history "surfaces again and again" had done so, again.

Capitalism and its perceived promise of prosperity also was part of the appeal. Back in the late 1950s when Soviet leader Nikita Khrushchev had threatened the West that "we will bury you," he was speaking in part about the economic competition and the sense that socialism was in the process of demonstrating its superiority. The Soviet system at that time had piled up impressive rates of economic growth. But this simply reflected the suitability of command economies for the initial stages of industrialization concentrated in heavy industries like steel; over the ensuing three decades the inefficiencies of the Soviet economy both in itself and as a model had become glaringly clear. Meanwhile, for all its economic problems in the 1970s, capitalism was on the rebound in the 1980s. The postcommunist governments were quick to start selling off state enterprises, opening their economies to Western foreign investment, and taking other measures to hang out the sign "open for business," capitalist style. The results were not uniformly positive—growth rates were lower than expected, unemployment was higher, and corruption was more rampant in a number of countries. But there was no going back to communist economic systems.

Overall this view confirms the validity of the U.S. Cold War position and policies. "We now know," as historian John Lewis Gaddis argues, that the Soviets and their leaders really did bear most of the responsibility for the Cold War. Stalin *was* an evil megalomaniac with aspirations to global domination. Marxism-Leninism *was* an ideology with limited appeal that declined even more over time. The Soviet Union was, as Gaddis puts it, "a state uniquely configured to the Cold War—and it has become a good deal more difficult, now that that conflict has ended, to see how it could have done so without the Soviet Union itself having passed from the scene."[50]

SOVIET REFORMISM AND OTHER REVISIONIST THEORIES   Just as revisionist theories of the origins of the Cold War put more blame on the United States, revisionist theories of the end of the Cold War give the United States less credit. Much greater credit in these explanations goes to Gorbachev. In 1982, after eighteen years in power, Soviet leader Leonid Brezhnev died. He was replaced first by Yuri Andropov, the former head of the KGB (the Soviet spy agency), but Andropov died in 1984. His successor, Konstantin Chernenko, an old *apparatchik* (party bureaucrat) in the Brezhnev mold, was very ill most of the time he was leader and died barely a year later. Gorbachev was a relative unknown when he came to power in 1985, but immediately was billed by no less a figure than conservative British prime minister Margaret Thatcher as "a man we can do business with." And she didn't just mean business deals, she meant the whole foreign policy agenda.

At age 51, Gorbachev was of a different generation than his predecessors. He quickly proclaimed a "new thinking" based on *glasnost* (openness) and *perestroika* (restructuring). In terms of Soviet domestic policy *glasnost* meant greater political freedoms, including a degree of freedom of the press, the release of such leading dissidents as Andrei Sakharov,[51] and an end to the Communist Party's "leading role" in society. *Perestroika* meant changes in the Soviet economy allowing for more open markets with some private enterprise and foreign investment. In Soviet foreign policy the "new thinking" was manifest in numerous initiatives aimed at reducing tensions and promoting cooperation. Under Gorbachev the Soviets became much more amenable to arms control. They signed the INF treaty in 1987 and moved forward with negotiations in the Strategic Arms Reduction Talks (START), which were the successor to SALT. While there were doubts as to whether it was more than rhetoric, Gorbachev declared the goal of eliminating all nuclear weapons by the year 2000. It was also Gorbachev who agreed in 1988 to the U.N.-mediated accord under which the Soviets withdrew their military forces from Afghanistan. And whereas Khrushchev had crushed the 1956 Hungarian Revolution and Brezhnev had done the same against the "Prague Spring" in Czechoslovakia in 1968, Gorbachev did not send a single tank into any East European country as the people in one country after another overthrew their communist governments.

So at least part of the answer to the question of why the Cold War ended when it did, and especially to the question of why it ended peacefully, is Gorbachev. While the triumphalists contend that U.S. pressures and strengths left Gorbachev with little choice other than to do what he did, revisionists argue that this is too simplistic. How many other times in history have leaders responded to crises at home and declining strength abroad by choosing repression and aggression? The central concept of foreign policy choice that frames our entire discussion of U.S. foreign policy in this book also applies to other countries. Gorbachev had choices: he could have sought to put down the rebellions in Eastern Europe. This may not have worked but it could have been tried. The popular revolutions still may have prevailed, and the Cold War still may have come to an end—but it would have been a much less peaceful end. The same argument applies to many other aspects of the Gorbachev foreign policy. The choices he made were not the only ones he had.

Three other points are made by revisionist theories. One gives American and European peace movements shares of the credit. They tempered the Reagan hard-line policies, keeping him, for example, from spending even more on SDI and possibly from a direct military intervention in Nicaragua. With the Reagan policies moved back toward the center, there was more of a basis for finding common ground with the Soviets. Peace activists also built relationships over many years with intellectuals, activists, scientists, and others within the Soviet Union. Even in some of the dark days of the early 1980s, Reagan's "evil empire" rhetoric notwithstanding, various groups kept up efforts to exchange ideas, maintain communications, and try to find common ground with colleagues, counterparts, and friends within the Soviet Union. Many of these counterparts came into positions of influence under Gorbachev; even those who did not were important as sources of support and expertise for Gorbachev's liberalizing policies.

Second, other international actors also get some of the credit. West German chancellor Helmut Kohl was instrumental in the reunification of Germany following the fall of the Berlin Wall. The United Nations played such a key role in helping bring peace in Afghanistan and elsewhere that its peacekeeping units won the 1988 Nobel Peace Prize. Another Nobel Peace Prize went to Oscar Arias, president of Costa Rica, whose peace plan was the basis for the settlements in Nicaragua and El Salvador. Principal focus on the two superpowers is warranted but the roles of these other key international actors are not to be ignored.

A third point concerns nuclear weapons and nuclear deterrence. Some revisionists take issue with any suggestion that nuclear weapons ultimately were part of the solution to the Cold War, seeing them more as a major part of the problem, causing close calls like the Cuban missile crisis and the overhanging specter of the arms race. Others give some credit to nuclear deterrence as having ensured the avoidance of a major-power war, but still argue that the ratcheting up of the nuclear arms race to ever higher levels prolonged the Cold War.

A final point distinguishes between the Soviets having lost the Cold War and the United States having "won." The assessment of the victory needs to be more nuanced, or the wrong lessons can get drawn. Containment in Europe can be assessed as a successful policy, whereas aspects of Third World containment like the Vietnam War and support for the Nicaraguan contras were misguided and failed. So too with various CIA covert actions, which even when they accomplished their objectives in the field had some dangerous domestic political reverberations. And some short-term successes turned out to have longer-term negative consequences—for example, in Afghanistan, where the same Stinger missiles the United States supplied to the mujahideen to shoot down Soviet aircraft later were used by anti-American terrorists and international narcotics traffickers, and in "failed states" like Somalia and Zaire, where corrupt dictators took advantage of their "ABC" credentials to rob and repress their people, knowing that U.S. support would continue in the same name of global containment.

This is one of those debates in which there is no single right answer. And just as we still debate the origins of the Cold War, so too will the debate over its end continue.

What must be acknowledged is how humbling the end was, or should have been, for "experts." It was not uncommon in the mid-1980s for professors to assume that any student who imagined a post–Cold War world was just young, naive, and idealistic. The Cold War was with us and, students were told, apt to have its ups and downs, its thaws and freezes, but it was not about to go away. Yet it did.

We need to bear this lack of certainty in mind as we consider our new era and enter the twenty-first century, and think about what the possibilities may be.

Summary

Dynamics of Choice, below, summarizes the main characteristics of U.S. foreign policy strategy in the early Cold War period, the Vietnam-détente–

DYNAMICS OF CHOICE

A Summary of U.S. Cold War Foreign Policy Strategy

	Early Cold War	Vietnam, détente, economic shocks	Reagan-Gorbachev era
Peace	United Nations	Détente	Peace through strength
Power	Containment, arms race	Lessons of Vietnam, arms control	Reagan doctrine, arms race–arms control
Principles	Ideological bipolarity, Third World "ABC"	Human rights	Evil empire, "ABC"
Prosperity	LIEO	OPEC, NIEO, Japan shocks	Boom and deficits

economic shocks period, and the Reagan-Gorbachev period. We can see elements of both continuity and change in both the emphasis placed on and the strategies chosen for each of the 4 Ps:

- *Peace:* pursued first principally by creating the multilateral structure of the United Nations, then in the 1970s through the bilateral superpower diplomacy of détente, then under Reagan by reverting more to unilateral assertion of peace through strength.
- *Power:* containment starting in Europe and then extending to Asia and more globally, the 1970s dominated by the debate over the lessons of Vietnam, the 1980s pushing for rollback through the Reagan Doctrine; deterrence first seen as a matter of U.S. nuclear superiority to be maintained by winning the arms race, then to be assured through arms control, then requiring a renewed arms race as a prerequisite to more effective arms control.
- *Principles:* the original conception of the Cold War as not just typical great-power politics but also deeply ideological, and the attendant equation of "ABC" with democracy in the Third World; the 1970s shift to human rights and questioning of the ABC rationale; the 1980s "evil empire" ideological warfare and reversion to ABC.
- *Prosperity:* to be assured by the LIEO; then shaken by OPEC, the NIEO, and other 1970s economic shocks; and restored in the 1980s boom albeit amid massive trade and budget deficits.

We also saw varying patterns in the foreign policy politics of the different subperiods (Dynamics of Choice, p. 180). As long as the Cold War consensus held, Pennsylvania Avenue was largely a one-way street in the White House's direction, making for an imperial presidency. This was as much because of congressional deference as presidential usurpation. The executive branch grew dramatically in the size, scope, and number of foreign and defense policy agencies. Societal influences were limited and mostly supportive of official policy, the media included; they also included the extremism of McCarthyism. But the consensus was shattered by the Vietnam War. Other issues and factors also came into play, with the net effect of more conflictual Pennsylvania Avenue diplomacy, with a more assertive Congress, in the eyes of some a less imperial and more imperiled presidency, more divisive intra–executive branch politics, more interest-group pressures, much more critical media, and more "dissensus" than consensus in public opinion. Foreign policy politics in the 1980s became even more contentious, to the point

DYNAMICS OF CHOICE

A Summary of U.S. Cold War Foreign Policy Politics

	Early Cold War	Vietnam, détente, economic shocks	Reagan-Gorbachev era
Presidency	Imperial	Imperiled	Resurgent
Congress	Deferential	Assertive	Confrontational
Executive branch	Expanding	Bureaucratic warfare	Bureaucratic warfare
Interest groups	Supportive	Oppositional	Proliferating
News media	Cheerleader	Critic	Critic
Public opinion	Consensus, McCarthyism	"Dissensus"	Polarized

where many questioned whether, as one prominent book put it, we had become "our own worst enemy."[52]

We now have a picture of the dynamics of foreign policy choice during the entire Cold War era, both the foreign policy strategy choices that were its essence (drawing on the Chapter 1 framework) and the foreign policy politics that were its process (Chapter 2). Chapter 3 gave us the historical context. And looking toward Part II, Chapters 4 and 5 provide the contemporary context for the foreign policy choices that the United States faces in the post–Cold War era.

Notes

[1]Dean G. Acheson, *Present at the Creation: My Years at the State Department* (New York: Norton, 1969), 674.

[2]Dwight D. Eisenhower, *Mandate for Change* (New York: Doubleday, 1963), 372–73.

[3]Theodore C. Sorensen, *Kennedy* (New York: Harper and Row, 1965), 639.

[4]Cited in Stanley Karnow, *Vietnam: A History* (New York: Viking, 1983), 629.

[5]Robert S. McNamara, *In Retrospect: The Tragedy and Lessons of Vietnam* (New York: Times Books, 1995), 322.

[6]Statement by General Bruce Palmer, Jr., cited in Bruce W. Jentleson, "American Commitments in the Third World: Theory vs. Practice," *International Organization* 41:4 (Autumn 1987), 696.

[7]Both cited in Col. Harry G. Summers, Jr., "How We Lost," *New Republic,* April 29, 1985, 22.

[8]Frank Snepp, *Decent Interval: An Insider's Account of Saigon's Indecent End* (New York: Random House, 1977); Arnold Isaacs, *Without Honor: Defeat in Vietnam and Cambodia* (Baltimore: Johns Hopkins University Press, 1983).

[9]William Appleman Williams, Thomas McCormick, Lloyd Gardner, and Walter LaFeber, *America in Vietnam: A Documentary History* (Garden City, N.Y.: Anchor Books, 1985), 122.

[10]"Address at Johns Hopkins University: Peace Without Conquest," April 7, 1965, *Public Papers of the Presidents: Lyndon B. Johnson, 1965,* Vol. 1 (Washington, D.C.: U.S.Government Printing Office, 1966), 395.

[11]Henry A. Kissinger, "The Vietnam Negotiations," *Foreign Affairs* 47:2 (January 1969), 218–19.

[12]"Address to the Nation on the Situation in Southeast Asia," *Public Papers of the Presidents: Richard M. Nixon, 1970* (Washington, D.C.: U.S. Government Printing Office, 1971), 409.

[13]Cited in Snepp, *Decent Interval,* 175.

[14]Hans J. Morgenthau, "To Intervene or Not Intervene," *Foreign Affairs* 45:3 (April 1967), 434.

[15]Cited in James A. Nathan and James K. Oliver, *United States Foreign Policy and World Order,* 2d ed. (Boston: Little, Brown, 1981), 322.

[16]"Telephone Remarks to the Delegates to the AFL-CIO Convention," December 9, 1965, *Public Papers of the Presidents: Lyndon B. Johnson, 1965,* Vol. 2 (Washington, D.C.: U.S. Government Printing Office, 1966), 1149.

[17]"Address to the Nation on the War in Vietnam," November 3, 1969, *Public Papers of the Presidents: Richard M. Nixon, 1969* (Washington, D.C.: U.S. Government Printing Office, 1970), 908–909.

[18]Cited in Doris Kearns, *Lyndon Johnson and the American Dream* (New York: New American Library, 1976), 264. See also Larry Berman, *Planning a Tragedy: The Americanization of the War in Vietnam* (New York: Norton, 1982); and Berman, *Lyndon Johnson's War* (New York: Norton, 1989).

[19]J. William Fulbright, "Congress and Foreign Policy," in Murphy Commission, *Organization of the Government for the Conduct of Foreign Policy,* Vol. 5, Appendix L (Washington, D.C.: U.S. Government Printing Office, 1975), 59.

[20]Arthur M. Schlesinger, Jr., *The Imperial Presidency* (New York: Atlantic Monthly Press, 1974), 11–12.

[21]Thomas M. Franck and Edward Weisband, *Foreign Policy by Congress* (New York: Oxford University Press, 1979).

[22]I. M. Destler, Leslie H. Gelb, and Anthony Lake, *Our Own Worst Enemy: The Unmaking of American Foreign Policy* (New York: Simon and Schuster, 1984), 137.

[23]Fulbright, "Congress and Foreign Policy," 60.

[24]James Aronson, *The Press and the Cold War* (New York: Bobbs Merrill, 1970), 195.

[25]Michael Roskin, "From Pearl Harbor to Vietnam: Shifting Generational Paradigms and Foreign Policy," *Political Science Quarterly* 89:3 (1974), 569.

[26]Graham Allison, "Cool It: The Foreign Policy of Young America," *Foreign Policy* 1 (Winter 1970–71), 156.

[27]Speech by Secretary of Defense Robert S. McNamara, October 1967, reprinted in Bruce W. Jentleson, *Documents in American Foreign Policy: A Reader* (Davis: University of California at Davis, 1984), 48–53.

[28]One was the Antarctic Treaty of 1959, prohibiting the testing or deployment of nuclear weapons in the South Pole area. Another was the Limited Test Ban Treaty of 1963, with Great Britain and France also signees, prohibiting nuclear-weapons testing in the atmosphere, under water, or in outer space, and imposing some limits on underground testing.

[29]Peter G. Peterson, *U.S.-Soviet Commercial Relations in a New Era* (Washington, D.C.: U.S. Government Printing Office, 1972), 3–4.

[30]Peterson, *U.S.-Soviet Commercial Relations,* 14.

[31]Cited in Bruce W. Jentleson, *Pipeline Politics: The Complex Political Economy of East-West Energy Trade* (Ithaca, N.Y.: Cornell University Press, 1986), 142.

[32]"Inaugural Address of President Jimmy Carter," January 20, 1977, in *Public Papers of the Presidents: Jimmy Carter, 1977* (Washington, D.C.: U.S. Government Printing Office, 1977), 1–4.

[33]Walter Isaacson, *Kissinger: A Biography* (New York: Simon and Schuster, 1992). See also the three volumes of Kissinger's memoirs: *White House Years* (Boston: Little, Brown, 1979); *Years of Upheaval* (Boston: Little, Brown, 1982); and *Years of Renewal* (New York: Simon and Schuster, 1999).

[34]Cited in James M. McCormick, *American Foreign Policy and Process,* 2d ed. (Itasca, Ill.: F. E. Peacock, 1992), 414.

[35]Quoted in Gaddis Smith, *Morality, Reason and Power: American Diplomacy in the Carter Years* (New York: Hill and Wang, 1986), 223.

[36]"State of the Union Address Delivered Before a Joint Session of the Congress," January 23, 1980, *Public Papers of the Presidents: Jimmy Carter, 1980–1981* (Washington, D.C.: U.S. Government Printing Office, 1981), 194–200.

[37]Raymond L. Garthoff, "Détente," in *Encyclopedia of U.S. Foreign Relations,* ed. Bruce W. Jentleson and Thomas G. Paterson (New York: Oxford University Press, 1997), Vol. 2, 10–11.

[38]Cited in Bruce W. Jentleson, "Discrepant Responses to Falling Dictators: Presidential Belief Systems and the Mediating Effects of the Senior Advisory Process," *Political Psychology* 11:2 (June 1990), 371.

[39]Quoted in Seymour Hersh, *The Price of Power: Kissinger in the Nixon White House* (New York: Summit Books, 1983), 462.

[40]Cited in Jentleson, "Discrepant Responses to Falling Dictators," 371.

[41]Cited in Bruce W. Jentleson, "American Diplomacy: Around the World and Along Pennsylvania Avenue," in *A Question of Balance: The President, the Congress and Foreign Policy,* ed. Thomas E. Mann (Washington, D.C.: Brookings Institution Press, 1990), 149.

[42]Miroslav Nincic, "The United States, the Soviet Union and the Politics of Opposites," *World Politics* 40:4 (July 1988), 452–75.

[43]Cited in Jentleson, "Discrepant Responses," 372.

[44]Jentleson, "Discrepant Responses," 372.

[45]Cited in Jentleson, "American Diplomacy," 179.

[46]Cited in Jentleson, "American Diplomacy," 151.

[47]U.S. Congress, *Report of the Congressional Committees Investigating the Iran-Contra Affair,* 100th Congr., 1st sess., November 1987, 11, 411, 19.

[48]See, for example, Richard Ned Lebow and Thomas Risse-Kappen, eds., *International Relations Theory and the End of the Cold War* (New York: Columbia University Press, 1995); Richard K. Betts, ed., *Conflicts after the Cold War: Arguments on Causes of War and Peace* (New York: Macmillan, 1994); Raymond L. Garthoff, *The Great Transition: American-Soviet Relations and the End of the Cold War* (Washington, D.C.: Brookings Institution Press, 1994); Jay Winik, *On*

the Brink: The Dramatic Saga of How the Reagan Administration Changed the Course of History and Won the Cold War (New York: Simon and Schuster, 1997).

[49]Intermediate-range nuclear missiles are those with attack ranges of between 500 and 5,500 kilometers (320 to 34,000 miles). This included most of the nuclear missiles stationed in NATO countries and those in the Soviet Union that could attack Western Europe. It did not include either long-range missiles the United States and the Soviets had aimed at each other, or shorter-range and battlefield nuclear weapons in the European theater.

[50]Quote from John Lewis Gaddis, "The New Cold War History," lecture published by Foreign Policy Research Institute, *Footnotes,* 5 (June 1998), 1–2. See also John Lewis Gaddis, *We Now Know: Rethinking Cold War History* (New York: Oxford University Press, 1997).

[51]Andrei Sakharov was known around the world for his courageous opposition to the Soviet regime. He actually was the physicist who, earlier in his career, had developed the Soviet hydrogen bomb. But he became a leading advocate of arms control and, later, of human rights and political freedom. He was awarded the Nobel Peace Prize in 1973, but was denied permission to leave the country to go to Stockholm, Sweden, to receive it. He was harassed by the KGB and, following his opposition to the Soviet invasion of Afghanistan, was put under house arrest. That was where and how he was forced to stay until Gorbachev freed him in 1986.

[52]Destler, Gelb, and Lake, *Our Own Worst Enemy.*

PART **II** *American Foreign Policy in the Twenty-First Century: Choices and Challenges*

Foreign Policy Politics: Diplomacy Begins at Home

Introduction: Politics without an Enemy

The absence of an Enemy is the defining feature of post–Cold War American foreign policy politics. Despite all the other dangers that the Soviet Union posed, having an Enemy (capital letter intentional) helped American presidents garner the domestic political support necessary for a strong and active foreign policy. Without the Soviet threat—indeed, without a Soviet Union at all—the U.S. foreign policy debate has split wide open.

Some want to heed the cry, "Come home, America." Who needs foreign policy anyway? these neo-isolationists ask. Why not just take advantage of the opportunity provided by the end of the Cold War to "put America first"? Reduce our international commitments and, for those commitments the United States does keep, make them more self-centered. Get beyond the old debate about whether politics should "stop at the water's edge"; just stay on our side of the water.

Yet the paradox of the post–Cold War era is that international affairs affect America and Americans at least as much, if not more than, during the Cold War. Recall the five major reasons stated at the outset of this book for the continued importance of foreign policy:

■ The United States still faces significant potential threats to its national security.

■ The U.S. economy is more internationalized than ever before.

- Many other areas of policy that used to be considered "domestic" also have been internationalized.
- The increasing ethnic diversity of the American people makes for a larger number and wider range of groups with personal bases for interest in foreign affairs.
- It is hard for the United States to claim to be true to its most basic values if it ignores their violation around the world.

None of these rationales resonates in tones anything close to the clarion calls of the Truman Doctrine or the Reagan Doctrine. Nor can American presidents point to the likes of a Hitler, Stalin, or Mao as personification of the Enemy—even Saddam Hussein filled the bill only somewhat and for a while. It is because the importance of foreign policy is less evident but still significant that both its strategy and its politics are so complex and so challenging.

In Part II we examine the principal questions of strategy and politics raised by these and other aspects of American foreign policy in the twenty-first century—the *essence of choice* as it pertains to the core national interest goals of peace, power, prosperity, and principles, and the *process of choice* in the domestic politics of American foreign policy in this new era. What are the differences as well as the similarities in foreign policy politics today as compared with earlier eras (Chapter 6)? Can a post–Cold War peace and world order be built (Chapter 7)? Despite everything that has changed, is power still the name of the game (Chapter 8)? What are the key foreign economic and social policy challenges for assuring and enhancing prosperity in this age of globalization (Chapter 9)? Will the twenty-first century be a democratic one, an era in which principles can and should play ever greater roles in American foreign policy (Chapter 10)? Our study of these questions takes us into many new issues and debates while staying grounded in the theoretical and historical contexts established in Part I.

One note regarding this chapter: Here we focus on broad patterns in post–Cold War foreign policy politics involving the roles and dynamics of the five major sets of actors: the president and Congress, intra–executive branch politics, interest groups, the news media, and public opinion. We then move on to the politics of specific foreign policy issues in each of the succeeding chapters: e.g., the United Nations as an issue in U.S. domestic politics (Chapter 7), the politics of post–Cold War military interventions (Chapter 8), and the politics of trade issues (Chapter 9) and human rights issues (Chapter 10).

Presidential-Congressional Relations: Post–Cold War Pennsylvania Avenue Diplomacy

For most of the 1990s, foreign policy, like other areas of policy, has suffered from "divided government," the situation in which one political party controls Congress and the other the White House. In 1991–92 there was a Republican president (Bush) and a Democratic Congress; from 1995 to 2000 a Democratic president (Clinton) and a Republican Congress. The only exception was 1993–94, when Democrats controlled both ends of Pennsylvania Avenue. Thus to some extent the tensions in "Pennsylvania Avenue diplomacy" have been an extension of broader partisan politics.

Yet in a more fundamental sense what continues to be manifested is the basic structural problem of *separate institutions sharing power*. As stressed in earlier chapters and as seen historically, the problems created by this sharing of powers are greater than they would be if it really were a separation of powers. Herein lies the continuity as well as the change. The specifics of many of the issues have changed, and politics seems to have become more of a blood sport. But the basic dynamic remains the same, of separate institutions still trying to figure out how to share powers. This plays out according to four main patterns: conflict, competition, constructive compromise, and cooperation.

Interbranch Conflict

Conflict continues to be the principal dynamic in presidential-congressional foreign policy politics. Although many issues could be cited here, the most glaring and recurring continues to be that of *war powers*. As discussed in Chapter 5, when the 1973 War Powers Resolution (WPR) was passed, overriding a veto by President Nixon, it was regarded by many as the salvation of the American political system. In practice, though, it has been ignored far more than it has been invoked. Dynamics of Choice on p. 189 provides a list of the major uses of military force by the United States since passage of the WPR. In not a single case has the WPR been fully applied. Not by Republican presidents Ford, Reagan, or Bush, and not by Democratic presidents Carter or Clinton. Nor by Congress—Republican or Democratic or split.

Two reasons explain why. One is the institutionally rooted attitudes of both branches. For presidents, opposition to the WPR has been almost an institutionally instinctual response. The WPR's very existence, let alone its specific provisions, were and are seen as an infringement on the role of the commander in chief and other aspects of the presidency's constitutional share

Major Uses of Force since the 1973 War Powers Resolution

Year	President	Country(ies)	Use of force
1975	Ford	Cambodia	U.S.S. *Mayaguez* incident
1980	Carter	Iran	Attempt to rescue American hostages
1982–84	Reagan	Lebanon	Peacekeeping
1983	Reagan	Grenada	Invasion to topple Marxist government and rescue American medical students
1986	Reagan	Libya	Air strikes in retaliation for terrorism
1987–88	Reagan	Iran	Naval forces to protect Kuwaiti oil tankers
1989–90	Bush	Panama	Invasion to topple and capture Panamanian leader Manuel Noriega
1990–91	Bush	Saudi Arabia, Kuwait, Iraq	Persian Gulf War—Operations Desert Shield, Desert Storm
1991–	Bush, Clinton	Iraq	Operation Provide Comfort—peacekeeping in northern Iraq to protect Kurds
1992–94	Bush, Clinton	Somalia	Operation Restore Hope—27,000 soldiers to maintain peace between warring factions
1993–95	Clinton	Bosnia	U.S. and NATO enforcement of no-fly zone, initial air strikes
1993–99	Clinton	Macedonia	U.S. troops as part of U.N. peacekeeping force

(Continued on page 190)

Major Uses of Force (Continued from page 189)			
Year	**President**	**Country(ies)**	**Use of force**
1993, 1994, 1996, 1997, 1998, 1999	Clinton	Iraq	Air strikes and other limited military actions
1994–95	Clinton	Haiti	Military intervention, occupation, restoration of elected president, Jean-Bertrand Aristide, to power
1995–	Clinton	Bosnia	U.S. troops part of NATO Implementation (peace-keeping) Force (IFOR), then Stabilization Force (SFOR)
1998	Clinton	Sudan, Afghanistan	Retaliation for terrorism
1999	Clinton	Yugoslavia	U.S. and NATO war against Yugoslavia (Serbia) to stop its ethnic cleansing in Kosovo

of war powers. This was evident, for example, in the early months of the Clinton administration, when proposals for reforming the WPR to make it more usable were rejected by White House political operatives worried that Bill Clinton would look "soft" if he were perceived as any less assertive of presidential prerogatives than his predecessors had been. Within Congress what is most interesting is that, despite many criticisms of presidents for not abiding by the WPR, Congress always has stopped short of taking action itself to invoke the WPR. This reflects congressional ambivalence between wanting to assert its role but being reluctant for political reasons to take responsibility for actually blocking military action. Here, too, political party has not mattered—the pattern has held when Democrats have been in the majority, when Republicans have, and when the two houses have been split between the two parties.

The WPR's other problem lies in the ambiguity of its language. Some examples from the 1980s illustrate that this problem was apparent even before the end of the Cold War.

In 1987–88, during the Iran-Iraq War, the Reagan administration sent the U.S. Navy into the Persian Gulf to protect Kuwaiti oil tankers. Iran launched a series of attacks, and the American naval forces counterattacked. More than just one incident occurred, and there were casualties on both sides. Section 2 of the WPR, the law's statement of purpose, states that it is to apply to situations in which "imminent involvement in hostilities is clearly indicated." Yet there was no clear definition in the law of what level of attack was necessary to be considered not just "skirmishes" but actual "hostilities." Thus Congress had no definitive basis for challenging the Reagan administration's claim that the Kuwaiti re-flagging operation was below the threshold of "hostilities," and thus did not fall under the strictures of the WPR. This incident was one of the cases mentioned in Chapter 2 in which congressional opponents turned to the federal judiciary as "referee," but the courts ruled that it was a political question that the legislative and executive branches had to work out between themselves.

Ambiguity also is inherent in Section 3 of the WPR and its provision for consultation with Congress "in every possible instance . . . before introducing U.S. armed forces into hostilities or into situations where imminent involvement in such is clearly indicated." When is consultation "possible"? Perhaps it was true that the troops sent to Grenada in 1983 to rescue the American medical school students threatened by the chaos there had to be dispatched immediately, leaving little time for consultation with Congress. But what about the 1989 invasion of Panama, which clearly had plenty of lead time for planning? And when consultation does occur, does it meet the requirement of being "before" if, as in 1986 when attacks were launched against Libya, congressional leaders are called in once the planes are on their way, but before they have dropped their bombs?

One doesn't have to be a linguist or a lawyer to see the problems that arise when these terms are left open to interpretation. It is true that the option was there when the law was written in 1973–74, and is there today for those who would rewrite it, to use tighter and more precise language. One could, for example, define "hostilities" as the firing of any first shot at a U.S. soldier, or "imminent involvement" as a U.S. solider being within range of an enemy's weapon—say 50 feet for a gun, 10 miles for a bomb, 100 miles for a missile. Clearly, though, such language-tightening can present its own problems by taking too much discretion away from a president, straightjacketing the president's ability to formulate strategy.

The 1990–91 Persian Gulf War was another case in which the WPR was more ignored than invoked. When President Bush first made the Operation Desert Shield commitment of about two hundred thousand troops to Saudi Arabia following Saddam Hussein's invasion of Kuwait, he did report to

Congress on the commitment but said that he was doing so only "consistent with," and not as required by, the WPR. His report denied that hostilities were imminent, and the same language game was played a few weeks later in granting higher salaries for the deployed troops according to the Pentagon's pay scale for personnel placed in "imminent danger," not that for "hostilities," even though the Pentagon was busily drawing up war plans and Bush likened Saddam to Hitler. In January 1991, with the deadline given Saddam for withdrawing from Kuwait approaching, Bush indicated that he had no intention of invoking the WPR or asking for congressional approval before moving to military action. He had gone to the United Nations more than a month earlier for a Security Council resolution authorizing "all necessary means" for getting Iraq out of Kuwait. With reference back to President Truman and the Korean War, Bush claimed that the U.N. Security Council resolution gave him all the authority he needed. Some in his administration however, argued for a middle path of encouraging Congress to vote on some form of a resolution, short of invoking the WPR, to indicate its support. Bush agreed, although he stated up front that if the resolution was defeated he would not consider it binding. Congress did pass the resolution with strong Republican support and enough Democrats to provide the margin of victory.

On January 16 the Bush administration launched Operation Desert Storm. The war against Iraq was on. We will never know whether the political coalition would have held had the war not gone as well as it did. It wasn't politically difficult to stand behind a war with so few American casualties and such a quick and overwhelming military victory. In fact, those in Congress who voted against the war were the ones who paid politically. The key analytic point, though, was that the American political system showed yet again that it lacked accepted procedures for inter-branch cooperation on the most fundamental issue a democracy must confront. We will see in Chapter 8 how this problem has grown even worse in the 1990s over such issues as Somalia, Bosnia, Kosovo, and Iraq.

Another major source of conflict has been over trade and other issues of *foreign economic policy.* This is the area of foreign policy for which the Constitution most explicitly grants Congress the principal share of authority. Article I, Section 8, endows Congress with the power "to regulate commerce with foreign nations." Presidential authority over trade policy thus has been more dependent than in other areas of foreign policy on what and how much authority Congress chooses to delegate. As the old free-trade consensus has eroded further, presidential-congressional conflict has grown greater.

The general pattern is threefold.* First are the intraparty splits, as the lines between protectionist and free-trade wings have been drawn more sharply within both the Republican and the Democratic parties. On a number of issues, President Clinton got less cooperation from House Democratic leader Richard Gephardt, closely allied with labor and long known as a critic of free trade, than he got from Republican Speaker Newt Gingrich. Second are the intra-Congress differences, with the Senate tending to be more pro–free trade than the House. Most studies attribute this to the differences in the sizes of their constituencies; the larger scope of senators' statewide constituencies leaves more room for balancing the costs and benefits of trade than do the smaller, more concentrated House districts. Third are regional differences, with senators and representatives from the East and West coasts tending to be more internationalist than those from the South and the Midwest.

Institutional Competition

A second significant pattern in presidential-congressional foreign policy politics is that of institutional competition. This competition reflects the "invitation to struggle" set out by the Constitution (see Chapter 2); this struggle goes beyond substantive policy differences and partisan politics to assertions of institutional prerogatives even in the day-to-day conduct of foreign policy.

One example of this competition can be seen in the increased forays of Congress into *direct diplomacy*, where legislators deal directly with foreign heads of state in ways that are not coordinated with and are often inconsistent with official administration policy. This problem has arisen before, as in the 1987 controversy when Speaker of the House Jim Wright (D-Tex.) opened up his own "alternative track" negotiations with Nicaraguan president and Sandinista leader Daniel Ortega. Congressional efforts at direct diplomacy became especially pronounced following the Republican sweep of Congress in the 1994 elections. In the first six months of 1995, when Speaker of the House Newt Gingrich's power was at its apex, foreign leaders who came to Washington didn't just stop on Capitol Hill for courtesy calls but did a large share of their business there. In January the prime minister of Japan stopped by Gingrich's office. In February the prime minister of Pakistan did. In April the British prime minister did the same. Then, in June 1995, French President

---

*Specific issues such as the North American Free Trade Agreement (NAFTA), fast-track authority, and the International Monetary Fund (IMF) are raised in Chapter 9.

Jacques Chirac found himself "pleading with Congress" to support an agreement he and President Clinton had reached for increased funding of the U.N. Peacekeeping Force (UNPROFOR) in Bosnia. "'It is up to the U.S. Congress to give the green light to the initiative,' the French President said, while the American president stood at his side in a striking scene."[1]

Nor is it only heads of foreign government who have to deal with Congress. In January 1997, shortly after his appointment as the new U.N. secretary-general, Kofi Annan met with Senator Jesse Helms (R.-N.C.), chairman of the Senate Foreign Relations Committee and an ardent opponent of the U.N. "Annan had said earlier in the day he did not think such direct consultations with Congress on U.N. reform would be proper," the *Washington Post* reported, "because traditionally the secretary general has dealt with member nations through their executive branches rather than legislatures." But he was told by President Clinton, according to a U.N. official, that "it is necessary to make friends in Congress and sell them on the idea of U.S. support."[2]

A line needs to be drawn separating even the most contentious battles over legislation from direct diplomacy practiced by members of Congress. The ends being pursued by Speaker Gingrich and Senator Helms no more justified their means than did Speaker Wright's. There is nothing wrong with key members of Congress being included by the executive branch as "observers" on U.S. negotiating teams, whether the issues are arms control, trade, the global environment, or others. Where the line gets crossed is if a member of Congress—*any* member of Congress—attempts an alternative track of diplomacy circumventing the president. Battles over U.S. policy through constitutional processes are one thing; raising questions about who is in charge of the actual carrying out of U.S. diplomacy is quite another. The immediate effects and the precedents set when that line is not observed cannot be healthy ones for American foreign policy.

Another example of institutional competition is in the *appointments process* for Cabinet posts and other major foreign policy positions. Whereas in the past a contentious nomination was pretty much the exception, in recent years it has become almost the rule. Presidential nominees still do get confirmed in most instances, but the Senate tends to probe deeper into their pasts, Senate questioning seems more like a cross-examination, and the Senate's agenda more often veers from a nominee's foreign policy qualifications to partisan politics.

A pointed example involved the nomination in 1997 of Anthony Lake as CIA director. Lake had been national security adviser in Clinton's first term. While it is fair to say that there were some substantive bases for questioning

Lake's CIA nomination, most observers felt these issues were not sufficient to disqualify him. Some leading Republican senators announced their support for Lake, and the votes seemed to be there to confirm him. But Republican senator Richard Shelby of Alabama, chair of the Senate Intelligence Committee, carried on what seemed to many to be a vendetta, repeatedly delaying Lake's confirmation hearings, then dragging them out and bombarding the nominee with questions, demands for documents, and other obstructionism. Lake ultimately asked President Clinton to withdraw his nomination. His letter to President Clinton went beyond his own case to raise the broader concern that "Washington has gone haywire" (see At the Source, p. 196).

Constructive Compromise

One of the myths noted back in Chapter 2 was that presidential-congressional conflict is necessarily a bad thing. To the contrary, when both branches give a bit they may come together on a policy that proves better than either original position—a "constructive compromise." The dynamic can even be deliberately used in foreign policy negotiations, along the lines of the proverbial "good cop/bad cop." This version of constructive compromise occurs when the president and his diplomats make it known to another government that they really would like to provide certain aid or other benefits, but that the Congress is insistent that the foreign nation meet certain conditions, take certain reciprocating actions, etc. This strategy may be coordinated behind the scenes, with the two branches really sharing the same goal and agreeing that this ploy is the best way to achieve it. Or it may be that the executive really is less insistent on the conditions, or too concerned with not offending the other country, but that Congress has a different sense of the national interest.

Two recent cases exemplify this pattern. One involved Russian troop withdrawal in the early 1990s from Baltic states that used to be part of the Soviet Union, such as Estonia and Latvia. This was a difficult issue because both sides had legitimate claims: the Estonian and Latvian governments to their rights as (newly) independent countries to not have Russian troops on their soil, and Russia for assurances that the rights of the Russian ethnic minorities living in these countries would be protected. The Russian government also was reluctant to lose access to its Baltic Sea naval ports, which are of significant military value. An agreement had been reached setting a deadline for the Russian troop withdrawal and pledging guarantees for the Russian minorities. But as the deadline approached, Russian president Boris Yeltsin was under strong nationalist pressure at home not to withdraw the troops.

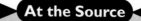

►◄ **At the Source** ►◄

"WASHINGTON HAS GONE HAYWIRE"

Letter from Nominee Anthony Lake

Anthony Lake was National Security Adviser in the first Clinton adminis-tration (1993–97). For Clinton's second term Lake was nominated as direc-tor of the Central Intelligence Agency (CIA). Although his nomination was controversial on some issues, it was supported by a number of prominent Republican senators, including Richard Lugar (R-Ind.), as well as Dem-ocrats. But Richard Shelby (R-Ala.), chair of the Senate Intelligence Com-mittee, sought to block Lake's nomination and resorted to highly partisan tactics to do so. The following excerpts from Lake's letter to President Clin-ton asking that his nomination be withdrawn raise broader concerns about the excessive politicization of the shared appointments power.

❝ Dear Mr. President:

I am writing to ask that you withdraw my nomination to be Director of Central Intelligence.

I do so because . . . [my nomination] is a political football in a game with constantly moving goal posts. . . .

I have gone through the past three months and more with patience and, I hope, dignity. But I have lost the former, and could lose the latter as this political circus continues indefinitely. As Senator Richard Lugar, perhaps the most respected member of the Senate, has said with regard to my nomination and its treatment, 'The whole confirmation process has become more and more outrageous.' It is nasty and brutish without being short. . . .

I have believed all my life in public service. I still do. But Washington has gone haywire.

I hope that, sooner rather than later, people of all political views be-yond our city limits will demand that Washington give priority to policy over partisanship, to governing over 'gotcha.' It is time that senior offi-cials have more time to concentrate on dealing with very real foreign policy challenges rather than the domestic wounds Washington is in-flicting on itself. ❞

Source: "Text of Lake's Sharply Worded Letter Withdrawing as the CIA Nominee," *New York Times*, March 18, 1997, B6.

The Clinton administration had been trying to mediate, but with little success. Some critics saw the problem as the administration not exerting enough pressure on Russia, and perhaps implying that an arrangement short of full troop withdrawal might be acceptable. Congress, however, issued strong threats to cut off economic aid to Russia if the troops were not withdrawn. And while other factors also came into play in Russia's ultimately fulfilling its troop-withdrawal pledge, the congressional "bad cop" was an important factor.

The 1994 peace treaty between Israel and Jordan is another example. Following the historic 1993 breakthrough of the initial peace agreement between Israel and the Palestine Liberation Organization (PLO), Jordan and Israel had been moving closer to their own peace treaty.* King Hussein of Jordan, however, was being very cautious about moving toward a full and formal peace with Israel. Among the key incentives the United States was offering Jordan was potential forgiveness of its $700 million debt. The executive branch was giving signals that it would grant debt forgiveness for a step short of full peace. But Congress would not. It had been Congress that had cut off aid to Jordan in 1991 when the king sided with Iraq in the Gulf War, and it was Congress that would have to turn aid back on.

Here, too, without overclaiming causal influence, the role of the congressional "bad cop" did have a positive effect. In the July 1994 "Washington Declaration," King Hussein and Israeli prime minister Yitzhak Rabin declared an end to their nations' state of war and their intent to sign a full peace treaty. Hussein and Rabin made an unprecedented appearance before a joint session of Congress. Their speeches "so moved lawmakers of both parties," the *New York Times* reported, "that Representative Bob Michel, the Republican leader, removed his eyeglasses several times to wipe away the tears, and Senator Barbara Boxer, the California Democrat, couldn't put her white handkerchief away."[3] Three days later Congress approved the first tranche of $220 million in debt forgiveness for Jordan. Three months later, Israel and Jordan signed their peace treaty.

Cooperation

Although far from the norm, there are some issues in which inter-branch cooperation prevails. In foreign policy this means that Congress supports or at least defers to the president, and a reasonably common, coordinated policy is pursued. It is a bit ironic that defense policy, the area in which bitter battles were fought for most of the 1980s, became a focal point of presidential-congressional

---

*See Chapter 7 for a discussion of the Israeli-Palestinian accords.

cooperation in the 1990s. Although there has been conflict on some items, such as a missile defense system, which Republicans have favored more than Democrats, overall there has been striking cooperation along Pennsylvania Avenue on the post–Cold War defense budget.* Dynamics of Choice on p. 199 reveals this by comparing the differences between the defense budgets as proposed by the president and those passed by Congress. The rightmost column shows the percentage change from the president's budget for each year, with indication of whether Congress made increases (+) or decreases (−) from the president's original proposal. The multi-year average given for each administration is a raw score, since the point here is the size of the variation, irrespective of whether it involved cuts or increases.

The Carter and Reagan differentials (5.21 percent, and 3.7 percent, respectively) were much larger than for Clinton, reflecting the more extensive interbranch conflict that defense budgets used to engender. Clinton's differential was only 1.18 percent, reflecting a much greater policy consensus. Both sides had finally agreed that cuts in defense spending are needed but that these cuts should be gradual and limited.

For a while arms control also broke with the past and was marked by cooperation. The first two treaties agreed to in the U.S.-Russian Strategic Arms Reduction Talks (START) were ratified by large margins: START I, signed by President Bush in 1991, was ratified 93 to 6 by a Democratic-led Senate; START II, signed by President Bush and then pushed by President Clinton, was ratified 87 to 4 by a Republican-led Senate. Clinton also got a Republican-led Senate to ratify the Chemical Weapons Convention, 71 to 29, and the 1998 NATO expansion treaty, approved 80 to 19. In 1999, however, old conflictual patterns reemerged as the Senate defeated the Comprehensive Test Ban Treaty. Indeed, the defeat was particularly contentious because of the brusque manner in which the Senate handled its deliberations, holding only a few days of hearings and voting largely along party lines.

Executive-Branch Politics: Issues of Leadership and Bureaucracy

The most important assessment of a foreign policy process within the executive branch is whether it meets the five criteria of a rational process, as was

---

*See Chapter 8 for a detailed discussion of defense policy issues.

Presidential-Congressional Relations on the Defense Budget

President	President's proposal (in billions of dollars)	As passed by Congress (in billions of dollars)	Percentage change
Carter			
1977	$112.3	$107.6	−4.2%
1978	117.8	114.5	−2.8
1979	125.8	130.4	+3.7
1980	146.2	161.1	+10.2
Average	125.5	128.4	5.21
Reagan			
1981	184.4	187.5	+1.7
1982	221.1	214.8	−2.8
1983	245.3	237.5	−3.2
1984	272.0	253.8	−6.7
1985	285.7	265.8	−7.0
1986	282.2	282.0	0.0
1987	297.6	285.4	−4.1
1988	294.0	298.3	+1.5
Average	260.3	253.2	3.37
Clinton			
1993	276.9	279.8	+1.0
1994	270.7	271.6	+0.3
1995	261.4	265.5	+1.6
1996	258.7	267.2	+3.3
1997	259.4	264.1	+1.8
1998	252.9	250.5	−0.9
Average	263.3	266.4	1.18

Source: Based on data reported in *Congressional Quarterly Almanac*, various years.

laid out in Chapter 2: (1) adequate and timely information provided to policy-makers through intelligence and other channels; (2) thorough and incisive analysis of threats posed, interests at stake, and other significant aspects of the issues; (3) identification of a range of policy options, and analysis of the relative pros and cons of each; (4) effective follow-through and implementation; and (5) a feedback loop for making adjustments and drawing lessons. Whether these criteria are met depends primarily on the leadership provided by the president, the roles played by his senior foreign policy advisers, and the bureaucratic politics and organizational dynamics of the executive branch.

Presidents as Foreign Policy Decision-Makers: George Bush and Bill Clinton

Of all the actors who influence foreign policy, the president remains the principal decision-maker. In Chapter 2 we also identified the key characteristics that affect presidential foreign policy leadership styles: prior relevant experience and expertise, cognitive belief systems, and political calculations. With regard to these characteristics, Presidents George Bush and Bill Clinton have a few similarities, but mostly differences.

EXPERIENCE   Bush ranks among the presidents with the most prior relevant foreign policy experience, and Clinton among those with the least. Bush had served in the military in World War II, the Navy's youngest pilot at the time and recipient of a medal for heroism. He had been a member of the House of Representatives (1966–70), ambassador to the U.N. in the Nixon administration (1971–73), head of the first U.S. liaison office in the People's Republic of China when diplomatic relations were first established (1974–75), and director of the CIA in the Ford administration (1976–77). He also served eight years as Ronald Reagan's vice president. Clinton, on the other hand, had spent his political career as governor of Arkansas (1978–80, 1982–92), the foreign policy component of which amounted to an overseas trade mission or two. Many attributed the foreign policy failures of his first year as president to his inexperience: "passive and changeable . . . like a cork bobbing on the waves," was one leading journalist's characterization.[4] In addition, the controversies over whether he had dodged the draft during the Vietnam War gave Clinton personal credibility problems as commander in chief.

BELIEF SYSTEMS The comparison of Bush's and Clinton's cognitive belief systems (see Dynamics of Choice, below) is less a matter of which is better or worse than of showing the contrasts. Bush's conception of the international system was of the old bipolar order in transition, giving way to unipolarity with the United States sitting at the top. His national-interest hierarchy put power first and peace second, albeit not to the exclusion of principles or prosperity. He was inclined toward interventionist strategies, whether in his assertive style of diplomacy or his willingness to use military force when vital national interests were deemed to be at stake. Clinton holds a more multilateralist conception of the international system, in which the United States is still the most powerful actor, but other major states and international institutions like the U.N. play substantially increased roles. His national-interest hierarchy prioritizes prosperity and principles, although also not ignoring the other core objectives. The principal strategy marking his various policy initiatives is neither as noninterventionist as was Jimmy Carter's, nor as

DYNAMICS OF CHOICE

Presidential Cognitive Belief Systems

	Bush	Clinton
Conception of the international system	Bipolarity to unipolarity	Multilateralism
National interest hierarchy	Power, peace	Prosperity, principles
Strategy	Interventionist	Negotiations
Policy examples	Persian Gulf War	U.N. peacekeeping
	Invasion of Panama	Peace brokering (Middle East, Northern Ireland)
	China after Tiananmen Square	Emphasis on foreign economic policy

interventionist as were Bush's or Reagan's; Clinton's strategy emphasizes negotiations.

The value of belief-system analysis is that it helps identify patterns in the foreign policies of different presidents. The policy examples listed in Dynamics of Choice on p. 201 show both how various Bush and Clinton foreign policies are consistent with each president's belief system, and how they contrast with each other.

POLITICAL CALCULATIONS   The third key factor affecting presidential foreign policy leadership is one of political calculations. On this count most analysts see Bush as having seriously miscalculated. His reputation as a "foreign policy" president hurt him in the 1992 election because the public perceived him as not paying enough attention to domestic policy. Clinton ran on the campaign slogan, "It's the economy, stupid," and his focus on the economy and domestic policy proved the better electoral calculation.

However, once in office Clinton made the mirror-image mistake. It was one thing to give greater priority to domestic policy, but quite another to make foreign policy as low a priority as Clinton initially tried to do in 1993–94. "Foreign Policy Morass," "Wobbling Dangerously," "Running from Foreign Policy"—these were typical headlines from Clinton's first year, and his foreign policy approval ratings fell as low as 33 percent. To his credit Clinton grew in office and became a better foreign policy leader. The president made more foreign trips in the first eighteen months of his second term than he had in his entire first term. Although he still encountered doubts and criticisms, as he entered the final years of his presidency he had shown sufficient foreign policy leadership to have worked past the earlier "failure" rating. But unlike his predecessor, Bill Clinton would never be known as a "foreign policy president."

The Senior Advisory Process: Greater Consensus, and Its Positives and Negatives

Neither the Bush nor the Clinton administration has had anything like the battles that Henry Kissinger fought with other Nixon and Ford administration officials, or those between National Security Adviser Zbigniew Brzezinski and Secretary of State Cyrus Vance in the Carter administration, or between Secretary of State George Shultz and Secretary of Defense Caspar Weinberger in the Reagan administration. Both the Bush and Clinton senior advisory processes largely show the positive effects of consensus within the executive branch. Yet they also show some of the drawbacks.

THE BUSH TEAM   Bush's principal foreign policy appointees had two characteristics in common.[5] They all had prior foreign policy and other relevant government experience, and all were longtime friends or associates of George Bush. Secretary of State James Baker had served as White House chief of staff and secretary of the treasury in the Reagan administration, and had been friends with Bush since their early days together in Texas politics. National Security Adviser Brent Scowcroft had served in the same position in the Ford administration, when his friendship with Bush began, and was a retired Air Force lieutenant colonel with a Ph.D. from Columbia University. Secretary of Defense Dick Cheney had been White House chief of staff for Ford, represented Wyoming in Congress for ten years, and had served as a member of the House Intelligence Committee. General Colin Powell, chair of the Joint Chiefs of Staff, emerged during the Reagan years first as a top Pentagon official and then as the national security adviser appointed in the wake of the Iran-contra scandal, a man in uniform who stood for everything that Oliver North did not.

As a team Bush and his top appointees generally were regarded as highly competent and quite cohesive. Even those who disagreed with their policies did not question their capabilities. After all the messy internal fights of prior administrations, the solidarity of the Bush team was a welcome relief. Some critics raised the concern over whether the Bush team was too tightly drawn and too homogeneous. Conservative columnist William Safire remarked on the "absence of creative tension [which] has generated little excitement or innovation. . . . As a result of the Bush emphasis on the appearance of unanimity, we miss the [Franklin] Rooseveltian turbulence that often leads to original thinking."[6] Overall, though, the Bush senior advisory process is seen as having been much more positive than negative.

THE CLINTON TEAM   The Clinton team (see Table 6.1) has also been marked more by consensus than by conflict. Illustrative of this was a *New York Times* profile of National Security Adviser Samuel ("Sandy") Berger, full of complimentary quotes from his colleagues. Secretary of Defense William Cohen lauded Berger as an "honest broker." Secretary of State Madeleine Albright dubbed him "the glue for the system." Joint Chiefs of Staff Chair General Hugh Shelton praised his ability to "run a great meeting." Hardly the comments one would have heard about Henry Kissinger in his day![7]

TABLE 6.1   The Clinton Foreign Policy Team

Position	First term (1993–97)	Second term (1997–2000)
National security adviser	Anthony Lake	Samuel (Sandy) Berger
Secretary of state	Warren Christopher	Madeleine Albright
Secretary of defense	Les Aspin (1993) William Perry (1994–97)	William Cohen
CIA director	James Woolsey (1993–95) Michael Carns* John Deutch (1995–97)	Anthony Lake* George Tenet
Ambassador to the U.N.	Madeleine Albright	Bill Richardson (1997–98) Richard Holbrooke (1999–)
Secretary of the treasury	Lloyd Bentsen (1993–95) Robert Rubin (1995–)	Robert Rubin (1997–99) Lawrence Summers (1999–)
Secretary of commerce	Ron Brown (1993–96) Mickey Kantor (1996–97)	William Daley
U.S. trade representative	Mickey Kantor (1993–96) Charlene Barshefsky (1996–)	Charlene Barshefsky
Chair, National Economic Council	Robert Rubin (1993–95) Laura D'Andrea Tyson (1995–97)	Gene Sperling

*Nominated for position, but nomination withdrawn before Senate vote.

Nevertheless, the Clinton team has had its rivalries and its weaknesses. Les Aspin, Clinton's first secretary of defense, did not even last a year, in part because he ended up with much of the blame for the military failure in Somalia. Warren Christopher will be remembered as a hardworking and gracious secretary of state but not the right man for the nature of the times. Anthony Lake, Clinton's first national security adviser, earlier in his career had worked both for Henry Kissinger and Cyrus Vance. He thus was especially conscious of the damage bureaucratic warfare could cause. Some critics, though, felt he may have learned these lessons too well, and played too low-key a role himself.

The initial sense was that the second-term team was stronger. The appointment of Madeleine Albright as the first woman ever to serve as secretary of state brought with it a sense of historic importance and excitement. Defense Secretary Cohen, previously a Republican senator from Maine, brought a sense of bipartisanship and good relations with his former colleagues on Capitol Hill. And Berger, who moved up from deputy national security adviser to national security adviser, already had a close relationship with President Clinton.

In addition, throughout the Clinton presidency Vice President Al Gore played a role unprecedented in a job that its first holder, John Adams, called "the most insignificant office that ever the invention of man contrived." Previous vice presidents typically had not had much of a substantive foreign policy role; trips to attend funerals of foreign dignitaries were pretty much the portfolio. Gore, who had earned a reputation for foreign policy expertise during his sixteen years in Congress, took on two types of major foreign policy responsibilities. First, to a much greater extent than any previous vice president, he was "in the loop" on a regular basis on policy formulation and "at the table" for virtually every major foreign policy decision. Second, he maintained an ongoing policy role with the various "Gore commissions" set up with foreign leaders of key countries (specifically, with Russia, Ukraine, South Africa, and Egypt) as mechanisms for ensuring that agreements made and agendas set at summits and other presidential-level meetings would not just sit there as pieces of paper once those events were over. These types of meetings get much less publicity than the big summits, but in substantive terms they have more importance than is often appreciated. Whether the Gore vice presidency will prove a model for future ones, and thus transform the institution, remains to be seen.

Although the Clinton foreign policy benefited in many respects from minimizing bureaucratic warfare, here, too, consensus has had negative aspects. For example, no one among the senior advisers has effectively provided strategic vision. Henry Kissinger pointed out that, although he liked National Security Adviser Berger, Berger is more a "trade lawyer" than a "global strategist."[8] Secretary of State Albright has been a much more effective communicator than Secretary Christopher was, and has come the closest to being a figure the public could "connect" with, but she also has come across as more focused on the issue of the day than on any overarching strategy.

The other pattern characteristic of the senior advisory process under Clinton has been frequent indecisiveness on the use of military force. In Somalia in 1993 the Clinton team wavered over defining the mission, with tragic and humiliating consequences. In Haiti, although the decision was finally made in September 1994 to send U.S. troops in, this was only after such incidents as the one in October 1993, when the naval ship U.S.S. *Harlan County,* carrying about one hundred U.S. and Canadian police trainers, turned tail as it entered the Port-au-Prince harbor at the sight of jeering mobs on the docks. In Bosnia, although the U.S.-brokered Dayton Accords did end the war and more than twenty thousand U.S. troops were included in NATO's peacekeeping forces, these actions came only after numerous threats had not been delivered on, and ethnic cleansing had been allowed to go on for too long. In the 1997 and 1998 crises with Iraq, the Clinton team's decision-making again was less than decisive, and the conviction and credibility of American threats to use force were widely questioned. And then in Kosovo in 1999, in launching the most massive use of force in the history of NATO, the administration was so slow to act and so indecisive about the use of ground troops that, although Serbia ended up paying a major price, the Kosovar Albanians paid much more dearly, losing their homes, their livelihoods, and for many, their lives.

Bureaucratic Politics: Assertive New Actors, Troubled Old Ones

THE RISE OF THE FOREIGN ECONOMIC POLICY BUREAUCRACY   The Clinton administration is the first to have consistently brought top foreign economic policy officials onto the foreign policy "first string." But the decision to include them in the formation of foreign policy has introduced two bureaucratic challenges. One is a matter of coordination. Even when policy is reasonably consensual, the multiple foreign economic policy departments and agencies must be harnessed into a coordinated effort. To help with this task, one of the bureaucratic innovations of the Clinton administration was the creation of the National Economic Council (NEC), mandated to do on the foreign economic policy side what the National Security Council (NSC) does on the political-diplomatic-military side.

The other challenge arises on issues for which there is no consensus; here, the strengthening of the economic voice can make for more divisive bureaucratic politics. The NEC now can compete with the NSC because it, too, is within the White House, close to the president, and able to speak for a number of executive-branch departments and agencies. On some foreign policy issues, the Commerce Department, the Agriculture Department, the U.S. Trade Representative, the Export-Import Bank, and the Overseas Private Investment Corporation (OPIC) will be arrayed on one side, and the State Department and the Defense Department will oppose them on the other.

This type of division was seen when China's most-favored-nation (MFN) status came up for renewal. Among all the bureaucratic battles fought over this issue, perhaps the most startling was the display of competitive speech-making in Beijing in early 1994, where a top Commerce Department official gave a strong pro-MFN speech, only to be followed shortly by Secretary of State Christopher with a "tough on human rights" message. Taking the conflict even further, both sides fed stories to the news media, often not just advocating their own view but also disparaging their fellow administration colleagues. Another example of such infighting arose over Japan policy, specifically the relative priority to be given to trade issues (Commerce, U.S. Trade Representative) versus protecting the U.S.-Japan security relationship (State, Defense). Here too the policy differences were substantial, and at times the intrabranch cross-accusations were no less derogatory than interbranch ones.

THE MORASS AT THE CIA   The CIA is particularly critical to the first two of the rational-process criteria—providing both high-quality intelligence and thorough and incisive analysis. Yet it has been beset by enormous problems that call into question its ability to do either.

Some of these have been fallout from recent scandals. Most glaring was the one involving Aldrich Ames, a CIA agent turned traitor who worked as a "mole" for the Soviet Union in the 1980s. Not only did the secrets Ames sold to the Soviets damage national security, the fact that he was so open about his lavish lifestyle, including driving to work at CIA headquarters in his Jaguar, raised concerns about why the CIA had not discovered him much sooner.

Other problems have arisen following exposure of the unsavory relationships the CIA maintained during the Cold War with some of its "ABC" (anything but communist) partners. For example, stories broke in 1994–95 about CIA knowledge and possible involvement in massive human rights violations and killings by the Guatemalan military, including the murders of an American innkeeper living in Guatemala and a leftist guerrilla leader who was married to an American.

The CIA's troubles have been in part due to a lack of leadership. During the Clinton administration the CIA has had three different directors, plus two nominated directors whose names had to be withdrawn because of Senate opposition—not exactly a formula for clear and consistent leadership.

In three other respects, though, the CIA's problems run much deeper. First is the continuing problem of democratic accountability. The 1970s reforms were supposed to have made the CIA more subject to congressional oversight. The Iran-contra scandal in the Reagan years, in which Congress yet again was lied to by executive-branch officials, revealed that accountability was still not reliable. A question asked during the Iran-contra investigations sums up the dilemma: "Can [intelligence] operations, and particularly covert action, be authorized and conducted in a manner compatible with the American system of democratic government and the rule of law?"[9] This question bears especially on the distinction between the two principal reasons for keeping an action covert and secret. One is because it is an *operational necessity,* for which political support might be there if it were possible to share the information but for which secrecy is essential to the policy's success. The other use of secrecy is mostly as a *political cover* for an operation that likely would engender more opposition than support. The former is a much stronger rationale in a democratic political system than the latter.

Second are problems of current performance and whether the CIA is providing the information and analyses that policy-makers need. The CIA was caught totally unaware by India's May 1998 nuclear-weapons tests. This was in part a technical matter, arising from the limitations of its monitoring equipment. But it also revealed shortcomings in the agency's analyses, for the political signals were there, even in the media and other open sources, that the new Hindu nationalist government of India had development of nuclear weapons as a major part of its political platform. Nor was this episode an isolated instance—a special investigative commission criticized "the underlying mindset" that hampered the overall quality of intelligence analyses.[10]

Third is the broader questioning of the CIA's mission in the post–Cold War world. Do we really still need the CIA? Some who see the CIA as a relic go so far as to question the very need for covert action as a power strategy in this new era. Others base their critique more on redundancy: the Pentagon has its "special operations" forces for commando and other covert actions, the FBI is playing a larger role with its own foreign investigative operations, and foreign intelligence is being collected by agencies within the State and Defense Departments. Shouldn't these suffice for the kinds of threats the United States faces? Why drain the federal budget with the costs of the CIA?

Those on the other side of the debate stress the need for major reform but argue against abolition. Given the uncertainties of this new era and the myriad of forces and threats out there—ethnic conflict, terrorism, weapons proliferation, economic espionage—policy-makers still have pressing needs for intelligence, just intelligence of a different sort. Thus satellites that used to spy on the Soviet Union can be reprogrammed to gather global environmental data on ozone depletion and global warming, thereby matching a satellite fleet in need of a new mission and a new mission in need of satellites. As to covert action, some argue that it is still useful, but with a different focus. The players have changed and the stakes are different, but the global power game continues to be played, and covert action is still one of the strategies used both by other states and by nonstate actors. So although the potential for abuse always will be there, the optimal policy is to try to minimize this problem while still maintaining the necessary capacity to undertake covert action when and where U.S. interests warrant it.

Foreign Policy Interest Groups: Proliferation and Intensification

Two main trends have characterized foreign policy interest groups in recent years: *proliferation,* in that there are many more of them than ever before, and *intensification,* in that they are more active not only in seeking to bring pressure on Congress and the executive branch, but also in taking more direct action of their own. These dynamics are another manifestation of broader post–Cold War trends: absent an overriding national security threat, there is little to constrain groups from pressuring for their own interests, and the foreign policy agenda has expanded to include so many more issues that there are more groups whose interests are being affected.

Economic Globalization and Interest Groups

As recently as 1970, trade accounted for only 13 percent of the U.S. gross domestic product (GDP). Today it amounts to more than 30 percent. And trade now comprises much more than goods and services. Companies scour the world, not just their own country, in deciding where to build factories and make other foreign investments. Millions of dollars in stock investments and other financial transactions flow between New York and Frankfurt, Chicago and London, San Francisco and Tokyo every day. Overall there are now more foreign economic issues on the agenda, and those issues are much more politically salient than they used to be. Whereas during the Cold War most foreign economic policy issues were relegated to "low politics" status in contrast to political and security "high politics" issues, in recent years issues such as NAFTA, fast-track, IMF funding, and other international economic issues have been as hotly contested and as prominent as any other foreign policy issues in recent years.

Following from the greater number and higher salience of the foreign economic policy agenda, more and more interest groups have become involved in the political competition. On an issue like NAFTA, for example, more than 180 different groups testified at congressional hearings. This included such major pro-business groups as the National Association of Manufacturers (NAM) and the U.S. Chamber of Commerce, as well as major labor organizations such as the AFL-CIO and the United Auto Workers. It also included groups specific to particular sectors of the economy, such as the National Association of Wheat Growers, the Gulf Citrus Growers Association, the American Apparel Manufacturers Association, and the Chemical Manufacturers Association. So, too, individual companies like ConAgra, Gillette, Fruit of the Loom, Eastman Kodak, and an array of others.

Interestingly, environmental groups (the Sierra Club, the Defenders of Wildlife, the Environmental Defense Fund, for example) also were very involved in formulating NAFTA. The involvement of groups such as these in trade issues is a relatively new development, and is another main trend to be noted. Whereas recognition of the interconnectedness of economics and the environment within domestic policy began to take hold in the 1970s, it is only in recent years that this linkage has begun to be a significant factor within foreign economic policy. In the NAFTA case pressure from environmental groups forced the Clinton administration to negotiate side agreements with Mexico for improved air quality, hazardous-waste disposal, and other "greening" of the trade agreement. We also saw the involvement of public interest groups, like Ralph Nader's Public Citizen, concerned with consumer product safety and other public interest issues, and human rights groups like Amnesty International concerned with political repression in Mexico.

Identity Groups

Identity groups—i.e., groups motivated less by material economic interests than by bonds of ethnic or religious identity to other countries—provide another example of the proliferation of interest groups. The increasing racial and ethnic diversity of the American populace, resulting both from new trends in immigration (see Table 6.2) and increasing empowerment of long-present minorities, is making for a larger number and wider range of groups with personal bases for seeking to influence foreign policy.

We discussed the Jewish-American lobby in Chapter 2; it continues to be highly influential on Middle East policy. The various Slavic American groups (e.g., Polish, Lithuanian, Latvian, and Estonian Americans) are another exam-

TABLE 6.2　Changing Immigration Patterns

Place of origin	Percentage of all immigrants originating in selected areas	
	1920	1996
Europe	87%	17%
Canada	8	3
Latin America	4	50
Asia	1	27

Source: U.S. Census Bureau, as reported in the *Washington Post*, May 25, 1998, p. A1.

ple. Influential during the Cold War in hardening U.S. policy toward the Soviet Union, these groups got a new lease on life with the end of the Cold War in support of policies geared toward helping the former communist states democratize, build their economies, and ensure their security against any future Russian threat through mechanisms such as NATO expansion. For example, in late 1993, when the Clinton administration was "dragging its feet on NATO expansion, Polish lobbying groups flooded the White House with telegrams and telephone calls. The Polish-American Congress put out a 'legislative alert' to its 34 divisions around the country to prevent a 'new Yalta,' political shorthand for the 'betrayal of Poland by the Western allies that occurred after the end of World War II.'" As the head of on lobbying group put it, "there are 23 million Americans who trace their heritage to Eastern Europe," and, even more important, "there are a dozen [U.S.] states—very important states for any presidential election—where they constitute more than 5 percent of the electorate."[11]

African Americans, led by TransAfrica and the Congressional Black Caucus, emerged as a strong foreign policy lobby on the issue of economic sanctions against apartheid South Africa. Another case in which they also played an influential role was in U.S. policy toward Haiti following the 1990 military coup that overthrew President Jean-Bertrand Aristide, a policy that culminated in the September 1994 U.S. military intervention. There was said to be "grumbling" in Congress "that [Clinton] administration officials consult more with key members of the Black Caucus about the [Haiti] crisis than they do with the chairmen and ranking members of House and Senate committees with jurisdiction over foreign policy or Caribbean affairs."[12]

The Cuban American lobby, and in particular its lead organization, the Cuban-American National Foundation (CANF), counts among its leadership a number of people who fled the island when Fidel Castro took power in 1959 and who were involved in the 1961 Bay of Pigs invasion and other covert efforts to overthrow Castro. Over the years the CANF has staunchly and repeatedly opposed efforts at lifting the economic embargo or otherwise liberalizing U.S.-Cuba relations.

As cohesive as these identity groups are, one cannot always assume purely consensual views within any one of them. Although the vast majority of Jewish Americans are strongly supportive of Israel, deep and fundamental splits have emerged among them over what that means in policy terms, with some more willing to support a peace agreement with the Palestinians than others. Few Cuban Americans are pro-Castro, but there are deep disagreements between those like the CANF, who want to keep the full squeeze on Castro, and those who favor an improvement in relations as a better way to help the Cuban people and ultimately to promote democratization. Similar conflicts have arisen among Vietnamese Americans over the normalization of diplomatic relations with the communist government there. Opposition was strongest among former South Vietnamese officials who still recall having had to flee as refugees, and for some having been jailed and tortured as political prisoners. Others, particularly of the younger generation, believed that normalization could provide benefits to people still living in Vietnam and also promote democratization.

Other groups could be mentioned here as well: Greek Americans on the issues of Cyprus and Macedonia; Irish Americans and the Northern Ireland issue; Arab Americans and their concerns about the Middle East; Pakistani Americans and Indian Americans and issues involving the tensions between Pakistan and India. More will emerge over time, as the American population increasingly reflects the shifts in overall immigration patterns noted in Table 6.2. For just as the proliferation of groups concerned with trade policy reflects the broader economic changes of the internationalization of the American economy, more and more Americans are interested in influencing U.S. relations with the countries from which they or their ancestors came.

The Explosion of NGOs

The rise of *non-governmental organizations,* or NGOs, is one of the most important developments of this new era. NGOs usually are unofficial, citizen-run, nonprofit organizations whose "business" is some aspect of foreign policy—e.g., promoting human rights, for Amnesty International and Human Rights Watch; building democracy, for the Open Society Institute and the American Bar Association; helping refugees, for Refugees International; protecting the global environment, for the Climate Action Networks; conflict resolution and "track-two diplomacy," for Search for Common Ground and the Carter Center. Although NGOs have been around for a long time, in the post–Cold War era vast numbers of NGOs have been formed. One expert estimates "about 600 U.S. NGOs with annual budgets in excess of $1 million [each] that either operate internationally or focus on international policy issues. . . . The combined expenditures of these NGOs probably exceeded $11 billion in 1996."[13]

In one sense NGOs fit in the "political issue group" category in our interest-group typology (see p. 45). One of their principal roles is *advocacy*—lobbying, endorsing candidates, mounting media campaigns, etc. Many NGOs operate in international forums like the United Nations. For example, at the 1995 U.N. World Conference on Women held in Beijing, China, more than 4,000 NGO delegates were officially accredited, just slightly fewer than the total number of government delegates.

The other major NGO role is *direct action.* Many NGOs don't just lobby governments to take action, they themselves are out on the front lines providing humanitarian assistance, monitoring human rights, supervising elections, helping with economic development, and taking on countless other global responsibilities. Proponents such as Jessica Mathews, president of the Carnegie Endowment for International Peace, a research institution in Washington, D.C., argue that NGOs "can outperform government in the delivery of many public services," and "are better than governments at dealing with problems that grow slowly and affect society through their cumulative effect on individuals."[14] The U.S. government has recognized this in some respects, for example, by increasing the percentage of economic development aid channeled through NGOs from barely 20 percent in 1990 to nearly 40 percent in 1995. The Clinton administration has pledged to increase this to 50 percent by 2000.[15]

The Madisonian Dilemma of Interest-Group Influence

"Are Politics Destroying Policy? Polarization and Interest Groups Stymie Change, Experts Say." So read the press-release headline for a 1998 book published by the Brookings Institution.[16] This takes us back to the dilemma pondered by James Madison in Federalist Paper no. 10, of when and how interest-group pressure becomes "the violence of factions." Madison saw nothing wrong with group interests per se; what made a group a faction was when its interests were "adverse to the rights of other citizens, or to the permanent and aggregate interests of the community." Thus the question is whether interest-group influence here in the post–Cold War world is normal and appropriate to the range of interests affected by foreign policy, or whether it has reached the point of factionalization.

Valid arguments can be made on both sides. On the positive side it is argued that, other than on issues of the utmost national security, foreign policy should be looked at the same way as domestic policy, with a much more encompassing sense of the legitimacy of group interests. Many of the issues pushed by groups actually are in the broad national interest as well, such as human rights and protecting the global environment, but are not given appropriate priority within the government and thus need outside pressure to bring them to the fore.

The negative view sees the national interest getting superseded by domestic politics when interest groups have too much influence. Among other problems, allowing interest groups too much influence undermines U.S. credibility in trying to persuade other governments on an issue. Why should we go along, those governments often ask, in cases such as U.S. economic sanctions against Cuba, when your policy is little more than the externalization of U.S. domestic politics? Moreover, to come back to Madison, it bears remembering that he was more in favor of efforts to "control the effects" of factions than he was of efforts to "remove the causes." In contemporary terms "controlling the effects" would include such measures as campaign-finance reform and efforts to engage and educate the general public.

The News Media: General Trends and the Persian Gulf War Case

The three main issues delineated in Chapter 2 regarding the role of the news media in the politics of foreign policy concerned their overall role, the modes of their influence, and tensions between freedom of the press and national security. Here we first examine general trends in these areas and then focus on the media coverage of the 1990–91 Persian Gulf War as a case both important in its own right and with broader implications.

General Trends

The most significant change regarding the news media since the end of the Cold War has been in what "the media" are and how they operate. For coverage of foreign policy, first rank still goes to major newspapers (the *New York Times*, the *Washington Post*), major television networks (ABC, NBC, CBS), and major newsmagazines (*Time, Newsweek*). Two newer developments have had their own dramatic effects. One has been the rise of cable and satellite television, led by CNN and increasingly involving more and more new networks. CNN made its name for its coverage during the Persian Gulf War. It was on the scene before the traditional networks and its twenty-four-hour news coverage made it a constant presence. Although on this and other foreign policy issues there are many benefits to the close and constant coverage of CNN and other cable news organizations, this constant attention brings intense "real time" pressure. An American soldier gets taken prisoner, and his face flashes on the television time and again, all day, all night. A terrorist incident occurs, and the video plays over and over. Policy-makers often must respond with little prior notice, in some cases actually first hearing about a major event on CNN rather than through official channels. They also must do so within the immediacy of the churning news cycle. This makes for a very different and more difficult dynamic in television's impact on key foreign policy choices.

The other major development involves the Internet. More and more people also are getting news on the Internet; one study showed a tremendous recent increase in the number of people who went on-line to get their news at least once a week, especially among eighteen to twenty-nine year olds, where the increase was from 7 percent to 30 percent.[17] Even more than just a medium for the communication of daily news, the Internet has substantially enhanced the capacity of NGOs, think tanks, and others to become independent sources of information, analysis, and advocacy. Nik Gowing, a journalist with the British Broadcasting Corporation, calls this development a breaking of the "information dominance" of governments, be they repressive regimes that would prefer to cut their people off from outside communication or democratic governments that must respond to the new dynamics of pressure.[18]

THE ROLE OF THE MEDIA   At first glance it seems that the old "cheerleader" role of the media can be dismissed as totally anachronistic. No president today could or would make a statement like Woodrow Wilson's during the 1916 military intervention into Mexico, asking the press "to be good enough to assist the Administration" in building and maintaining support for its policy. Presidents might still like to be able to make such a request, and as in the Persian Gulf War they may try to control news coverage to a similar effect, but they surely never would be able to so matter-of-factly ask for some cheerleading.

A number of leading scholars stress that the media still can be very deferential in their treatment of official policy.[19] Reporters still need the government officials who are their sources; government officials know that although good relationships with reporters do not guarantee favorable reporting, they may well help when trying to "spin" a story.

Still, the media as critic seems to have become more the norm. Scandals like the Aldrich Ames spy story get broken in the press. Investigative reporters dig into controversies like China's role in the Clinton campaign-finance scandal and cost overruns at the Pentagon. Daily reporting often seems focused less on conveying information about major foreign policy issues and events than on parceling out credit for who gains politically and apportioning blame for policy failures. For these and other reasons some scholars see the relationship as having become much less symbiotic and more one of "interdependent mutual exploitation."[20] The media and the government still are interdependent, but have less common ground and make more efforts to manipulate each other.

To say that the media's role as critic is in many aspects positive is not simply to defend the media, it is to affirm the Bill of Rights and one of the fundamental principles of democracy. At times in recent years, though, the media seem to have become more cynical, the ramifications of which can be more negative. Sorting these roles out and seeking a better balance is one of the crucial political challenges Americans face.

MODES OF MEDIA INFLUENCE   Television in particular has a major agenda-setting impact. Studies by media scholar Shanto Iyengar and others show that when people are asked to identify the most significant problem facing the nation, they name something that has been on television news recently.[21] Mass starvation was plaguing many parts of Africa in the mid-1980s, but the outside world, the United States included, was paying little attention. However, when NBC News came into Ethiopia and aired footage of parched fields and ravaged children to millions of television viewers back home, suddenly the Ethiopian famine was on the foreign policy agenda. Of course, the famines elsewhere in Africa where the TV cameras did not go did not make it onto the agenda.

Reference often is made to the "CNN curve," whereby coverage by CNN or the other television news networks raises public awareness of an issue and can help increase support for providing aid, sending troops, or taking other action to deal with the problem. But the curve also has a downside, in which negative coverage, especially of a major policy disaster, can fuel a precipitous drop in public support. The October 1993 killing of the American troops in Somalia was a graphic example of this phenomenon.

Newspapers, too, can have agenda-setting impact, largely through investigative reporting or other lead stories that break major news. The first reports of "ethnic cleansing" in Bosnia were published, replete with shocking reports and photos, in mid-1992 by *Newsday,* a New York newspaper. Newspapers can also set the agenda through steady and solid reporting, sticking with an issue and making sure that it not only gets on the agenda but doesn't go away.

In addition to the indirect effects on policy-makers via these influences on public opinion, the media's direct influence on policy-makers also is quite evident. Take, for example, the "Early Bird," a thick compilation, usually about sixty pages long, of newspaper articles that circulates every morning to State and Defense Department officials and other Washington policy-makers. Many regard it as no less essential reading than the daily intelligence reports. "What will the press think?" is a question now regularly asked in executive-branch foreign policy meetings. Editorials and op-ed articles also have a remarkable influence. Highly critical opinion pieces in a major paper like the *New York Times* or the *Washington Post* have been known to prompt hastily called State Department meetings or to have made officials forget about whatever else was on their schedule in order to draft a response.

FREEDOM OF THE PRESS VS. NATIONAL SECURITY   This tension has been exacerbated in the post–Cold War era for a number of reasons. One is another manifestation of politics without an Enemy. The rationale for restrictions on freedom of the press in the name of national security is not as strong when the threats the nation faces are less compelling. Another is that the national-security rationale was so abused in the past that it carries less credibility than before. Past abuses have led many to believe that politics often has more to do with why documents and proceedings get classified than policy does. Is freedom of the press being limited because the issue at hand genuinely requires secrecy in the name of the national interest? Or is secrecy being resorted to more because if the action or policy were known there would be political fallout?

On the other hand there do continue to be genuine national-security needs for limiting media access. Sometimes this is because of the inherent sensitivity of the information in question—is there not, for example, a national interest in preventing terrorists from gaining access to information that could be used to develop biological weapons or other weapons of mass destruction? Sometimes a highly sensitive and important process, if not kept secret at a particular stage, will wither under the light of public exposure. This was the case with the "Oslo" talks that led to the first Israeli-Palestinian peace agreement in 1993. These secret talks were held mostly in a secluded country inn outside Oslo, Norway, away from the lights of television. They were revealed publicly only when they had made significant progress. Had there been early media reports about this dialogue taking place, the criticisms from the extremes on both sides would have been so great that both the Palestinians and the Israelis would likely have had to disown the peace process before its first fruits were ready to be reaped.

Historian Michael Beschloss stresses the value, especially in times of crisis, of "a cocoon of time and privacy."[22] He speculates as to how different the Cuban missile crisis might have turned out if the media coverage had been as intrusive and intense as it is today. What if TV network satellites had discovered the Soviet missiles on their own and broke the story on the evening news, sparking congressional and public outcry and increasing pressure on President Kennedy to take immediate but precipitous and potentially escalating action like an air strike? Could ExCom have deliberated over so many days without leaks? Kennedy was able to shape his own story rather than being caught on the defensive; today his position would have been much tougher to sell, and he probably could not have gotten away with a number of gambits that balanced toughness with understanding of Khrushchev's situation if every move was independently and immediately reported and discussed on radio talk shows.

The Persian Gulf War Case

A number of these issues were manifested during the 1990–91 Persian Gulf War.[23] Of course, no agenda-setting role was needed in this case; Saddam Hussein took care of that. During the buildup of Desert Shield and especially once Desert Storm was launched and war began, the Bush administration and the military sought to manage the news coverage with two principal goals: to limit the independence of the media coverage, and to shape it to be as positive as possible. War correspondents were confined to "pools" of limited numbers and restricted to designated locations. Film footage released for TV was carefully screened so as to give the impression of a near-flawless bombing campaign—"smart" bombs going through ventilation shafts, high "target-kill" ratios, very few civilian sites hit. General Norman Schwarzkopf, commanding officer of the U.S. and allied forces in the Gulf, proved to be not only an excellent military strategist but also a whiz at media briefings and TV communication, and became a new folk hero.

The media protested that, while certain restrictions were understandable during war, the measures taken to control the coverage "go far beyond what is required to protect troop safety and mission security."[24] *Newsweek* called it "the propaganda war. . . . In theory, reporters in democratic societies work independent of propaganda. In practice they are treated during war as simply more pieces of military hardware to be deployed."[25] The military essentially was saying to the media that, with the nation at war, our intention is to limit and direct your role to the cheerleader one, not the critic one. In pursuit of cheerleader coverage, the military limited the amount and accuracy of information provided to the media. It was later learned that in fact the air campaign had not been nearly as successful as portrayed. Later information revealed that only 7 percent of the bombs were precision-guided munitions, and while these did hit their targets 90 percent of the time, more than 90 percent of the bombs were "dumb" conventional ones that missed their targets 75 percent of the time. Data such as these sharply contrasted with "the high-tech, never-miss image that the Pentagon carefully cultivated during the war."[26]

Perhaps the greatest impact the press did have in this case was an anticipatory one. President Bush, Joint Chiefs of Staff Chair Powell, and General Schwarzkopf all later acknowledged that one reason for ending the war when they did, and not going further to remove Saddam from power, was concern with media coverage of what could have been a more difficult and bloodier stage of the war. Whether one argues that this was an appropriate constraint or sees it as a negative halfway measure, the point of the media's influence on policy and policy-makers is the same.

Public reaction to the Gulf War media restrictions was mixed. Many viewed them as appropriate and necessary; some even lambasted the media as "unpatriotic" for some of their more critical reports. Others were more supportive of the media's role and wary of the restrictions on press freedom that were imposed, especially as the glory of the victory faded over time. Similar issues arose during the 1999 Kosovo War.[27]

The most important conclusion, both from the Persian Gulf War case and the more general trends, is that the news media are integral to the foreign policy process. They no longer play just an indirect role as an influence on public opinion. Through old modes like newspapers, somewhat aging modes like television, and newer modes like cable and satellite TV and the Internet, the media are playing a direct role in foreign policy politics to a greater extent than ever before.

Because the media are so much a part of the policy-making process, the government also seeks to be as much a part of the media process as possible. Efforts at news management are not usually as blatant as during the Persian Gulf War. But read the minutes of major foreign policy meetings, and you'll see significant attention paid to media-related issues. Check out staff rosters in the State and Defense Departments, and you'll see numerous media advisers. Look at the curriculum taught at the Foreign Service Institute and the National Defense University, and you'll see courses on the role of the media. And, if anything, given constantly advancing technology, these emphases will only grow with time.

Post–Cold War Public Opinion: Currents and Cross-Currents

6.3

What does the public think about foreign policy these days? As befits a period of historic transition, this question as yet has no definitive answer. No new consensus has emerged. The best characterization is of currents flowing in one direction, and cross-currents in the other.

Our discussion herein focuses on general patterns in public opinion with regard to the overarching debate over internationalism vs. isolationism, and the "nexus" issues that exemplify the growing interconnection between foreign and domestic policy. Specific issues that will be discussed in later chapters include public opinion about the United Nations (Chapter 7), military force (Chapter 8), trade (Chapter 9), and democratization and human rights (Chapter 10).

Neo-Isolationism vs. Neo-Internationalism

Should the United States seek to minimize its involvement in world affairs, to "isolate" from the rest of the world? Or should it take an active, "international" role? We saw in Chapter 3 the deep historical roots of the isolationist-internationalist debate over these core questions. Back to Washington's farewell address, through the nineteenth century, whether to try to stay out of World War I, whether to keep out of the League of Nations, whether to say "not our problem" as Hitler marched across Europe—now again with the end of the Cold War, this fundamental question has been raised anew.

Americans seem to be giving a mixed answer to this question today. *Neo-isolationists* see the end of the Cold War as reason for the United States to re-strict its involvement in international affairs. *Neo-internationalists* see new bases for an actively engaged foreign policy notwithstanding the end of the Cold War. To take the analysis a step further, within the two basic categories, two subgroups can be distinguished: "apathetics" and "antagonistics" on the one side, "attentives" and "activists" on the other.

Apathetics are those who just don't care very much about foreign policy. They not only see domestic issues as more important, but barely see the rele-vance of foreign policy and consider it a distraction from the domestic agenda. They are unlikely to support and may well oppose most foreign policy initiatives. They are the ones who are most receptive to the "come home, America" cry. They also are evident in surveys that show that Americans have limited knowledge about foreign affairs, compared not just to elites but to publics in other countries. A 1989 study by the National Geographic Society found Americans able to correctly identify only 8 of 16 locations on a world map, achieving no better than sixth place out of ten countries surveyed. Bro-ken down by age, American eighteen to twenty-four year olds came in last. A more general foreign policy knowledge survey done in 1994 had Americans ranking sixth out of seven, behind Germany, Italy, France, the United King-dom, and Canada, and ahead only of Spain.[28]

Antagonistics constitute smaller numbers but are more strident in their opposition. They are the "American First-ers," whose views resonate with re-sentments, against allies like Europe and Japan for not paying for their own defense, and against the United Nations for corruption, inefficiency, and anti-Americanism. The militia groups that got so much publicity in the wake of the 1995 Oklahoma City bombing are a particularly extreme version of antag-onistics. These groups hold to an "extremist catechism" that, as described in *U.S. News and World Report,* includes such tenets as "the United Nations is threatening to take over the United States. . . . [F]oreign troops under UN command are training on American soil, and black helicopters are spying on Americans. . . . [T]he United States is secretly building or supporting 'concen-tration camps' to house resisters to the new world order. . . . [R]oad signs contain secret codes to direct foreign invaders."[29] These groups are not that large—although they are larger than many realized before Oklahoma City.

Among internationalists, the *attentives* are those who pay the most attention to foreign policy, see its relevance, and generally support the need for the United States to continue to play a leadership role. They include both Republicans and Democrats, from the moderate center of both parties. Representative positions include support for the United Nations (including paying off the rather large U.S. debt to the U.N.), for NATO expansion, for NAFTA and other trade liberalization, for the International Monetary Fund, and for other diplomatic, economic, and military initiatives and leadership roles. As in the past, the demographics of the attentives reveal higher levels of education and income, professional occupations, more urban than rural, and concentrated most heavily in the Northeast and on the West Coast.

Activists are those who engage in lobbying and other action geared to influencing official U.S. foreign policy, whether as individuals, through protest movements, or as members of various identity, economic, and other interest groups. They include the individuals and groups that go beyond seeking to influence policy and take direct action, such as through NGOs dealing with poverty, refugees, democracy-building, etc. They also include more and different types of people: doctors, lawyers, nurses, teachers, business administrators, city managers, and others who have skills and experience that allow them to play a hands-on role helping foreign countries and peoples.

What, then, is the balance of opinion between the neo-isolationist and the neo-internationalist groups? As seen in Figure 6.1, in one poll after another a strong majority still comes out as internationalist. The main reason for this is that the public has learned the lessons of the twentieth century—of how both world wars inevitably pulled the United States in, and the crucial contributions the United States made to both victories; of the folly of isolationist moves like not joining the League of Nations and passing the 1929 Smoot-Hawley protectionist tariff; of the indispensable role the United States played in the Cold War; of OPEC oil crises and the interdependence of the American economy with the global economy. And, fundamentally, it understands that the United States has come to be so interconnected in so many ways with the rest of the world that isolationism is not just undesirable—it simply is not possible.

Yet at times and on certain issues this general internationalist current can be swamped by neo-isolationist cross-currents. Part of the dynamic is that the neo-isolationists often are more vocal, more active, and better organized. This can mislead policy-makers who may see the public as more isolationist than it really is. A study by the University of Maryland Program on International Policy Attitudes found that 74 percent of policy-makers believed that the public favored "disengagement," only 32 percent believed that the public wanted the

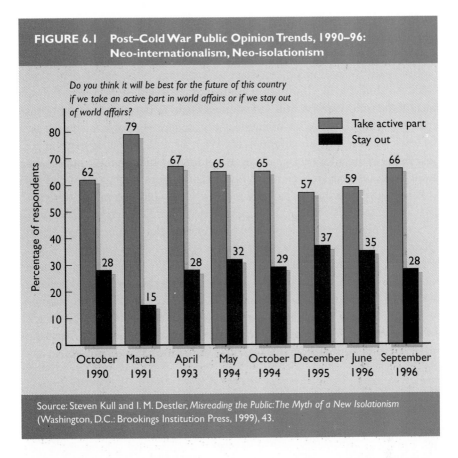

FIGURE 6.1   Post–Cold War Public Opinion Trends, 1990–96: Neo-internationalism, Neo-isolationism

Do you think it will be best for the future of this country if we take an active part in world affairs or if we stay out of world affairs?

Take active part
Stay out

Percentage of respondents

October 1990 · March 1991 · April 1993 · May 1994 · October 1994 · December 1995 · June 1996 · September 1996

Source: Steven Kull and I. M. Destler, *Misreading the Public: The Myth of a New Isolationism* (Washington, D.C.: Brookings Institution Press, 1999), 43.

United States to be an international leader, and only 15 percent believed that the public could be convinced to support engagement.[30] These perceptions are quite out of sync with the actual opinion data as seen in Figure 6.1. Yet in political terms perceptions often matter more than the actual numbers. So we end up with public opinion constraining internationalist policies more than the polling data might lead us to believe it would.

Foreign-Domestic "Nexus" Issues

One of the polling questions often cited to "show" how little the public cares about foreign policy asks about the biggest problems facing the country. Whereas in the mid-1980s 26 percent cited a foreign policy issue, only 7.3 percent did so in 1998. For social problems the pattern was the reverse, going up from 39 percent to 62 percent.[31] Yet this question is more useful to us as an example of how flawed conclusions can be drawn from poll data than for any major insights into public opinion.

Is it any wonder that more people cite problems close to home as the "biggest" ones today? Look at the state of American cities, public education, health care, and the like. Indeed the problem may well have been that during much of the Cold War too little attention was paid to these kinds of problems on the home front. But to say domestic issues are more important is not to say that foreign policy ones are unimportant. What we especially need to get at are those issues at the intersection, or "nexus," of foreign and domestic policy—issues such as jobs, drugs, economic competitiveness, illegal immigration, and oil.

And indeed, it is these issues in which the post–Cold War public is particularly interested (see Table 6.3). As a group they have a 68 percent "top priority" score, a higher average than the 58 percent for global interests and much higher than the 19 percent for global altruism or the various individual scores in the "other" category. Moreover, ranked individually, the nexus issues have five of the top seven scores. This type of opinion data shows especially well the basic understanding that the distinctions between foreign and domestic policy have become increasingly blurred, making it impossible to solve such problems without *both* domestic and foreign policy components. Personal security, not just national security, is at stake, and in ways that do not stop at national borders.

TABLE 6.3   Foreign-Domestic Policy "Nexus" Issues

	Percentage of Americans considering issue to be a top foreign policy priority
Nexus issues	
Protecting the jobs of American workers	80%
Stopping international drug trafficking	75
Strengthening our domestic economy to improve the U.S. international position	67
Stopping illegal immigration into this country	61
Insuring adequate energy supplies for the U.S.	59
Average	68
	(Continued)

TABLE 6.3 Foreign-Domestic Policy "Nexus" Issues *(Continued)*

	Percentage of Americans considering issue to be a top foreign policy priority
Global interests	
Reducing the threat of international terrorism	71
Preventing the spread of weapons of mass destruction	68
Improving the global environment	56
Strengthening the United Nations	36
Average	58
Global altruism	
Protecting weaker nations against foreign aggression	21
Promoting and defending human rights in other countries	21
Helping improve living standards in developing nations	16
Promoting democracy in other nations	16
Average	19
Other foreign policy problems	
Better managing our trade and economic disputes with Japan	40
Ending the warfare in Bosnia	32
Helping Mexico become more stable politically and economically	16
Ensuring democracy succeeds in Russia and other former Soviet states	14

Source: Times Mirror survey, June 1995, cited in Alvin Richman, "American and Russian Publics View Global Issues as Top Foreign Policy Goals," U.S. Information Agency report, August 2, 1996.

Summary

There is a natural human tendency, especially when feeling beset by problems of the moment, to hark back to the "good old days." In foreign policy circles there is a great deal of such longing for the "golden age of bipartisanship," that period usually delineated as stretching from the Truman Doctrine to the early days of the Vietnam War. But as understandable as such sentiments are, as the basis for serious discussions about the post–Cold War politics of U.S. foreign policy they are highly misleading.

First of all, the basic dynamic between the president and Congress remains as the Constitution set it up, an "invitation to struggle for the privilege of directing American foreign policy,"[32] within a relationship that is less a genuine separation of powers than one of separate institutions sharing powers. This does not mean that consensus is impossible, nor that all interbranch conflict has to have negative policy effects. But it does convey how and why presidential-congressional conflict is "normal" for the American political system.

Second, executive-branch decision-making and foreign policy formulation may strive to be a rational process, but they continue to be characterized more by their own politics. A number of bureaucratic players—diplomatic and military and economic—are involved, bringing their own pulls and pushes of consensus and conflict. The most important one remains the nature and quality of the foreign policy leadership the president provides.

Third, among the broader societal influences, interest groups have proliferated and intensified their pressures. This is evident in a number of ways, including on economic issues as a consequence of the internationalization of the American economy, among a widening range of ethnic and religious identity groups, and with the huge increase in the number and impact of NGOs. These trends are unlikely to slacken in the future.

Fourth, the news media are having an even greater impact on foreign policy politics than in the past. Some of this is due to technological change, some to commercial and industry-based economic factors, and some to political and policy factors. The net effect is that the news media are viewed by policymakers as first-order parts of the policy process, to be taken into account much more often than not in setting foreign policy.

Fifth, public opinion is not easily typed one way or the other, but rather is marked by currents and cross-currents. A "neo" form of isolationism is evident, which has been an important political factor but not as widespread as many fear. A basic commitment to internationalism has been sustained among the American public, although it has been uneven and at times tentative.

All in all, we should not forget that disagreements over issues as important and complex as foreign policy are to be expected. When a nation faces a clear and present danger, as the United States did after Pearl Harbor and arguably as it did in the early days of the Cold War, it is quite logical that its politics stop at the water's edge. But under less extreme conditions, it is altogether logical that there be full, substantive debate. It is precisely because foreign policy issues so often raise such vital concerns and pose choices between such core American values that they take on such political importance. Working those types of debates out is what diplomacy is all about—at home as well as abroad.

Notes

[1] Michael Dobbs and John F. Harris, "French President Chirac Asks Congress to Fund More Peacekeeping in Bosnia," *Washington Post*, June 15, 1995, A34.

[2] John M. Goshko, "In Shift, UN Chief Meets with Helms on Reforms," *Washington Post*, January 24, 1997, A1, A30.

[3] Elaine Sciolino, "Old Foes Carve Plowshares before Emotional Congress," *New York Times*, July 27, 1994, A8.

[4] Elizabeth Drew, *On the Edge: The Clinton Presidency* (New York: Simon and Schuster, 1994), 158, 283.

[5] This section draws on Larry Berman and Bruce W. Jentleson, "Bush and the Post–Cold War World: New Challenges for American Leadership," in *The Bush Presidency: First Appraisals*. ed. Colin Campbell and Bert A. Rockman (Chatham, N.J.: Chatham House, 1991), 93–128.

[6] Cited in Berman and Jentleson, "Bush and the Post–Cold War World," 103.

[7] Elaine Sciolino, "Berger Manages a Welter of Crises in the Post–Cold War White House," *New York Times*, May 18, 1998, A9.

[8] Sciolino, "Berger Manages a Welter of Crises," A9.

[9] U.S. Congress, *Report of the Congressional Committees Investigating the Iran-Contra Affair*, 100th Cong. 1st sess., November 1987, 375.

[10] Tim Weiner, "CIA Study Details Failed Spy System," *New York Times*, June 3, 1998, A1, A8.

[11] Michael Dobbs, "Enthusiasm for Wider Alliance Is Marked by Contradictions," *Washington Post*, July 7, 1995, A1, A24.

[12] Steven Holmes, "With Persuasion and Muscle, Black Caucus Reshapes Haiti Policy," *New York Times*, July 14, 1994, A10.

[13] John J. Stremlau, "Non-governmental Organizations," in Bruce W. Jentleson and Thomas G. Paterson, eds., *Encyclopedia of U.S. Foreign Relations* (New York: Oxford University Press, 1997), Vol. 3, 258. See also Margaret E. Keck and Kathryn Sikkink, *Activists Beyond Borders: Advocacy Networks in International Politics* (Ithaca, N.Y.: Cornell University Press, 1998).

[14] Jessica Mathews, "Power Shift," *Foreign Affairs* 76:1 (January/February 1997), 63.

[15] Stremlau, "Non-governmental Organizations," 259.

[16] Margaret Weir, ed., *The Social Divide: Political Parties and the Future of Activist Government* (Washington, D.C.: Brookings Institution Press, 1998).

[17] From a 1998 study by the Pew Center for the People and the Press, available at http://www.people-press.org.

[18] Nik Gowing, presentation at "Managing Information Chaos," conference held at the United States Institute of Peace, Washington, D.C., March 12, 1999.

[19] W. Lance Bennett and David L. Paletz, eds., *Taken by Storm: The Media, Public Opinion, and U.S. Foreign Policy in the Gulf War* (Chicago: University of Chicago Press, 1994).

[20]Patrick O'Heffernan, "A Mutual Exploitation Model of Media Influence in U.S. Foreign Policy," in Bennett and Paletz, eds., *Taken by Storm,* 232–33.

[21]Shanto Iyengar, *Is Anyone Responsible? How Television Frames Political Issues* (Chicago: University of Chicago Press, 1991).

[22]Michael R. Beschloss, *Presidents, Television and Foreign Crises* (Washington, D.C.: Annenberg Washington Program, 1993).

[23]Jerel A. Rosati, *The Politics of United States Foreign Policy* (New York: Harcourt, Brace, 1993), 307–9; see also Bennett and Paletz, eds., *Taken by Storm.*

[24]John T. Rourke, Ralph G. Carter, and Mark A. Boyer, *Making American Foreign Policy,* 2d ed. (Dubuque, Ia.: Brown and Benchmark, 1996), 362.

[25]"The Propaganda War," *Newsweek,* February 25, 1991, 38.

[26]Rosati, *The Politics of United States Foreign Policy,* 507.

[27]Within a few weeks of the beginning of the Kosovo war, the editors and executives of seven major news organizations wrote a letter of protest to Defense Secretary William S. Cohen urging a loosening of controls on information: "Detailed information about the allied operation is vital to an informed public discussion of this matter of national interest." Felicity Barringer, "Editors Seek More Information on the Air War," *New York Times,* April 16, 1999, A13.

[28]Gilbert S. Grosvenor, "Superpowers Not So Super in Geography," *National Geographic,* December 1989, 816.

[29]Joseph P. Shapiro, "An Epidemic of Fear and Loathing," *U.S. News and World Report,* May 8, 1995, 37–44.

[30]Steven Kull and I. M. Destler, *Misreading the Public: The Myths of a New Isolationism* (Washington, D.C.: Brookings Institution Press, 1999), 9–32.

[31]John E. Rielly, ed., *American Public Opinion and U.S. Foreign Policy, 1999* (Chicago: Chicago Council on Foreign Relations, 1999), 8.

[32]Edward S. Corwin, *The President: Office and Powers, 1787–1957,* 4th rev. ed. (New York: New York University Press, 1957), 171.

CHAPTER **7** *Peace: Building a Post–Cold War World Order?*

Introduction: The Liberal Internationalist Paradigm and the Post–Cold War Era

Initial visions of the peace that was to follow the Cold War were in large part post–Cold War manifestations of Liberal Internationalism. The essence of this paradigm, as laid out in Chapter 1, is an emphasis on the building of a system of international institutions, organizations, and regimes that provide the basis for cooperation among states to resolve tensions, settle disputes, and work together in ways that are mutually beneficial and, above all, to avoid war (see Dynamics of Choice, below).[1] With reference to the relatively peaceful end that the Cold War came to, Liberal Internationalist scholars such as John Ruggie contend that "there seems little doubt that multilateral norms and institutions have helped stabilize [the] international consequences." And as to the

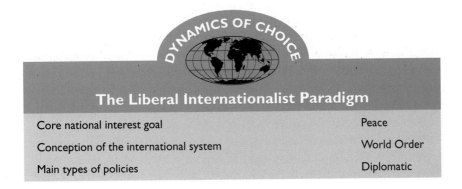

DYNAMICS OF CHOICE

The Liberal Internationalist Paradigm

Core national interest goal	Peace
Conception of the international system	World Order
Main types of policies	Diplomatic

post–Cold War world, "such norms and institutions appear to be playing a significant role in the management of a broad array of regional and global changes in the world system today."[2] We are entering the post–Cold War era, in this view, with international institutions that, while well short of "world government" and not without their weaknesses, are quite strong and have the potential to be made stronger.

Professors Robert Keohane and Lisa Martin lay out in functional terms the theoretical basis for why international institutions develop: "Institutions can provide information, reduce transaction costs, make commitments more credible, establish focal points for coordination and, in general, facilitate the operation of reciprocity."[3] In so doing international institutions help states overcome the difficulties of collective action, which as discussed earlier, can persist even when states have common interests. This is a very rational argument, much more pragmatically grounded than classical Wilsonian idealism. The world envisioned is not one strictly free of tensions and conflicts. But it is one in which the prospects for achieving cooperation are greater than Realism and other power-based theories foresee. Liberal Internationalists also see the constraints on a state's own freedom of action that come with multilateralism as less than the capacity gained to achieve shared objectives and serve national interests in ways that would be less possible unilaterally.

Another key part of the Liberal Internationalist paradigm is the peace-brokering role the United States plays. This, too, both goes back in history (e.g., President Theodore Roosevelt's role in brokering the peace that ended the 1906 Russo-Japanese War, for which he won the Nobel Peace Prize) and has a strong Cold War lineage (e.g., Secretary of State Henry Kissinger's 1970s Middle East "shuttle diplomacy"). And, as we will see, in the Middle East, among Russia and some of the other former Soviet republics, in the former Yugoslavia, and elsewhere, post–Cold War American diplomats have had quite a full peace-brokering agenda.

How much have international institutions achieved, and how much can they achieve, in building and maintaining a post–Cold War peace? How can the United States best play its peace-brokering role? What have been the main tensions between peace and the other national-interest objectives (power, prosperity, principles)? With these central questions in mind, this chapter examines

- the United Nations, and in particular U.N. peace operations;
- regional multilateral organizations in each of the world's major regions;
- nonproliferation regimes against weapons of mass destruction; and
- the U.S. peace-brokering role in general and as seen in three recent cases.

The record that comes through is mixed, showing strengths as well as weaknesses. We want to understand both the strengths and the weaknesses, the reasons for them, and the factors that affect them, so as to better assess the Liberal Internationalist paradigm and to be able to draw pertinent lessons for American foreign policy.

The United Nations

The only way to effectively study the United Nations is to get beyond both the idealized views and the caricatures. Sweeping visions, such as that of Secretary of State Cordell Hull at the U.N.'s founding in 1945, of cooperative and harmonious world government that would alleviate "the need for spheres of influence, alliances, balances of power," freeing the world from its "unhappy past," never were very realistic.[4] On the other hand, right-wing conspiratorial views of the U.N. plotting to take over the United States, including supposed sightings of U.N. "black helicopters" on secret maneuvers in the U.S. hinterland, are pretty far out, too.

Figure 7.1 sketches the main components of the United Nations. As an institution, the U.N. has three unique strengths. First is its *near-global membership*. At the U.N.'s founding in 1945, there were only 51 members of the General Assembly. As of 1999, there are 185. The first major wave of growth came with decolonization, starting in the late 1950s. Another surge came in the 1990s, a manifestation of the many new nations formed after the breakup of the Soviet Union (where one state became seventeen), Yugoslavia (where one became five) and Czechoslovakia (which divided into two states). Its inclusive membership makes the U.N. the one place where representatives of all the world's nation-states regularly meet. As Gareth Evans, former Australian foreign minister, put it, "the world needs a center. . . . The United Nations is the only credible candidate."[5]

Second, resolutions passed by the U.N. Security Council (UNSC) carry a *normative legitimacy* that no other institution can convey. The UNSC holds the international community's ultimate "seals of approval and disapproval."[6] Its resolutions are particularly important in justifying the use of military force, both for major wars (e.g., the Korean War, the Persian Gulf War) and for peace operations (e.g., Somalia, Haiti, Bosnia).

Third is the *scope of U.N. programs, geared to the full global agenda*, including not only peace, but also economic development, the environment, human

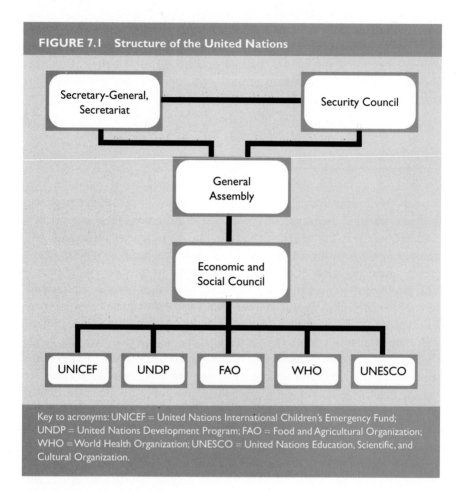

FIGURE 7.1   Structure of the United Nations

Key to acronyms: UNICEF = United Nations International Children's Emergency Fund; UNDP = United Nations Development Program; FAO = Food and Agricultural Organization; WHO = World Health Organization; UNESCO = United Nations Education, Scientific, and Cultural Organization.

rights, and public health. Although issues like the crises in Somalia and Bosnia get the most publicity, arguably the most meaningful work the U.N. does is in seeking, as stated in its Charter, "to employ international machinery for the promotion of the economic and social advancement of all peoples." It does this through specialized agencies and programs, some of which are shown in Figure 7.1.

For U.S. foreign policy, debates regarding the U.N. focus on three areas: the peace-power tension between the ways in which the U.N. can enhance American foreign policy and the ways in which it can limit U.S. prerogatives, questions about the U.N.'s institutional and programmatic effectiveness, and domestic political controversies evoked by the U.N.

Peace and Power: Policy Enhancement vs. Prerogative Encroachment

It is one thing to say that both the United States and the United Nations seek peace. The more difficult question from a U.S. perspective is whether their efforts toward peace are complementary and reinforcing, or whether they are in tension and pose tradeoffs. To what extent does working with and through the U.N. enhance the U.S. capacity to achieve peace; to what extent does it encroach on the prerogatives of American power? Some argue that this is an arrogant question for Americans even to pose. Others see it as essential and justified by both the interests and the responsibilities of U.S. leadership.

The 1990–91 Persian Gulf War against Iraq was a strong example of how working with and through the U.N. can further U.S. policy. Soon after Saddam Hussein's invasion of Kuwait in 1990 the UNSC imposed economic sanctions, condemned Saddam diplomatically, and took other measures to show that it was not just the United States but the broad international community that opposed him. As the crisis wore on and Saddam remained intransigent, the threat to use military force, initially made by President George Bush, was affirmed and enhanced by a UNSC resolution authorizing "all necessary means" to get Saddam out of Kuwait, including the use of military force. So when Operation Desert Storm was launched in early 1991, it had the benefits of both U.N. legitimization and of the burden-sharing of twenty-seven coalition nations sending troops or providing other assistance. Yet both the military command for fighting the war and the diplomatic initiative for negotiating the terms of the peace were left to the United States.

This positive experience in the Persian Gulf War, along with the general aura of U.S. triumph at the end of the Cold War, led to a real bullishness about the U.N. In January 1992 President Bush joined other world leaders at the first-ever summit of the heads of state of UNSC members. The summit called for a major new study proposing "ways of strengthening . . . the capacity of the United Nations" for the new era.[7] The ensuing report by U.N. Secretary-General Boutros Boutros-Ghali, appropriately titled *An Agenda for Peace*, received a great deal of attention from the Bush administration and then from the newly installed Clinton administration. Bill Clinton, his U.N. ambassador Madeleine Albright, and other figures in this new administration went even further than their predecessors in stressing the enhancing effects and other benefits of an expanded role for the U.N.

Then, however, came the crises in Somalia and Bosnia, and a sharp disillusionment with the U.N. within the United States. Among the issues raised by the failures of U.N. peacekeeping missions in these countries was the prerogative-encroachment one. For in these cases, although some benefits did come with UNSC sponsorship, major problems arose over constraints on the definition of the mission, the structure of military command, and other issues. In Bosnia, for example, the "dual-key" arrangement, by which prior to the December 1995 Dayton Accords the United States and NATO could not take military action without prior U.N. approval, undermined the credibility of the military threat and complicated military operations. The whole setup was "insane," Assistant Secretary of State Richard Holbrooke lamented in July 1995 when U.N. authorities wouldn't let NATO retaliate even when U.N. peacekeepers were taken hostage.[8]

The recurring crises with Iraq after the Gulf War also raised dissatisfaction with the U.N. role. Iraq had been kept under severe restrictions after the war had ended. A series of UNSC resolutions kept economic sanctions on Iraq, created the United Nations Special Commission on Iraq (UNSCOM), which had unprecedented authority for on-site inspection and other measures to force Iraq to eliminate its weapons of mass destruction, and took other steps to isolate and contain Iraq. The United States could have done little if any of this on its own. The U.N.'s legitimacy was essential. But as Iraq challenged and defied the U.N. resolutions, the need to consult with the U.N. was one of the constraints on the U.S. capacity to take military action or exert its power in other ways. In February 1998 U.N. Secretary-General Kofi Annan mediated an agreement with Saddam Hussein that defused a looming crisis, but the agreement fell apart later in the year. As tensions mounted again in November 1998, and American bombers were within minutes (literally) of attacking Iraq, Saddam headed them off with a letter to Secretary-General Annan yet again pledging to cooperate. While many felt President Clinton still should have attacked—including officials within his own administration—a primary reason that he did not was concern about a potential backlash at the U.N. When the United States finally did launch air strikes the next month, Secretary-General Annan was very critical, as were the French and Russian ambassadors to the U.N. We thus see within the same case both the policy-enhancing and prerogative-encroaching dynamics of working with the U.N.

EXPANSION OF THE SECURITY COUNCIL   An ongoing issue that also reveals this enhancement-encroachment tension is the debate over whether the UNSC should expand its number of permanent members.[9] The structure of the UNSC reflects the global balance of power as it was left by World War II: there are five permanent members—the United States, Russia (formerly the

Soviet Union), Britain, France, and China (the Republic of China on Taiwan until 1971, and since then the People's Republic)—who in addition to their permanent seats also have the power to veto any UNSC action; and there are ten other UNSC seats, which rotate among countries for three-year terms and which do not carry the veto.

But for some, this World War II–era structure now seems outdated. Tremendous changes have taken place in the international system during the intervening decades. With this in mind, calls have been made for granting other countries permanent membership on the UNSC. What about Japan and Germany, some ask: given their great importance in global affairs and their rank as the second- and third-largest contributors to the U.N. budget, shouldn't they now have permanent seats? Should it be with or without the veto? And what about major Third World countries like Brazil, India, Nigeria, and South Africa, from regions that now only get rotating seats? Shouldn't their interests be represented by permanent seats?

The Clinton administration has publicly supported permanent membership for Japan and Germany, but has remained noncommittal as to whether they should have the veto. This reflects U.S. willingness to more broadly share the responsibilities for peace, but a reluctance to impinge on the significant power lever of the veto. As to Third World states, the U.S. position is carefully phrased in diplomatic language: "The U.S. sees further scope for a modest expansion of the Security Council to enable fair representation of all the world's regions," with the added qualifier of "a firm requirement that any changes should not reduce the Council's effectiveness, and that the prerogatives of the current permanent members should be maintained."[10] One of India's motivations for its May 1998 nuclear-weapons test was to express its dissatisfaction with its lack of progress toward a permanent UNSC seat despite being the second most populous country in the world and one of the most ancient civilizations. The same five nations that are the world's nuclear-weapons powers also are the UNSC permanent members. Now India, its leaders asserted, had nuclear weapons, and so now it also should receive the same status. Others contended that India's nuclear-weapons tests, carried out in defiance of the will of the international community, should instead weaken its claim to a UNSC permanent seat, because dangerous precedents would be set by condoning this path to permanent membership.

There had been some pressure to deal with the Security Council expansion issue in time for the U.N.'s fiftieth anniversary in 1995. That didn't happen, and so the issue continues to brew, amid American ambivalence about the potential value of a larger and more representative Security Council on the one hand, and the concerns about encroachments on U.S. prerogatives on the other.

CREATION OF THE INTERNATIONAL CRIMINAL COURT   Following World War II, special international war-crimes tribunals were created to prosecute the Nazis (the Nuremberg trials) and Japanese military leaders. The U.N. General Assembly had considered creating a permanent international criminal court at various times since then, but no such action was taken. Nuremberg-like temporary war-crimes tribunals were set up in the 1990s to deal with atrocities committed during civil wars and ethnic conflicts in the former Yugoslavia and Rwanda. In their wake, proposals to create a permanent International Criminal Court (ICC) gained increasing support. The purpose of a permanent court is both to avoid the delays and other problems of having to create a new special tribunal each time a new set of atrocities occurred and to try to deter such occurrences in the first place.

The ICC was approved at a U.N. conference held in Rome in mid-1998. Very few countries voted against it, but the United States was one of them. Originally the Clinton administration had supported the idea of an ICC, in large part because a permanent international court would potentially enhance U.S. foreign policy in cases against aggressors, gross violators of human rights, and rogue states. But the treaty that was proposed at the 1998 Rome conference was seen as encroaching on U.S. prerogatives. One issue was the relationship between the ICC and the Security Council. The United States wanted the UNSC to have authority over the ICC, so that with its veto the United States could block ICC actions that it opposed. Another was the concern that U.S. soldiers might be subjected arbitrarily, unfairly, and in politically explosive ways to the ICC's jurisdiction. The United States argued that subjecting Americans to an international trial would violate the U.S. Constitution and that, as one opponent of the ICC put it, "we're the ones who respond when the world dials 911, and if you want us to keep responding you should accommodate our views."[11] Most other nations found the U.S. positions unjustified, and the votes on these and other issues went overwhelmingly against the United States, on the order of 75 to 21 and 115 to 17. The conference concluded with a treaty to create the ICC, but the United States has refused to sign.

The ICC is thus another issue that both demonstrates the tensions between policy enhancement and prerogative encroachment in the U.S. relationship with the U.N. and in its own substantive terms remains a major foreign policy controversy.

How Effective Is the U.N.?

A second debate regarding the U.N. deals with concerns about its effectiveness. How well do its programs and policies work? When it declares goals and objectives, how capable is it of achieving them? We consider these questions through three main areas of U.N. programs and policies.

ECONOMIC AND SOCIAL PROGRAMS   As noted earlier and seen in Figure 7.1, the U.N. has a wide array of economic and social programs. Although other U.N. departments and actions get more publicity, these programs are in many ways the most meaningful work the U.N. does. UNICEF (the United Nations International Children's Emergency Fund), for example, is working to ensure that 90 percent of the world's children are immunized against diseases, to eradicate polio, to prohibit genital mutilation, to reduce child deaths from diarrhea by 50 percent, and to eliminate iodine-deficiency disorders. In late 1998 UNICEF, along with two other U.N. agencies, the World Health Organization (WHO) and the U.N. Development Program (UNDP), plus the World Bank, launched a major new program to eradicate malaria. One child dies every 30 seconds, and 3,000 children under five die every day, from malaria.

Although other positive examples could be cited, not all U.N. socioeconomic development programs win such praise. For example, until recent reforms were initiated at the WHO and former Norwegian prime minister Gro Harlem Brundtland was made its new director-general, this "once-proud agency" had achieved "notoriety for bad management, a marked deterioration of its programs, and a measure of cronyism and favoritism verging on the corrupt."[12] Quite a few other U.N. programs have been hampered by excessive bureaucracy, corruption, and similar problems. Some reform has begun, and it clearly is needed. "While the United Nations is not the inefficient, incompetent body unfair critics depict it to be," wrote Yale professors Paul Kennedy and Bruce Russett, "it clearly requires a serious overhaul to prepare it for the years ahead."[13]

Another activity that has drawn both praise and criticism has been the numerous global conferences convened by the U.N. in the 1990s. Each was intended to focus attention and provide a launching pad for concerted action in an area of global concern: for example, the global environment was the topic of the 1992 Rio Earth Summit, population planning the focus of the 1994 Cairo conference, and women's rights the topic of the 1996 Beijing conference. But these conferences have drawn mixed reviews, getting credit for some achievements and for bringing important issues to the world's attention, but also criticized for being quite expensive, in some aspects extravagant, and having diverted the already limited funds available away from U.N. programs and policies.

A study by the Carnegie Commission on Preventing Deadly Conflict raised the question, "How expensive is the U.N.?" The commission's report provides some interesting comparisons. For example, the U.N.'s core budget is only $1.3 billion a year, which is almost $1 billion less than the annual budget for the city of Tokyo's fire department. Americans spend about $5.3 billion a year on spectator sports; the U.N. spends $4.6 billion on economic and social development. The entire U.N. system employs only about one-third as many people as McDonald's and less than Disneyland, Disney World and Euro Disney combined![14] These comparisons are not intended to justify waste or other problem areas, but they do help check common assumptions about the U.N.'s size and resources.

HUMAN RIGHTS AND THE NORMATIVE TENSION BETWEEN UNIVERSALITY AND SOVEREIGNTY   One of the core political normative tensions for the U.N. is between *state sovereignty* and *universality.* The state sovereignty norm stresses the rights and interests of the individual nation-states that constitute the membership of the U.N. It is based on the principle that, as Professors Robert Art and Robert Jervis write, "no agency exists above the individual states with authority and power to make laws and settle disputes."[15] As stated in Article 2, Section 7 of the U.N. Charter, "nothing contained in the present Charter shall authorize the United Nations to intervene in matters which are essentially within the domestic jurisdiction of any state."

Yet other portions of the U.N. Charter manifest norms of the universality of the rights of individuals, irrespective of the state in which they reside or whether threats to those rights come from foreign forces or their own governments. Article 3 affirms that "everyone has the right to life, liberty and the security of person"; Article 55 commits the U.N. to "promote . . . universal respect for, and observance of, human rights and fundamental freedoms"; Article 56 pledges all members "to take joint and separate action toward this end." In addition, documents such as the Universal Declaration of Human Rights, adopted by the U.N. General Assembly in 1948 by a unanimous vote, provide a sweeping affirmation of the "equal and inalienable rights of all members of the human family."

Sovereignty not only confers rights on states, it also imposes responsibilities.[16] Concerns that abridgements of state sovereignty could become guises for power politics are understandable. But in this age of ethnic cleansings, state authority cannot be totally unconditional or absolutely normatively superior to the fundamental human rights of people.

This inherent normative tension between state sovereignty and the universality of human rights complicates the U.N.'s role. The U.N. Commission on Human Rights reflects this tension; its operation has been characterized by a leading scholar as subject to "substantial political constraints" and only "occasionally" effective.[17] States that violate the human rights of their peoples often are able to block or limit U.N. action against them, assisted by other repressive states that, while not involved in the case at hand, are concerned about precedents that might be used against them in the future. A similar issue came up with the ICC: whether permission of the state where the crimes are committed would be required in order for the ICC to have jurisdiction. Despite strong criticisms that this requirement would severely limit the ICC's effectiveness, letting brutal leaders kill their own people yet protect themselves from international judgment, member states were unwilling to opt for universality, and the state sovereignty constraint prevailed. But as U.N. Secretary-General Annan reminds us, "the [U.N.] Charter was issued in the name of 'the peoples', not the governments of the U.N. . . . . It was never meant as a license for governments to trample on human rights and human dignity. . . . The fact that a conflict is 'internal' does not give the parties any right to disregard the most basic rules of human conduct. . . . While paying full respect to state sovereignty, [we] assert the overriding right of people in desperate situations to receive help, and the right of international bodies to provide it."[18]

U.N. MILITARY PEACE OPERATIONS   Table 7.1 lists the 50 U.N. peace operations since 1948. Whereas only 13 of these missions were authorized prior to 1988, since 1988 another 37 new missions have been undertaken. The number of U.N. troops shot up from 9,570 in 1988 to 73,393 in 1994; U.N. peacekeeping budgets went from $230 million to $3.6 billion.

Amid the controversies over its failures in Somalia and Bosnia in the early 1990s, the U.N.'s past peacekeeping successes often get forgotten. Indeed, their record was so strong that the U.N. Peacekeeping Forces received the 1988 Nobel Peace Prize. These forces "represent the manifest will of the community of nations," the Nobel Committee's citation read. Through and because of them, the U.N. "has come to play a more central role in world affairs and has been invested with increasing trust."[19]

The recent peacekeeping record, though, has drawn more condemnations than commendations. Part of the U.N.'s problem has been sheer overload. The huge number of operations going on simultaneously made for an enormous agenda, especially for an institution with so little of the military infrastructure of command and control, communications, intelligence, training, and logistics. Furthermore, the structure of decision-making authority often proved

TABLE 7.1 United Nations Peacekeeping Operations, 1948–99

Year(s)	Mission	Location
1948–	U.N. Truce Supervision Organization (UNTSO)	Palestine
1949–	U.N. Military Observer Group in India and Pakistan (UNMOGIP)	India/Pakistan
1956–67	U.N. Emergency Force (UNEF I)	Egypt/Israel
1958	U.N. Observation Group in Lebanon (UNOGIL)	Lebanon
1960–64	U.N. Operations in the Congo (ONUC)	Congo (Democratic Republic)
1962–63	U.N. Security Force in West New Guinea (UNSF)	West New Guinea
1963–64	U.N. Yemen Observation Mission (UNYOM)	Yemen
1964–	U.N. Peacekeeping Force in Cyprus (UNFICYP)	Cyprus
1965–66	U.N. India-Pakistan Observer Mission (UNIPOM)	India/Pakistan
1965–66	Mission of the Representative of the Secretary-General in the Dominican Republic (DOMREP)	Dominican Republic
1973–79	U.N. Emergency Force (UNEF II)	Egypt/Israel
1974–	U.N. Disengagement Observer Force (UNDOF)	Israel/Syria
1978–	U.N. Interim Force in Lebanon (UNIFIL)	Lebanon
1988–90	U.N. Good Offices Mission in Afghanistan and Pakistan (UNGOMAP)	Afghanistan/Pakistan
1988–91	U.N. Iran-Iraq Military Observer Group (UNIMOG)	Iran/Iraq
1989–90	U.N. Transition Assistance Group (UNTAG)	Namibia
1989–91	U.N. Angola Verification Mission (UNAVEM I)	Angola
1989–92	U.N. Observer Group in Central America (ONUCA)	Central America
1991–92	U.N. Advance Mission in Cambodia (UNAMIC)	Cambodia
1991–95	U.N. Angola Verification Mission (UNAVEM II)	Angola
1991–95	U.N. Observer Mission in El Salvador (ONUSAL)	El Salvador
1991–	U.N. Mission for the Referendum in Western Sahara (MINURSO)	Western Sahara
1991–	U.N. Iraq-Kuwait Observation Mission (UNIKOM)	Iraq/Kuwait
1992–93	U.N. Transitional Authority in Cambodia (UNTAC)	Cambodia

Date	Mission	Location
1992–93	U.N. Operation in Somalia (UNOSOM I)	Somalia
1992–94	U.N. Operation in Mozambique (ONUMOZ)	Mozambique
1992–95	U.N. Protection Force (UNPROFOR)	Former Yugoslavia
1993–94	U.N. Observer Mission Uganda-Rwanda (UNOMUR)	Rwanda/Uganda
1993–95	U.N. Operation in Somalia (UNOSOM II)	Somalia
1993–96	U.N. Mission in Haiti (UNMIH)	Haiti
1993–96	U.N. Assistance Mission in Rwanda (UNAMIR)	Rwanda
1993–97	U.N. Observer Mission in Liberia (UNOMIL)	Liberia
1993–	U.N. Observer Mission in Georgia (UNOMIG)	Georgia
1994	U.N. Aouzou Strip Observer Group (UNASOG)	Chad/Libya
1994–2000	U.N. Mission of Observers in Tajikistan (UNMOT)	Tajikistan
1995–97	U.N. Angola Verification Mission (UNAVEM III)	Angola
1995–96	U.N. Confidence Restoration Operations in Croatia (UNCRO)	Croatia
1995–99	U.N. Preventive Deployment Force (UNPREDEP)	Macedonia
1995–	U.N. Mission in Bosnia & Herzegovina (UNMIBH)	Bosnia & Herzegovina
1996–97	U.N. Support Mission in Haiti (UNSMIH)	Haiti
1996–98	U.N. Transitional Administration for Eastern Slavonia, Baranja, and Western Sirmium (UNTAES)	Eastern Slavonia
1996–	U.N. Mission of Observers in the Prevlaka (UNMOP)	Croatia
1997	U.N. Transition Mission in Haiti (UNTMIH)	Haiti
1997	U.N. Verification Mission in Guatemala (MINUGUA)	Guatemala
1997–99	U.N. Observer Mission in Angola (MONUA)	Angola
1997–2000	U.N. Civilian Police Mission in Haiti (MIPONUH)	Haiti
1998–2000	U.N. Mission in the Central African Republic (MINURCA)	Central African Republic
1998–99	U.N. Mission of Observers in Sierra Leone (UNOMSIL)	Sierra Leone
1998	U.N. Civilian Police Support Group (UNPSG)	Croatia
1999–	U.N. Interim Administration Mission in Kosovo (UNMIK)	Kosovo
1999–	U.N. Transitional Administration in East Timor (UNTAET)	East Timor
1999–	U.N. Mission in the Democratic Republic of the Congo (MONUC)	Congo
1999–	U.N. Mission in Sierra Leone (UNAMSIL)	Sierra Leone

Source: GAO/NSIAD 97-34, Appendix II, pp. 31–4, and "Fifty Years of United Nations Peacekeeping," on United Nations Web site· http://www.un.org/Depts/DPKO/pk50.htm, accessed October 4, 1999.

too slow and indecisive to either carry out complex and speedy military operations or convey credibility to an aggressor. This was the point Assistant Secretary of State Holbrooke was making in his lambasting of the dual-key U.N./NATO command authority in Bosnia.

Additionally, all of these peace operations involved soldiers assembled on a temporary basis from the national armies of U.N. member countries. The original idea that the U.N. would have its own standing army of troops and officers assigned to it on an ongoing basis was never realized, as was discussed in Chapter 4. Each time there is need for a U.N. peace operation, it thus is necessary to assemble a new force. This adds to the problems of timely response, unit cohesiveness, and effective training.

The more fundamental problem, however, has been the difference in missions between peace*keeping* and peace *enforcing*. Most of the "first generation" U.N. successes had been on peacekeeping missions. In these situations the U.N. forces are brought in after the parties have agreed to the terms of peace, and with the consent of those parties, to ensure and facilitate the keeping of that peace. The peacekeepers' rules of engagement are neutral and impartial: to use force only for their own self-defense, and not to interfere in the internal affairs of the parties. But in Somalia and Bosnia the conflicts were still raging when U.N. troops landed. There was no peace to be kept; it had to be imposed and enforced. To the extent that the parties had reached any agreements, they were but partial ones—holding actions, gambits, even outright deceptions. In such situations the U.N.'s limited rules of engagement do not work very well; neutrality and impartiality can let aggressors off the hook. Even a Nobel laureate method will not succeed when applied to purposes as fundamentally different as is peacekeeping from peace-making and peace enforcing. By late 1995 even U.N. Secretary-General Boutros-Ghali was acknowledging that "[peace] enforcement is beyond the power of the U.N. . . . In the future, if peace enforcement is needed it should be conducted by countries with the will to do it."[*][20]

The U.N. and U.S. Domestic Politics

GENERAL PATTERNS   Figure 7.2 shows how strong U.S. public support was for the U.N. from the 1950s through the 1960s. This is consistent with our analysis so far in this chapter. In those years the U.N.'s role was viewed by the

---

*We return to this issue in Chapter 8 as a question also for the United States and its post–Cold War use of military force.

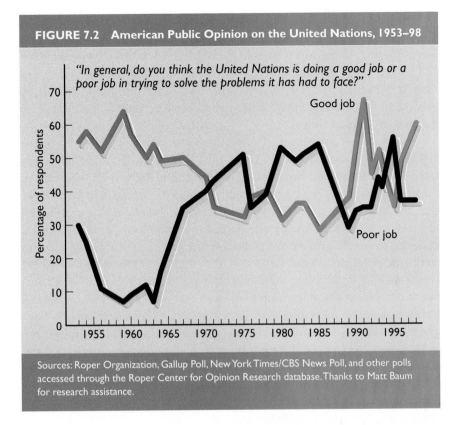

FIGURE 7.2   American Public Opinion on the United Nations, 1953–98

"In general, do you think the United Nations is doing a good job or a poor job in trying to solve the problems it has had to face?"

Good job

Poor job

Percentage of respondents

Sources: Roper Organization, Gallup Poll, New York Times/CBS News Poll, and other polls accessed through the Roper Center for Opinion Research database. Thanks to Matt Baum for research assistance.

American public as enhancing U.S. foreign policy. The U.N. generally supported U.S. positions during the Cold War. The strongest example of this support was in the Korean War, when the very same day that North Korea invaded South Korea, the UNSC ordered it to cease and withdraw, and then made the defense of South Korea a U.N. operation led by the United States and with troops from other U.N. member countries.* On many other issues as well, a pro-U.S. tilt generally characterized U.N. decisions. Furthermore, people felt that the U.N. largely was effective in achieving its programmatic goals.

---

*The Soviet Union was absent from the vote due to its boycott of the UNSC, stemming from the refusal of the Security Council to take China's seat away from the government of Chiang Kai-shek and give it to the People's Republic of China following the communist triumph in the Chinese civil war the previous October. Chiang's government had fled mainland China and had relocated on the island of Formosa (Taiwan).

The "good job"/"poor job" lines first cross in Figure 7.2 in the early 1970s. The "poor job" view dominated public opinion through the mid-1980s. This was the period during which votes in the General Assembly often were critical of U.S. foreign policy and criticisms of U.N. inefficiencies and corruption mounted. The late 1980s–early 1990s turnaround was prompted initially by peacekeeping successes in Afghanistan and elsewhere, and then especially by the 1990–91 Persian Gulf War.

The "poor job" gap reopened in reaction to Somalia and Bosnia. In August 1995 only 35 percent of Americans rated the U.N. positively, while 56 percent rated it negatively. Polls began to even out again in 1996 as the situation in Bosnia improved and the U.N. got credit at least for agreeing to let NATO take charge. Other factors, such as internal reforms and the election of a new secretary-general, Kofi Annan, also helped the "good job" rating recapture a majority. Indeed, no doubt to the dismay of many of the U.N.'s most ardent congressional critics, a separate 1995 poll by the Times-Mirror Center for the People and the Press asking about favorable and unfavorable views of a number of different political institutions showed that 67 percent of the American public gave a favorable rating to the U.N. but only 53 percent to the U.S. Congress. And in a Gallup poll a few months later asking about who has "too much power," 63 percent of Americans said the Internal Revenue Service and 62 percent the advertising industry, but only 21 percent the U.N.[21] Still, part of the political problem is that those who are anti-U.N.—the segment of the public we characterized as "antagonistics" in Chapter 6—tend to be the most vocal and active, at times violently so.

U.S. DEBT TO THE U.N.   The most politically contentious domestic debate about the U.N. has been over repayment of the back dues the United States owes to the U.N. Although the precise amounts are disputed, most estimates put the U.S. arrears at over $1.5 billion by early 1999. The "Richest Deadbeat" was how a *New York Times* headline described the situation. The United States was in a group of countries whose debts were so high that they risked losing their votes in the General Assembly—countries such as Bosnia, Cambodia, Congo, Iraq, Somalia, Togo, and Yugoslavia. The policy effects of this debt were quite real. For example, when Yugoslav Serb attacks on ethnic Albanians in Kosovo began intensifying in mid-1998, the U.N. reaffirmed its arms embargo against Yugoslavia. But the U.N.'s lack of funds made enforcement of the embargo very difficult.

Congress, not the president, has the final say on repaying the U.S. debt, because Congress has the power of the purse. Thus Senator Jesse Helms and other congressional critics have been well positioned on this issue. Their points to some extent are serious and substantive, raising concerns about the need for U.N. reform. Yet the issue has also been highly political. In 1998, for example, conservatives in Congress attached an anti-abortion clause to the U.N. funding bill, specifying that funds from the United States could not be used for any U.N. program that facilitated or provided abortions. Even American allies were outraged. "It's preposterous," the Dutch ambassador to the U.N. stated, that the United States should try to set conditions for what it is obligated to pay under international law. "It's as simple as that."[22]

U.S. TROOPS UNDER FOREIGN COMMAND   The question of whether U.S. troops should be placed under non-American command was the hottest issue raised by the Somalia and Bosnia experiences. The dominant perception in the United States of the Somalia debacle was that it was caused principally by the failures of U.N. commanders, and American soldiers paid the price with their lives. In fact, the decision to launch the commando operations that resulted in American deaths was made without the knowledge of the U.N. force commander. The political pressure after U.S. soldiers were killed was so high that the Clinton administration retreated, not only withdrawing U.S. troops from Somalia but also changing its policy on whether U.S. troops would serve under foreign command. Just a few months earlier the administration had been reported to be leaning toward putting American troops under U.N. commanders "on a regular basis." But in the wake of Somalia it issued a major policy statement that "the United States does not support a standing UN army nor will it earmark specific military units for participation in UN operations."[23]

While there is plenty to debate on this issue, it is not the case that U.S. troops have never served under foreign command. U.S. troops served under foreign command in World Wars I and II, and in some successful Cold War–era U.N. peacekeeping operations. It still can be argued that these were mostly exceptional and high-stakes situations, with more vital U.S. interests at stake than in most post–Cold War situations. But the historical record at least should be clear.

The role of the U.N. in the post–Cold War era thus raises a number of important and continuing issues for U.S. foreign policy. The useful debates, however, are not about whether the United States should withdraw from, or turn its foreign policy over to, the U.N. Rather they are about how strong an institution the U.N. is and can be for building and maintaining peace.

Regional Multilateral Organizations

Regional multilateral organizations (RMOs) have become increasingly important parts of the structure of peace in the post–Cold War era. There are three reasons why this has been generally true from region to region.

First, *the sources of instability now tend to be more regionally rooted than globally transmitted.* During the Cold War much of the world's instability was connected to the global geopolitics of bipolarity and the U.S.-Soviet rivalry. In the post–Cold war era, instability tends much more to be rooted in regional issues and rivalries.

Second, *there is increasing recognition of the interconnection between regional security and domestic instability.* Ethnic conflicts, civil wars, and other conflicts that start out as internal problems can draw in regional states, spread across borders, set off massive refugee migrations, and create other general "contagion" effects that destabilize other parts of the region. RMOs thus have been making broader claims of legitimacy for intervening in domestic affairs in the name of regional security.

Third, given these regional roots and effects, it follows that *direct cooperation among the regional actors themselves is more crucial to peace and stability* than in the past, when the key actors usually were Washington and Moscow. On the one hand this means that countries and regions must confront long histories of rivalry and even hatred. On the other hand there can be common cultural ties, shared economic interests, and other relationships on which to try to build regional security institutions.

It is because the United States is in the unique position of being a "member" in one way or another of almost every world region that strengthening regional security is a key objective of post–Cold War U.S. foreign policy. This objective has been the highest U.S. priority in Europe, where the United States has membership in NATO, its principal security alliance (discussed in Chapter 8) as well as in the Organization for Security and Cooperation in Europe. As a Western Hemisphere nation, the United States is a member of the Organization of American States. As a Pacific nation, it is a member of Asia-Pacific Economic Cooperation and the Regional Forum of the Association of Southeast Asian Nations. The United States has been "sponsor" of efforts to create new regional multilateral institutions in the Middle East. Only in Africa, with the Organization for African Unity, has the U.S. role been less central, although even there it has been an important one.

Europe: The Organization for Security and Cooperation in Europe

The Conference on Security and Cooperation in Europe (CSCE) was established in 1975 during détente as the only European institution with full East-West regional membership. Its principal impact was through the Helsinki Final Act, the main parts of which established norms and principles for humans rights within and peaceful resolution of conflicts among member countries. For the most part the CSCE was just that, a "conference," which met from time to time as a forum for consultation and discussion. But when the East European revolutions came in 1989, it became clear in retrospect how important the CSCE had been in providing "a political platform and moral support for the champions of democratic change," such as Solidarity in Poland and Charter 77 in Czechoslovakia, that brought communism down.[24]

The name change made in 1994 to the *Organization* on Security and Cooperation in Europe (OSCE) was intended to convey greater institutionalization. A primary motivation for institutionalizing has been the increased recognition of the link between regional security and the peaceful resolution of ethnic and other internal conflicts. These linkages were a major theme of the 1990 Charter of Paris for a New Europe, which established the first permanent organizations under the CSCE. "We are convinced," one provision of the charter reads, "that in order to strengthen peace and security among our states, the advancement of democracy and respect for and effective exercise of human rights are indispensable." The charter thus mandated "new forms of cooperation . . . in particular a range of methods for the peaceful settlement of disputes, including mandatory third-party involvement."

On this basis the OSCE has been taking on a greater role in "preventive diplomacy" and other political and diplomatic efforts at conflict management and conflict resolution. It does so through such structures as its Office for Democratic Institutions and Human Rights, which monitors elections, provides assistance in the drafting of constitutions and other laws, and promotes the development of civil society; the High Commissioner on National Minorities, which seeks to protect the rights of ethnic minorities, in part through the deployment of human rights observers; and third-party mediators and other diplomatic strategies for conflict resolution.

Its record thus far of preventing tensions and conflicts from leading to mass violence and ethnic war is a mixed one. One major study of the OSCE concludes that it can have the most success "in relatively low-level situations."[25]

Consistent with this pattern, its 1990s successes include cases in which tensions had not yet crossed the Rubicon of widespread violence, and the OSCE gets a substantial share of the credit for keeping them relatively peaceful: in Estonia and Latvia, where explosive issues have arisen over withdrawal of Russian troops and human rights protections for Russian ethnic minorities; tensions between Hungary and Romania over treatment of their respective ethnic minorities; and in Macedonia, like Bosnia a former Yugoslav republic with deep ethnic splits, but which has managed to avoid ethnic war. But in cases like Bosnia, Croatia, Kosovo, and Nagorno-Karabakh (an enclave with a large Armenian population that is geographically separate from but ruled by Azerbaijan that was mired in ethnic war from 1991–94, and has had a shaky truce since then), the conflicts ran too deep and had degenerated too much for the limited tools of the OSCE to accomplish much.[26]

The Western Hemisphere: The Organization of American States

During the Cold War virtually all of U.S. policy toward Latin America, including creation of the Organization of American States (OAS) in 1948, was geared to the global containment strategy. The OAS largely was seen as being under the U.S. thumb. It dutifully supported the U.S. anticommunist interventions in Guatemala in 1954 and the Dominican Republic in 1965, and the expulsion of Cuba from its membership following Castro's revolution. With so many of its members being military dictatorships, the OAS could be seen as pro-democracy only if one accepted the "ABC" (anything but communist) definition of democracy.

With the Cold War over and anticommunism no longer the Western Hemisphere's organizing principle, and with all its member states now democracies (albeit some quite limited ones), in June 1991 the OAS adopted a resolution on its "Commitment to Democracy and the Renewal of the Inter-American System." Called the Santiago Resolution (the meeting took place in Santiago, Chile), this resolution was the OAS's version of the OSCE's Charter of Paris. While including qualifiers about "due respect for the principle of nonintervention," it legitimized as grounds for OAS intervention "the sudden or irregular interruption of the democratic political institutional process, or of the legitimate exercise of power by the democratically elected government in any of the Organization's member states." The measures to be considered included military intervention.

However, when the first test came a few months later in Haiti, the OAS took only limited action. It authorized some trade sanctions, but not even comprehensive ones. Memories of past U.S. interventions in Latin America were still too strong for it to authorize military force even against the brutal military regime in Haiti. (The U.N. eventually did.) The OAS did somewhat better in one of its next tests, which came in 1996 when the Paraguayan military attempted a coup. The OAS joined the United States in threatening diplomatic and economic sanctions, and it did so immediately and comprehensively. The coup was put down in an excellent example of how regional cooperation can be quite effective.

It is doubtful that the OAS will ever be as robust a regional security institution as the OSCE, given the U.S. dominance in the region. But for it, too, the challenge and the open questions are whether it can play a more significant regional security role than it has in the past.

Africa: The Organization for African Unity

The Organization for African Unity (OAU) was established in 1963 as part of the struggle for decolonization. It originally had thirty-two members. Today there are fifty-three. Here, too, the threats are now far more from within than outside the region. Africa has paid a dear price at the hands first of European colonial powers and then of the Cold War superpowers. Although the legacies of both eras still are significant factors, the driving forces in so many of Africa's wars and so much of its instability are its own ethnic conflicts, anti-democratic and corrupt leaders, and interstate rivalries.

Given this colonial past, the OAU has been especially sensitive to infringements on strict conceptions of state sovereignty. Yet this sensitivity has often been manipulated to protect dictatorial and corrupt leaders, thus working against the interests of Africa's peoples. In 1993, amid the ravages of wars in Somalia, Liberia, the Sudan, and other African countries, the OAU decided that it needed to take additional steps if it was to meet the demands of this new era to play a leadership role in helping forge peace and stability in Africa. The undeniability of the regional security consequences of conflicts traditionally considered domestic had reached the point that African leaders began to reassess traditional norms prohibiting external intervention for the purpose of preventing or managing domestic conflicts.[27]

The OAU thus established its "Mechanism for Conflict Prevention and Resolution," geared to multilateral interventions, both diplomatic and military. As with the OAS's Santiago document, this resolution still had significant qualifiers about "respect of sovereignty" and functioning "on the basis of con-sent and the cooperation of the parties to a conflict." Nevertheless it repre-sented a relative strengthening compared to the OAU's past. In addition, the United States has made some effort to assist the OAU and its members in strengthening their regional security capacity, through such programs as pro-viding U.S. military training and funding for African multilateral peace oper-ations. There remains a long way to go, though, before the OAU can be considered a strong regional organization.

Asia: The Association of Southeast Asian Nations and Its Regional Forum

The Association of Southeast Asian Nations (ASEAN) was established in 1967 largely to promote economic cooperation among its members, which at that time were Indonesia, Malaysia, the Philippines, Singapore, and Thai-land.* Security threats then largely arose from Cold War politics, and since most countries in ASEAN were U.S. allies, the United States took care of the region's security.

Here, too, some shifts came in the early 1990s. The 1992 ASEAN summit declared that "ASEAN shall seek avenues to engage Member States in new areas of cooperation in security matters." As part of this effort, the ASEAN Re-gional Forum (ARF) was created in 1993 with the major Asia-Pacific pow-ers—the United States, Japan, China, and Russia—as quasi-members ("dialogue partners" and "consultative partners" were the technical diplomatic terms). These powerful countries' regional rivalries could threaten the peace and stability of the region on the one hand; on the other, their cooperation could make the region as peaceful and as secure as any.

Structurally, the fact that the major powers are not full-fledged members of the organization makes ASEAN and the ARF weaker than their counter-parts in other regions. But it was a start. By 1996 the ARF had begun to de-velop a number of security cooperation initiatives, and had been recognized as an important forum through which the Asia-Pacific major powers could work. However, when it comes to issues involving the internal affairs of states, such as human rights in small states like Burma and big ones like China, and the instability in Cambodia, the states in this region have been extremely re-luctant to encroach on strict conceptions of sovereignty.

---

*Today its membership also includes Brunei and Vietnam.

The Middle East: The Multilateral Peace Process

As hard as the bilateral peace talks have been between Israel and its neighbors (specifically, the Palestinians and Syria), even reaching an agreement would not be sufficient for regional security in the Middle East. Regional security agreements and institutions need to be created, involving not just Israel and its immediate neighbors but a wider range of Arab states from the region. This is why the peace talks launched at the October 1991 Middle East peace conference in Madrid included multilateral as well as bilateral tracks. The multilaterals tracks were structured along five issue areas: regional economic development, water, environment, refugees, and arms control and regional security.

The Arms Control and Regional Security (ACRS) talks are of particular interest.[28] They have not involved all the states in the region—Iran, Iraq, and Libya were not invited to participate, and Syria and Lebanon boycotted them. But they did involve Israel and fourteen Arab states, including Egypt, Jordan, Saudi Arabia, Tunisia, and others, as well as the Palestinians. From 1992 to 1994, negotiations held under U.S. auspices made progress on some initial measures at a surprisingly fast pace. There even were drafts of an "ACRS Declaration of Principles," including such pledges as to "refrain from the threat or use of force" and achieve "equal security for all," which in 1993–94 came very close to agreement. However, for a number of reasons, including both the Israeli-Palestinian problems and a worsening Israeli-Egyptian rivalry despite their peace treaty, the ACRS talks stalled well short of creating the hoped-for regional security institution. Moreover, the problem remained of what to do about states like Iran, Iraq, and Libya, which were not included in this process but posed security threats not just to Israel but also to other states in the region, especially with respect to weapons of mass destruction.

One of the important questions as we consider different regions is how much the regional security institutions in one region can serve as a model for those in another. The Middle East ACRS talks drew somewhat on the European experience with the CSCE. Some leaders, such as former Israeli prime minister Shimon Peres and former Jordanian crown prince Hassan, have pushed for even more extensive emulation of Europe through a "Conference on Security and Cooperation in the Middle East" (CSCME). The Peres and Hassan proposals included similar sets of norms of peaceful resolution of conflict, similar proposals for cooperative security through arms control and other measures, and a number of other ideas drawn from the European experience. However, partly because of the difficulties in making further progress in the bilateral peace talks and partly because of doubts about whether something so closely based on the European model really fit the Middle East, the CSCME has remained more vision than reality.

No other region has developed its regional multilateral organizations as extensively as has Europe. But all the world's regions have made efforts toward this end, in recognition of the points made at the beginning of this section about the sources of instability being more regionally rooted than globally transmitted, the interconnectedness of regional security and domestic instability, and of potentially strong regional bases for cooperation. The United States is involved in important ways in all of them.

Nonproliferation Regimes

"International regimes" is the term used for combinations of norms, rules, and enforcement mechanisms set up by treaties and other agreements that seek to regulate key areas of international relations.[29] International regimes tend to be less formal organizationally than the U.N. and the RMOs, but still can be said to be institutionalized to the extent that their norms, rules, and enforcement mechanisms are widely accepted.

Nonproliferation regimes are directed at preventing the spread of weapons of mass destruction (WMD), particularly nuclear, chemical, and biological weapons. Strengthening nonproliferation regimes has been a major goal for American foreign policy, because WMD proliferation threatens American security and interests in four areas: (1) a WMD attack directly on the United States; (2) an attack on U.S. forces overseas; (3) an attack on U.S. allies; and (4) the general threat to international peace and stability.*

Nuclear Nonproliferation

Efforts at preventing the proliferation of nuclear weapons began during the Cold War. In 1957, in one of the first major international nonproliferation agreements, the International Atomic Energy Agency (IAEA) was created to ensure that, as nations developed nuclear energy, it would be used only for

---

*We also take up nonproliferation in Chapter 8 as a power issue.

peaceful purposes (i.e., power plants). In 1968 the U.N. General Assembly approved the Nuclear Non-Proliferation Treaty (NPT), which entered into force in 1970. The NPT allowed the five states that already had nuclear weapons—the United States, the Soviet Union, Britain, France, and China—to keep them, but prohibited all other member states from acquiring or developing them. Despite these stringent restrictions, 185 countries have signed the treaty.

The original treaty stated that twenty-five years after coming into force, there would be a U.N.-sponsored conference to determine "whether the Treaty should be extended indefinitely, or for an additional fixed period or periods." When this conference was held in 1995, the decision was made to make the NPT permanent (the term used was "indefinite extension"). The United States was the principal drive behind the success of that vote.

A persisting question, though, is how strong the nuclear nonproliferation regime actually is. North Korea brought the world to the brink of a major crisis in 1993–94 when intelligence reports showed that its ostensibly peaceful nuclear program was being used to develop nuclear weapons, despite North Korea's having signed the NPT. Furthermore, some countries that are known or believed to have nuclear weapons have not signed the NPT. Israel, which does not admit to having nuclear weapons but is widely believed to have them, has maintained that its security concerns make it imprudent to sign the NPT. Then there are India and Pakistan, which in May and June 1998 defied the international community by conducting nuclear-weapons tests. This development was particularly alarming in light of the fact that these countries had already fought two wars against each other and tensions between them had spiraled into numerous crises. Now there was the added risk that the next war could go nuclear. Additionally, the example set when countries defy the nonproliferation regime without paying a significant price damages the regime's credibility.

Other weaknesses in the nonproliferation regime involve problems of verification and enforcement. It needs to be verified, not just assumed, that countries that have agreed to the NPT actually are abiding by their commitments. The IAEA is principally responsible for verifying countries' compliance. In the 1980s Iraq, despite being party to the NPT, managed to get around IAEA inspections and come close to bringing its nuclear-weapons programs to completion. (The Iraq case is discussed further later in this chapter.) In the 1990s Iran and Libya have been suspected of seeking to develop nuclear weapons despite being NPT signees. The problem of enforcement also pertains to the supplier end. There has been great concern, for example, about "loose nukes" in Russia falling into the wrong hands. The United States has sought to counter this threat by creating an economic assistance program to pay for the destruction and deactivation of former Soviet missiles, by buying up the plutonium from the dismantled Russian nuclear weapons, and by employing out-of-work Russian nuclear scientists; the goal of these efforts is to reduce any incentives to sell these supplies and services to would-be proliferators.*

There are a number of other issues that also bear upon the strength of the nuclear nonproliferation regime. These include treaties such as the Comprehensive Test Ban Treaty, nuclear export controls, the Missile Technology Control Regime, and others, as summarized in the box on p. 255.

There is an argument in some policy and academic circles that at least some nuclear proliferation could strengthen peace.[30] One of the factors that kept the United States and the Soviet Union from engaging in direct war with each other during the Cold War, it is argued, was the possibility of escalation to nuclear war. Following such reasoning, some believe that war would also be less likely between a nuclear India and a nuclear Pakistan, and perhaps in the Middle East as well. While this type of argument is made by a number of prominent scholars, the prevailing view still stresses the risks and dangers of nuclear proliferation, and thus the need for as strong a nonproliferation regime as possible.

Chemical and Biological Weapons

Many view chemical and biological weapons as even scarier than nuclear ones. One reason is that chemical and biological weapons are less expensive to produce—the "poor man's nuclear weapon," some call them. Another is that the level of technology and military capability required for their use is much less sophisticated, and thus they are more accessible to terrorists. This latter fact was demonstrated in 1995 by a Japanese cult called Aum Shinrikyo, which unleashed a chemical-weapons attack on a busy subway train in Tokyo. The cult had intended to kill millions of people. Although the actual death toll was limited, as a *New York Times* headline put it, the "Japanese Cult's Failed Germ Warfare Succeeded in Alerting the World."[31] Investigation of the cult found a veritable arsenal of chemical weapons, as well as labs equipped to produce lethal germs and bacteria for biological weapons.

---

*These measures are part of the Nunn-Lugar program, named for its two original Senate sponsors, Sam Nunn (D-Ga.) and Richard Lugar (R-Ind.). It is an example of a case in which bipartisanship still prevails.

THE NPT AND OTHER KEY COMPONENTS OF THE NUCLEAR NONPROLIFERATION REGIME

Nuclear Nonproliferation Treaty (NPT): entered into force in 1970, extended indefinitely in 1995. Commits non–nuclear weapons states not to acquire or make nuclear weapons. Has 185 signatories; main holdouts are India, Pakistan, Israel, Brazil, and Cuba

Comprehensive Test Ban Treaty (CTBT): approved in 1996, bans all nuclear weapon test explosions; builds on earlier treaties such as the 1963 Limited Test Ban Treaty. Signed by 149 nations; main holdouts are India, Pakistan, and North Korea. The United States was the first to sign but in 1999 the Senate voted against ratification.

International Atomic Energy Agency (IAEA): international organization established in 1957 with principal responsibility for monitoring and verifying that nuclear energy is used for peaceful purposes and not weapons development

Nuclear Suppliers Group: informal group of nuclear supplier nations that maintains multilateral controls on nuclear-related exports

Zangger Committee: also part of multilateral nuclear export controls, maintains a "trigger list" of items that can be exported but for which the recipient state must comply with IAEA-supervised safeguards

Missile Technology Control Regime (MTCR): established in 1987, restricts exports of missiles that could carry nuclear weapons; members are states with missile technology and capacity, principally the United States, Russia, Britain, and France; among nonmembers is China.

Source: Zachary Davis and Carl Behrens, *Nuclear Nonproliferation Policy Issues in the 105th Congress,* Congressional Research Service (CRS) Issue Brief, Library of Congress, May 13, 1998.

The Chemical Weapons Convention (CWC), signed in 1997, did substantially lessen the threat from chemical weapons, at least from states. The CWC is more far-reaching than the NPT in three main respects. First, it applies to all states—no exceptions, no previous possessors grandfathered in like the five major-power nuclear-weapons states. By 2007 all states must have destroyed all their chemical weapons. Second, it has tougher and more intrusive enforcement provisions. It mandates short-notice, anytime, anywhere "challenge inspections" of sites where cheating is believed to be taking place. The Organization for the Prohibition of Chemical Weapons (OPCW) is the CWC's version of the IAEA, but has greater authority. Third, states that do not join the treaty face automatic trade sanctions. This was a primary reason why most of the U.S. chemical industry, while not advocating the additional regulations imposed by the CWC, calculated that American companies had more to lose if the United States was not part of the treaty and therefore supported it during the Senate ratification debate.

The key tests of the CWC will be in whether these tough provisions work in practice. Russia signed and ratified the CWC, but doubts remain about whether it will fully follow through with eliminating its arsenal of 40,000 metric tons of chemical weapons. During the 1999 Kosovo war, fears arose that Serbia, a non-signatory, would use its chemical weapons. Iraq has not signed, nor has Syria, nor has North Korea. Egypt has linked its signing of the CWC to Israeli signing of the NPT. We must wait to see whether non-signatories can be brought into the fold and, if signatories do not abide by the treaty's terms, whether the OPCW has the political will and technical ability to enforce the provisions.

Biological weapons (also called germ warfare) were legally banned by the 1972 Biological Weapons Convention, but this treaty is seen by many as weak and hard to enforce and verify. U.S. intelligence agencies estimate that the number of countries with germ-warfare research programs has increased from only three back in 1979 to seventeen in 1998.[32] The very nature of biological weapons—growable in small laboratory settings, and deliverable on a handkerchief rather than a missile—poses even greater problems for their detection and prevention. Some feared scenarios get a bit like science fiction, but some are all too realistic. Indeed, in major cities such as New York the police and other public-safety authorities have begun running practice drills on what to do in case of a biological weapons attack.

Lessons of the Iraq Case

The case of Iraq demonstrates important lessons about the risks and dangers of not maintaining a strong overall nonproliferation regime.[33] By the time he invaded Kuwait in August 1990, Saddam Hussein had assembled an astounding complex for developing the full WMD arsenal—nuclear, chemical, and biological weapons, and ballistic missiles. Where had he acquired this? Much of it from the West, including from the United States.

There definitely was some strategic logic in the U.S. "tilt" toward Iraq in its 1980–88 war with Iran, given the greater threat posed by Iran's Islamic fundamentalists and the deep animosity of its anti-American leader, Ayatollah Khomeini. But the Reagan and Bush administrations failed to see past the old adage, "the enemy of my enemy is my friend." Indeed, the enemy of my enemy *may be* my friend, but he also may still be *my enemy, too.* It thus was one thing to feed the Iraqi population while it was at war with Iran, or to provide some industrial equipment, or even to share military intelligence and to bolster Iraqi defensive military capabilities. It was quite another matter to loosen controls on technology and equipment exports with "dual uses" (i.e., both commercial and military applications). The United States did this, to a degree that significantly and substantially contributed to Iraqi development of offensive military capabilities, especially its nuclear, biological, and chemical weapons.

Even after the Iran-Iraq War was over, thus lessening the strategic rationale, and amid reports of Saddam's having used chemical weapons against the Kurdish minority in Iraq, new licenses for dual-use technology exports were being granted by the United States. Later, following the Iraqi invasion of Kuwait, one former Reagan official would lament that "it would have been much better at the time of their use of poison gas [in 1988] if we'd put our foot down."[34] What was a dictator such as Saddam to think, when even the use of chemical weapons fell within the bounds of behavior that the United States considered tolerable? If this new relationship with the United States was not affected by an issue as salient as chemical warfare, then what would it be conditioned upon?

The Bush administration continued this looseness on nonproliferation. It did so despite repeated warnings of what Saddam was up to. For example, a series of top-secret intelligence reports from the U.S. Defense Intelligence Agency and the CIA in mid-1989 provided extensive evidence that Saddam had developed a network of front companies across Europe and in the United States through which he was acquiring essential WMD technology. Nor was the United States alone in selling dual-use technologies to Iraq. Germany was far and away the biggest supplier. Britain also was a major one.

At the end of the Gulf War in February 1991, as part of the terms of surrender, Saddam had to agree to allow UNSCOM into Iraq with unprecedented authority to search for and dismantle his WMD complexes. For a few years UNSCOM was able to uncover a great deal, and some of what they found was quite shocking. Yet by around 1996–97 Saddam stepped up his obstruction of

UNSCOM, playing cat-and-mouse with the inspectors, periodically kicking them out of the country, and precipitating repeated crises and tests of will with the U.N., the United States, and the international community. It thus proved exceedingly difficult to undo the WMD threat that had been allowed to develop over the preceding decade. Moreover, a question persisted: What if Saddam had not invaded Kuwait when he did, and his WMD programs had had another year, maybe more, to keep going?

Land Mines and the Regime-Creating Role of NGOs

While not a WMD per se, anti-personnel land mines are included here because they exemplify a new and different pattern in the fight against weapons proliferation. The 1997 treaty banning land mines came about less because of independent decisions by governments than from the pressure brought by the International Campaign to Ban Landmines (ICBL), a network of approximately a thousand nongovernmental organizations (NGOs) from more than sixty countries. Moreover, the treaty was signed by 133 governments despite U.S. opposition.

Anti-personnel land mines, buried in the ground in fields and along roads where children and other innocent civilians accidentally trigger them, had been taking a huge toll in human life. Estimates were of twenty-six thousand people a year—five hundred per week—most of them civilians, being killed or maimed by land mines. An exact count of the number of land mines buried across the globe is impossible, but reliable estimates put the number at about 110 million. Although some demining efforts were going on, they could barely keep up with new mines being planted. And even if no new mines were planted, the demining rate was so slow that it would have taken 1,100 years![35]

Governments and the U.N. were concerned but were not acting expeditiously. The ICBL used a number of strategies to pressure countries to support the treaty. It documented the problem through numerous studies. It lobbied governments in Washington and other major capitals, and worked particularly closely with governments like Canada that were strong supporters. It worked through the U.N. It used the media skillfully, as in the public display of veritable mountains of shoes (children's shoes especially) to symbolize those who had been killed by land mines. It also got support from celebrities, most notably Princess Diana.

The main reason why the United States did not sign the land mine treaty was because of Pentagon concerns over risks to American troops, especially those still stationed along the demilitarized zone (DMZ) between North and

South Korea. The Clinton administration was not entirely opposed to a land mine treaty, but it contended that until North Korea was ready to provide credible assurances that it would not attack South Korea, land mines would continue to be an essential part of the deterrence and defense posture along the DMZ. But, as with the ICC, the U.S. position did not prevail.

When the Nobel Peace Prize for 1997 was announced, it went to Jody Williams, an American who was coordinator of the ICBL coalition. For this and other reasons the land mine campaign is serving as a model for NGOs concerned with other arms control and disarmament issues, such as an international campaign launched in 1998 targeted at assault rifles and other light weapons.

The United States as a Peace Broker

There are three principal reasons why the United States often has been playing the role of peace broker in the post–Cold War era. First are its *leadership responsibilities*. The sole surviving superpower may be too strong a term, but as the most powerful country in the world the United States has responsibilities to support and foster peace as much as possible. Sometimes this means acting on its own, unilaterally. At other times it means providing the leadership that is critical to forging multilateral efforts.

Second is its *acceptability to the parties in conflict*. During the Cold War the United States rarely was seen as a neutral broker. Now, though, even when it may be more allied with one side than the other (e.g., in the Middle East with Israel), it still tends to be seen by the parties involved as sufficiently balanced to play a brokering role. Furthermore, the United States is still the key to delivering the goods that the parties to the conflicts want and need, be they security guarantees or economic assistance. Here, too, it is not just what the United States itself provides directly, but its capacity to mobilize multilateral action and support.

Third is that *U.S. interests are at stake* in many of these conflicts. Peace-brokering is not altruism. It serves the interests of others, but it also serves U.S. foreign policy interests. These interests vary from case to case, as we will see, but they are there in almost every case.

It is one thing to seek to broker peace, however, and another to succeed at it. Many factors affect whether peace is achieved. In the following three cases we will analyze how the United States has played the peace broker role, and with what effectiveness.

The Middle East Peace Process

September 13, 1993. The lawn of the White House. Bright blue sky, warm with a touch of late-summer crispness in the air. On one side of President Clinton, Israeli prime minister Yitzhak Rabin; on the other side, Palestine Liberation Organization (PLO) Chair Yasir Arafat. Sworn enemies, but there at the White House for a symbolic first handshake and to sign their first peace agreement, the Israeli-Palestinian Declaration of Principles (DOP).

"It is time to put an end to decades of confrontation and conflict," the DOP stated, "and strive to live in peaceful coexistence and mutual dignity and security and achieve a just, lasting and comprehensive peace" (see At the Source, p. 261). This document in itself was a historic breakthrough. Over the next few years other significant progress was made, including the signing of a full peace treaty between Israel and Jordan and a series of follow-on agreements between Israel and the Palestinians, including the 1998 Wye River agreement. The United States played the lead diplomatic role in all of these negotiations.

U.S. LEADERSHIP   One of the main reasons the Middle East peace process took off in the early 1990s was the transformed regional context caused by the double-barrel effects of the end of the Cold War and the U.S.-led victory in the Gulf War. Without the Soviet Union, Middle East "rejectionists" (those who reject peace with Israel) like the PLO were bereft of a superpower patron. In contrast, with its profound political victory in the Cold War and overwhelming military victory of the Gulf War, U.S. prestige was at an all-time high. Seeking

Yitzhak Rabin and Yasir Arafat shake hands after signing the Israeli-Palestinian Declaration of Principles at the White House. (*AP/Wide World Photos*)

At the Source

ISRAELI-PALESTINIAN
DECLARATION OF PRINCIPLES (1993)

❝ The Government of the State of Israel and the Palestinian team (in the Jordanian-Palestinian delegation to the Middle East Peace Conference) (the 'Palestinian Delegation'), representing the Palestinian people, agree that it is time to put an end to decades of confrontation and conflict, recognize their mutual legitimate and political rights, and strive to live in peaceful coexistence and mutual dignity and security and achieve a just, lasting and comprehensive peace settlement and historic reconciliation through the agreed political process. . . .

Article I, *Aim of the negotiations*

The aim of the Israeli-Palestinian negotiations within the current Middle East peace process is, among other things, to establish a Palestinian Interim Self-Government Authority, the elected Council (the 'Council') for the Palestinian people in the West Bank and the Gaza Strip, for a transitional period not exceeding five years, leading to a permanent settlement based on Security Council Resolutions 242 and 338. . . . ❞

Accompanying letter from Palestine Liberation Organization (P.L.O.) Chairman Yasir Arafat to Israeli Prime Minister Yitzhak Rabin

❝ Mr. Prime Minister,

The signing of the Declaration of Principles marks a new era in the history of the Middle East. In firm conviction thereof, I would like to confirm the following P.L.O. commitments:

The P.L.O. recognizes the right of the State of Israel to exist in peace and security.

The P.L.O. accepts United Nations Security Council Resolutions 242 and 338.

The P.L.O. commits itself to the Middle East peace process and to a peaceful resolution of the conflict between the two sides and declares that all outstanding issues relating to permanent status will be resolved through negotiations.

The P.L.O. considers that the signing of the Declaration of Principles constitutes a historic event, inaugurating a new epoch of peaceful coex-

(*Continued on page 262*)

(Israeli-Palestinian Declaration   *Continued from page 261)*
istence, free from violence and all other acts which endanger peace and stability. Accordingly, the P.L.O. renounces the use of terrorism and other acts of violence and will assume responsibility over all P.L.O. elements and personnel in order to assure their compliance, prevent violations and discipline violators. . . .

   In view of the promise of a new era and the signing of the Declaration of Principles and based on Palestinian acceptance of Security Council Resolutions 242 and 338, the P.L.O. affirms that those articles of the Palestinian Covenant which deny Israel's right to exist and the provisions of the Covenant which are inconsistent with the commitments of this letter are now inoperative and no longer valid. Consequently, the P.L.O. undertakes to submit to the Palestinian National Council for formal approval the necessary changes in regard to the Palestinian Covenant. **"**

Accompanying letter from Prime Minister Rabin to Chairman Arafat

"Mr. Chairman,
In response to your letter of Sept. 9, 1993, I wish to confirm to you that in light of the P.L.O. commitments included in your letter the Government of Israel has decided to recognize the P.L.O. as the representative of the Palestinian people and commence negotiations with the P.L.O. within the Middle East peace process. . . . **"**

Source: "Declaration of Principles on Interim Self-Government Arrangements," Stockholm International Peace Research Institute, *SIPRI Yearbook 1994* (New York: Oxford University Press, 1994), appendix 3A.

---

to capitalize on this, the Bush administration called a Middle East peace conference for October 1991 in Madrid, Spain.* While the Soviet Union officially was the co-chair, it was clear that the main role lay with the United States.

   The initial peace agreement Rabin and Arafat signed that day at the White House, the DOP, actually had been negotiated in secret talks in Oslo, Norway.

---

*The venue was symbolic because both Jews and Arabs (Moors) had been driven out of Spain in the fifteenth century during the Spanish Inquisition.

This led some to see the "Oslo agreement" as evidence that the U.S. role as Middle East peace broker had lessened. But this was too superficial an analysis. The personal role of Norwegian Foreign Minister Johan Jorgen Holst, who had built trust with both sides, definitely was an important factor in the decision to hold the talks in Oslo, and a good reminder that Americans do not have a monopoly on peace-brokering. Another factor was the need to conduct the talks somewhere where they would be out of the limelight, which would have been nearly impossible in the United States. Once the talks were completed, though, it was Washington where the signing ceremony took place. And the United States has played the major diplomatic role in the years since, in brokering the follow-on agreements and in trying to move the process along toward a comprehensive peace.

ACCEPTABILITY TO THE PARTIES IN CONFLICT   Israel long had held that it would not negotiate peace unless the United States played a key role in the process. It had, for example, rejected a number of U.N.-led initiatives because it believed the U.N. did not give sufficient consideration to Israeli security and other interests. The United States and Israel have had their differences, but one president after another, Republican and Democrat alike, has affirmed American support for Israel's security.

Prior to 1993 Arafat and the PLO considered the United States an enemy, and the United States condemned and opposed them as terrorists. But for a number of reasons those views had changed. For Arafat, although other world leaders had received him for many years, the invitation to the White House conferred a degree of legitimacy and status that could only come from Washington. The United States also has been the key to unlocking international economic assistance, as for example with the two Donors Conferences, the first convened at the State Department within weeks of the 1993 DOP, at which $2.2 billion in economic assistance was pledged to the Palestinians by more than forty nations and international institutions such as the World Bank; and the second in December 1998 shortly after the Wye agreement, at which an additional $3 billion to $4 billion in aid was pledged to the Palestinians. Arafat also knew that if there ever were to be peace and independence for his people, only the United States could provide the combination of reassurance, persuasion, and pressure for Israel to agree.

U.S. INTERESTS   Cold War or post–Cold War, the interests the United States has at stake in the Middle East have been vital. No region has been more important to the American economy nor more capable of causing profound disruptions than the Middle East, because of its oil (prosperity). For this and other reasons the region remains geopolitically important (power). It has had more wars than any other region since 1945, and is home to the most ominous WMD proliferation threats (peace). It also has domestic political importance, given the influence both of the Jewish American lobby and of the oil companies and other major corporations with commercial interests in the Arab world.

President Clinton's Middle East diplomacy came in for criticism at various times over both overall strategy and specific tactics. Was the White House being tough enough on Arafat when he didn't fulfill his commitments? Or on Israeli prime minister Benjamin Netanyahu for moves that unnecessarily antagonized the Palestinians? On these and other issues there has been plenty of room for debate. The point of consensus, though, has been that the Middle East continues to be a region that sorely needs peace-brokering, and that the United States continues to be the one that needs to play that role.

Russia, Ukraine, and the Soviet Union's Nuclear Weapons, 1991–94

Among the consequences of the breakup of the Soviet Union in 1991 was that, where there had been a single nuclear-weapons power, there now were four: Russia, Ukraine, Belarus, and Kazakhstan. As the principal successor state to the Soviet Union, Russia had the principal claim to Soviet nuclear weapons. Deals were struck with Belarus and Kazakhstan to give up the old Soviet nuclear weapons left on their territories. But Ukraine was more reluctant.

There were a number of reasons for Ukraine's stance. Ukraine and Russia had a long history of rivalry and hostility. Ukraine had briefly been an independent nation (1917–19) before Soviet forces forcibly absorbed it into the Soviet Union. Now independent again, Ukraine was contesting a number of military and security issues with Russia in addition to the nuclear-weapons issue. Both countries also had their own antagonistic domestic politics, with extremist nationalists in Russia such as Vladimir Zhirinovsky threatening to reabsorb Ukraine, and Ukrainian nationalists in the Rada (its legislature) quite vitriolic in their anti-Russia rhetoric. Mixed in also were each country's concerns for its prestige. Nuclear weapons conferred international importance and status, and Ukraine was reluctant to give these up. It was, after all, the second largest Soviet successor state, and was bigger and only slightly less populous than Britain or France, Europe's other nuclear powers.

U.S. INTERESTS   U.S. interests were at stake in a number of ways. Fear of a "Yugoslavia with nukes," of a country breaking up and potentially becoming embroiled in ethnic and other conflicts, only this time with nuclear weapons present, was high on everyone's list. Even short of that, the START I arms-control treaty just signed by Presidents Bush and Gorbachev after years of painstaking negotiations was at risk of being undermined. So, too, possibly with the global NPT, for if ex-Soviet republics other than Russia retained nuclear weapons, it would weaken the case against other countries elsewhere doing so.

LEADERSHIP AND ACCEPTABILITY TO THE PARTIES   Only the United States had the prestige and leverage to act as broker on such a major issue between such major countries. If Ukrainian president Leonid Kravchuk was to go against the anti-Russian nationalists, he needed to be able to assure his people that their security would not be threatened and also show that Ukraine gained something from the deal. Although not willing to grant the full security guarantees Ukraine wanted, the Clinton administration did provide some security assurances, took a number of steps to develop closer U.S.-Ukrainian bilateral relations, and helped get Russia to pledge to respect Ukraine's sovereignty and security. Clinton visited Kiev, the Ukrainian capital, and Kravchuk was invited to Washington. And in more concrete terms, Ukraine was given substantial sums of foreign aid, and special initiatives were taken to promote American trade with and investment in Ukraine.

In January 1994, after much negotiation, the Trilateral Agreement between the United States, Russia, and Ukraine was signed by Presidents Clinton, Yeltsin, and Kravchuk. And on June 1, 1996, the last nuclear weapon was removed from Ukraine. As President Clinton said that day, "in 1991 there were more than 4,000 strategic and tactical nuclear warheads in Ukraine. Today there are none . . . [a] historic contribution in reducing the nuclear threat."[36] U.S. peace-brokering had worked well.

Bosnia and the Dayton Accords, 1995

The Dayton accords ended the war in Bosnia. They were signed by the presidents of Bosnia, Croatia, and Serbia after negotiations led by the United States and held at a military base in Dayton, Ohio. In ending such a brutal war, the Dayton accords were an important success. Yet they came only after tens of thousands had been killed, and hundreds of thousands left as refugees by more than three years of the worst warfare in Europe since World War II.

CS7

U.S. LEADERSHIP   The United States did show leadership in bringing the parties together at Dayton. No other country had the power and prestige to be able to do this. Various U.N. peace initiatives had achieved various cease-fires, but not much more, and the cease-fires rarely lasted long. But it took a long time for the United States to actually undertake a major initiative. In 1991–92, when the wars in the former communist Yugoslavia were starting, the Bush administration largely held to the view that the conflicts were a European problem, and the western Europeans should be the ones to take the lead. Presidential candidate Bill Clinton was harshly critical of the Bush policy, and promised to be more assertive by, among other things, lifting the arms embargo against the Bosnian Muslims and launching air strikes against the Bosnian Serbs ("lift and strike"). But once in office, Clinton backed off, showing indecisiveness and succumbing to political concerns about the risks involved.

By mid-1995 the urgency of the situation no longer could be denied. The Bosnian Serbs had become so brash as to take several hundred U.N. peacekeepers hostage. Congress was threatening to cut off aid to the U.N. peacekeeping mission. This not only endangered what was left of any semblance of peacekeeping and humanitarian assistance, but threatened a crisis within NATO, because British and French troops were among the U.N. forces such abandonment would endanger. Then three top American officials were killed in Bosnia when their jeep hit a land mine. Realizing that there no longer was much of a middle option, that the choices now were give up or get serious, the Clinton administration finally asserted American leadership. NATO air strikes were launched against Bosnian Serbs, and with more firepower than the earlier "pinprick" strikes. Military support was given to the Croatian army for a major offensive against the Serbs. Economic sanctions were ratcheted up. And diplomacy was stepped up, culminating in the Dayton peace conference.

ACCEPTABILITY TO THE PARTIES   The United States had been the principal Western supporter of the Bosnian Muslims, so their leader, Alija Izetbegović was more receptive to negotiations led by the United States than by others. So, too, with Croatia, which also had been receiving significant American military aid and assistance. U.S. relations with Serbia and its president, Slobodan Milošević, had been more conflictual, but Milošević knew that only Washington could lift the sanctions that were ravaging the Serbian economy and turn off the NATO air strikes against the Bosnian Serbs. This was another case in which the parties to the conflict knew that they needed to deal with the only country that could deliver.

U.S. INTERESTS   The question of interests was at the heart of the U.S. policy and political debate over Bosnia. Were the interests at stake sufficient to warrant the risks of involvement in the conflict? The initial answer from the Bush and early Clinton administrations was "no." Many other policy makers strongly disagreed, which is why Bosnia was such an intense political issue. As the war intensified, as it threatened to spread, as it set a dangerous precedent for other parts of Europe, as it split NATO, and as the horrors kept being shown on CNN, it became increasingly hard to deny that the United States had important interests at stake. These interests were well served by the peace, however limited and imperfect, that the Dayton accords brought.

Summary

We began this chapter with a summary of the Liberal Internationalist paradigm and its main arguments as to why and how U.S. foreign policy can and should seek to build a post–Cold War peace. We have focused on the key components of such a peace and representative cases and examples within each.

With regard to the United Nations, it is essential to get beyond both the idealized views that underemphasize the limits and problems the U.N. does have as a global institution, and the caricatures and castigations that certain groups and political figures too often propagate. Arguments about whether the United States should withdraw from, or turn its foreign policy over to, the U.N. really are straw men. The substantively important debates are on questions concerning how strong an institution the U.N. is and can be for building and maintaining peace. These debates bear especially on U.S. foreign policy on issues such as human rights, peace operations, and global social and economic development.

A second main set of players in building peace comprises the increasingly important regional multilateral organizations. Because instability, conflict, and threats of war now tend to be much more regionally rooted than globally transmitted, RMOs like the OSCE, the OAU, and others need to play more important roles than in the past. This is being recognized in almost every region of the world, albeit with varying rates of progress. Here, too, the American foreign policy interest is in the potential for policy enhancement and complementarity between what the United States can do through its own initiatives and what can be better done through collective or coordinated action. Yet as with the U.N., RMOs also bring up issues of prerogative encroachment and conflicting interests.

Nonproliferation regimes are less formal institutions but ones that address one of the post–Cold War era's most dangerous threats. A balanced perspective is especially important with regard to such an ominous issue. On the one hand, back in the 1960s predictions claimed that as many as fifteen to twenty states would acquire nuclear weapons. Today, even counting suspected ones, the actual figure is probably fewer than ten. The NPT is in large part responsible for these numbers' being so low. The Chemical Weapons Convention also represents significant nonproliferation progress. Yet WMD threats remain, and in some respects are growing worse, both from certain states and from the risks of WMD terrorism.

Claims of success for U.S. peace-brokering at times are overblown, just as blame for failures sometimes gets exaggerated. Issues like the Middle East peace process continue to pose complex policy challenges and engender debates over what U.S. policy should be. Whatever the strategy, both the U.S. interests at stake and the needs of a post–Cold War peace make the U.S. role as peace broker a crucial one. This was evident in the cases discussed herein.

In sum, the Liberal Internationalist paradigm and the policies that follow from it have been and will continue to be integral to post–Cold War American foreign policy. There is great potential for going further in building a post–Cold War peace; there also are formidable challenges. Meeting these not only involves issues discussed in this chapter, it also raises questions of power, to which we turn in the next chapter.

Notes

[1] Among the major works are Robert O. Keohane, *International Institutions and State Power: Essays in International Relations Theory* (Boulder, Colo.; Westview, 1989; Robert O. Keohane and Lisa L. Martin, "The Promise of Institutional Theory," *International Security* 20:1 (Summer 1995), 39–51; John G. Ruggie, "Multilateralism: The Anatomy of an Institution," *International Organization* 46:2 (Spring 1992); Ruggie, *Winning the Peace: America and World Order in the New Era* (New York: Columbia University Press, 1996); and Stephen D. Krasner, ed., "International Regimes," special edition of *International Organization* 36:2 (Spring 1982).

[2] Ruggie, "Multilateralism: Anatomy of an Institution," 561.

[3] Keohane and Martin, "The Promise of Institutionalist Theory," 42.

[4] Quoted in Thomas J. Paterson, J. Gary Clifford, and Kenneth J. Hagan, *American Foreign Relations: A History since 1895* (Lexington, Mass.: D.C. Heath, 1995), 243–44.

[5] Quoted in Michael N. Barnett, "Bringing in the New World Order: Liberalism, Legitimacy, and the United Nations," *World Politics* 49:4 (July 1997), 541.

[6] Barnett, "Bringing in the New World Order," 543.

[7] Boutros Boutros-Ghali, *An Agenda for Peace* (New York: United Nations, 1992), 1.

[8]Cited in Bruce W. Jentleson, "Who, Why, What and How: Debates over Post–Cold War Military Interventionism," in *Eagle Adrift: American Foreign Policy at the End of the Century,* ed., Robert J. Lieber (New York: Longman, 1997), 63–64.

[9]Bruce Russett, ed., *The Once and Future Security Council* (New York: St. Martin's, 1997).

[10]U.S. Department of State, Bureaus of International Organizations and Public Affairs, "Fact Sheet: UN Security Council Expansion," September 19, 1997.

[11]Thomas W. Lippman, "America Avoids the Stand," *Washington Post,* July 26, 1998, C1, C4.

[12]"No Third Term at the U.N.," *Washington Post,* May 2, 1997, A18.

[13]Paul Kennedy and Bruce Russett, "Reforming the United Nations," *Foreign Affairs* 74:5 (September/October 1995), 50–71; Independent Working Group on the Future of the United Nations, *The United Nations in Its Second Half Century* (New York: Ford Foundation, 1995).

[14]Carnegie Commission for Preventing Deadly Conflict, *Preventing Deadly Conflict: Final Report* (Washington, D.C.: Carnegie Commission, 1997), 135.

[15]Robert J. Art and Robert Jervis, *International Politics: Enduring Concepts and Contemporary Issues,* 3d ed. (New York: HarperCollins, 1992), 2.

[16]Francis M. Deng, Sadikel Kimaro, Terrence Lyons, Donald Rothchild, and I. William Zartman, *Sovereignty as Responsibility: Conflict Management in Africa* (Washington, D.C.: Brookings Institution Press, 1996); Bruce W. Jentleson, "Preventive Diplomacy: Analytic Conclusions and Policy Lessons," in *Opportunities Missed, Opportunities Seized: Preventive Diplomacy in the Post–Cold War World,* ed. Jentleson (Lanham, MD.: Rowman and Littlefield, 1999).

[17]Jack Donnelly, "Humanitarian Intervention and American Foreign Policy: Law, Morality and Politics," in *Human Rights in the World Community: Issues and Actions,* eds. Richard P. Claude, and Burns H. Weston (Philadelphia: University of Pennsylvania Press, 1992), 63.

[18]Kofi Annan, "Intervention," Ditchley Foundation Lecture 35, reprinted as "Supplement to the Ditchley Conference Reports 1997/98," 2, 4–5.

[19]Jentleson, "Who, Why, What and How," 55.

[20]John M. Goshko, "Balkan Peacekeeping Exposes Limits of UN, Boutros-Ghali Says," *Washington Post,* October 10, 1995, A21.

[21]Shoon Kathleen Murray, Louis Klarevas, and Thomas Hartley, "Are Policymakers Misreading Public Views towards the United Nations?" paper presented at the 38th Annual Convention of the International Studies Association, Toronto, Canada, March 1997, 6.

[22]Steven Lee Myers, "Plan to Pay Off UN Dues Stalls," *New York Times,* May 21, 1997, A1, A8.

[23]Cited in Jentleson, "Who, Why, What and How," 62–63.

[24]"From CSCE to OSCE: Historical Retrospective," OSCE Web site, http:/www.osceprag.cz/info/facts/history.htm, accessed September 23, 1998.

[25]Abram Chayes and Antonia Handler Chayes, eds., *Preventing Conflict in the Post-Communist World: Mobilizing International and Regional Organizations* (Washington, D.C.: Brookings Institution Press, 1996), 10.

[26]P. Terrence Hoppmann, "The Organization for Security and Cooperation in Europe," *Peaceworks* (Washington, D.C.: U.S. Institute of Peace, forthcoming); and chapters in Jentleson, ed., *Opportunities Missed, Opportunities Seized.*

[27]Edmond J. Keller, "Transnational Ethnic Conflict in Africa," in *The International Spread of Ethnic Conflict: Fear, Diffusion, and Escalation,* ed. David A. Lake and Donald Rothchild (Princeton: Princeton University Press, 1998), 275–92.

[28]Bruce W. Jentleson, *The Middle East Arms Control and Regional Security (ACRS) Talks: Progress, Problems and Prospects,* Policy Paper 26, University of California Institute on Global Conflict

and Cooperation, September 1996; Joel Peters, *Pathways to Peace: The Multilateral Arab-Israeli Peace Talks* (London: Royal Institute of International Affairs, 1996).

[29]Krasner, *International Regimes;* Andreas Hasenclever, Peter Mayer, and Volker Rittberger, *Theories of International Regimes* (New York: Cambridge University Press, 1997).

[30]See Scott D. Sagan and Kenneth N. Waltz, *The Spread of Nuclear Weapons: A Debate* (New York: Norton, 1995).

[31]*New York Times,* May 26, 1998, A1.

[32]William J. Broad and Judith Miller, "Germ Defense Plan in Peril as Its Flaws Are Revealed," *New York Times,* August 7, 1998, A1, A16.

[33]Bruce W. Jentleson, *With Friends Like These: Reagan, Bush and Saddam, 1982–1990* (New York: Norton, 1994).

[34]Quoted in Jentleson, *With Friends Like These,* 93.

[35]Richard Price, "Reversing the Gun Sights: Transnational Civil Society Targets Land Mines," *International Organization* 52:3 (Summer 1998), 618.

[36]James E. Goodby, "Preventive Diplomacy for Nuclear Nonproliferation in the Former Soviet Union," in Jentleson, ed., *Opportunities Missed, Opportunities Seized.*

8 *Power: Still the Name of the Game?*

Introduction: The Realist Paradigm and the Post–Cold War Era

There is no question that the United States enters the twenty-first century as the world's most powerful nation. But there are many questions about the strategies for shaping, sustaining, and using that power.

From a Realist perspective, the end of the Cold War meant the closing of a particular era of "power politics," but not the elimination of the struggle and rivalry for power that are the essence of international relations. To think otherwise, as political scientist John Mearsheimer and other leading Realists argue, is ahistorical and dangerously naive.[1] Power politics has been the way of the world for twelve hundred years, through many historical transitions no less sweeping than our own—on what basis would one conclude that our era is so fundamentally different? We must not forget the lessons learned the hard way from the 1920s and 1930s. That was a time when power supposedly didn't matter as much because there was an international institution like the League of Nations and treaties like the 1928 Kellogg-Briand Pact (named in part for the American secretary of state, Frank Kellogg), which simply declared war illegal. Yet, as British scholar Martin Wight wrote, such views were "a chimera. . . . International politics have never revealed, nor do they today, a habitual recognition among states of a community of interest overriding their separate interests, comparable to that which normally binds individuals within the state. . . . The only principle of order is to try to maintain, at the price of perpetual vigilance, an even distribution of power."[2]

Today, no less than then, as far as Realists are concerned, "international institutions have minimal influence on state behavior, and thus hold little promise for promoting stability in the post–Cold War world." Foreign policy competition is an inherently stronger dynamic among states than is foreign policy cooperation. States always have sought and always will seek "opportunities to take advantage of one another" as well as to "work to insure that other states do not take advantage of them."[3] The United States therefore should seek to maintain its "primacy," as some theorists call it, or "preponderance," as others call it.[4] Power is still the name of the game. The Realist paradigm still prevails (see Dynamics of Choice, below).

For Realists, consequently, three points are central. First, states pursue interests, not peace per se. If their interests are better served by war, aggression, and other such coercive means, appeals to peace as an objective won't work very well. Peace is best served by using power to affect the calculations states make.

Second, political and military power remain the major currencies of power. They are crucial to a strong national defense, to credible deterrence, and to other effective means of statecraft. The requirements of each of these strategies have changed with the change in the nature of threats, but the need for the basic strategies remains. As for economic power, it is valued by Realists less as its own international currency than as the "bullion" on which military power ultimately rests. The American economy has to be kept strong and competitive primarily so that the advanced technologies needed for next-generation weapons can be provided, and so that the political support for a large defense budget and other global commitments can be maintained.

Third, while other issues such as trade and human rights are more important than they used to be, war and aggression still are at the heart of the inter-

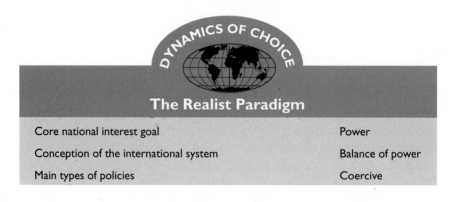

DYNAMICS OF CHOICE

The Realist Paradigm

Core national interest goal	Power
Conception of the international system	Balance of power
Main types of policies	Coercive

national agenda. The 1990–91 Persian Gulf War made this abundantly clear. The Berlin Wall had come down, the Soviet Union was taking its last gasps, democracy was being proclaimed in one country after another—but the invasion of Kuwait by Saddam Hussein was age-old military aggression. The wars in the former Yugoslavia were the worst in Europe since World War II. Africa endured more wars in the 1990s than during any previous decades in its history. The progress toward peace in the Middle East has not eliminated the threat of another major war there. The Korean demilitarized zone remains one of the tensest spots on the globe.

Four sets of power-related issues present themselves for U.S. foreign policy today. The first concerns *the geopolitics of the post–Cold War era.* Russia and China no longer are U.S. enemies, but to what extent are they new friends, and to what extent great-power rivals? And what about relations with longtime allies in Europe and Japan? The second involves the need for *rethinking defense strategy.* Lessons can be drawn from the Persian Gulf War in this regard. More generally, the key question concerns what adjustments are needed in the basic strategies of deterrence to meet the threats and challenges of this new era. This question pertains to nuclear weapons and strategy, to NATO, and to regional deterrence in such key regions as the Persian Gulf and East Asia. It also raises the latest version of the historical "great debate" on defense spending—how much is enough?

The third concerns U.S. policy toward the *ethnic and other deadly conflicts* that have been so pervasive in this post–Cold War era. This problem involves questions of military intervention, including both strategy and politics, as well as of preventive statecraft. The fourth is *security threats from nonstate actors.* It is necessary not only to bring U.S. power to bear against other states in the international system, but also to meet challenges and threats from nonstate actors such as terrorists, drug lords, and global crime rings.

Major-Power Geopolitics

For a while in the early 1990s U.S. power was so dominant that the post–Cold War system was being characterized as "unipolarity." The Soviet Union had fallen, and the United States was the sole surviving superpower. The Persian Gulf War left no doubts about American military might. The United States seemed in a class by itself.

Post–Cold War geopolitics, though, has proven more complex and varying than depicted in the unipolarity model. The United States is not as consistently influential and not as dominant in its relations with other major powers as this model suggests. But multipolarity doesn't fit either, as it implies that other major countries have much the same power as the United States does. Some analysts have tried blended characterizations, such as "uni-multipolarity," but while these help make the point about geopolitical complexity, they end up saddling us with more jargon.

To analyze the geopolitics of this new era, we need to look more closely at U.S. relations with each of the other major post–Cold War powers: Russia, China, western Europe, and Japan.

Russia

The great uncertainty about Russia and its future really should not surprise us. Think about it: Russia has not gone through a change just of policy, or of leadership, or ruling party. The Union of Soviet Socialist Republics, proclaimed in 1922 by Vladimir Ilyich Lenin as a new and revolutionary empire setting out to revolutionize the entire world, collapsed and fell apart in 1991. Democracy was proclaimed, capitalism replaced socialism: change swept through every part of Russian society. The first free elections in Russian history were held. A stock market opened in Moscow. Cultural freedom came out of the shadows, and Western influences were let in, including even the Rolling Stones, live and in concert in the summer of 1998 in Moscow (see Perspectives, p. 275).

But the process has been a deeply unsettling one in almost every way. There is value to democratic elections having been held, but they have allowed anti-Western demagogues and old-line communists to gain influence in the Russian Duma (the lower house of the legislature). Boris Yeltsin held on to the presidency for almost a decade, but at times resorted to means of questionable constitutionality, did not govern very effectively, and periodically lapsed from the scene due to health problems. Russian capitalism has been shaky at best, deeply corrupt at worst, with workers and government employees and even soldiers going months without receiving their paychecks while robber-baron company heads have made millions for themselves. The Russian economy has shrunk by almost 40 percent since the breakup of the Soviet Union. International investors have had recurring crises of confidence, and Wall Street and other Western stock markets have felt the shocks from Russian economic instability.

PERSPECTIVES
PERSPECTIVES

PERSPECTIVES

CHANGE IN RUSSIA SIGNIFIED BY THE ROLLING STONES

MOSCOW, Aug. 12 — Mick Jagger said it all, in Russian. "At last, we are here," the 55-year-old rock star yelled into the microphone, his voice booming across a sports stadium filled with 50,000 cheering Russians. Many had waited 20, even 30 years to see the Rolling Stones, live and in Moscow.

Many fans at tonight's concert—an extravaganza of smoke, lights and special effects dampened only somewhat by a cold rain—had been teenagers when the Stones were at the peak of their popularity. In those days, their records—or copies of their records, ingeniously made on X-ray film—were traded like illicit treasure in Moscow's subway tunnels and dark courtyards, out of sight of the Soviet police. . . .

"I thought I wouldn't live long enough," said Andrei, 42, a Moscow businessman who came to the concert tonight at the Luzhinksi stadium. "For me," echoed Simeon, 40, a television producer who, like Andrei, declined to give his last name, "it is enough if they just walk out on stage. Why? Because for us they are a legend."

The Stones began their concert with "Satisfaction," and the crowd happily joined in, word for word. By trying to keep their youth away from Western mass culture, the Soviet authorities succeeded only in making them commit its lyrics and music to memory.

The ban on rock music meant that there were no locally produced records. Western labels were brought in, in small quantities, by tourists, diplomats and sailors and sold on the black market for as much as a student's monthly stipend. Copies were made on reel-to-reel tapes, or on disks cut from used X-ray film—known as "bones" because of the vaguely visible X-ray images—on which the grooves of vinyl records could be etched. . . .

For Moscow, a city still struggling to achieve normality, the stopover by the Stones here during their much-touted "Bridges to Babylon" European tour was a sign that it too makes the grade. "Having seen the Rolling Stones live, we become like everyone else, at least in this field of

(*Continued on page 276*)

(Change in Russia   *Continued from page 275)*
human endeavor," noted a commentator in the newspaper *Moscow News*. It was left to papers close to the now-enfeebled Communist Party to note that the Stones came here only "in their declining years."

But it was a local radio station, in a zany talk-show broadcast after the concert, that put the Moscow appearance of the Stones in new historical perspective by staging an imaginary photo linkup between Lenin, the founder of the Soviet state fictitiously resurrected and performing at Carnegie Hall in New York, and Mick Jagger, talking from Moscow, comparing concert notes.

Source: Celestine Bohlen, "For the Rolling Stones' Fans, Satisfaction at Last," *New York Times*, August 12, 1998, p. A4. Copyright © 1998 by the New York Times. Reprinted by permission.

How should the United States respond? There are three possible scenarios for Russian-American relations.

RUSSIA AS FRIEND   "Ron and Mikhail," "Bill and Boris"—the end of the Cold War brought quite a bit of chumminess between American and Soviet/Russian leaders. There was much mutual praise, lots of amiable photo ops, plenty of pledges to work together. Both the Bush and Clinton administrations, with bipartisan support in their respective Congresses, granted Russia large amounts of foreign aid. A number of cooperative military programs were initiated, even including American economic assistance to pay for housing for former Soviet troops returning home from East Germany and elsewhere in Eastern Europe. These were not just economic assistance programs, but defense by other means.

The major nuclear-weapons cuts agreed to in the Strategic Arms Reduction Treaties (START) were a centerpiece of this new friendship and strategic partnership. START I, signed in 1991 by Presidents Bush and Gorbachev and ratified by both the U.S. Senate and the Russian Duma, made major cuts in both sides' nuclear arsenals: from Cold War levels of 13,000 U.S. and 11,000 Soviet strategic nuclear weapons to 6,000 on each side. START II, signed in January 1993 by Presidents Bush and Yeltsin, would cut almost another 50 percent, to 3,000–3,500 warheads per side. The U.S. Senate ratified START II in 1996, but it took until 2000 for the Russian Duma to do so. Some of the reasons were issue-specific, such as the costs of making the cuts and dismantling nuclear weapons at a time of major fiscal and economic crisis for Russia. Some of the opposition was retaliation from parties and factions angered by NATO expansion and then the Kosovo war. A more general disquietude about Russian-American relations as too one-sided also was a factor, and as such was indicative of the limits to the Russian-American friendship. Even so, efforts continue for further cuts in American and Russian nuclear weapons, through negotiations on a START III treaty to lower weapons ceilings to 2,000–2,500 by the year 2008. Proposals also are being considered for even deeper cuts to minimal levels of deterrence.

RUSSIA AS GREAT-POWER COMPETITOR   Although its current economic and other problems handicap Russia at the moment, its sheer size, resource endowments, geopolitical position, and history ensure that Russia again will be a great power. Even when the Russian-American friendship was at its peak in the early 1990s, Russia saw some of its foreign policy interests as in competition and even conflict with those of the United States.

This has been especially evident regarding the former Yugoslavia, where the Russians have supported their fellow Slavs, the Serbs, while the United States has opposed them. Russian troops did join with NATO troops in the Bosnia peacekeeping mission, but only after the Serbs had agreed to the Dayton accords. The same dynamic was evident in 1998–99 over Kosovo: Russia blocked U.S. efforts to get a U.N. Security Council resolution authorizing air strikes, and sharply condemned the NATO military action against the Serbs.

Another set of tensions has been over the "near abroad," the term Russia uses to refer to the other former Soviet republics. To Russia this is its sphere of influence, an area in which it claims a right to exert political pressure and even intervene militarily to protect its interests, as it already has done in Georgia, Moldova, Tajikistan, Armenia, and Azerbaijan (as well as Chechnya, which is within Russia's own territory). This is one of the reasons why even the limited support Russia gave to the first wave of NATO expansion may not continue if the next group of prospective NATO members includes any ex-Soviet states, such as the Baltics (Latvia, Lithuania, and Estonia).

The foreign policy competition also has been becoming increasingly evident in the Middle East. Because this region had been such a major front in the Cold War, American-Russian cooperation against Iraq during and after the Persian Gulf War, as well as their cooperation in the Arab-Israeli peace process, was of tremendous significance. But by the mid-1990s, differences over relations with Iraq were mounting, as Russia pushed to lift the U.N.-imposed economic sanctions and opposed U.S. threats and uses of military force against Iraq. So, too, with Iran, over which differences reached the point that the United States imposed economic sanctions against Russia for helping Iran develop ballistic missiles.

RUSSIA AS ADVERSARY   In a third possible scenario Russia could become an adversary in one of two ways. One would be through the rise of a nationalist leader who might go beyond the normal great-power competition and seek to rebuild an empire and regain global influence through an aggressive and militaristic foreign policy. Expansionism is rooted deep in Russian history, it is argued; it did not just start with Lenin and the communists. Moreover, the instabilities of Russian politics raise concerns that, as with Hitler in Weimar Germany in the 1930s, an aggressively nationalist leader will be brought to power promising to restore the motherland's greatness. The extremist Vladimir Zhirinovsky, with promises to restore the old Russian empire (including taking back Alaska!), caused a scare with the gains he and his party made in the December 1993 Duma elections. The communist Gennadi Zyuganov raised new fears with the political support he was showing leading up to the June 1996 presidential elections. Neither prevailed, but that hasn't alleviated the concern that they or others like them may come to power, whether through elections or nondemocratic means such as a military coup.

The other scenario involves Russia becoming a major threat more out of weakness than of strength. The concern here is of a Russia that is less and less able to govern itself effectively. Most urgent in this regard is the safety and security of Russia's nuclear arsenal. Numerous studies have warned of the increasing dangers of accidental or unauthorized nuclear launches. The officers and soldiers in charge of the nuclear arsenal, ranked as an elite during the Cold War and treated accordingly, now suffer from low pay, food and housing shortages, deteriorating discipline, and the like. Furthermore, safety measures, maintenance systems, and replacement of aging technology and equipment all have been drastically scaled back because of Russia's budget crisis. The gravity of this situation raises troubling specters: an accidental launching after a false alarm that is not checked out properly amid the breakdown of discipline or of equipment; an intentional but unauthorized launching by disgruntled officers; a terrorist group stealing or buying a nuclear weapon.

China

In Chapter 5 we discussed the Nixon-Kissinger opening to China and how the principal basis for it was the geopolitical calculus of the common enemy: the

Soviet Union. Trade and other relations between the United States and China also developed over the 1970s and 1980s. However, three main developments made the 1990s a period of greater U.S.-China differences.

One was greater conflicts over human rights precipitated by the 1989 massacre in Beijing's Tiananmen Square of Chinese students and other pro-democracy demonstrators. The Chinese government unleashed a brutal military crackdown after the students staged a mass protest, sending tanks and soldiers into the streets to fire on the protesters, killing many of them. For the Bush and Clinton administrations this atrocity raised the issue of economic sanctions and linkages between human rights and most-favored-nation (MFN) trading status (see Chapter 9). More generally, it showed the limits of political change in China and became a major issue in Sino-American relations.

Second was that, with the end of the Cold War and the disappearance of the shared Soviet enemy, China and the United States entered the post–Cold War era with their global, geopolitical differences more apparent than their commonalities. Given China's extraordinary economic growth and modernization as well as its assertive style of diplomacy, many analysts believe it may be even more of a possible challenger for global-power status in the coming decades than Russia. Globally, China has often sided with Iraq, Iran, and other U.S. adversaries by supplying them with advanced weaponry and technology for weapons of mass destruction, for example. Chinese-Russian relations also have shown signs of growing closer, albeit well short of restoration of their early Cold War alliance.

Third, China's further emergence as a regional power in East Asia threatens to upset the regional balance of power. States like Japan that worry about a too-powerful China must be made to feel secure, yet China's own concerns about its security and a too-powerful Japan must also be taken into account. The United States and China also have differences over North Korea and how best to manage the threat it poses to regional stability. But the tensest issue in U.S.-China relations continues to be Taiwan and its future. The crux of this issue is the same as it has been since the 1949 Chinese communist victory. Will Taiwan be absorbed into mainland China, or will it retain its separateness and perhaps even become a recognized independent nation? And will the issue be settled peacefully?

The main options for dealing with China as defined in the U.S. policy debate have been containment and engagement. *Containment* is a variation, albeit milder and more limited, of the Cold War strategy toward the Soviet Union. The strategy that follows from this analysis is short of confrontational but is firm, cautious, attentive to threats and relative power—i.e., geared to containment. It rests on the same logic as George Kennan's original 1947 formulation of containment of the Soviet Union (Chapter 4): that the internal changes needed to make China both less of a threat and more of a democracy are more likely to occur if the country's external ambitions are contained and the system is thus forced to fall on its own contradictions. Summits are OK, as they were for Kissinger with the Soviets, but the U.S. posture should be kept strong. Historically the international system has tended to have problems absorbing major new powers, so caution is the watchword.

A number of recent crises and controversies have reinforced the containment posture toward China. In 1998 word spread that China had used contacts developed through military, scientific, and economic cooperation with the United States to steal secrets about American nuclear weapons design and development. Tensions over Taiwan again flared in mid-1999 after the Taiwanese president made pro-independence statements and China responded with barely veiled threats. These controversies heightened concerns about the Chinese military buildup and about Chinese provocations on a number of regional security issues.

Those who support *engagement* take a different view of China, although not a polar opposite. They are wary about Chinese regional interests but assess them as less threatening. China wants the role in the Asia-Pacific to which, based on its size and history, it feels entitled. This does create tensions, and the United States must stand by it allies and its interests, but these issues can be worked out through diplomacy and negotiations. Besides, militarily, China doesn't come close to matching the United States, even with its recent advances. Taiwan is acknowledged as a more contentious issue, although policymakers are cautioned to be careful that the Taiwanese don't exploit U.S. support to be provocative. As to the Persian Gulf and other areas, more can be accomplished through quiet diplomacy than through China-bashing.

This view makes the argument for a strategy that emphasizes integration and diplomacy. China needs to be brought into more multilateral organizations, both economic ones such as the World Trade Organization and strategic ones such as the Missile Technology Control Regime. This integration will provide structured and peaceful mechanisms for dealing with China's own concerns, and will also encourage China to adopt international norms and abide by international rules. On a bilateral basis the United States should continue with periodic summits, other diplomacy, trade, and other areas of engagement. Human rights issues and democratization are not to be ignored, and other approaches pursued, but the MFN–human rights linkage is strongly rejected. Too many issues are involved to allow overall relations to pivot strictly on this issue. Trade and investment interests are not least among these: American investment in China has grown enormously in the 1990s, and future prospects are for even greater growth.

Western Europe

In addition to issues related to the North Atlantic Treaty Organization (NATO, see below), there are other aspects to transatlantic geopolitics. One is the extent to which the European Union (EU) achieves its goal of a common foreign and security policy. Although most of the publicity has been going to the new common European currency, the euro, and other areas of economic policy in which the EU has been moving toward greater cooperation, the EU has stated its intention to pursue a common foreign and security policy. Britain and France have been taking new initiatives to lead the way toward this goal. Such efforts will not necessarily put the EU in opposition to the United States. They could, though, make it more of an independent force and a stronger one in its own right.

Of the three main west European powers—Britain, France, and Germany—Britain and the United States have had the closest, most cooperative foreign policies in the 1990s. It is not quite the "special relationship" of FDR and Churchill during World War II, but in the Persian Gulf, against Libyan terrorism, in Kosovo, and on a number of other issues, British and American interests have strongly coincided. France and the United States, however, have had numerous foreign policy tensions. U.S.-French difficulties are not totally new; it was right in the middle of the Cold War that President Charles de Gaulle took France out of the NATO military command. U.S. leaders often see France as an irksome ally, a country that hasn't come to grips with its faded imperial status. The French side, in turn, often views the United States as naive, arrogant, still an upstart. In more specific terms, policy conflicts have arisen over such issues as relations with Iran and Iraq, the Arab-Israeli peace process, and a number of African conflicts, particularly in countries that used to be French colonies.

As for Germany, one of the old sayings about NATO as cited in Chapter 4 was that, in addition to keeping the Russians out of Europe and the Americans in, its tacit purposes was also to keep the Germans down. Debate continues over whether Germany has become a stable democracy committed to peace or whether there need be concern about Germany turning again to aggression. Nor is this just a historically based question. Noted Realist scholar Kenneth Waltz has argued that, given the increases in their power and stature, it would be a historical aberration for Germany and Japan not to seek to become great powers again. "When a country receives less attention and gets its way less often than it feels it should," Waltz contends, "internal inhibitions about becoming a great power are likely to turn into public criticism of the government for not taking its proper place in the world."[5] Other scholars, though, see Germany as understanding that its historical legacy will continue to limit the role it plays to that of a major power, but not one that could again become a great-power challenger to the United States.[6]

Japan

For U.S.-Japan relations as well, the end of the Cold War has caused change but not a fundamental redefinition. The old security concern of a Soviet invasion no longer pertains; Russia and Japan still have some outstanding issues, including territorial disputes dating from World War II, but their relations now are well within the bounds of diplomacy. Nevertheless, the U.S.-Japan security alliance has at least as much if not more importance today for maintaining the Asia-Pacific regional balance of power. "Our security relationship with Japan is the linchpin of United States security policy in Asia," the Pentagon has stated. "It is seen not just by the United States and Japan, but throughout the region, as a major factor for securing stability in Asia."[7] A new U.S.-Japan defense agreement was signed in 1997, and about 40 percent of the one hundred thousand American military personnel in the Asia-Pacific region continue to be based in Japan.

Within this basic alliance, however, there are some tensions. One is over the interrelationship between security and economics—i.e., ensuring that the strong sense of shared interests on security matters does not suffer too much fallout from the more contentious economic side of U.S.-Japan relations. The trade disputes that began in the 1970s and grew especially heated in the 1980s have persisted through the 1990s. Japan continues to be the largest source of the American trade deficit. And while Japan's economic problems in recent years have taken away from its image as an economic powerhouse, this has ended up adding to the economic disputes. Its government's weakness in dealing with its own economic problems exacerbated the overall Asian financial crisis of the late 1990s and, because of the much greater size of the Japanese economy, reverberated even more than the Russian economic instability on Wall Street.*

A second issue concerns, to borrow from the title of a popular Japanese book, "the Japan that can Say No." Say "no," that is, to the United States, a sentiment that reflects resentments on that side of the Pacific that mirror the Japan-bashing on this side. Whereas some in the United States have felt that Japan takes advantage of American support, some in Japan feel that the United States is too domineering and that their country needs to show that it can't be taken for granted to always follow the American lead. An issue on which these sentiments have been especially strong has been the presence of U.S. military bases in Japan, especially on the island of Okinawa.

Third is Japan's post–Cold War military role. The "peace constitution" written for Japan by the United States during the post–World War II occupation limited Japan's military forces strictly to self-defense. The question now is whether those limits can be loosened somewhat. The 1997 U.S.-Japan defense agreement took some steps in this direction, allowing the Japanese military to provide such additional assistance to the United States in the region as providing minesweepers, conducting search-and-rescue missions in international waters, and helping enforce U.N.-mandated economic sanctions. Japanese military units also have begun serving in U.N. peacekeeping missions, albeit in limited roles. There is little chance in the foreseeable future, though, that Japan would be allowed to develop its military into a major offensive force. Americans often don't appreciate the extent to which anti-Japan sentiments and fears persist in China, in South Korea, in the Philippines, and elsewhere in the region; these fears draw not only on the World War II experience, but go back further in history.

Rethinking Defense Strategy

During the Cold War U.S. defense planners had a strong sense of who the enemy was: the Soviet Union. They had a basic strategy for defending the United States, its allies, and its interests: nuclear deterrence, combined with regional deterrence through NATO and other parts of a global network of military alliances and bases. Without the Soviet enemy, though, and with a

---

*We discuss this more in Chapter 9.

number of other emerging threats and challenges, some major rethinking of U.S. defense strategy has been needed—indeed, it has only just begun.

The Persian Gulf War and Its Lessons

The 1990-91 Persian Gulf War against Iraq had three main lessons with regard to both the scope and limits of American power. The most immediate was that aggression was still a fact of international life. Troops marched and tanks rolled as Iraq took over Kuwait, its smaller and militarily weaker neighbor.

Second was that the twenty-seven-nation international coalition the Bush administration put together was both a manifestation and a multiplier of American power. That is, the willingness of so many countries to join with the United States demonstrated how much the rest of the world looked to Washington for leadership. And being able to make this not just George Bush vs. Saddam Hussein, but a coalition of the world's major nations, including some of Saddam's Arab brethren, forged under U.N. auspices made the U.S. position that much stronger.

Third was that the military victory left no doubts about American military power. It is important to recall how dire many of the predictions were of the risks that going to war might bring. But these predictions did not come to pass, and with the help of CNN the whole world watched the vivid images of American military might.

There were, however, limits to the Gulf War's significance. As a military operation, for all the technological innovations the U.S. military displayed, it was fundamentally a classical strategy of armed forces against armed forces on the battlefield. It closely followed the "Powell doctrine" (named for General Colin Powell, who at the time was chair of the Joint Chiefs of Staff) of ensuring that when military force is used, it is used decisively and overwhelmingly—a fundamental lesson the Pentagon had drawn from Vietnam. But the nature of this war would prove to be more the exception than the rule. Somalia, Bosnia, Haiti, Kosovo, and the other ethnic conflicts and internal wars in which the United States has been involved were much more politically based uses of military force, and much less battlefield-based—more like Vietnam than Desert Storm, and thus presenting different challenges for the use of military force (these military interventions will be discussed further later in this chapter).

Another limitation on the significance of the Gulf War is that it left Saddam in power in Baghdad. A number of factors went into the decision to stop the ground war after only one hundred hours, before reaching Saddam himself; and while in some respects this decision was understandable, the succeeding years would show the problems and threats Saddam still could cause. Moreover, precisely because of how decisive and overwhelming the military victory was, its political limits were all the more striking.

Finally, there were the lessons of the enemy-of-my-enemy-is-my-friend "over-tilting" toward Iraq in the 1980s (see Chapter 7).[8] Some argued that these prewar mistakes really didn't matter since the U.S.-led forces won the war. Some even argued that the United States and the world in general were better off that the war had been fought. At best this was a cold power-politics calculus that too readily dismissed the death toll, other human suffering, economic costs, environmental destruction, and further consequences of the war. Yet over time, as the conflicts with Iraq persisted, even this strategic logic came into question. Thus, along with the military lessons to be learned from how the war was fought, there were important lessons to be learned about why the war occurred.

The Future of NATO

Time and again during the Cold War and at its end, warnings were sounded about the demise and possible death of NATO. But when the Berlin Wall fell, the Warsaw Pact was torn up, and the Soviet Union came asunder, NATO was still standing. Its central goal—to "safeguard the freedom, common heritage and civilization of [its] peoples, founded on the principles of democracy, individual liberty and the rule of law" (see the excerpts from the North Atlantic Treaty in Chapter 4)—had been achieved, and without a single shot having been fired in anger. No wonder NATO has been touted as the most successful peacetime alliance in history.

The ensuing question has been whether NATO's very success would lead to its demise. "Alliances are against, and only derivatively for, someone or something," according to an old international relations axiom.[9] With the Soviet enemy gone, was there really a strong enough reason to keep NATO going? Given the budgetary costs and other factors, should it just be showered with testimonials, given its "gold watch," and sent into retirement? All these questions boil down to two issues about NATO's future: its membership and its mission.

THE EXPANSION OF NATO MEMBERSHIP At the end of the Cold War NATO faced a problem that was the fruit of its success: its former adversaries had been defeated. Indeed, their major alliance, the Warsaw Pact, had fallen apart; their major empire, the Soviet Union, had crumbled. Confrontation had ended, and cooperation was now a possibility. The challenge for NATO now was how to build new cooperative relationships with these former adversaries, and with Russia in particular.

The initial transitional strategy started by the Bush administration and furthered by the Clinton administration was to create new institutional mechanisms linked to NATO but not fully part of it. In 1991 all of the former Soviet and Soviet-bloc states were invited to join the North Atlantic Cooperation Council, later renamed the European-Atlantic Partnership Council (see Table 8.1). This was to be a mechanism for consultation on political and security issues. Then in 1994 the Partnership for Peace (PFP) was created, also involving most Soviet and Soviet-bloc states and geared toward building cooperation among the members' militaries and defense establishments. The PFP also made possible participation in actual NATO peace operations; for example, thirteen PFP members sent troops to Bosnia as part of the NATO peacekeeping force there.

Although these institutional linkages confer the right to consult with NATO if a state feels its security is threatened, this is not the same as the "Article 5" collective-security guarantee that full NATO members give one another. Article 5 of the NATO treaty defines an attack on one state as an attack on all and pledges members to come to each other's defense. This is why the actual expansion of NATO membership has been such a tough issue. We saw this in 1997–98 in the debate over the first set of new members: Poland, Hungary, and the Czech Republic. We will continue to see it, since pledges have been made by the United States and other NATO leaders to continue to bring in other new members.

One argument in favor of NATO expansion is based on the concept of a *security community.* A security community is defined as an area "in which strategic rivalries are attenuated and the use of force within the group is highly unlikely."[10] NATO expansion would enlarge the area of Europe in which this sense of security and stability would prevail. Czech President Vaclav Havel, who spent many years in prison as a dissident in the communist era, took this concept further, stressing the political, cultural, and even psychological benefits for the countries of eastern Europe of finally becoming genuine and full members of the Western community.

The other main pro-expansion argument stresses the continued, albeit changed, need for deterrence. NATO doctrine still calls for a deterrence posture to ensure collective security against a potential aggressor. The main concern, although it is sometimes left implicit, is a resurgent Russia. It is not so

TABLE 8.1   NATO: Its Evolution, Cold War to Post–Cold War

NATO members

Charter members	Joined during the Cold War	Joined after the Cold War
Belgium	Greece (1952)	Czech Republic (1998)[‡]
Canada	Turkey (1952)	Hungary (1998)[‡]
Denmark	Federal Republic of	Poland (1998)[‡]
France*	Germany (1955)[†]	
Iceland	Spain (1982)	
Italy		
Luxembourg		
Netherlands		
Norway		
Portugal		
United Kingdom		
United States		

NATO-Russia Permanent Joint Council

Members of NATO, Russia

Partnership for Peace (PFP) members

Former republics of the Soviet Union	Former Warsaw Pact members	Former republics of Yugoslavia	Former neutral European states
Armenia	Albania	Macedonia	Austria
Azerbaijan	Bulgaria	Slovenia	Finland
Belarus	Romania		Sweden
Estonia	Slovak Republic		Switzerland
Georgia			
Kazakhstan			
Kyrgyz Republic			
Latvia			
Lithuania			
Moldova			
Turkmenistan			
Ukraine			
Uzbekistan			

Euro-Atlantic Partnership Council Members

Albania	Estonia	Lithuania	Sweden
Armenia	Finland	Macedonia	Switzerland

(*Continued on page 288*)

TABLE 8.1 NATO: Its Evolution, Cold War to Post–Cold War *(Continued)*			
Euro-Atlantic Partnership Council Members			
Austria	Georgia	Moldova	Tajikistan
Azerbaijan	Kazakhstan	Romania	Turkmenistan
Belarus	Kyrgyz Republic	Slovak Republic	Ukraine
Bulgaria	Latvia	Slovenia	Uzbekistan

*Withdrew from NATO military command in 1965 but maintained political membership
†As a condition of German reunification in 1990, NATO agreed not to station military forces in the territory of the former German Democratic Republic (East Germany).
‡Former Warsaw Pact members

much a fear that the Soviet Union would be reconstituted, although this possibility is not totally dismissed. The more salient concerns about Russia run deeper historically—Russia does have a precommunist history of regional expansionism—and grow out of the uncertainties and instabilities of Russia's own postcommunist transition and the possibility of more aggressively nationalist leaders coming to power.

Critics of NATO expansion stress their own two points. One is that NATO expansion may make an aggressive Russia more, rather than less, likely. Antagonistic nationalist forces within Russia may be strengthened in the face of an enlarged NATO, and appeals to traditional Russian fears of encirclement may end up bringing to power leaders much less pro-Western than Boris Yeltsin. The special charter signed with Russia in 1998, the NATO-Russia Founding Act, was intended as reassurance that NATO expansion was not directed against them. But if the next rounds of NATO expansion involve the Baltic states or other ex-Soviet countries, there may be greater backlash within Russia.

Second is the concern that adding new members will dilute the cohesion that has made NATO function so effectively. This is less a criticism of any specific new members than a basic organizational precept: as the number of members goes up, making decisions and carrying out policies becomes that much harder. "If one country after another is admitted," a former U.S. ambassador to NATO argues, "it will no longer be today's functioning and cohesive NATO that the new members will be joining but rather a diluted entity, a sort of league of nations."[11]

NATO'S POST–COLD WAR MISSION   There is a subtle but significant shift in the use of the terms "threats" and "risks" in defining NATO's mission. During the Cold War NATO was focused on deterring and defending against the threat posed by the Soviet Union and the Warsaw Pact. Its central mission was to meet this threat with the necessary forces, weapons, and doctrine. Post–Cold War NATO doctrine has come to recognize that security threats are less likely to come from "classical territorial aggression" than from the risks of "the adverse consequences that may arise from the serious economic, social, and political difficulties, including ethnic rivalries and territorial disputes, which are faced by many countries in Central and Eastern Europe."[12] This meant both that deterrence strategy needed to be reformulated and that peace operations needed to be a new and major part of NATO's mission.

The wars in the former Yugoslavia posed the first tests of how well NATO would handle this new mission of peace operations. These wars—first in Croatia and Bosnia, and then in Kosovo—posed a number of difficult issues for NATO, and the results have been decidedly mixed. The former Yugoslavia was "out of area" in terms of the North Atlantic Treaty's provisions pertaining to attacks on or within the territory of member countries. On the other hand, the underlying purpose of the alliance was to keep the peace in Europe, and these were the most gruesome and destructive wars in Europe since World War II. They also were a different type of conflict than NATO had been formed to fight. NATO doctrine, training, deployments, battle plans, and equipment were geared to conventional warfare against the Warsaw Pact forces, armies against armies, along demarcated battle lines, relying on technology and classical strategy. In Bosnia and Kosovo, though, the wars were marked by ethnic passion more than military professionalism, and they were driven by ethnic cleansing not classical invasion.

From 1992 until late 1995 the United States and western Europe mostly hurled accusations and cross-accusations across the Atlantic as wars raged in Croatia and in Bosnia—"three years of collective buck-passing," as Joseph Lepgold puts it.[13] NATO finally did intervene in Bosnia following the signing of the Dayton accords in December 1995. It did so with a 60,000-troop Implementation Force (IFOR), which was followed about a year later with a somewhat smaller Stabilization Force (SFOR). IFOR and SFOR succeeded in restoring stability to Bosnia, and as such demonstrated that NATO could play an important peacekeeping role. Both operated much more efficiently and conveyed much more of a deterrent threat than had the crazy-quilted U.N. force that had preceded them. They also were noteworthy in including Russian and other former Soviet-bloc troops.

Yet what was the lesson? That NATO would intervene only late in such conflicts, only after ethnic cleansings had run their horrific course? What about initiating earlier peace-making and peace-enforcing operations, which might prevent so many lives from being lost, so many rapes from being committed, so many villages from being plundered? New mechanisms and strategies were being developed to enhance NATO capabilities for peace operations, such as the Combined Joint Task Forces of ad hoc military commands of some NATO partners for specific military operations. But even if NATO could enhance its capabilities for peace operations, would it have the political will to act early when the risks might be higher but deterrence and prevention were still possible?

The 1999 Kosovo war added to the dilemmas in a number of respects. Its action against Serbia was the most extensive military action NATO had ever undertaken—not just a few air strikes, not just peacekeeping, but a war. Yet the war was undertaken with a mix of forcefulness and hesitation that reflected ambivalence and confusion about the nature of the mission and the depth of commitment to it. The bombing campaign against Serbia was massive, and the political rhetoric was tough. But the mission stayed defined as "degrading" Serbian capabilities, as measured in buildings, bridges, and military assets, all while Serb forces proceeded with their ethnic cleansing of Kosovo. The reluctance to commit ground troops could not but lead the Serbs to question just how committed NATO was.

Thus, questions regarding NATO's new mission still are open ones—and unless one believes that Europe's ethnic conflicts are over, they are questions for which answers will need to be found.

Another key issue is whether NATO should extend its reach even further to deal with broader global threats such as weapons of mass destruction and terrorism. This would constitute even more of a shift beyond NATO's original mission, as such threats often emanate from the Middle East and other far out-of-area locales. One view is that, although their point of origin is out of area, their impact is felt well "within area" and they constitute some of the most serious threats NATO member states face. The other view is that this is too broad an extension of NATO's domain to be consistent with its main mission. A broader issue raised is whether such extended mandates would benefit the United States and accentuate American power by providing broader support and more burden-sharing on some key global issues, or whether the consensus-building that would be needed within the alliance would end up inhibiting U.S. power by reducing the capacity to act unilaterally.

Deterrence and the "Two MRC" Strategy

"MRC" is the Pentagon acronym for "major regional contingency"—i.e., major regional war. U.S. military doctrine calls for the ability to fight two

MRCs at any time. American forces in all their aspects—size, force structure, deployment, weaponry—are to be maintained at levels and capabilities sufficient to pose a strong enough deterrent to prevent such wars from happening, but if necessary also to fight and win them quickly and *even simultaneously.* The scenarios on which the two-MRC strategy is based are another war in the Middle East started by Iraq and another Korean war. These were said to be only illustrative, and the Defense Department report announcing the two-MRC doctrine acknowledged that planning assumptions were not based on repeating past experiences. Nevertheless these were the regional deterrence scenarios most often invoked to justify the two-MRC strategy.

Is this the right strategy? Both regions do continue to be quite unstable. Even if Saddam Hussein were no longer in power, and even if the Arab-Israeli peace process were to succeed—big "ifs" in their own right—the Middle East still would suffer from numerous other sources of instability and would continue to pose serious threats to U.S. interests. And with North Korea, although the war scare in 1993–94 in the crisis over nuclear proliferation was defused, there have been numerous tensions since, including fears of a major implosion by a regime whose people have been suffering massive starvation and which remains the most inscrutable in the world. The East Asia region also has other potentially explosive issues, such as China-Taiwan, that could pose dangerous military situations.

Even so a number of questions about the two-MRC strategy are debated. One is whether forces this large really need to be maintained. Cold War doctrine had required the capability to fight two and one-half wars, with the "half" war being a guerrilla one. But is a half war all that can be reduced? Isn't the assumption of fighting simultaneously a bit improbable? Or is this just being prudent?

Another question raised is about the political viability of the continued global "forward deployment" of U.S. forces at overseas military bases. Japan is not the only place where political problems have arisen over American bases. Key bases in the Philippines had to be shut down because of domestic political opposition. In the Persian Gulf, even after the Gulf War the only governments willing to allow American troops to be based on their soil were Kuwait and Saudi Arabia. A number of other countries have wanted American protection, but have been so fearful of fundamentalist-led anti-Americanism that they concocted such arrangements as floating docks for U.S. forces just off their shores. And in Saudi Arabia there were two major terrorist attacks in 1995–96 against the U.S. forces stationed there.

A third question is whether, by planning for these kinds of large-force conventional wars, U.S. strategy becomes less equipped for dealing with peacekeeping, peace enforcement, and other "operations other than war" (Pentagonese again). This goes back to the point made earlier about the limits of the Gulf War model, and is taken up more fully later in this chapter.

Nuclear Deterrence, Nuclear "Abolition," Nuclear Defense?

Nuclear deterrence strategy has changed in three principal respects. One is that, as a top Clinton National Security Council official put it, "nuclear weapons now play a smaller role in our national security strategy than at any point during the nuclear era." This official went on to stress that "it would be a mistake to think that nuclear weapons no longer matter;" nuclear deterrence does continue to be an integral component of U.S. defense strategy, but a less dominant one than during the Cold War. The second change is the abandonment of the nuclear-war-fighting doctrine adopted by the Reagan administration. The document on which the post–Cold War policy is based "removes from presidential guidance all previous references to being able to wage a nuclear war successfully or to prevail in a nuclear war."[14] Nuclear weapons might still be used as retaliation or in some other way, but U.S. policy has done away with the Reaganesque notion that a nuclear war could be fought almost like a regular war. One exception is the willingness to use nuclear weapons as retaliation for the use of nuclear or other weapons of mass destruction (WMD). During the Persian Gulf War, for example, analysts suspect that Saddam Hussein was deterred from using chemical or biological weapons by the Bush administration's threat of nuclear retaliation.

This leads us to the third change, which is greater focus on global WMD threats. Although the nonproliferation regimes discussed in Chapter 7 have achieved a great deal, the Pentagon nevertheless estimates that more than twenty-five countries, many of which are hostile to the United States or its friends and allies, possess or are developing WMD. Dealing with these threats requires going beyond traditional deterrence postures to develop *counterproliferation* strategies. These strategies are being developed with a number of U.S. allies, including NATO, Israel and other allies in the Middle East, and allies in the Asia-Pacific region. Intelligence is shared, counterproliferation technologies are exchanged and developed cooperatively, and joint actions are planned by defense and military establishments. These range from developing intelligence and military capacities to locate and destroy a proliferator's weapons and other strategic sites, to anthrax vaccination programs for troops and development of protective suits and equipment against chemical weapons.

Notwithstanding these changes and adaptations, nuclear deterrence has been set as a "cornerstone" of U.S. foreign policy for the "indefinite future."[15] The basic need to deter aggression remains, and maintaining U.S. nuclear superiority is seen as a crucial component of a credible deterrence posture. "Having the most powerful weapons and deterrent plays an essential role," as one strategist put it, "in attaining the number one security policy objective of the United States, which is to preserve our central interests abroad without involving us in a war. Nuclear weapons are not all that is needed to make war obsolete, but they have no real substitute."[16] Toward these ends, and within the U.S.-Russia START weapons cuts, the basic "triad" force structure of land-based ICBMs (intercontinental ballistic missiles), submarines, and air bombers and cruise missiles has been continued. The nuclear deterrence portion of the defense budget still runs more than $30 billion annually.

Yet two main critiques have been offered.

NUCLEAR "ABOLITION" Serious questioning of nuclear deterrence has come from those who believe the end of the Cold War presents a historic opportunity for deep cuts and even "abolition" of nuclear weapons. Even the 80 percent cuts proposed for START III are said not to be enough. Why do the United States and Russia even need that many nuclear weapons? Surely we can feel secure with many fewer. Indeed, why not come as close to totally abolishing them as possible?

These questions have not been raised just by "peaceniks." In January 1997 sixty retired generals and admirals from the United States and more than a dozen other countries issued a statement calling for much deeper cuts and a commitment to move toward total elimination of nuclear weapons (see Perspectives, p. 294). Among the most outspoken of this group was retired general George Lee Butler, the former head of the Strategic Air Command (SAC), which is in charge of the major part of the U.S. nuclear force.

Three main arguments are made by General Butler and others who take this position.[17] One is that the United States could make its own deeper cuts unilaterally and actually be more, not less, secure. The American nuclear arsenal still would be well above what is needed for second-strike capacity and to pose a credible deterrent. Such reductions would also help alleviate the risk of Russia turning further toward a "first use" doctrine to compensate for the widening U.S. advantage in the face of the disarray and crumbling of Russia's capacity to maintain its nuclear arsenal.

Second is a fundamental questioning of whether nuclear deterrence really still has the credibility it claims. How believable is the threat that the United States would respond to an attack, especially a non-nuclear one, with nuclear weapons? Not very, according to critics: the disproportionality of such a response would make it very difficult to actually carry out.

Third is a concern about accidents. There have been many false alarms for both the United States and Russia over the years, no doubt many more than

---

PERSPECTIVES

"RETIRED NUCLEAR WARRIOR SOUNDS ALARM ON WEAPONS"

OMAHA, Dec. 4 — Three years ago, Air Force Gen. George Lee Butler commanded a military headquarters on the outskirts of this city with the power to propel the world to a nuclear conflict. At his direction, bombers laden with 2,800 warheads could have raced down runways and flown toward the former Soviet Union or anyplace else Washington targeted for ruin.

Today, Butler is slated to give a lunchtime speech in Washington in which he will make a dramatic departure from the views he publicly espoused as commander in chief of America's nuclear arsenal—the pinnacle of his 37-year career in military uniform. He is to describe U.S. nuclear policy as "fundamentally irrational" on grounds that such arms pose a great threat to mankind.

Butler, who once personally approved thousands of targets for U.S. nuclear weapons, now advocates that Washington urgently pursue the elimination of such arms around the globe. He says taking such an extreme measure is the only way to forestall a horrible nuclear accident and prevent warheads from falling into the hands of rogue states or terrorists. . . .

"Nuclear weapons are inherently dangerous, hugely expensive, militarily inefficient and morally indefensible," Butler says now. He acknowledges that this view is a kind of heresy for a former CINCSAC, or commander in chief of the Strategic Air Command—a job that often has gone to some of the country's most hawkish military leaders, such as Gen. Curtis E. LeMay, the model for Jack D. Ripper in *Dr. Strangelove*. . . .

Butler says those who argue such arms are still needed in the aftermath of the Cold War are victims of the "intellectual smog" that justified the absurd pressures of having to decide in less than 30 minutes whether to order a nuclear retaliatory strike and wipe out an entire nation.

(*Continued on page 295*)

("Retired Nuclear Warrior" *Continued from page 294*)

Today, however, after reflecting more on his experiences, Butler is more angry at what he calls the persistent "terror-filled anesthesia" about nuclear arms. With "the luxury to step back mentally and think about the implications of having spent four trillion dollars producing 70,000 nuclear weapons . . . I realize that the notion nuclear weapons bring security—the idea that somehow we were in charge, that somehow all of this was infallible and manageable and we could make it work— . . . is fatally flawed."

Source: R. Jeffrey Smith, "Retired Nuclear Warrior Sounds Alarm on Weapons," *Washington Post*, December 4, 1996, A1. © 1996, The Washington Post. Reprinted with permission.

we know. In one such incident, in early 1995, a Norwegian research rocket was mistakenly taken by Russia for an incoming U.S. nuclear missile, and Yeltsin came very close to ordering a counterattack. Both sides still follow a "launch on warning" policy, which can mean that decisions on whether the blip on the screen is an incoming missile or a research rocket or a flock of birds have to be made in a matter of minutes. Here, too, proposals are made for the United States to act unilaterally to take its weapons off hair-trigger alert. This both would reduce the chances of a mistake on the U.S. side and could prompt the Russians to follow suit.

Fourth is a moral argument about having lost sight of what Jonathan Schell, a leading nuclear abolitionist, calls the "singularity" of nuclear weapons. "Their singularity, from a moral point of view, lies in the fact that the use of just a few would carry the user beyond every historical benchmark of indiscriminate mass slaughter. . . . The use of a mere dozen nuclear weapons against, say, the dozen largest cities of the United States, Russia or China, causing tens of millions of deaths, would be a human catastrophe without parallel."[18]

Some of the counterpoints made by defenders of nuclear deterrence can be inferred from the previous discussion. One main point to emphasize is the concern about cheating and "break-out." If cuts go very far, especially if full abolition were to be tried, such that countries have no nuclear weapons or only a very few, a state or perhaps a terrorist organization that "broke out" by having secretly kept or developed some would have an enormous advantage. Moreover, even if every weapon is eliminated from the face of the earth, the knowledge of how to build nuclear weapons would still rest in the minds of humankind.

Nonetheless, the very fact that the debate has gone to this level is yet another example of the profound changes brought by the post–Cold War era. It is a debate that surely will continue.

NUCLEAR DEFENSE   Another critique of U.S. strategy focuses on the need for a ballistic-missile defense (BMD) system to protect against a nuclear attack if deterrence fails. Current proposals are mostly for more limited missile defense than the "Star Wars" system of the 1980s. The main impetus comes from the threats associated with nuclear and missile proliferation in such countries as Iraq, North Korea, and Iran. In 1993 American intelligence agencies concluded with great certainty that no country outside the five major nuclear powers "will develop or otherwise acquire a ballistic missile in the next 15 years that could threaten the contiguous 48 states or Canada."[19] However, advances made in the ensuing two to three years by Iran and North Korea in their missile programs, and by Pakistan and India in their nuclear-weapons programs, made this statement seem much less of a certainty.

Three issues define the debate over BMD. One is about technological effectiveness. A 1998 report to the Pentagon revealed that only 4 out of 17 tests of a prototype BMD system were successful, and these were under the benign conditions of a planned test, wholly unlike the stressful conditions of actual combat and the "fog of war." Recent tests have been more successful, but still mixed. The technological challenges of this version of BMD are not as great as for the Reagan "Star Wars" system, which was based in space and was to provide a full national shield. Nevertheless they are formidable, and the margin of error is exceedingly small.

The second issue is cost. Experts estimate that more than $100 billion already have been spent on BMD research, and in 1999 the Clinton administration and the Republican Congress agreed on an increase from $4 billion to $10 billion just for that year.[20]

Third is a possible strategic "boomerang" of negative reactions from Russia and China. The Russians contend, and many U.S. experts concur, that U.S. BMD plans are inconsistent with the original 1972 Anti-Ballistic Missile (ABM) treaty that was part of the U.S.-Soviet SALT I agreements. The ABM treaty was based on the doctrine of "mutually assured destruction," by which nuclear war could best be avoided if neither side had extensive BMD systems (so that whichever side attacked first still would be vulnerable to nuclear retaliation). If agreement cannot be reached with Russia on amending the ABM treaty, the debate is over whether the security gains justify going ahead anyway. As for China, it is concerned both about the strategic balance and about proposals to provide theater BMD systems to Japan and Taiwan.

Defense Spending: How Much Is Enough?

One of the historical "great debates" (Chapter 3) and a recurring controversy during the Cold War, this question is still with us. Part of the problem is what measures to use. The late 1990s defense budget is approximately $260 billion per year. That number can be seen as high or low, depending on your perspective. It looks high compared to the $53 billion in the federal budget for education, training, employment, and social services; or compared to Russia, which only now spends $82 billion, or China at $32 billion, or the whole rest of the world, which combined spends only about $2 total for every $1 in the U.S. defense budget. On the other hand, it looks low as a percentage of the federal budget, now about 15 percent, compared to 28 percent in the late 1980s; or as a percentage of U.S. gross domestic product (GDP), about 3 percent, compared to 6.2 percent in the late 1980s; or in looking at defense budget projections for 2002, which are almost 50 percent less than 1990 levels in inflation-adjusted dollars.

Another part of the debate is over specific allocations within the defense budget. How much spending on new weapons? The need for maintaining technological supremacy for the American military is a point of consensus. But on how much spending is enough to achieve that, analysts disagree. Estimates vary from assessments of the $45 billion to $50 billion budgeted in 2002 for technology development as about $15 billion too little, to others that see room for saving as much as $100 billion in weapons procurement and related areas by 2002. Congressional politics also enter in. One member of Congress slipped $250,000 into the defense budget for a study of a caffeinated chewing gum that might help sleep-deprived troops—and that is manufactured by a company in his district. Another added $5 million for retrofitting locks used on classified documents to meet stricter specifications—as manufactured (you guessed it!) by a company in his district.[21]

Overall troop levels also are a key issue. Active-duty troops already have been cut from more than 2 million at the end of the Cold War to about 1.45 million. The 1997 Quadrennial Defense Review proposal took that number down only another 60,000. As a budget issue there are pressures to cut more to save more. But as a political issue, troop reductions lead to domestic base closings, and no member of Congress wants to approve bases being closed in his or her district or state.

Ethnic and Other Deadly Conflicts

How to deal with the ethnic and other deadly conflicts that so marked—or, more to the point, marred—the first decade of the post–Cold War world is another key dilemma for American power. Of the major conflicts shown in Map 8.1, the vast majority are fundamentally ethnic in nature. We noted earlier the limited applicability of Powell doctrine decisive warfare strategies, such as were used in the Persian Gulf War, to these types of conflicts. Nor does the two-MRC regional deterrence strategy fit these conflicts very well. They pose their own challenges both for the use of military force and for diplomacy.

Military Intervention

The question of when and where the United States should intervene militarily is especially difficult when the horrors of ethnic cleansing and genocide seem to urge action in the name of American principles, but involve areas that, as the U.S. ambassador to Somalia put it about that country, are "not a critical piece of real estate for anybody in the post–Cold War world."[22] The argument was well framed in the "Mother Teresa" exchange of articles in *Foreign Affairs* by Michael Mandelbaum and Stanley Hoffmann. Mandelbaum argued that giving national-interest weight to humanitarian concerns is being "too much like Mother Teresa" and turns foreign policy into "social work." Hoffmann countered that the very distinction between interests and values is "largely fallacious," in that "a great power has an 'interest' that goes beyond strict national security concerns and its definition of world order is largely shaped by its values."[23]

THE LESSONS OF EXPERIENCE   The Clinton administration's mishandling of the 1993 Somalia intervention greatly exacerbated this debate. A much-ballyhooed report issued in 1994, *A National Security Strategy of Engagement and Enlargement* (the "En-En" strategy, to its critics), read more like a statement of when and why the United States *would not* intervene militarily than as a delineation of when and why it *would*.[24] When the administration did finally intervene in Haiti in 1994 and Bosnia in 1995 it pointed to these cases as evidence that it did have a guiding conception of when and how to use military force. In actuality, though, both of these cases were more negotiated, last-minute occupations than coercive, preventive interventions.

In Haiti, among other missteps, there had been the especially embarrassing incident (mentioned in Chapter 7) in October 1993 of the U.S.S. *Harlan*

Major Conflicts of the 1990s

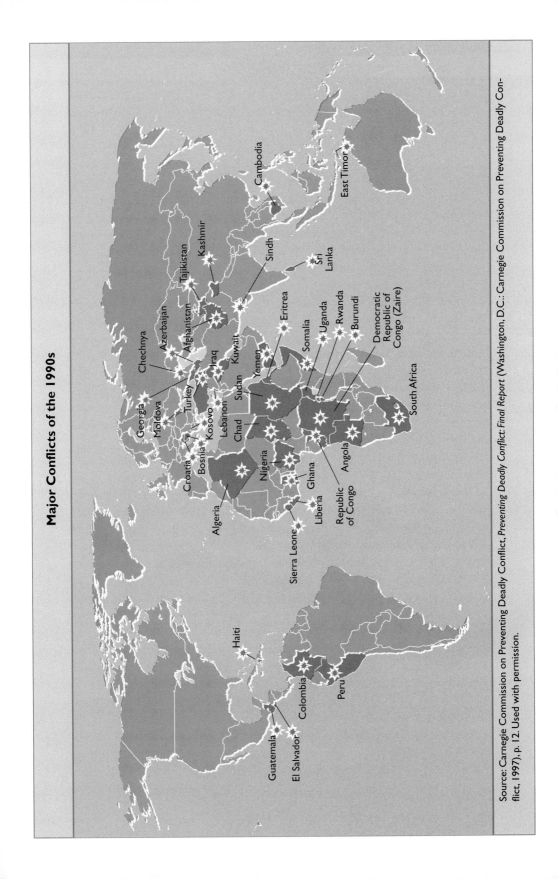

County fleeing the Port-au-Prince harbor when met by demonstrators on the docks. In September 1994, President Clinton dispatched former president Jimmy Carter, Senator Sam Nunn, and retired general Colin Powell to Haiti as a last-ditch negotiating effort to avoid U.S. forces having to shoot their way onto the island. The Carter-Nunn-Powell mission succeeded in getting the Haitian military-coup leaders to step down although, in large part because of the *Harlan County* and other credibility-sapping incidents, it wasn't until they were absolutely convinced that the American assault planes were in the air and naval forces on their way that the coup leaders agreed to go. The "invasion" thus became more of a peaceful landing and an agreed-upon temporary occupation.

In the Bosnia case, credit is due for the U.S.-led NATO peacekeeping mission begun in late 1995. About one-third of the sixty thousand NATO troops first sent to enforce the Dayton accords were American. And for all the killing that took place between 1991 and 1995, there has been very little since in Bosnia. Still there was a sense that the United States acted only when forced to do so, when most if not all other options had been exhausted, and only when the aggressor's defiance and disregard for the West had reached the brazen extremes that the Serbs' did. If it was then and only then that the United States would commit its military forces, this was not all that credibility-enhancing an example in the long run.

In Kosovo the United States and NATO acted sooner than they had in Bosnia, but still not soon or effectively enough to prevent massive killings and other violence. The threat of air strikes was made only in late 1998, many months after the first wave of Serbian aggression against the Kosovar Albanians and despite numerous warnings and calls for earlier preventive action. When the air campaign did get launched in March 1999, despite the massive tonnage dropped, the many sorties flown, and the number of physical targets hit, it was too little and too late to stop the full ethnic cleansing of Kosovo.

It remains to be demonstrated if and when the timing and strategies may be different in the future.

REQUIREMENTS FOR A MORE EFFECTIVE STRATEGY   A number of factors are essential to an effective military intervention strategy for dealing with ethnic and other such conflicts. One is the need to bear in mind the distinction between the political and the genuinely humanitarian dimensions in humanitarian crises. Back in April 1991, when a deadly cyclone hit Bangladesh, killing 139,000 people and doing $2 billion worth of damage to this already impoverished country, and American military forces were sent to provide relief and help with reconstruction, this genuinely was a humanitarian intervention. But the starvation in Somalia, the outbreak of plague in Rwanda, the fears of annihilation of the Kurds in Iraq and the Muslims in Bosnia and Kosovo—all were *politically precipitated* humanitarian crises. This by no means diminishes the need for humanitarian relief to alleviate people's suffering, but it does point to important differences in how the mission needs to be defined, the forces structured, and the political and military components of the overall strategy woven together.

Another issue is what Professor Richard Betts has called the "delusion of impartiality."[25] Impartiality is pretty straightforward in genuinely humanitarian situations like the Bangladesh cyclone. So, too, in genuine peacekeeping situations, when both sides need to be confident that the international party will not take sides and assured that each will not be disadvantaged so long as it abides by the terms of the peace. It is when the parties are still in conflict, and the problem is peace-making or peace-enforcing, that impartiality is a delusion.* Impartiality in such cases would mean applying the same strictures to both sides, even if this leaves one side with significant military advantages over the other. It also would mean not coercing either side, irrespective of which one is doing more killing, seizing more territory, or committing more war crimes. "Such lofty evenhandedness may make sense for a judge in a court that can enforce its writ, but hardly for a general wielding a small stick in a bitter war."[26]

Instead the strategy must be "fair but firm." The parties to the conflict must know both that cooperation has its benefits and that noncooperation has its consequences. They must be assured that the benefits of cooperation will be fully equitable. And they must be convinced that the United States and any other international parties involved are prepared to enforce the consequences differentially, as warranted by who does and who does not cooperate. This does not mean that force must be used, but that it must be an option, and it must be seen by the parties as a credible one.

There also needs to be a questioning of the conventional wisdom of using force only as a last resort. Although all would prefer to avoid having to use military force, it is extremely unrealistic to believe that these rogue leaders will agree to peaceful methods of conflict resolution if they think they can achieve their goals militarily at costs they deem acceptable. Each situation will have to

---

*See Chapter 7 to review the distinction between peacekeeping and peace-making or peace enforcement.

be analyzed to assess whether and how preventive military action or the threat thereof is likely to deter and not exacerbate oppression, but "preserving force as a last resort implies a lockstep sequencing of the means to achieve foreign policy objectives that is unduly inflexible and relegates the use of force to *in extremis* efforts to salvage a faltering foreign policy."[27]

Finally, there must be a more balanced assessment of the limits of air power. The utility of air power has been overestimated throughout the twentieth century; the Clinton administration apparently learned very little from this history.[28] It made more frequent use of air power than ever before in U.S. foreign policy, but with only limited success in transforming military might into political objectives. Air strikes were launched against Iraq and Saddam Hussein time and again, but with very little lasting effect. The Kosovo war was fought principally through air power, yet the Serbian ethnic cleansing went on. Most wars simply cannot be fought just from the air. Ground troops do carry risks, but they often are essential for results.

The Politics of Military Intervention

PENNSYLVANIA AVENUE FUMBLING   War-powers tensions between the president and Congress have been even more difficult than usual with regard to these types of conflicts. Somalia was Bill Clinton's first war-powers issue, and it was a disaster. The original troop commitment had been made by President Bush in December 1992, with the mission defined largely as a short-term humanitarian one of relief from starvation (Operation Provide Comfort). The troops were sent by executive action, outside the procedures of the War Powers Resolution, although with strong bipartisan support. The Clinton administration later would be criticized for keeping the troops in and taking on the broader mission of "nation-building." Had it withdrawn the troops according to the original schedule, however, the risk of reversion to chaos was high. In this regard the administration's mistake may have been less taking on the broader mission per se than not paying enough attention to the requirements of a more effective strategy (as just discussed), and not sufficiently consulting with Congress and bringing it in to have some "co-ownership" for the policy.

Once the policy started to go badly, and especially in October 1993 when eighteen American soldiers were killed, and one dead soldier was ignominiously dragged through the streets of the capital city, Mogadishu, a political firestorm was set off on Capitol Hill, on the airwaves, and with the general public. Within hours the president felt he had no choice but to get on television with a hastily prepared speech promising to withdraw the American troops. Whether this was the right decision, and whether the mistake was not having withdrawn the troops sooner or not having made a more concerted effort to accomplish the mission, the picture conveyed to the world was of an American political system still fumbling the war power.

The September 1994 Haiti intervention went better, but actually was a close call. Had the Carter-Nunn-Powell mission not succeeded in persuading the Haitian military to step down, and had the invasion brought casualties, the outcry on Capitol Hill likely would have been deafening. Other than the Congressional Black Caucus and some other liberal Democrats who had been pushing for military action, most others in Congress were nonsupportive if not outright opposed to a Haiti intervention. Moreover, the Clinton administration had not bothered to come to Congress, despite the consultation clause of the WPR, not even for a resolution like the one Bush got for the Persian Gulf War.

The usual presidentialist claim of the demands of a crisis situation was not very convincing in this case, given all the advance planning and the fact that the Clinton administration had gone to the U.N. Security Council almost two months earlier for an "all necessary means" resolution authorizing the intervention. The real reason for not consulting Congress was that the administration was afraid it would lose. In the end, and yet again, the ambiguities of the WPR and the reluctance of Congress to act on its own allowed the president to go his own way, with plenty of criticism but few biting procedural constraints.

The politics of the deployment of U.S. troops to Bosnia as part of IFOR following the Dayton accords largely adhered to the same pattern. The president was not stopped from deploying the troops, but he was not exactly supported in doing so, either. The House did pass a resolution that was at best a mixed message; it stated support for the troops themselves but "disowned the deployment decision."[29] The Senate resolution was more supportive, but it too contained far more caveats, criticisms, and reservations than presidents usually get when putting American troops on the ground. Moreover, to get even this Clinton had to state that the deployment was only for one year. Yet it was clear from the outset that this was an unrealistic timetable. Indeed, a year later the president announced that, although he would make some cuts in numbers, the American troops needed to stay in Bosnia another year. Another year later came yet another extension; this one was left more open-ended. Congress criticized, and passed various measures affecting the deployment at the margins, but didn't stop them.

In the Kosovo case as well there was neither strong and explicit congressional support nor a concerted effort to stop the military action. When a few House members pushed to have at least some formal legislative action, whether a declaration of war or an invocation of the provisions and procedures of the War Powers Resolution, they garnered little support.

The war-powers issue thus still is unresolved, and full of potential for further interbranch conflict. The immediate political costs and constraints have been contained, but only by deferring the central issue—indeed, the most central issue any democracy must grapple with—for yet another day.

PUBLIC OPINION ON THE USE OF MILITARY FORCE   During the early Cold War the public generally was willing to support the use of military force. In Chapter 5 we saw how, as part of the "Vietnam trauma," public support for the use of force became extremely weak. Starting in the 1980s and then in the 1990s, the pattern became more mixed, with public support having increased for the use of force for certain objectives but not for others. The picture we get is of a public that is neither as trigger-happy as during parts of the Cold War, nor as gun-shy as in the wake of Vietnam; the American public has become "pretty prudent."[30]

Behind these trends we can see three general patterns. First, public support tends to be greatest when the principal policy objective for which force is being used is to coerce *foreign policy restraint* on an aggressor threatening the United States, its citizens, or its interests. The Persian Gulf War is an example. When the first deployments were made to Saudi Arabia, public-opinion polls registered in the range of 60–70 percent support, which was higher than support for Vietnam ever was. Polls also showed that public support was not strictly dependent on expectations of low casualties. In one poll posing hypothetical questions about possible casualties, only at the level of ten thousand or more deaths did support fall significantly—but even then at 60 percent this was still something much less than an antiwar movement. Belief in the importance of the objective of restraining aggression provided at least some tolerance for the risks of casualties.

Second, the public tends to be least supportive of military force when the principal objective is to engineer *internal political change* in another country's government. The low levels of support for aiding the Nicaraguan contras in the 1980s are one example. Haiti in the 1990s is another: only about 35 percent of Americans supported the military intervention when it was launched in September 1994. Even with the halo effect of the casualty-free occupation, approval ratings only went up to about 45 percent. The public still had doubts about using force to remake a government.[31]

Third are *humanitarian interventions,* for which public support tends to fall in between. In Somalia, for example, which started out as the veritable "pure" humanitarian intervention case, initial polls showed 70 percent support or higher. However, as perceptions of the mission changed to "nation-building"—i.e., internal political change—public support dropped to 47 percent, and then to 35 percent when the American soldiers were killed. This was indicative of the much lower public tolerance for casualties when the objective was remaking governments rather than restraining aggression. Then when, six months later, the Rwandan genocide began, the "Somalia effect" worked against getting involved in a conflict that was strikingly similar, and to many seemed more protracted and dangerous. On the other hand it was difficult not to be moved by the killing and suffering shown on television. Post-Rwanda support for humanitarian intervention did come back up, although not as high as pre-Somalia. The humanitarian objective explains why support for the use of ground troops was higher than many expected in the early stages of the Kosovo war. The American public was not eager to send ground forces in, but it was willing to do so given the nature of the principal policy objectives.

This basic pattern of what the public is and is not inclined to support does have an underlying logic based on conceptions of *legitimacy* and calculations of *efficacy.* On the first point, using force to restrain aggression has a much stronger normative claim than does trying to remake governments. Humanitarian intervention falls in between, with some situations so dire that claims to legitimacy can be made even if the intervention is within a state and without the consent of the state's government. As to prospects for effectiveness, foreign policy restraint objectives have the inherent advantage of being more readily translatable into an operational military plan. Internal political change objectives, however, tend to require strategies more political in nature and less suitable to an operational military plan. Humanitarian interventions fall in between on this point as well; they usually have discrete missions and objectives but are difficult to keep from crossing over into state-building.

Other factors may also come into play in any particular case. Multilateral support and burden-sharing is one; the public often wants to know that other countries are also bearing some of the risks and costs.* The reactions of congressional leaders, newspaper editorialists, television pundits, and other elites

---

*This can cut both ways, however, as with the strong opposition to U.S. troops serving under foreign command as discussed in Chapter 7.

are also a factor.* Fundamentally, though, the American public is hardly eager to use military force, but is not invariably opposed to it. It still lacks lots of information, and may not even be able to find the relevant places on a map, but it manages to show "good judgment in the use of resources" and "caution and circumspection as to danger and risk"—exactly how the dictionary defines "prudence."

Preventive Statecraft

The basic logic of "preventive statecraft" seems unassailable: Act early to prevent disputes from escalating or problems from worsening.[32] Reduce tensions that if intensified could lead to war. Deal with today's conflicts before they become tomorrow's crisis. Preventive statecraft follows the same logic as preventive medicine: Don't wait until the cancer has spread or the arteries are fully clogged. Or, as the auto mechanic says in a familiar television commercial, as he holds an oil filter in one hand and points to a seized-up car engine with the other, "Pay me now or pay me later."

Yet despite the unassailability of the basic logic, the post–Cold War track record thus far, both for the United States and for the rest of the international community, is very mixed. Too often we hear that nothing else could have been done, that nothing more or different was viable than the policies as pursued. But there are a number of bases for arguing that preventive statecraft could have worked, that deadly conflicts like those in Rwanda, Bosnia, and Kosovo could have been limited, if not prevented.

PURPOSIVE SOURCES OF ETHNIC CONFLICT   A starting point for understanding how and why preventive statecraft could have worked better involves the debate between "primordialist" and "purposive" theories of the sources of ethnic conflict. The primordialist view sees ethnicity as a fixed and inherently conflictual historical identity; thus the 1990s conflicts were primarily continuations of ones going back hundreds of years—e.g., "Balkan ghosts" going back to the fourteenth century, the Somali clan rivalries dating from the precolonial pastoral period, the medieval *buhake* agricultural caste system of Tutsi dominance over Hutu in what is now Rwanda. Yugoslavia was an "intractable problem from hell," as Secretary of State Warren Christopher put it, "tribal feuds, ancient hatreds, steeped in a history of bloodshed."[33]

---

*"Cueing," "framing," and "priming" were discussed more generally in Chapter 6.

If this were true, then it would be hard to hold out much hope for preventive statecraft. The histories, though, are not nearly so deterministic. A number of studies have shown that ethnic identities are much less fixed over time, and the frequency and intensity of ethnic conflict much more varying over both time and place than primordialist theory would have it. In Bosnia, for example, the ethnic intermarriage rate in 1991 was around 25 percent, and there were very few ethnically "pure" urban residents or ethnically homogeneous smaller communities. As a Bosnian Muslim schoolteacher put it, "we never, until the war, thought of ourselves as Muslims. We were Yugoslavs. But when we began to be murdered because we are Muslims things changed. The definition of who we are today has been determined by our killing."[34]

An alternative explanation of the sources of ethnic conflict is the "purposive" view. This view acknowledges the deep-seated nature of ethnic identifications and the corresponding animosities and unfinished agendas of vengeance that persist as historical legacies. But the purposive view takes a much less deterministic view of how, why, and if these identity-rooted tensions become deadly conflicts. It focuses the analysis on forces and factors that intensify and activate historical animosities into actions and policies reflecting conscious and deliberate choices for war and violence. The dominant dynamic is not the playing out of historical inevitability but, as another author put it, "the purposeful actions of political actors who actively create violent conflict" to serve their own domestic political agendas by "selectively drawing on history in order to portray [events] as historically inevitable."[35]

The conflicts thus were not strictly "intractable problems from hell." They were fed, shaped, manipulated, directed, and turned toward the purposes of leaders and others whose interests were served by playing the ethnic card.

Missed Opportunities   A second point in support of the potential of preventive statecraft is the strong evidence from a number of recent cases that the international community *did* have specific and identifiable opportunities to try to limit if not prevent these conflicts. But its statecraft was flawed, inadequate, or even absent. We cannot know for sure that conflict could have been prevented; this is what is called a "counterfactual argument," and its limits must be acknowledged.[36] Such arguments must be based on what genuinely was known and possible *at the time,* not just in retrospect— otherwise they would be vulnerable to the charge of "Monday-morning quarterbacking." Nevertheless the evidence in virtually every case is that different policies were possible, and such policies had plausible chances of positive impact.

In Somalia, for example, although "no amount of preventive diplomacy could have completely pre-empted some level of conflict," there is solid evidence of "a virtual litany of missed opportunities" implying "that timely diplomatic interventions at several key junctures might have significantly reduced, defused and contained that violence."[37] Similarly in Rwanda, a whole series of missed opportunities has been identified, beginning a few years before the April 1994 genocide and continuing up to its eve, when the Hutu-dominated military still was divided and "an important factor in their decision to act was the failure of the international community to respond forcefully to the initial killings in Kigali and other regions."[38] In the Bosnia case experts provide varying analyses as to what the most egregious international policies were (perhaps because the list from which to select is so long). But few disagree that there was a "failure to prevent what was preventable."[39] So, too, with Kosovo, on which numerous warnings had been sounded and many proposals made for preventive action, especially during 1998 when Serbian leader Slobodan Milošević was launching his firstwave of ethnic cleansing, and some even going back a number of years earlier.[40]

CASES OF SUCCESSFUL PREVENTIVE STATECRAFT   In addition to the failures that could have been successes, there were other cases that quite plausibly could have become deadly conflicts, but in which preventive statecraft worked. The former Yugoslav Republic of Macedonia, which had its own quite significant ethnic tensions and vulnerabilities in the wake of the breakup of Yugoslavia but did not fall into mass violence, is a good example.[41] Analysts credit the maintenance of peace to the fact that an international presence was established on the ground in Macedonia in 1993. The Conference on Security and Cooperation in Europe sent an observer mission headed by a skilled American diplomat and with a broadly defined mandate. A number of nongovernmental organizations also established themselves in Macedonia, both providing an early-warning system and helping establish conflict-resolution mechanisms and other multiethnic programs. Most significant was the actual deployment of a multinational military force before significant violence had been unleashed. This force included U.S. troops, which, despite their small number and their being confined to low-risk duties, "carry weight," as Macedonian President Kiro Gligorov stressed. "It is a signal to all those who want to destabilize this region."[42]

Still, we must ask, even if preventive statecraft is doable, is it worth doing? It may be viable, but does it have sufficient value for the United States to justify the risks and the costs of undertaking it? Why not just wait and see, kick it down the road, and see if action really is necessary? If it were the case that the fires of ethnic conflicts, however intense, would just burn themselves up, and not threaten to spread regionally or destabilize more systematically, then in strict Realist terms one could argue that the United States could afford to just let them be. But we should realize by now that that is not always or even frequently the case.

Even though many of the ethnic conflicts of the 1990s did not involve inherently strategic locales, the damage to U.S. interests proved greater than anticipated as they escalated and spread. And whereas the costs of waiting tend to be assumed to be less than the costs of acting early, they have proven to be much greater than expected, arguably higher than those for preventive action would have been. For as difficult as preventive statecraft can be, the onset of mass violence transforms the nature of a conflict. A Rubicon gets crossed, on the other side of which resolution and even limitation of the conflict become much more difficult. The addition of revenge and retribution to other sources of tension plunges a conflict to a fundamentally different and more difficult depth. Foreign policy strategies that might have been effective at lower levels of conflict are less likely to be so amid intensified violence. The Croatia-Bosnia conflicts never were going to be easy to resolve, but after all the killings, the rapes, and the other war crimes, the tasks were vastly harder. So, too, in Rwanda, Somalia, and elsewhere where mass violence was not prevented.

For this and other reasons options do not necessarily stay open over time. A problem can get harder down that road to where it has been kicked. It thus is altogether Realist to act today rather than tomorrow. Moreover, the United States cannot not take a position. It follows from the earlier point about the purposive nature of these conflicts that, to the extent that the United States and other international actors can be expected to act (such as through military intervention or other measures such as economic sanctions and tough diplomacy) in ways that raise the costs and risks for ethnic leaders who would turn to mass violence, a moderating effect on these domestic actors' calculations is possible. If there is no such expectation, the calculation is left without a major constraint against turning to war and mass violence. Thus even "staying out" has an impact, especially when you are the most powerful country in the world. U.S. policy affects these conflicts one way or the other. The choice is how it will have its impact.

Security Threats from Nonstate Actors

Thus far our focus has been principally on security threats and issues involving the United States and other states in the international system. But we also need to take into account security threats from *nonstate actors,* such as terrorists, drug lords, and global crime rings. These groups often get support from states, but they are constituted and act independently, pursuing their own agendas and posing their own threats to American security interests. Such groups are by no means totally new to international affairs and American foreign policy, but they have become more prevalent in the post–Cold War era— and they pose difficult challenges for bringing American power to bear.

Terrorism

It is a basic fact that more Americans die from being hit by lightning than from terrorism. So why is so much attention paid every time a terrorist strikes? This question is intentionally rhetorical, but it does make a point. Terrorism does not actually threaten that many Americans, but its randomness and the sense of injustice it evokes, as well as the drama that it entails and the media's full klieglight attention, ensure that it will continue to be a major security issue.

Terrorism against the United States and Americans in recent years has had three main characteristics. First, while state sponsors of terrorism still play an important role (e.g., Iraq, Iran, Sudan), the major perpetrators against the United States have been extremist Islamic fundamentalist groups. An example is the group led by Osama bin Laden that bombed the American embassies in Kenya and Tanzania in mid-1998 and that also was involved in a number of other anti-American terrorist acts in the 1990s. "We believe the biggest thieves in the world are Americans and the biggest terrorists on Earth are Americans," bin Laden declared on ABC's *Nightline* about two months before the embassy bombings. The fervor of such anti-Americanism is fed by U.S. support for Israel, U.S. support for such conservative Arab regimes as Saudi Arabia, and other aspects of U.S. foreign policy.

Second, terrorism increasingly is penetrating U.S. borders. The 1993 bombing of the World Trade Center in New York City was a frightening demonstration of how terrorism was no longer something that happened overseas. In that bombing, Islamic fundamentalists drove a rental truck loaded with explosives into one of the building's basement parking garage. Its detonation shook these massive buildings, prominent parts of the New York skyline, to their foundations. Five people were killed and about a thousand others were hurt; it could have been many more. In mid-1997 the New York City police broke up a Palestinian radical group's terrorist plot to bomb the New York City subway system. If not for a good tip, this attack would have been launched within days. No doubt there are numerous other instances of failed terrorist plots about which we don't even know.

Third, an increasing danger is posed by WMD terrorism. Polls show that Americans worry more about nuclear terrorism than about nuclear war; a 1998 poll revealed that 50 percent saw the former as likely, but only 36 percent the latter. In one actual incident of such terrorism, when Aum Shinrikyo, a Japanese quasi-religious cult, killed twelve and injured thousands when it released sarin, a lethal chemical agent, on a crowded subway train in Tokyo in March 1995. It is all too easy to imagine all sorts of similar scenarios within the United States and against Americans abroad. Some of these involve homegrown terrorists such as right-wing militias. Indeed, a former Clinton administration official cited such actual incidents as a right-wing extremist group planning to kill federal government officials with a biological weapon, and a white-supremacist group convicted of purchasing three vials of freeze-dried bubonic plague.

"The fight against terrorism must be a national security priority," President Clinton has declared.[43] The budget for various aspects of counterterrorism increased to close to $10 billion in 1999. But developing strategies has been difficult. Deterrence against terrorists can be even more difficult than against states: where should the weapons be aimed and to whom the threat delivered? Furthermore, no one knows how deterrable terrorists are. Deterrence is based on a rational calculation that the costs of aggression exceed the benefits. Suicide bombers and other fanatical believers may be impervious to such a calculation.

When deterrence fails and retaliation is undertaken, the purposes are both to inflict punishment on the perpetrators and in so doing to try to harden the deterrent posture against future acts by them or by other terrorists. This was the case with the 1998 air strikes against Osama bin Laden and his supporters in Afghanistan and the Sudan. Such uses of military force are consistent with U.S. public opinion, since the objective is to restrain aggression: 70 percent of Americans supported the strikes against bin Laden. Ensuring effectiveness, though, can be difficult. Even with all the intelligence the United States had, it was difficult to know for sure the "return address" for targeting the military retaliation against bin Laden. Air strikes against a Sudanese factory alleged to be a chemical weapons plant raised the issue of causing harm—"collateral damage"—to innocent people.

Increasing domestic preparedness is the other main counterterrorism strategy. The FBI, which plays a key role in this area, has had an increase of over 400 percent in its counterterrorism budget since 1993. State and city governments also are becoming increasingly involved. New York City, for example, has developed special training programs for its police as well as medical personnel to cope with chemical or biological terrorism. "While there is no known immediate threat," the city's director of emergency management said, "we would be irresponsible if we did not plan for one.[44]

This emphasis on domestic preparedness has raised questions of what if any role the Pentagon should have against terrorist threats at home. The military is organized into "command structures" as the basis for defense against threats to U.S. interests and security in various parts of the world. Is it now necessary to have a "continental U.S. command" for defense against terrorism at home, so that the military can aid and possibly take charge of federal agencies in a time of crisis?

On the one hand, in addition to its defense capabilities, the military has unparalleled capacity for the managerial and logistical aspects of an emergency situation. "If there's a bona fide chemical attack in the subway system in New York, it's going to quickly go beyond what the local police can handle," one Pentagon official said. Only the military, another official said, has the capacity to transport thousands of hospital cots, tons of clean water, or "10,000 people who have been inoculated against anthrax" to the site of a biological attack where civilians have been stricken. On the other hand, the possibility of domestic use of the military raises major civil-liberties concerns. By law the military is prohibited from domestic law enforcement. Exceptions have been made in circumstances deemed to warrant this extended power, albeit only in very limited domains. But with something like a terrorist WMD attack that could spur widespread panic and extended periods of crisis, the concern of abuse is acute. "The danger is in the inevitable expansion of authority so the military gets involved in things like arresting people and investigating crimes," warned an official of the American Civil Liberties Union. "It's hard to believe that a soldier with a suspect in the sights of his M-1 tank is well positioned to protect that person's civil liberties."[45]

Drug Wars

To the extent that the measure of a security threat is its impact on the everyday lives of the American people, illegal narcotics rank quite high. They have penetrated the nation's cities, schools, workplaces, and families. Although the war against drugs does have a "demand-side" domestic policy component, the "supply side" is largely a foreign policy problem. It tends to focus on Latin America, particularly Mexico, Colombia, Panama, Peru, and Bolivia. But the problem is virtually global: the "golden triangle" in southeast Asia of Burma, Thailand, and Laos; Afghanistan and Pakistan; former Soviet republics in central Asia; Lebanon and Syria; Nigeria.

Three principal strategies have been pursued to fight the international narcotics trade, and with only mixed results all around. One strategy of course has been to try to use diplomacy. The State Department has a special bureau dealing with international narcotics ("drugs and thugs," some call it), and the White House has its "drug czar," who coordinates efforts both within the U.S. government and with other countries. Diplomatic efforts go on all the time at working levels, and on occasion even at the head-of-state level. Such efforts include programs to provide assistance for drug eradication, crop substitution, and police training. One problem, though, has been concern about the reliability of diplomatic partners, as with Mexico in 1997, when the army general who headed the national drug-fighting agency was arrested for himself being on the payroll of the drug cartels. Another problem arises when diplomacy degenerates to finger-pointing, as with American accusations that Mexico or Colombia or some other supplier country isn't doing enough to stop the flow of drugs, and their countercharges that the United States isn't doing enough to curtail demand.

Another strategy is a form of economic sanctions known as *decertification*. Every year the State Department presents to Congress reports on every country known to be a source of drugs. If a country is deemed not to be doing enough against drugs, it can be "decertified," which means that it loses eligibility for a number of U.S. economic and trade-assistance programs. There have been some instances in which this coercive pressure has been effective, prompting countries to step up their anti-drug efforts to avoid decertification and countries that have been decertified to do more to regain eligibility for U.S. assistance. Some countries have reacted nationalistically against the whole process, seeing it as another demonstration of American arrogance— the very term "decertification" to some means the United States is putting itself in an overlord position. This also has led to charadelike and credibility-weakening situations in which the State Department has certified a country to avoid a diplomatic dispute even though its anti-drug record was highly questionable.

A third main strategy has been military. It is not just rhetoric when we speak of "drug wars." Some of the largest post–Cold War U.S. military assistance programs have been to the Colombian and other Latin American militaries for anti-drug operations. American military personnel have been stationed in Colombia, Peru, and elsewhere, in small but still significant numbers. There even have been U.S. military casualties. "This is not a one-night stand," said General Charles E. Wilhelm, commander of U.S. military forces in Latin American and the Caribbean. "This is a marriage for life."[46] Others, however, warn that these military commitments risk drawing the United States deeper into these countries' internal political conflicts. Colombia, where American military involvement has been the greatest, is a particular concern because of the interweaving of the drug war with a long-festering guerrilla war, and because of the Colombian military's history of human rights violations and other undemocratic practices that make them a questionable partner.

Global Crime Rings

"Most Americans still refuse to believe just how well-organized global crime has become," writes Senator John Kerry, a senior member of the Senate's main anticrime subcommittee. "The new global criminal axis is composed of five principal powers in league with a host of lesser ones. The Big Five are the Italian Mafia, the Russian mobs, the Japanese *yakuza,* the Chinese triads and the Colombian cartels. They coordinate with smaller but highly organized gangs with distinct specialties in such countries as Nigeria, Poland, Jamaica and Panama." The threats have become so severe that they go well beyond "being exclusively in the realm of law enforcement; they also become a matter of national security."[47]

One of the reasons for this heightened concern about crime as a foreign policy issue is that, as a former head of the CIA warned, "international organized crime can threaten the stability of regions and the very viability of nations."[48] The annual income of many of these global crime rings exceeds the GDP of many a country; the United Nations estimates that international crime costs $750 billion a year. This gives criminals enormous economic power with the ability to, among other things, finance major weapons purchases for building formidable military arsenals of their own and providing plenty of money in bribes and kickbacks to public officials. It is the same basic pattern as with terrorists and drug lords—money and guns, both critical power resources, are more and more in the hands of nonstate actors.

Another reason for the heightened concern is that, while there long have been international dimensions to U.S. "domestic" crime, as with the Mafia, the international-domestic interconnection has become more pervasive. As FBI Director Louis Freeh put it, whereas the FBI made its initial reputation after its founding in the 1920s by fighting "interstate crime," its future reputation depends on how effective it is against "transnational crime." The United States now is being "ravaged by foreign criminals originating in partial or complete sanctuaries abroad." In years past the FBI's "Ten Most Wanted" list consisted mostly of bank robbers, big-city racketeers, and kidnappers. In 1997 eight of the ten fugitives on it were international criminals who had committed crimes in the United States. The FBI thus has vastly expanded its overseas role, from 70 special agents in 23 nations in 1994 to a planned 129 special agents in 46 nations by 2000. Its Moscow office, as one example, had 35 cases when it opened in 1994; by 1998 its caseload was up to 284.[49]

Summary

The United States is the world's most powerful nation. It is number one in military might. Its nuclear arsenal is second to none. Its armed forces are the best trained and have the best military technology available. The United States also has the most active diplomacy, drawing on a broad range of strategies of statecraft.

But to what extent can it convert its power to influence? Foreign policy requires being able to influence other countries, influence events, and influence other forces that affect U.S. interests. In this chapter we have studied the strategies and relationships affecting U.S. capacity to convert its power to influence.

We identified the key issues and dynamics in major-power geopolitics. Unipolarity was a passing phase. While not just one among multipolar equals, the United States also cannot automatically dominate all aspects of its relations with the other major powers. Its relations with Russia, China, western Europe, and Japan are complex and at times uncertain.

American defense strategy is undergoing rethinking. Cold War–era strategies and doctrines need revising and updating, although not necessarily discarding. The core questions remain the same—how best to deter and defend against threats to the United States, its citizens, interests, and allies.

Issues of military intervention pose difficult problems of strategy for meeting the ethnic and other conflicts that constitute most post–Cold War wars. Such issues are some of the most difficult decisions a democracy can face, especially American democracy, with its history of political tensions over war-powers issues. Preventive statecraft is an additional strategy for trying to deal with ethnic and other deadly conflicts before they become violent; while more viable than is often assumed, preventive statecraft does have its own requirements for being effective.

The threats from nonstate actors, such as terrorists, drug lords, and international criminals, while not totally new, are of a much greater scope and magnitude than in earlier eras. Bringing American power to bear against them in some respects can be even more difficult than against state-based actors.

Overall, Realists go too far in their critique of the other paradigms. Liberal Internationalism is more important in building the peace than Realists give it credit for, as discussed in the preceding chapter. Prosperity and principles also have their importance, as we will see in the next two chapters. But there is much of worth in the Realist paradigm. The world has changed in a lot of ways, but power still is the name of at least a major part of the game.

Notes

[1]John J. Mearsheimer, "The False Promise of International Institutions," *International Security* 19:3 (Winter 1994–95); Robert J. Art, "A Defensible Defense: America's Grand Strategy after the Cold War," *International Security* 15:4 (Spring 1991); Christopher Layne, "From Preponderance to Offshore Balancing: America's Future Grand Strategy," *International Security* 21:4 (Spring 1997); Samuel P. Huntington, "Why International Primacy Matters," *International Security* 17:4 (Spring 1993).

[2]Martin Wight, "The Balance of Power," in *Diplomatic Investigations: Essays in the Theory of International Politics,* ed. Herbert Butterfield and Martin Wight (Cambridge, Mass.: Harvard University Press, 1966), 150–51.

[3]Mearsheimer, "False Promise of International Institutions," 7, 12.

[4]See Layne, "From Preponderance to Offshore Balancing."

[5]Kenneth N. Waltz, "The Emerging Structure of International Politics," *International Security* 18:2 (Fall 1993), 66.

[6]Andrei S. Markovits and Simon Reich, *The German Predicament: Memory and Power in the New Europe* (Ithaca, N.Y.: Cornell University Press, 1997); Peter J. Katzenstein, *Tamed Power: Germany in Europe* (Ithaca, N.Y.: Cornell University Press, 1997).

[7]U.S. Department of State, Bureau of East Asian and Pacific Affairs, "Fact Sheet: U.S.-Japan Security Relations," July 28, 1997.

[8]Bruce W. Jentleson, *With Friends Like These: Reagan, Bush and Saddam, 1982–1990* (New York: Norton, 1994).

[9]George Liska, *Nations in Alliance: The Limits of Interdependence* (Baltimore: Johns Hopkins University Press, 1962), 12.

[10]Joseph Lepgold, "NATO's Post–Cold War Collective Action Problem," *International Security* 23: (Summer 1998), 84–85.

[11]David Abshire, "A Debate for 16 Parliaments," *Washington Post*, February 19, 1997, A21.

[12]Lepgold, "NATO's Post–Cold War Collective Action Problem," 81.

[13]Lepgold, "NATO's Post–Cold War Collective Action Problem," 91.

[14]All quotes in this paragraph from R. Jeffrey Smith, "Clinton Directive Changes Strategy on Nuclear Arms," *Washington Post*, December 7, 1997, A1, A8–10.

[15]Smith, "Clinton Directive Changes Strategy on Nuclear Arms."

[16]Michael May, "Fearsome Security: The Role of Nuclear Weapons," *Brookings Review*, Summer 1995, 24.

[17]Jonathan Schell, "The Gift of Time: The Case for Abolishing Nuclear Weapons," *The Nation*, February 2–9, 1998.

[18]Schell, "The Gift of Time," 11–12.

[19]Cited in Bradley Graham, "Iran, N. Korea Missile Gains Spur Warning," *Washington Post*, July 15, 1998, A1, A23.

[20]Dana Priest, "Cohen Says U.S. Will Build Missile Defense," *Washington Post*, January 21, 1999, A1, A10.

[21]Charles R. Babcock, "Pentagon Budget's Stealth Spending," *Washington Post*, October 13, 1998, A1, A4.

[22]Quoted in Bruce W. Jentleson, "Who, Why, What and How: Debates over Post–Cold War Military Intervention," in *Eagle Adrift: American Foreign Policy at the End of the Century*, ed. Robert J. Lieber (New York: Longman, 1997), 52.

[23]Michael Mandelbaum, "Foreign Policy as Social Work," *Foreign Affairs* 75:1 (January/February 1996), 16–32; Stanley Hoffman, "In Defense of Mother Teresa: Morality in Foreign Policy," *Foreign Affairs* 75:2 (March/April 1996), 172–75.

[24]President William J. Clinton, *A National Security Strategy of Engagement and Enlargement* (Washington, D.C.: U.S. Government Printing Office, 1994).

[25]Richard K. Betts, "The Delusion of Impartial Intervention," *Foreign Affairs* 73:6, (November/December 1994), 20–33.

[26]Betts, "The Delusion of Impartial Intervention," 25.

[27]Jane E. Holl, "We the People Here Don't Want No War: Executive Branch Perspectives on the Use of Force," in *The United States and the Use of Force in the Post–Cold War Era: A Report by the Aspen Strategy Group* (Queenstown, Md.: Aspen Institute Press, 1995), 124 and *passim*.

[28]See, for example, Robert A. Pape, *Bombing to Win: Air Power and Coercion* (Ithaca, N.Y.: Cornell University Press, 1996).

[29]Pat Towell and Donna Cassata, "Congress Takes Symbolic Stand on Troop Deployment," *Congressional Quarterly Weekly Report*, December 16, 1995, 3817.

[30]This section draws on Bruce W. Jentleson, "The Pretty Prudent Public: Post Post-Vietnam American Opinion on the Use of Military Force," *International Studies Quarterly* 36:1 (March 1992), 49–74, Bruce W. Jentleson and Rebecca L. Britton, "Still Pretty Prudent: Post–Cold War American Public Opinion on the Use of Military Force," *Journal of Conflict Resolution* 42:4 (August 1998), 395–417.

[31]What about Panama 1989, the question might be asked, when polls showed over 80 percent support for the overthrow of the dictator General Manuel Noriega? Although this was a case of using force for internal political change, these polls all were taken after the fact and really reflected the "halo effect" of a quick success. More telling are polls taken in the months prior to the invasion, which showed only 32 percent support.

[32]This section draws on Bruce W. Jentleson, ed., *Opportunities Missed, Opportunities Seized: Preventive Diplomacy in the Post–Cold War World* (Lanham, Md.: Rowman and Littlefield, 1999). See also Carnegie Commission for Preventing Deadly Conflict, *Preventing Deadly Conflict: Final Report* (Washington, D.C.: Carnegie Commission, 1997), both for the report itself and its bibliography of the burgeoning literature in this field.

[33]Robert D. Kaplan, *Balkan Ghosts: A Journey through History* (New York: St. Martin's, 1993); Bruce W. Jentleson, "Preventive Diplomacy: A Conceptual and Analytic Framework," in Jentleson, ed., *Opportunities Missed, Opportunities Seized.*

[34]Chris Hedges, "War Turns Sarajevo away From Europe," *New York Times*, July 28, 1995, A4.

[35]V. P. Gagnon, Jr., "Ethnic Nationalism and International Conflict: The Case of Serbia," *International Security* 19:3 (Winter 1994–95). The Carnegie Commission for Preventing Deadly Conflict in its *Final Report* makes its own strong statement of the purposive view: "Mass violence invariably results from the deliberately violent response of determined leaders and their groups to a wide range of social, economic and political conditions that provide the environment for violent conflict, but usually do not independently spawn violence" (p. 39).

[36]Philip Tetlock and Aaron Belkin, eds., *Counterfactual Thought Experiments in World Politics: Logical, Methodological, and Psychological Perspectives* (Princeton: Princeton University Press, 1997).

[37]Kenneth Menkhaus and Louis Ortmayer, "Somalia: Misread Crises and Misread Opportunities," in Jentleson, ed., *Opportunities Missed, Opportunities Seized*, pp. 212–13, 233.

[38]Astri Suhrke and Bruce Jones, "Preventive Diplomacy in Rwanda: Failure to Act or Failure of Actions?" in Jentleson, ed., *Opportunities Missed, Opportunities Seized*, p. 259.

[39]Susan Woodward, "Costly Disinterest: Missed Opportunities for Preventive Diplomacy in Croatia and Bosnia and Herzegovina, 1985–1991," in Jentleson, ed., *Opportunities Missed, Opportunities Seized*, p. 139; and Woodward, *Balkan Tragedy: Chaos and Dissolution after the Cold War* (Washington, D.C.: Brookings Institution Press, 1995).

[40]United States Institute of Peace, "Kosovo: Escaping the Cul-de-Sac," Special Report, July 1998.

[41]Michael Lund, "Preventive Diplomacy for Macedonia, 1992–1998: From Containment to Nation-Building," in Jentleson, ed., *Opportunities Missed, Opportunities Seized.*

[42]Michael G. Roskin, "Macedonia and Albania: The Missing Alliance," *Parameters* (Winter 1993–94), 98.

[43]Speech by President Clinton, "On Keeping America Secure for the Twenty-First Century," delivered at the National Academy of Sciences, Washington, D.C., January 22, 1999.

[44]Judith Miller and William J. Broad, "New York Girds for Grim Fear: Germ Terrorism," *New York Times*, June 19, 1998, A1, A30.

[45]William J. Broad and Judith Miller, "Pentagon Seeks Command for Emergencies in the United States," *New York Times*, January 28, 1999, A19.

[46]Diana Jean Schemo, "Bogota Aid: To Fight Drugs or Rebels?" *New York Times*, June 2, 1998, A1, A12.

[47]Senator John Kerry, "Organized Crime Goes Global While the United States Stays Home," *Washington Post*, May 1, 1997, C1.

[48]Kerry, "Organized Crime."

[49]FBI Director Louis Freeh, testimony before the House Committee on International Relations, October 1, 1997, pp. 8, 10.

CHAPTER **9** *Prosperity: Foreign Economic and Social Policy in an Age of Globalization*

Introduction: The International Political Economy Paradigm and the Post–Cold War Era

We live in an age of globalization. The profound changes in the international political economy stand with the end of Cold War bipolarity and the spread of democracy as driving forces of this new era. Our focus in this chapter is on the challenges posed for U.S. foreign policy in its pursuit of prosperity amid the complex and powerful forces of globalization (see Dynamics of Choice, below).

One aspect of globalization is the greater importance of foreign economic policy. Trade now accounts for over 30 percent of U.S. gross domestic product (GDP), a much greater share than in the past. Imports are much more prevalent in the purchasing patterns of the average American consumer, be it a

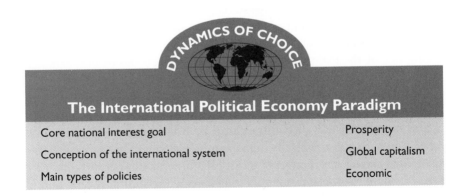

DYNAMICS OF CHOICE

The International Political Economy Paradigm

Core national interest goal	Prosperity
Conception of the international system	Global capitalism
Main types of policies	Economic

major purchase like an automobile or everyday items like clothing. And exports are increasingly important sources of jobs. One study found that exporting companies had almost 20 percent faster employment growth and were 9 percent less likely to go out of business than companies that did not export.[1] As to monetary policy, whereas in the past decisions by the Federal Reserve Board were based almost exclusively on domestic economic factors such as inflation and unemployment, now much greater attention is paid to the value of the dollar relative to that of other major currencies, to the impact of financial crises in other countries on U.S. growth rates, and to other international economic factors. In these and other ways globalization both has been raising the salience of foreign economic policy and making the line between it and domestic economic policy less and less distinct.

To the extent that globalization helps expand economic opportunities and increase economic wealth, it enhances U.S. prosperity and global welfare more generally. In other respects, though, globalization may not be so positive a force. Consider the widening gap between what one prominent investment banker has called the "awesome force of the global financial marketplace" and the more limited reach of the policies of national governments and international institutions like the International Monetary Fund (IMF).[2] With many more countries with market economies than ever before, and given how drastically new technology has reduced intracorporate costs of running distant operations, major multinational corporations (MNCs) have a much wider range of choices about where to build a new factory or make other foreign direct investments. Bankers, money managers, stockbrokers, and other international financiers don't just have Wall Street, or also just London and Frankfurt and Tokyo, but also Hong Kong, Moscow, Brasilia, and many other of the world's proliferated stock markets, currency markets, and other investment exchanges from which to choose. Whatever their choices, it takes just the click of a computer mouse to move huge sums of money instantly—often over $1 trillion going from one country to another in a single day. Although market-based principles dictate that private investors should be free to make such decisions, one of the main purposes both of U.S. policy and of international economic institutions has been to provide a degree of governance against instabilities, inequities, and other imperfections.

Globalization also is affecting the challenges of "social stewardship," the broader agenda of issues such as the global environment, world poverty, and public health, that deal with the human and social condition. As we will see later in this chapter, any number of statistical indicators show poverty, hunger, disease, and other problems not only still plaguing much of the world, but in many places growing worse. The United States does not bear exclusive responsibility for these problems, but it still is looked to for leadership. Moreover, with satellite telecommunications and the Internet carrying messages and images across the globe almost instantly, it is that much harder to ignore the starving children, destitute villages, and other shocking scenes. And whereas the first "Earth Day" was held in 1970 in the United States as a domestic protest on such issues as clean air and clean water, Earth Day 1998 was a worldwide movement dealing with issues such as climate change, ozone depletion, and biodiversity, all of which span national boundaries both in their impact and in the policy responses required to deal with them.

The increasing integration of the global economy also has made economic sanctions a much more controversial foreign policy tool. Countries are potentially more economically vulnerable to sanctions. Recognizing this fact, the United States has been using sanctions much more than ever before—so much so that at times they seem to be the weapon of choice for a wide array of foreign policy objectives. Yet sanctions' record of success is not very strong. They have succeeded in some cases but in others have failed, misfired (inflicting humanitarian crises on the civilian populaces of targeted regimes), and backfired (incurring substantial economic costs for the country that does the sanctioning).

In sum, globalization is neither wholly positive nor wholly negative. It is, however, an undeniable force and thus one for which the policy challenges need to be met. We will look at four areas—international trade, international finance, global social stewardship, and the use of economic sanctions—to examine in more detail the key issues facing U.S. policy.

International Trade

Table 9.1 shows the balance between U.S. imports and exports in the 1990s and the corresponding trade deficits. Trade deficits are not new to the 1990s; the United States has run a trade deficit every year since 1971. Some economists and other analysts don't see this as a major problem, arguing that the U.S. deficit actually helps the world economy since this puts more dollars in international circulation and the dollar serves as the principal transaction and reserve currency for world trade. Nevertheless, when the U.S. trade deficit jumped to $169 billion in 1998, more concern began to be expressed as to whether the signs indicated a weakening of the American trade position that might not bode well for the future.

TABLE 9.1	U.S. Trade Balance in the 1990s (in millions of dollars)		
	Imports	**Exports**	**Trade balance**
1990	495,311	393,592	−101,718
1991	487,129	421,730	−65,399
1992	532,498	448,157	−84,341
1993	714,990	642,953	−72,037
1994	802,682	698,301	−104,381
1995	891,593	786,529	−105,064
1996	959,349	850,775	−108,574
1997	1,047,799	937,593	−110,207
1998	1,100,314	931,026	−169,288

Sources: 1990–92 data from *Statistical Abstract of the United States: 1993* (Washington, D.C.: U.S. Department of Commerce, Bureau of the Census, 1993), pp. 815–16; 1993–97 data from *Statistical Abstract of the United States: 1996*, p. 796, and *Statistical Abstract of the United States: 1998*, p. 798; 1998 data from U.S. Department of Commerce, Bureau of the Census, *U.S. International Trade in Goods and Services*, series FT-900 (http://www.census.gov/foreign-trade/Press-Release/currentpressrelease/exh1.txt), accessed May 26, 1999.

What countries does the United States trade with? Figure 9.1 shows us, and also shows both change and continuity in American trade partners over the past two decades. The percentages are pretty much the same today for trade with western Europe, Latin America, and the former Soviet bloc as they were in 1980. The trade share of the Asia-Pacific region went up, in large part because of the growth in trade with China. Trade also went up with Canada and Mexico, a result of the North American Free Trade Agreement (NAFTA) having passed in 1993. Falling oil prices largely explain the relative declines in trade with both the Middle East and Africa (Algeria and Nigeria are major African oil producers).

However, as Figure 9.2 shows, U.S. dependence on imported oil has grown greater since 1973, the year that the first OPEC (Organization of Petroleum Exporting Countries) oil crisis hit. Despite the United States' having gone through one oil crisis after another—the 1979 OPEC crisis set off by the Iranian Revolution followed on the 1973 one, and there was another brief scare in 1990–91 during the Persian Gulf War—imports grew from about 20 percent of total U.S. oil consumption to over 44 percent. And within that the shares for OPEC as a whole and for the Persian Gulf OPEC countries both almost doubled. Falling oil prices have made this oil dependence less costly economically, but it poses serious issues for U.S. energy and economic security.

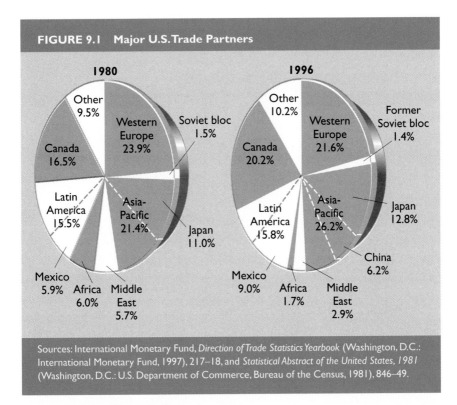

FIGURE 9.1   Major U.S. Trade Partners

Sources: International Monetary Fund, *Direction of Trade Statistics Yearbook* (Washington, D.C.: International Monetary Fund, 1997), 217–18, and *Statistical Abstract of the United States, 1981* (Washington, D.C.: U.S. Department of Commerce, Bureau of the Census, 1981), 846–49.

Making U.S. Trade Policy

Trade policy has been among the more politically contentious issue areas of post–Cold War U.S. foreign policy. The old free-trade consensus is not dead, but it has eroded and fractured. More Americans see themselves as either winners or losers; the latter sentiment feeds neo-protectionism. There is a sense, especially among labor unions and other workers, of "breaking the postwar bargain," as Professor Ethan Kapstein puts it, that "just when working people need the nation-state as a buffer against the world economy, it is abandoning them."[3] Manufacturing employment in the United States has been falling, and those who find new jobs often do so at much lower pay. Although this jobs shift is not solely due to trade competition, it often tends to be seen heavily in these terms.

Politics arise in each of three key areas in the making of U.S. trade policy: executive-branch negotiation and congressional approval of treaties and other trade agreements; the promotion of American exports and foreign

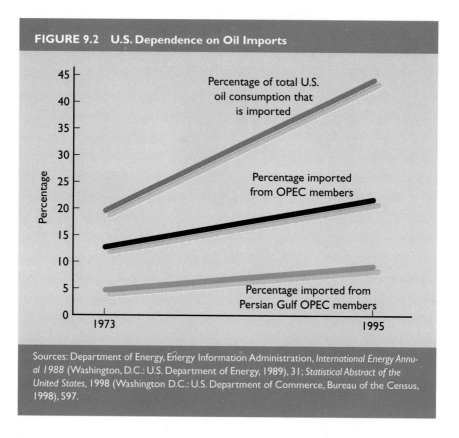

FIGURE 9.2   U.S. Dependence on Oil Imports

Percentage of total U.S. oil consumption that is imported

Percentage imported from OPEC members

Percentage imported from Persian Gulf OPEC members

1973   1995

Sources: Department of Energy, Energy Information Administration, *International Energy Annual 1988* (Washington, D.C.: U.S. Department of Energy, 1989), 31; *Statistical Abstract of the United States, 1998* (Washington D.C.: U.S. Department of Commerce, Bureau of the Census, 1998), 597.

investments; and the regulation of imports. Dynamics of Choice on p. 325 indicates the major executive-branch agencies involved in each of these areas.

TRADE AGREEMENTS   The executive branch agency that takes the lead in conducting trade negotiations is the U.S. Trade Representative (USTR). The office of the USTR was first established in 1962 and in the years since has grown in importance; the USTR now holds rank as an ambassador and a member of the president's Cabinet. Depending on the issue area, other executive-branch actors may also be part of the negotiating team: the Commerce Department for issues relating to industrial goods and technology, or the Agriculture Department on agricultural trade. The State Department may also be involved through its Undersecretary of State for Economics, Business, and Agricultural Affairs. On issues that may affect the environment, the Environmental Protection Agency (EPA) plays a role.

The Making of U.S. Trade Policy

Policy area	Key Executive-Branch Agencies
Negotiating trade agreements	U.S. Trade Representative (USTR) Commerce Department State Department, Undersecretary for Economic Affairs Agriculture Department Environmental Protection Agency (EPA)
Export promotion	U.S. Export-Import Bank Overseas Private Investment Corporation (OPIC) Trade and Development Agency (TDA) State Department Agriculture Department
Administrative trade remedies	U.S. International Trade Commission (ITC) Commerce Department Federal Trade Commission Labor Department

When trade agreements take the form of treaties, they require ratification by two-thirds of the Senate. Although the House of Representatives has no formal role in treaties, it usually finds a way to be involved—often through legislation providing the funds needed for treaty implementation, because all appropriations bills are required by the Constitution to originate in the House. Trade agreements that are not formal treaties require approval by both chambers, although only by simple majority votes.

NAFTA was a major political test in U.S. trade policy, one that showed broader patterns in post–Cold War trade politics.[4] A big protectionist push was made by NAFTA opponents, led by billionaire businessman Ross Perot, who at the time was riding high as an independent presidential candidate and national protest figure. The liberal wing of the Democratic Party and the neo-isolationist wing of the Republican Party also were part of the anti-NAFTA coalition. As they saw it, jobs would be lost as American companies closed factories and moved south to Mexico for its cheap labor, weak environmental regulations, and other selfish benefits. NAFTA proponents also came from the ranks of both parties. The original agreement was signed by President Bush. President Clinton pushed it through congressional approval, and did so with a coalition drawing much more support from Republicans than from Democrats (see Dynamics of Choice, below). In the end the margin of victory, 61 to 38 in the Senate and 234 to 200 in the House, was larger than expected. Although this amounted to a choice of free trade over protectionism, it also has to be noted that the decision was not based strictly on the policy merits of the case—there was plenty of wheeling and dealing, as senators and representatives linked their votes to related trade issues, to other pet projects, and even to invitations to White House dinners.

Renewal of *fast-track authority* has been another contentious issue in U.S. trade policy. In Chapter 2 we saw that the Constitution was unusually explicit in granting authority over trade to Congress, and that presidential authority in this area of foreign policy is much more subject to the limits of what Congress chooses to delegate. Fast-track authority gets its name from the guarantee that any trade agreements the president negotiates and submits to Congress under this authority will receive expedited legislative consideration within ninety days, and under the special procedural rule that the vote be "up or down," yea or nay—i.e., no amendments are allowed. Congress had granted fast-track authority to every president since Gerald Ford, but always subjected

The Congressional Vote on NAFTA, 1993

	Yea	Nay
House of Representatives		
Democrats	102	157
Republicans	132	43
Total	234	200
Senate		
Democrats	27	28
Republicans	34	10
Total	61	38

it to renewal every few years as a way for Congress to reclaim the authority if it were to so choose. When fast-track was up for renewal in 1997 the Clinton administration was unable to get Congress to renew it; labor unions lobbied strongly against fast-track. The immediate effect was to set back efforts to build from NAFTA to a hemispheric Free Trade Area of the Americas (FTAA). The broader effect was to delay initiation of a new round of global trade talks, because the credibility of U.S. leadership was undermined when the president could not show sufficient political strength at home to regain fast-track authority.

EXPORT PROMOTION   The opening of markets through trade treaties and agreements does not ensure that American exporters will be the ones that win the major sales. Nor is it purely a matter of economic competitiveness. All major industrial countries have government policies to promote the exports of their companies, although such efforts are subject to rules, established by the General Agreement on Tariffs and Trade (GATT), as to what is permissible. The 1979 GATT agreement included restrictions on the use of *subsidies,* which are special payments and other methods governments use to reduce exporters' costs so as to make their goods more price-competitive in international markets. These restrictions were strengthened and expanded in the 1994 GATT agreement. Still, plenty of room exists for export-promotion programs seeking a competitive edge.

As of the early 1990s the United States lagged behind its major Western economic competitors in export promotion. One Clinton administration study estimated that Britain spent $1.50 on export promotion for every $1 billion worth of nonfarm exports, and France $1.01, but the United States only $.33.[5] To change this imbalance, more funding was provided to certain export-promotion executive-branch agencies, such as the Export-Import Bank of the United States, which provides credit and other financing for foreign customers to buy American exports; the Trade and Development Agency, which helps American companies put together business plans and feasibility studies for new export opportunities; and the Overseas Private Investment Corporation, which provides insurance and financing for foreign investments by U.S. companies that will create jobs back home and increase exports. Even though agricultural exports account for less than 10 percent of American exports, the Agriculture Department gets more than 50 percent of the export-promotion budget, reflecting interest-group politics and the power of farm constituencies.

The State Department also has increased its role in export promotion as part of its post–Cold War retooling. "For a long time secretaries of state thought of economics as 'low policy' while they dealt only with high science like arms control," Secretary of State Warren Christopher stated in 1995. "I make no apologies for putting economics at the top of our foreign policy agenda."[6] As part of their training before assuming their embassy posts, U.S. ambassadors now go through a course entitled "Diplomacy for Global Competitiveness." Once in their posts, as described in *Newsweek,* the U.S. ambassador to South Korea "hosted an auto show on the front lawn of his residence, displaying Buicks and Mercurys like a local used-car huckster"; the U.S. ambassador to India "won a contract for Cogentrix, a U.S. power company, with what he calls 'a lot of hugging and kissing' of Indian officials"; and the U.S. ambassador to Argentina "called in Argentine reporters to inform them that he was there as the chief U.S. lobbyist for his nation's businesses."[7]

ADMINISTRATIVE TRADE REMEDIES   Administrative trade remedies are actions by executive-branch agencies in cases in which relief from import competition is warranted under the rules of the international trading system. From early on GATT had an "escape clause" that allowed governments to provide temporary relief to industries seriously injured by import competition that resulted from lower tariffs. GATT also provides "anti-dumping" provisions against a foreign supplier that exports goods at less than fair value. In such cases the importing country can impose an additional duty equal to the calculated difference between the asking price and the fair-market price. In cases involving unfair subsidies provided by a foreign government, the importing country can impose "countervailing duties," also according to an equalizing calculation. The U.S. government also provides "trade adjustment assistance" (TAA), special economic assistance to companies, workers, and communities hurt by import competition, which is supposed to help them adjust by either becoming more competitive or shifting to new industries. TAA programs are the province of the Department of Labor.

The U.S. agency that administers escape clause, anti-dumping, and countervailing duty cases is the International Trade Commission (ITC). The ITC is an independent regulatory agency with six members, evenly divided between Republicans and Democrats, all appointed by the president subject to Senate confirmation. Its ability to decide its cases objectively rather than politically is further aided by the seven-year length of the members' terms. The Commerce Department is also involved in anti-dumping and countervailing duty cases. Headed as it is by a member of the president's Cabinet, it is more political, but unless the ITC concurs Commerce alone cannot provide the import relief.

These administrative trade remedies also provide a good example of how Congress can shape policy through legislative crafting. Take the escape clause remedies. The 1962 Trade Expansion Act has set the criteria for escape clause relief as imports being the "major cause" of the injury suffered by an industry. This meant *greater* than all the other causes combined, a difficult standard to meet. The 1974 Trade Act changed "major" to "substantial," which meant that the injury from imports now had only to be *equal* to any of the other individual factors, a much less stringent criterion on which the ITC was to base its rulings.[8]

A reverse example involved the Federal Trade Commission (FTC), another independent regulatory agency, and a recent case involving the "Made in the U.S.A." label.* In 1997 the FTC announced that it was lowering the standard required for a product to be considered made in the United States from its being "all or virtually all" made of American parts by American labor, to allowing the label when 75 percent of the product met these standards. Reaction was strong from labor unions and their congressional supporters, who saw this as taking away an incentive for industries to invest and create jobs at home. The FTC was forced to back down.

The Uruguay Round and the WTO System

U.S. policy continues to support the same fundamental principles and practices on which the international trade system has been based since the General Agreement on Tariffs and Trade (GATT) was first signed in 1947. There is to be continued progress toward freer trade and more open markets through periodic "rounds" of multilateral negotiations based on nondiscrimination and reciprocity. (These rounds are named for the locales [countries, cities] in which negotiations are held.) How to make this progress and abide by these principles while also advancing the U.S. national interest amid the dynamics of globalization poses a number of policy challenges.

The 1994 Uruguay Round agreement was significant in two respects. One was its extensive provisions for freer trade, including in sectors that never before had been included in GATT agreements. The other was the creation of the *World Trade Organization* (WTO) as a stronger multilateral institution than GATT had been. Whereas GATT always was more of a set of agreements

---

*The FTC's name is a bit deceptive. It deals primarily with fair advertising, consumer protection, economic competition, and other aspects of domestic commerce and "trade."

than an international institution per se, the WTO has full legal standing and is very much a formal organization, with more than five hundred employees at its headquarters in Geneva, Switzerland. The main debate in U.S. policy has been over the extent to which these developments help or hurt U.S. economic interests.

One way in which most people think American economic interests benefit is in the extension of free-trade policies to additional economic sectors. Whereas the GATT principally had covered trade in industrial and manufactured goods, the Uruguay Round also included agreements on trade in services (e.g., banking, insurance, some investment areas), intellectual property (e.g., movies, books, computer software, other inventions), and agriculture. The term "GATT" still is used to refer to the trade agreements covering industrial goods; it has now been supplemented by the GATS, General Agreement on Trade in Services; TRIPs, Trade Related Aspects of Intellectual Property Rights; and TRIMs, Trade Related Investment Measures. The free-trade provisions on agriculture are still limited but quite significant since, as one noted authority puts it, "never before had there been anything more than token trade liberalization in this politically 'untouchable' sector."[9] And in the years since the Uruguay Round, additional agreements have been reached covering telecommunications and information technology equipment as well as further liberalization of financial services. All of these are areas in which American exporters are highly competitive and thus stand to gain from trade liberalization.

A second strengthening of the WTO trade regime is in its greater coverage of nontariff barriers (NTBs). Originally the GATT treaties dealt primarily with lowering tariffs. Since tariffs were the main barrier to trade, this made sense for a time. But as tariffs came down, some countries increasingly resorted to means other than tariffs for protecting their domestic markets from import competition—e.g., burdensome requirements for import licensing, special regulations and standards harder for imports to meet than for domestic products, quiet collusion among businesses, and cumbersome customs inspections. GATT did start to deal with NTBs in its 1979 Tokyo Round agreement, but the Uruguay Round went much further. Japan long has been the most egregious user of NTBs, and the United States was particularly interested in opening up Japanese markets. However, there is another side to this issue: the United States also has its own policies and practices that other countries see as NTBs.

The issue that has been the most controversial within the United States has been the greater regulatory authority given to the WTO. In the past the GATT secretariat could play an advisory and facilitative role in resolving trade disputes, but it lacked authority to impose a settlement. Now the WTO has been given dispute-settlement authority that is binding. Initial rulings by its panels can be appealed, at which point the final decision is made by a vote of the full membership. Each country has one vote, irrespective of its size. This is like the U.N. General Assembly, and quite different from other international economic institutions such as the IMF and the World Bank, where voting is proportional to a country's financial contribution. For the United States this means that, whereas it gets about an 18 percent vote in the IMF and the World Bank, in the WTO its vote counts no more than that of any other country.

Proponents believe a stronger trade-dispute settlement process benefits all countries, the United States included. It adds to the sense of order that is a critical for the growth of global trade. If American exporters are being treated unfairly, they now have a better chance of making their case on its merits to the WTO (a neutral third party) and having the dispute resolved in their favor. However, critics fear that any such benefits are outweighed by other countries' using and abusing the system against the United States, taking advantage of a forum in which the rules provide power in numbers. These critics would prefer the older way of doing things, whereby American power and status could be brought to bear, be it explicitly or implicitly, to help resolve trade disputes in the United States' favor. Moreover, in some of the other powers given to the WTO, such as the new "trade policy review mechanism," which for the first time subjects national trade policies to systematic and regular review, critics see the fostering of a global bureaucracy prone to inefficiencies and threatening American sovereignty. Proponents, on the other hand, see the WTO as a needed administrative and regulatory body for an age of such extensive trade interdependence.

Geo-Economics: Friends as Foes?

> The methods of commerce are displacing military methods—with disposable capital in lieu of firepower, civilian innovation in lieu of military-technical advancement, and market penetration in lieu of garrisons and bases. . . . It is true, of course, that, under whatever name, "geo-economics" has always been an important aspect of international life. In the past, however, the outdoing of others in the realm of commerce was overshadowed by strategic priorities and strategic modalities. . . . Now, however, as the relevance of military threats and military alliances wanes, geo-economic priorities and modalities are becoming dominant in state action.[10]

It is telling that this quotation is from a noted Cold War military strategist, Edward Luttwak. Luttwak does qualify his conception of geo-economics, noting that it does not mean that "World Politics is . . . about to give way to World Business," in the sense of private-sector MNCs and banks supplanting states as the key actors in international relations.[11] But it is a scenario of states competing with each other all the more to benefit from and influence the economic activities and choices of major corporations and banks in order to ensure states' own national economic positions.

And it is western Europe and Japan, the very countries that were the principal U.S. allies during the Cold War, that are now cast as the United States' principal competitors, and even potential adversaries. It isn't so much that economic tensions and conflicts with these countries are totally new. There had been quite a few trade disputes in the past, such as the 1960s "chicken wars" with western Europe over frozen chicken imports, or the 1970s "textile wrangle" and then the 1970s–80s Toyota-smashing auto wars with Japan. But as long as the common enemy of the Soviet Union lurked, these and other economic disputes were subordinated to the shared security interests of the Cold War. With the Soviet threat gone, though, relations have been opened to more divergence of interests, competition, and, at times, reinforcing cycles of resentment.

Japan in particular is seen as a potential economic adversary. One public-opinion poll found that 62 percent of Americans viewed economic competition from Japan as a "critical threat" to the United States.[12] Nor was this just some emotional reaction among the mass public. The challenge from Japan "is a real one," wrote one noted American strategist, citing the modified Clausewitz axiom that "economics is the continuation of war by other means."[13] These concerns were not just about the general trade balance, but were also about growing American dependence on Japan for technologies such as semiconductors that are key to the advanced weapons and communications systems on which American military might rests. Can the United States be sure, the nightmare question started to be asked, that in some future crisis when there might be disagreement, Japan wouldn't try to pressure the United States by embargoing semiconductors or other militarily vital technologies? Few see this as probable, but not everyone dismisses it as totally implausible.

With the Europeans, although there is less concern about spillover into the security realm, as NATO has shown its post–Cold War resilience, there is no shortage of economic disagreement and competition. U.S.-European differences over agricultural trade were one of the issues that held up completion of the Uruguay Round in 1994. Incidents of economic espionage and "walls that have ears," as recounted in Perspectives on p. 333, have exacerbated existing

PERSPECTIVES

"ECONOMIC SUMMIT SUBPLOT:
DO FRENCH WALLS HAVE EARS?"

LYON, France, June 29—As *Air Force One* descended the other night for the opening of the 22nd annual summit meeting of the world's biggest industrial nations, a security agent gathered the small army of Cabinet members and aides accompanying President Clinton and delivered a clear warning.

Enjoy the two- and three-star restaurants, he said, and the fine Beaujolais. But bring all your documents with you—not only classified material, but anything that sheds new light on Washington's economic strategies.

"He just wanted to remind us that this is France we're visiting," one of Mr. Clinton's economic aides said during the summit meeting. "When it comes to economic espionage, no one is any better."

As a result, Laura D'Andrea Tyson, the chairman of the National Economic Council, and Charlene Barshefsky, the acting United States trade representative, and other top Clinton aides toted briefing books and stacks of paper everywhere they went, tucking them under their chairs during a four-hour meal at Le Passage, a comfortable two-star in the old quarter of town. . . .

And more than ever before, wherever trade negotiators go, it is widely assumed that bugs, miniature video cameras and tapped telephones are there to greet them.

Whether those fears were justified in Lyons was impossible to judge. In private, American officials said they assumed that the French had lodged the President and his staff in the Sofitel, a comfortable but boxy hotel on the banks of the Rhone, because it was wired for sound. But at least one senior American official in a position to know said that to his knowledge, nothing was found when security agents swept the place.

"And we've certainly held summits in places where we've had a problem," he said.

It's not just summit meetings. Ms. Barshefsky visited Beijing two weeks ago to discuss Washington's accusations of piracy of software

(*Continued on page 334*)

("Economic Summit Subplot" *Continued from page 333)*
music and videos. When American security agents swept her room, others in the Administration say, they found so much electronic gear they started to laugh. How did she deal with it?

"I got dressed fast," Ms. Barshefsky said.

Surveillance is a two-way street, of course. Only last year the French caught the Central Intelligence Agency station in Paris trying to steal a variety of economic secrets, from the details of the French position on global trade talks to a host of other matters. They expelled several agents and the station chief. The incident led to a major internal investigation within the C.I.A., not only because of the embarrassment, but because the United States Ambassador in Paris, Pamela Harriman, had been kept in the dark about the operation until the arrests.

And last year in Geneva, American intelligence was working hard to discover up-to-the-minute details of Japan's position on a tense set of negotiations about selling more American cars and auto parts in Japan. When news of that operation leaked several months later, the Japanese felt compelled to feign shock and issue a protest. The Administration asked the Federal Bureau of Investigation to conduct an investigation— not of the espionage itself, but of how the word of it got out.

It was no surprise that the White House was just a touch more wary than usual when its huge summit delegation arrived here. France has been on the other side of one major deal after another in recent years: it fought hard to win a major contract in Brazil over monitoring the rain forest from space—the deal ultimately went to the Raytheon Company of Lexington, Mass.—and it has seized on the American tensions with Beijing to sell more aircraft built by Airbus Industrie, the European consortium in which France is a partner. Battles are pending over telecommunications equipment around the world, amid speculation, never easy to prove, about intelligence involvement in all those deals. . . .

Such back-room talks over chips or the proper powers of the World Trade Organization lack the drama of the arms control negotiations of the 80's and almost never involve issues of life or death. That is one reason American intelligence agencies are so reluctant to dive fully into the economic espionage business.

(*Continued on page 335*)

(**"Economic Summit Subplot"**   *Continued from page 334*)
But they know they have little choice: one study after another about the future of intelligence identifies economic threats—from a rising China, a resurgent Japan, a European Union that begins to act truly like a union—as a major challenge of the next decade, along with fighting terrorism and drugs.

Source: David E. Sanger, "Economic Subplot: Do French Walls Have Ears?" *New York Times,* July 1, 1996, pp. A1, D2. Copyright © 1996 by The New York Times. Reprinted by permission.

tensions. Although this account is of French economic espionage against the United States, the spying also has gone in the other direction; in one incident France expelled an American embassy official on economic espionage grounds. Major differences have also arisen over economic sanctions, especially when the United States has tried to punish European countries and companies for not going along with U.S. policies.

Still, concerns along these lines shouldn't become alarmist. The United States, western Europe, and Japan continue to share a fundamental consensus on the mutual benefits of the global free-trade system. Compliance with its rules is still the norm on all sides. When one or another trade dispute has brought the parties too close to the abyss of trade wars, they have shown the ability to find compromises and other working agreements. Moreover, broader foreign policy and security considerations still glue the alliance together and remind all parties that power and peace interests have not gone away and at times must be weighed against the benefits of opening another Toys 'R Us or selling more cellular phones. Finally, some argue that, while it is true that Japan and others don't play by strict free-market rules, focusing too much on retaliation diverts attention and resources from what the United States can and must do in its own domestic policy to maintain international competitiveness. Policies to promote the development and commercialization of new technologies, improve the educational system, and other such "self-help" measures are more essential to the U.S. geo-economic position than anything Japan or the European Union could or should do.

International Finance

U.S. goals for the international financial system remain fundamentally the same as when the system was set up at the end of World War II: help provide the monetary and financial stability necessary for global economic growth and particularly for the growth of international trade; avoid the monetary versions of economic nationalism and protectionism that lead countries to compete more than cooperate; and in these and other ways contribute to international peace and stability. The system as designed continues to be grounded in free-market principles but with sufficient international management and regulation to prevent or at least correct the imperfections of market forces. This management is carried out primarily through the multilateral institutional structure of the International Monetary Fund (IMF) with the United States in a lead role, and with Japan and western Europe also playing key roles.

Yet these efforts have become much more difficult with the increasing internationalization of financial markets. Starting in the 1980s and picking up steam in the 1990s, one country after another reduced regulations over financial markets and scaled back barriers to the inflow and outflow of private capital. In the United States and other Western countries this was part of the general trend toward deregulation. In developing and postcommunist countries the intent has been to attract the foreign capital deemed necessary for democratization and economic growth. For investors this meant an ever wider range of opportunities, particularly for short-term profits from currency fluctuations and stock and bond investments—opportunities that could be tapped easily thanks to the information technology and telecommunications revolution. These buy-and-sell, invest-and-disinvest decisions of private-sector economic actors have tremendous effects on governments and their citizens. Yet the capacity of governments and of the IMF to affect and respond to those decisions has been limited.

We see these dynamics and dilemmas in the recurring international financial crises of the second half of the 1990s, and in U.S. policy debates about the IMF and the future of international financial and monetary policy.

1990s Financial Crises

The world economy was wracked beginning in the mid-1990s by a chain of financial crises in Asia and Latin America. The first of these crises hit Mexico in

1995. The Mexican peso collapsed, losing almost half its value in less than a month. In this crisis as well as the others, primary responsibility lay with the national government itself. In the Mexican case a peasant uprising in the state of Chiapas, scandals involving the ruling PRI party, and doubts about the new government of President Ernesto Zedillo fed a climate of political instability. The problems of the Mexican economy were largely homegrown, the result of inefficient policies, government corruption, and profligate spending on imports. News that these problems were more severe than realized was the catalyst that pushed the peso into its plunge and set the crisis off.

A key factor making the crisis as bad as it was was the problem of "hot money"—short-term investments in stocks, bonds, and currencies seeking quick returns. Such investments are held by investors ready and able to shift these funds from one country to another at the slightest doubt about the rate of return. Hot money had been surging into Mexico, so much so that it was second only to China in the amount of foreign investment entering the country between 1990 and 1994. When the worse-than-expected economic news broke, on top of the concerns about political stability, both Mexican and foreign investors rushed their funds out of Mexican financial markets.

The Mexican crisis hit home for the United States. The success of NAFTA was at stake, just a year after the hard-fought political battle to pass the agreement. Concerns were raised about "contagion" effects spreading to other countries in the Western Hemisphere. In putting together a financial rescue package the Clinton administration faced substantial congressional opposition, which claimed that the proposed rescue plan was misusing American taxpayers' money to "bail out" Mexico and Wall Street. The administration therefore resorted to a bit of an end-run to provide much-needed aid to Mexico by drawing on the president's discretionary authority to meet an economic emergency without additional congressional legislation. Working with the IMF the administration put together a package of credits worth $50 billion, of which about $20 billion came from the United States.

At one level this was a success story: Mexico got its economy stabilized and growing again. It paid the credits back to the United States ahead of schedule. The U.S. Treasury even made a $500 million profit from the interest. The United States and the IMF showed the capacity for financial crisis management. But questions remained about crisis prevention. Why hadn't there been an earlier response, before the situation became a crisis? The top U.S. official at the IMF criticized the organization for failing to provide early warning, for not being "on top of" deteriorating economic conditions and not having "expressed more concern about the trend and urged Mexican authorities to be cautious in monetary policy."[14] Others criticized the United States for itself not being sufficiently attuned to the economic and political problems of its neighbor and trade partner. Furthermore, although the end run around Congress had worked this time, the overall issue of the IMF remained unresolved in Pennsylvania Avenue diplomacy. And, as we would soon see, the hot money problem was still there in other national and international markets.

The Asian financial crisis that struck in mid-1997 involved not just one country but a number of them. It started in Thailand and spread to Indonesia and South Korea. All had been success stories, "Asian tigers," exemplars of the newly industrialized countries that the United States hailed in the 1970s and 1980s as proof that capitalism worked better than socialism or other forms of statism. But the underside of East Asian capitalism, with its speculative investments, cronyism and corruption, overconsumption of imports, and excessive debt, now burst the bubbles. This crisis proved much less controllable than the Mexican one. In the last half of 1997 the Thai, Korean, and Indonesian stock markets fell by 33–45 percent. Their currencies (the baht, won, and rupiah, respectively) fell by even larger percentages, as shown in Figure 9.3. In all three cases overall growth of GDP was negative, meaning their economies were shrinking and massive numbers of working- and middle-class families were losing their jobs and most of their savings.

U.S. interests were affected in a number of ways by this crisis. American banks and mutual funds were heavily invested in Asian markets. American companies had factories, fast-food restaurants, computer programming, and other major investments at risk. American exporters lost some of their fastest-growing markets, accounting for a big chunk of the growth in the 1998 trade deficit. And politically all three countries were U.S. allies. In Indonesia the government of President Suharto fell; this had the potential to be a positive change, given Suharto's thirty-two-year-long corrupt and authoritarian rule, but the immediate effect was to cause more chaos and rising political violence. There also was continuing concern about the spread of the crisis to Japan, which was already having serious economic problems that, if worsened, could spiral the crisis dangerously downward.

Then two other major countries, Russia and Brazil, joined the list of financial crisis victims. The Russian crisis hit in late 1998; the ruble had tumbled by 282 percent by December 1998 and 324 percent by May 1999. Even though there was less foreign investment at stake in Russia than in the Mexican and Asian cases, the Russian crisis had a "last straw" effect on investor psychology and set off a sharp drop on Wall Street, with the Dow Jones industrial average plummeting more than 20 percent. Suddenly the crisis was brought home to

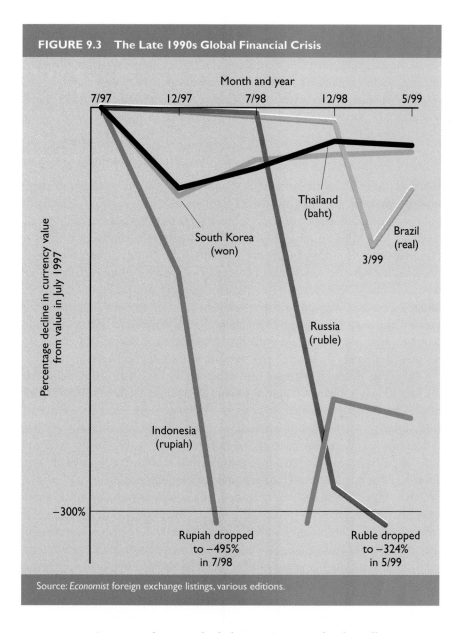

FIGURE 9.3   The Late 1990s Global Financial Crisis

Month and year

Percentage decline in currency value from value in July 1997

Thailand (baht)

South Korea (won)

Brazil (real)
3/99

Russia (ruble)

Indonesia (rupiah)

−300%

Rupiah dropped to −495% in 7/98

Ruble dropped to −324% in 5/99

Source: *Economist* foreign exchange listings, various editions.

average Americans, as they watched their retirement funds, college savings for their children, and other nest eggs shrink with each passing day. The stock market restabilized later in 1998 only to have Brazil—another heralded economic success story, the world's eighth-largest economy, and a potential contagion to other parts of Latin America—go into financial crisis in early 1999.

In the Asian, Russian, and Brazilian cases IMF packages were put together, but they were less effective than in the Mexican case. There were a number of reasons for this, among which were greater doubts than before about both U.S. and IMF policy.

Policy Debates over the IMF

When a country faces financial crisis, the IMF usually makes credits and other support available, but also insists that the recipient state agree to tight fiscal policies, outright austerity measures, and economic reforms as a condition of receiving the IMF assistance. To the IMF, overspending, inefficiency, corruption, and other economic ineptitude is what got the country into its financial fix, and unless major reforms are put in place the added money likely will be wasted. In the 1995 Mexican peso crisis, for example, the IMF conditioned its financing on Mexican agreement to implement stringent fiscal and monetary policies and take other steps to stabilize the exchange rate and reform the economy. In this and other cases the IMF disburses the financing in "tranches" at designated intervals, conditional on compliance and performance.

Two quite different critiques are offered of the IMF formula. One is that the medicine is too harsh, that in the name of saving the patient it risks killing him. Here are countries already in serious crisis and the immediate effect of IMF austerity is to ratchet up unemployment, push up the prices of food and other staples, and cut way back on the social safety net governments can provide. There has to be a better way to get reform, it is argued, a more graduated approach that still has room for necessary social services.

The other critique believes that the IMF's readiness to bail countries out when they get in financial trouble creates a version of the classic problem of a "moral hazard." This means that in the name of providing help, incentives for the very behavior and actions that are to be encouraged are in fact reduced by showing that, if things get bad enough, someone else will step in to reduce the risks and lower the costs. Might the very success of the 1995 bailout of Mexico have led the Thai, Korean, and Indonesian governments to think that they could continue on their profligate and corrupt ways, for if real trouble hit, the IMF would be there for them, too? Perhaps U.S. banks and mutual funds felt the same false sense of security. States and others in similar situations are more likely to learn and change their ways, this argument claims, if they have to pay the price of their mistakes.

Another level of the debate goes to the very viability of the IMF as the principal multilateral institution for managing the international financial system. Here, too, we get two quite contrasting sets of arguments. One view is that the IMF is not powerful enough, and that a much stronger international financial institution needs to be created, possibly a global central bank modeled after the U.S. Federal Reserve. International rules and norms also need to be changed to allow countries, as a French official put it, "to bring the Frankenstein of deregulated global financial markets under control."[15] This could include policies such as capital controls, long prohibited as inconsistent with free markets and unfettered capital flows, but now advocated by some in at least their partial form as a necessary check on the extraordinary power that markets wield.

Others, such as former treasury secretary Robert Rubin, concurred on the need for change but questioned whether such sweeping new proposals would not end up creating a host of their own problems. Instead they have been pushing for reforms to strengthen the IMF in a more step-by-step manner. Among their proposals are policies requiring greater "transparency," that is, more disclosure of financial information to the IMF both by banks and other private-sector actors and by national governments; new powers for the IMF to act preventively before a full financial crisis hits; and increases in the funds available to the IMF.

Further compounding this debate are broader shifts in international monetary power. Although the United States still is unquestionably the world's strongest financial power, Europe is seeing its relative financial power increase. With the European Union having developed a common currency (the euro), this is likely to be even truer in the years to come as the euro competes with the dollar as the currency of choice for international transactions and national financial reserves. As Joan Spero and Jeffrey Hart write, "although the United States is still necessary, it is not sufficiently powerful to fulfill its earlier role. . . . In a world in which monetary power is more widely dispersed, management will depend not on the preferences of a dominant power but on the negotiations of several key powers."[16]

Moreover, some blame the United States even more than the IMF for being too fervent about its free market-ism. Advocacy of open markets was not just a reasoned economic strategy; at times it was like a mantra for the United States, repeated over and over as a mix of interests and ideology. Indeed, many see U.S. policy and doctrine as a significant contributing factor in the 1990s financial crises.

Social Stewardship

9.2

Social stewardship includes the responsible use of natural resources—resource use that meets the needs of current generations without compromising the ability of future generations to meet their needs. . . . [It] also includes long-range efforts to improve public health . . . investments in human potential such as public education and micro-credit initiatives. . . . Social stewardship is also valued as a building block of economic growth. Certainly, people who are healthy and educated are better prepared to seize economic opportunity than those who are sick, malnourished or illiterate. . . . And social stewardship also has a moral value that cannot be quantified. . . . Social stewardship is an expression of our common humanity and the dignity and worth of each human being.[17]

Issues of "social stewardship" call for policy-makers to look beyond immediate pocketbook concerns, to look down the road and across the planet. Across the planet at poverty and the dire conditions in which billions of people live. Down the road to future generations for whom we are but stewards of the environment and creators of policies that have lasting legacies. While less immediate and less direct in their impact, social stewardship concerns also are crucial issues of prosperity, conceived as it needs to be in broad and long-range terms.

Poverty and the Human Condition

Although there were some economic-development success stories during the Cold War, overall not a lot of progress was made in reducing Third World poverty, in either absolute or relative terms. One of the most telling absolute measures is the World Bank's "human development index," which quantifies the quality of life for people around the world by tabulating income data (per capita GDP), basic nutrition, access to clean water and health services, life expectancy, adult literacy rates, and other indicators of the human condition. As of the early 1990s, of 127 Third World countries, only 26 made the "high" human development category, while 53 were in the "medium" and 48 in the "low" category. "Low" human development meant an average real GDP per capita of $1,269 per year or less, life expectancy of 57 years or less, only 68 percent or less of the population with access to such basic needs as clean water, and an adult literacy rate of less than half the population.[18]

The most telling relative measure is the widening of the income gap between North and South. Whereas in 1960 about 70 percent of global income went to the richest 20 percent of countries, by 1990 this was up to 83 percent.

Put another way, the ratio of the richest to the poorest had gone from 30:1—itself enormously unequal—to 64:1. Despite the end of the Cold War and other developments that seemed propitious for progress against Third World poverty and social ills, this overall trend continues. For every country that has had its per capita income go up in the 1990s, there are almost three that had it go down. The map on p. 344, showing regions and countries drawn according to income, shows how disproportional global income distribution continues to be.

Moreover, the intra-country income gap between the "haves" and the "have-nots" has been getting wider. In Latin America the income share of the richest 20 percent of the population now is more than 50 percent, while the poorest 20 percent receive only about 5 percent of the national income. One in three people in the region lives on less than $2 a day. Nor is the situation any better in economic-growth "success" stories like China, where the progress that was made in the 1980s in reducing poverty leveled off in the 1990s, leaving more than 25 percent of the population, some 350 million people, living on less than $1 a day.

The *global population problem* also keeps growing worse.[19] World population is now about 6 billion. Population growth over the past decade has been the fastest in the 250 years that such measurements have been taken. In 1800, world population was 1 billion. It took 125 years to reach 2 billion (1925). It then took 35 years to reach 3 billion (1960). Since then the intervals have been 14 years (4 billion, 1974), 13 years (5 billion, 1987), and 12 years (6 billion, 1999). Not only is the sheer size of these numbers a problem in itself, but more than 90 percent of this population growth is in the Third World. Contrast the map on p. 345, showing the world drawn proportional to population distribution, with the map on p. 344, based on income distribution. In part the situation in the income-distribution map is caused by that in the population-distribution one: rapid population growth means that economic growth rates must be even higher to register positive on a per capita basis. Nevertheless, the two maps together provide a graphic indication of global in equality.

Hunger also remains a huge problem around the world. An estimated 35,000 children die each day of malnutrition and disease. Close to one billion people, it is estimated, are chronically undernourished—that's one out of every six humans. The problem, though, is less one of food production than of food distribution. Mid-1970s predictions of falling food supplies have been proven wrong by advances in agricultural sciences and technology. But for a number of reasons, including declining foreign aid, other financial problems, the ravages of wars, and political actions by many Third World governments, the world's food does not reach the people that need it the most.

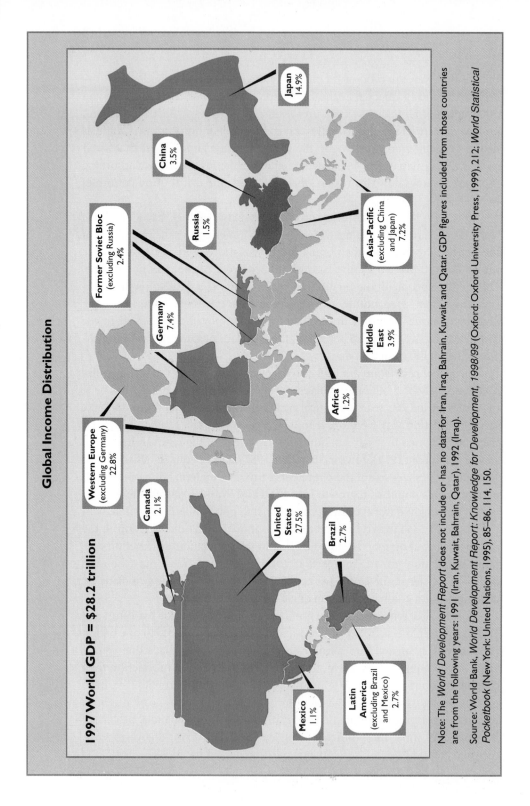

Global Income Distribution

1997 World GDP = $28.2 trillion

Japan
14.9%

China
3.5%

Asia-Pacific
(excluding China
and Japan)
7.2%

Former Soviet Bloc
(excluding Russia)
2.4%

Russia
1.5%

Germany
7.4%

Middle
East
3.9%

Africa
1.2%

Western Europe
(excluding Germany)
22.8%

Canada
2.1%

United
States
27.5%

Brazil
2.7%

Mexico
1.1%

Latin
America
(excluding Brazil
and Mexico)
2.7%

Note: The *World Development Report* does not include or has no data for Iran, Iraq, Bahrain, Kuwait, and Qatar. GDP figures included from those countries are from the following years: 1991 (Iran, Kuwait, Bahrain, Qatar). 1992 (Iraq).

Source: World Bank, *World Development Report: Knowledge for Development, 1998/99* (Oxford: Oxford University Press, 1999), 212; *World Statistical Pocketbook* (New York: United Nations, 1995), 85–86, 114, 150.

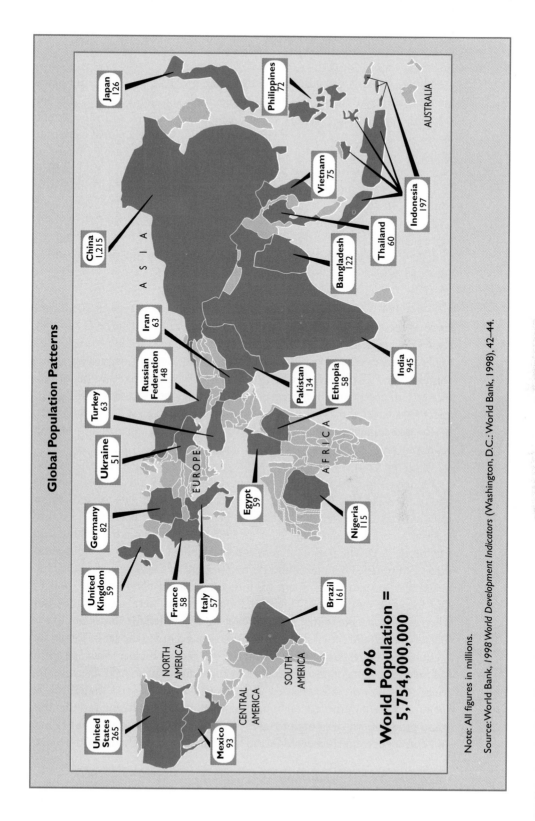

Global Population Patterns

**1996
World Population =
5,754,000,000**

Japan 126

Philippines 72

AUSTRALIA

Vietnam 75

Indonesia 197

China 1,215

Thailand 60

Bangladesh 122

A S I A

India 945

Iran 63

Russian Federation 148

Pakistan 134

Ethiopia 58

Turkey 63

Ukraine 51

EUROPE

A F R I C A

Germany 82

Egypt 59

Nigeria 115

United Kingdom 59

France 58

Italy 57

NORTH AMERICA

Brazil 161

SOUTH AMERICA

CENTRAL AMERICA

United States 265

Mexico 93

Note: All figures in millions.

Source: World Bank, *1998 World Development Indicators* (Washington, D.C.: World Bank, 1998), 42–44.

Finally, *global public health* has seen some progress, but still defies many attempts at improvement. In 1978 U.N. member states signed the "Health for All, 2000" agreement pledging to eradicate most diseases and raise public health standards. Since then AIDS has arisen and become a global epidemic. Some 30 million people worldwide are HIV-infected. About 66 percent of these people are in Africa, and another 20 percent in South Asia. Yet less than 10 percent of the money spent worldwide on AIDS is spent in Third World countries. In addition, even a disease such as tuberculosis (TB), considered under control, is again on the rise. Nearly 3 million people died of TB in 1995, more than in the worst years of the TB epidemic that struck around 1900. All told, 20 old diseases have re-emerged and 29 previously unknown ones have appeared in the last 20–25 years.[20]

U.S. POLICY   The United States is seen by many as bearing a significant share of the blame for Third World poverty. Officially, of course, U.S. policy always has favored Third World economic development. But in reality, for virtually the entire Cold War this goal was a much lower priority than global containment. This is evident when you consider who received the bulk of U.S. foreign aid: geopolitically strategic countries like South Vietnam in the 1960s and 1970s, Israel and Egypt since the late 1970s, and El Salvador in the 1980s. It also was evident in the much greater sums spent on military aid than on economic aid.

With the Cold War over, some hoped that more of U.S. foreign aid would be redirected to economic development. Instead, the United States used the end of the Cold War to cut back on rather than reallocate its foreign aid. In inflation-adjusted terms the decline has been close to 50 percent. U.S. aid to Central America, for example, fell from $226 million a year in the 1980s to $26 million in 1997. The politics here was predictable in some respects but paradoxical in others. One poll found that 75 percent of the American public believed that too much was spent on foreign aid, and only 4 percent thought that too little was spent (17 percent thought things were about right). But whereas most people thought that foreign aid accounted for 15 percent of the federal budget, the actual figure is less than 1 percent.[21] One set of follow-up questions asked respondents how much of the federal budget *should* be spent in foreign aid, and got the extraordinarily high answer of about 13 percent. Yet when the question was phrased differently—"Now imagine that the U.S. spends 1 percent of the federal budget on foreign aid. Would you feel that this is too little, too much or about right?"—46 percent said it was "about right," and only 34 percent considered it "too little." This is better than the 75 percent "too much" and 4 percent "too little" of the original poll cited, but neverthe-less gives some pause.

U.S. development policy continues to be split, pulled in different and somewhat contradictory directions. The official policy of the Agency for International Development (AID) has shifted toward *sustainable development* and its more social-stewardship approach to economic growth and development. Economic growth still is a goal, but greater weight than in the past is put on environmental factors, considerations of equity, and other societal effects within the developing country. Notwithstanding this shift in doctrine, however, the impact of U.S. policy is severely constrained by the limited foreign aid budget. In addition, policy-makers are divided between this doctrine and the tendency to rely more on classical free market-ism. Another limitation and internal contradiction has arisen out of domestic antiabortion politics: Congress has imposed constraints on U.S. funding for global birth control and other population programs.

Although the economic effects on U.S. prosperity interests are the primary motivation for U.S. development, other aspects of the national interest come into play as well. Many see principles at stake, in the very basic sense of humanitarianism and seeking to help those who need the help the most. Peace and power interests also are at stake, given how the persistence and exacerbation of Third World poverty can undermine political stability in countries of significant geopolitical interest to the United States. The peasant rebellion in Chiapas, one of Mexico's poorest states and one with a heavily indigenous population, is a good example.[22] When the Chiapas rebellion first broke out on New Year's Day 1994 it shocked those in Washington and Mexico City who were keen on celebrating NAFTA's coming into force. Even when for a few years the Mexican government seemed to have suppressed the rebellion, its counterinsurgency tactics and violations of human rights posed a serious problem for U.S. fealty to principles. Yet the rebellion has continued and even spread to other Mexican states; combined with Mexico's other problems, this situation poses the specter for U.S. peace and power interests of potentially even more serious and widespread instability in the United States' contiguous neighbor.

THE WORLD BANK   For its part the World Bank, the principal multilateral institution dealing with economic development, generally is regarded as less successful than the GATT and the IMF have been in their areas. Among the major criticisms are that the World Bank has invested too heavily in expensive infrastructure projects and has not provided enough funding for smaller-scale projects that more directly benefit the people, that it has looked the other way when faced with corruption, and that it has not paid enough attention to environmental concerns. Although much of this criticism is aimed directly at the World Bank, because the United States controls the largest voting bloc* and because the head of the World Bank has always been an American, the United States also often gets some of the blame here as well.

In recent years the World Bank has been undergoing significant reform and reassessment. As it does it faces three main sets of issues. One is resources. Given the scope and severity of global poverty, the World Bank's financial reserves need to be increased. But increased pledges and contributions of capital from the developed countries, the United States in particular, have not been sufficiently forthcoming.

A second issue is development doctrine and strategy. The World Bank long was seen by environmentalists as among the worst offenders, and much in need of "greening" in its policies and programs. Since the mid-1990s it has taken a number of steps in this direction. Critics have also pointed to the need to pay more attention to corruption, political repression, and other domestic political issues in recipient countries. Traditionally the World Bank claimed to be apolitical, that its decisions were economic ones to be made on economic criteria and whose success was to be evaluated based on growth rates and other hard economic data. By the mid-1990s, though, the World Bank had begun to shift its stand, based on the strong evidence that good government is a necessary part of sound economic development. This evidence was reinforced in 1997–99 by cases like Indonesia, a formerly vaunted success story that was then undermined in large part by massive corruption.

A third issue also is a political one, albeit at the level of the donor countries and the extent to which they should be allowed to attach political conditions to their lending and voting. In theory, as a multilateral economic development institution the World Bank is supposed to be detached from the politics of the international agenda. Yet the United States, its biggest donor, has also been the country most inclined to make political linkages and attach conditions to its funding. Some of this has been initiated by presidents, some imposed by Congress. Back when the U.S. voting share in the World Bank was

---

*Like in the IMF but unlike in the U.N. General Assembly, voting in the World Bank is not "one country, one vote" but is proportional to the size of a country's financial contribution. In past decades the U.S. share was more than 40 percent. As the relative share of U.S. funding has declined, so too has the U.S. voting share, now down to under 20 percent.

over 40 percent, it was much easier for the United States to impose its position. But with its voting share less than 20 percent now and without the bloc strength of the Cold War, other countries are both more willing and more able to oppose the United States on these issues. Moreover, the United States now also needs to be concerned about precedents; in the future other countries might also seek to impose political conditions on World Bank lending and be able to get 51 percent despite U.S. opposition.

DEVELOPMENT AND FREE MARKET-ISM   President Fernando Enrique Cardoso of Brazil was seen by many as epitomizing the ostensibly newly emerging Third World consensus in favor of capitalism. Back in the 1970s, as Professor Cardoso, he was the co-author of *Development and Underdevelopment in Latin America,* a leading book critiquing capitalism and favoring more socialistic policies that was used in college courses around the world. Yet as president of Brazil in the 1990s he was the champion of policies favoring private foreign investment, reducing the role of the state in the economy, and other strongly pro-capitalist and free-market measures. The initial popularity of these policies got him elected and re-elected. However, when the 1999 financial crisis hit Brazil, Cardoso's popularity fell and many began questioning whether free market-ism really was the optimal economic strategy. And far from being confined to one country, this debate was being reopened on a broadly global scale.

Nevertheless, most analysts still feel that whatever the ills and shortcomings of global capitalism, there is no future in returning to the inefficient statist policies of the past. Spero and Hart have shown a very strong correlation between economic growth rates and "outward" rather than "inward" national economic policies—i.e., policies open to foreign trade and investment rather than closed off through import substitution, expropriation of foreign investment, and the like. The difference was almost twofold between the 8–9 percent average growth rate for those Third World countries most outwardly oriented, and 3–4 percent for those most inward oriented.[23]

Many Third World countries have made substantial headway in economic reform toward more outward-oriented and free-market-based policies. Accordingly, they attract huge inflows of private capital, up from a mere $18.4 billion in 1987 to $225 billion in 1996. Yet this also means, as journalist Thomas Friedman put it, that countries now have to live by the credo "Don't mess with Moody's," referring to the investor service that establishes the credit ratings for companies and now for countries: "In the 1960s the most important visitor a developing country could have was the head of AID [the Agency for International Development], the U.S. agency that doled out foreign aid. In the 1970s and '80s the most important visitor a developing country could have was from the IMF to help restructure its economy. In the 1990s the most important visitor a developing country can have is from Moody's Investors Service Inc."[24] Since Moody's cares even less than the IMF about the social and economic inequalities of fiscal austerity, it is no wonder that the gap between the haves and the have-nots has been widening.

Another sense in which economic problems seem inherent to the very structure and dynamics of the global capitalist system are the declining terms of trade between the industrialized, technology-driven economies of the North and the raw materials–based economies of the South. Another empirical point made by Spero and Hart is that between 1965 and 1991 the average terms of trade deteriorated almost 50 percent for the poorest Third World countries and about 30 percent for those considered middle-income developing countries.[25] In other words, the poorest countries were getting half as much value for their exports to the developed world, in terms of the prices they could charge compared to the prices they had to pay; middle-income countries were getting only about 70 percent value compared to 1965.

We thus find a range of critics questioning free market-ism. Pope John Paul II, in a speech to the U.N. General Assembly, put much of the blame on the developed world—and by implication particularly the United States—for its "consumerist culture," its "unjust criteria in the distribution of resources and production," and its politics "to safeguard special interest groups." U.N. Secretary-General Kofi Annan, in a speech to the 1999 World Economic Forum, a conclave of the world's leading government officials and international business leaders, warned that until and unless people in poor countries can gain confidence in the global economy, it "will be fragile and vulnerable— vulnerable to backlash from all the '-isms' of our post–Cold War world: protectionism, populism, nationalism, ethnic chauvinism, fanaticism and terrorism." The key to gaining that confidence, he stressed, is to break away from the idea that the choice is only "between a global market driven . . . by calculations of short-term profit and one which has a human face."[26] As the leading proponent of free markets and the world's major capitalist country, the United States is always at least implicitly the focus of these and other such challenges.

Global Environmental Issues

In his best-selling book *Earth in the Balance,* then-senator Al Gore honed in on the global environment as "the central organizing principle of civilization."

Gore was critical of "violations of our stewardship" as manifested in such global environmental problems as ozone depletion and global warming.[27] Although Gore and others succeeded in raising the priority given to global environmental issues both in U.S. policy and globally, resulting in some important treaties and other progress, quite a bit more needs to be done to meet the standards of stewardship.

Global environmental issues pose four types of policy difficulties. First, they constitute a classic "collective action" problem. Collective action problems are those in which all would benefit by taking joint action to deal with a problem, and all suffer from not doing so, but collective action is impeded by each waiting for the other to act first or by lack of agreement on what should be done. It is the essence of interdependence that all countries will suffer if global warming, ozone depletion, and other global environmental problems grow worse, and that all countries therefore have interests in ensuring that they do not. But it is the essence of the problem of global governance that taking such action is so difficult.

Second, environmental issues raise the classic tradeoff between short-term and long-term gain. As with other issues we have discussed, like preventive statecraft (Chapter 8), global environmental issues require acting today, paying the costs today, for benefits that will be reaped only many years from now. Nor is the need to act today absolutely self-evident, the danger clear and present. The world is not yet in crisis. Some associations are made between present weather patterns and global warming, but the severe effects of climate change really won't be felt until well into the future. Yet if the international community waits until then to act it will be too late. The same short-term/long-term dynamic holds for species and biodiversity preservation, stopping desertification, curtailing air and water pollution, and other environmental issues. To the old axiom that "all politics is local" can be added that "all politics are short-term."

Third, issues of North-South equity further complicate global environmental negotiations. For example, on global warming, developing countries claim a right to higher ceilings on industrial emissions. They base their claim both on economic grounds that poor countries cannot afford more sophisticated emissions-scrubbing technologies, and on the historical justice argument that developed countries did more than their share of polluting during the nineteenth and early twentieth centuries. The United States and other developed countries have conceded on some of these points, as with the exemptions and lower standards for many Third World countries negotiated in the 1997 Kyoto global warming treaty. But such exceptions complicate the domestic politics of treaty ratification. Business and other groups opposed to the

Kyoto global warming treaty aired a very effective television spot showing scissors cutting out India, China, and other Third World countries from a world map while the voice-over talked about the unfairness of these countries's being exempted while the United States foots the bill.

Fourth is the problem of enforcement. This, too, is not just characteristic of global environmental issues; it is also part of a broader problem.* Once multilateral agreements are reached, norms affirmed, and actions mandated, how to ensure fulfillment and compliance? Most treaties and other agreements do call for sanctions or other penalties and consequences for states that do not meet their obligations, but these are not always enforced. Special multilateral bodies can be created, like the U.N. Sustainable Development Commission set up following the 1992 Earth summit. But as a practical matter such bodies have very limited authority and power.

This analytic context helps explain both the scope and the limits of progress by the United States and the international community on global environmental issues. The beginnings of an infrastructure of treaties and other global environmental agreements has been created: the Montreal Protocol on ozone depletion, the Rio Treaty on biodiversity, the Kyoto global warming treaty, the U.N. Law of the Sea treaty, and others. But although the Clinton administration has shown willingness to sign on to these treaties, only the Montreal Protocol has been approved by Congress. The United States is the only industrialized country that has not ratified the biodiversity treaty. It did not sign the Law of the Sea treaty until 1994, more than ten years after most other countries did, and Senate ratification has yet to happen. A ratification deadline was agreed to at the 1997 Kyoto conference, but although most countries made this deadline the United States did not. None of these treaties has been defeated in Congress; they have been held back by the Clinton administration for fear that they would be defeated.

These issues, and those that will succeed them, are crucial because of the range of U.S. interests affected. By presenting them in the context of the U.S. national interest in prosperity, the conventional formulation of economics vs. environment is rejected. Of course environmental protection is more expensive than allowing water pollution, air pollution, and excess use of nonrenewable resources to be treated as "externalities." This is not an open-ended justification for excess regulation and undue economic burdens, but also is not a rationalization for a private company's treating a cost borne by society as

---

*See, for example, Chapter 10 on human rights.

an externality. This is the essence of the concept of sustainable development. Moreover, there are profits to be made, jobs to be created, and export markets to be gained in the emerging industry of environmental-protection equipment and technology. And not all solutions are high tech: take Ben and Jerry's Rain Forest Crunch ice cream, which is made from Brazilian rain-forest nuts specially imported so as to create a market incentive for preserving the rain forest.

Environmental issues also merge with broader U.S. foreign policy concerns about political stability and security (peace). Environmental scarcity and degradation have been sources of conflict and violence in a number of wars, both recent and historical. They also further complicate the tasks of building strong and democratic states, not just in the Third World but everywhere. The environment is an issue for Russia, where for decades pollution standards for industries were close to nil, where entire bodies of water like the Aral Sea were totally destroyed, where nuclear and other wastes were disposed with much too little precaution. It also is an issue for China, five of whose largest cities are among the most polluted in the world, and where numerous other environmental problems continue to grow worse.

Economic Sanctions

Even a partial list of targets of 1990s U.S. economic sanctions includes Iraq, Libya, Iran, Serbia, North Korea, China, Russia, Nigeria, Burundi, the Sudan, Haiti, Guatemala, Colombia, Paraguay, Cuba, Burma, and Cambodia. Other countries also have been using sanctions—Russia against various ex-Soviet states, Greece against Macedonia, Israel against the Palestinians—but the United States far and away has been the most frequent user of sanctions.

Sanctions take a number of forms: trade sanctions through embargoes on exports to targeted countries and boycotts of imports from them; financial sanctions through freezes on assets held in foreign accounts and denial of international credits and loans; investment sanctions, including both bans on new investment and requirements to divest existing investments; curtailment of foreign aid; and others. Whatever the form or combination, what all these examples have in common is the effort to use international economic relationships for political purposes. As such the use of sanctions poses important questions about U.S. policy choices in two respects: first, with regard to 4 Ps tensions and tradeoffs between prosperity and other national interests; second, about when and how sanctions work.

Policy Choice: 4Ps Tensions and Tradeoffs

Table 9.2 lists the major economic sanctions the United States has imposed during the post–Cold War era. The principal policy objectives of U.S. sanctions cover the whole gamut of national interest objectives: *principles,* the justification for sanctions in democratization and human rights cases; *power and peace,* justifying the various controls on military and proliferation-related exports and technology against Iraq and other countries suspected of the proliferation of nuclear and other weapons of mass destruction (WMD); and *peace,* used to justify sanctions intended to stop or prevent wars and reverse invasions.

Since by definition sanctions carry economic costs for the United States as well as for the targeted country, imposing them means giving priority to other national-interest objectives over prosperity. Conversely, when decisions are made not to impose sanctions, it is often because of the interests of prosperity. And either way, the politics often are quite contentious. Back in Chapter 1 we highlighted the Tiananmen Square sanctions against China as a major case showing tensions between the 4 Ps. On the one side were human rights advo-

TABLE 9.2 Major Post–Cold War U.S. Economic Sanctions		
Year imposed	**Target**	**Principal objectives**
1989	China	Principles
1990	Iraq	Peace, power**
1991	Haiti	Principles**
1992	Serbia	Peace**
1992*	Iran	Power, peace, principles
1992	Somalia	Peace, principles**
1992*	Libya	Peace, power**
1993	Sudan	Power, principles
1994*	North Korea	Peace
1994	Rwanda	Peace**
1996*	Cuba	Principles, power
1996	Myanmar (Burma)	Principles
1997	Sierra Leone	Peace**
1998	India, Pakistan	Peace, power

*Indicates earlier sanctions going back to the Cold War era
**Indicates sanctions imposed through the United Nations, with allies or with other significant international support

cates in Congress and such nongovernmental organizations as Human Rights Watch Asia and Amnesty International pushing for suspension of most-favored-nation status and other sanctions in the name of American principles. Sanctions opponents made a claim to principles, arguing that trade liberalization ultimately would bring political liberalization to China. Some also made power and peace arguments along the lines of the overall engagement strategy (Chapter 8). Mostly, though, the battle was about trade and investment, about prosperity vs. principles.

Sanctions restricting trade in dual-use technologies and other exports that run risks of WMD proliferation are a good example of the prosperity vs. power and peace tension. Although no one really advocates exporting WMD per se, sanctions on the sale of technologies and other exports that have both commercial-civilian uses but also potential military applications are often controversial. American companies see substantial markets abroad for such dual-use technologies and products, with strong returns in both profits and job creation. Defense officials and nonproliferation advocates stress the potential dangers involved and argue for erring on the side of caution.

Another difficult choice involves issues of principle raised by the humanitarian effects of sanctions. In the cases of severe sanctions against Haiti and Iraq in the 1990s, the regimes managed to insulate themselves but the civilian populaces bore extreme suffering. In the Haiti case sanctions hit so hard as to push per capita GDP down 25 percent and raise unemployment to 60–70 percent and inflation to 60 percent, all in a country that already was the poorest in the Western Hemisphere. When sanctions were first imposed the Haitian people generally supported them, showing a willingness to bear some costs in the expectation that the military regime and its supporters would be brought down. Instead, in large part because the sanctions were so poorly enforced and targeted, the coup leaders bore so few of the costs that in Creole (the Haitian language) *anbago,* the word for "embargo," was cynically referred to as *anba gwo,* meaning "under the heels of the rich and powerful."[28]

In Iraq, too, the masses of people have suffered the most. In late 1996 UNICEF estimated that 4,500 children under the age of 5 were dying in Iraq every month. A U.N. Food and Agriculture Organization report in 1997 found food shortages and malnutrition in Iraq to have become ever more "severe and chronic."[29] Yet all along, going back to the first U.N. sanctions against Iraq in 1990, provisions were offered to allow for humanitarian relief with the caveat that the U.N. would control the funds to ensure that Saddam Hussein did not divert them for WMD or other such purposes. Moreover, while blaming the United States and the international community for the suffering of the

Iraqi people, Saddam kept managing to find funds to build and refurbish his multiple presidential palaces and to secretly import military equipment and technology. This does not relieve U.S. policy from concern for the humanitarian issues, but it does reveal the complexity of the policy choices and policy effects.

Policy Efficacy: Do Sanctions Work?

The evidence is that sanctions have worked in some ways and in some cases but not others.[30] They helped end apartheid in South Africa, but even after almost forty years have yet to bring Fidel Castro down in Cuba. They have helped contain Saddam Hussein from developing further his military power and especially his WMD programs, but they have contributed to the humanitarian crisis in Iraq, as just discussed. They had some impact on Serbia in ending the war in Bosnia, but couldn't have done it alone; the U.S.-led NATO air strikes were a necessary step. They didn't work in Haiti, but this may have been because of how erratically and poorly they were implemented and enforced.

The sanctions literature reflects this mixed assessment. "It would be difficult to find any proposition in the international relations literature more widely accepted," wrote Professor David Baldwin in the mid-1980s, "than those belittling the utility of economic techniques of statecraft."[31] One recent article was straightforwardly titled: "Why Economic Sanctions Do Not Work."[32] Baldwin's statement as quoted above, however, was a critical one, from which he went on to question whether sanctions are held to an "analytical 'double standard' . . . prone to accentuate the negative and downplay the positive aspects of such measures."[33] Other studies also have concluded that sanctions have worked and can work more often than often acknowledged.

Among the factors that affect whether sanctions work, one of the most important is the extent to which the sanctions are multilateral. If other countries serve as alternative trade partners for the target state, sanctions can have little or no impact. Alternative trade partners also can have a political effect by significantly reducing the credibility that sanctions convey. This works in different ways depending on whether the alternative partner is an ally or an adversary of the state initiating the sanctions, but either way it can have an important impact.

Another factor is the extent to which the target state has the economic capacity to defend itself against the sanctions. For example, Rhodesia (now Zimbabwe), which despite in the 1960s–70s becoming the first country to be hit with sanctions by the full United Nations, had sufficient domestic industrial capacity to substitute for most of the embargoed goods and ride the sanctions out for more than ten years. In other cases economic self-defense is not possible economy-wide, but the governing regime and supportive elites can lessen sanctions' effect on themselves through black markets, sanctions-busting, and other profiteering, as was seen in Iraq and Haiti in the 1990s. Thus sanctioning countries often freeze the foreign financial assets of regime leaders in order to better target the sanctions.

Third is whether sanctions are a good "fit" with the foreign policy objectives being pursued. One of the recurring problems in U.S. policy is that sanctions often are turned to as a default option, based more on the resistance to using force and constraints on other options than on careful analysis of sanctions themselves. "When in doubt, impose sanctions" assumes that there is nothing to lose by doing so, but in fact sanctions often can end up net negative for the United States, whether through misfiring and missing the regime but hitting the populace, or backfiring and hurting American exporters more than foreign regimes, or weakening rather than buttressing American credibility when the results fall well short of the threats.

What makes sanctions particularly vexing for U.S. post–Cold War policy is that the broad economic, strategic, and political systemic changes do not cut strictly one way or the other. On the one hand, target states are now more vulnerable to sanctions in three respects. First, in economic terms, while the impact of globalization does vary, few if any countries have been able to stay sufficiently insulated or isolated as not to be vulnerable to the economic disruptions set off by sanctions. Whereas the GNP impact of Cold War–era sanctions averaged less than 2 percent, a number of the 1990s cases involved double-digit effects. Second is the increased willingness of the United Nations to use its sanctions authority, broadening the coalition and establishing legitimacy in ways only the U.N. can. There were only two cases of U.N.-mandated sanctions prior to 1990, but since then there have been more than ten, many of which were in large part due to U.S. prodding, such as those against Iraq, Serbia, and Haiti. Third, because democratization has opened up more countries' political systems, groups whose interests are at risk are in more of a position to bring political pressure for policy change to avoid or end sanctions.

On the other hand other aspects of these same systemic trends have made the political viability of sanctions more problematic. Economically, the greater economic vulnerability of countries has been part of the reason for the sanctions-induced humanitarian crises. Strategically, although it is true that the U.N. has used sanctions more recently than in the past, at times they have been watered down or delayed by various countries. The United States also has had major disputes with western Europe in cases like Iran and Cuba, where the allies see their geopolitical as well as economic interests differently. As to the democratization trend, many of the regimes against which sanctions have been used have not been part of it (Iraq, Serbia, and Cuba, for instance).

In sum, it would be one thing if we simply could conclude that sanctions really just don't work, or that they are easy to wield. It even would be easier if we just could say that the patterns were largely the same as during the Cold War. But none of these statements hold up. Instead we have a paradox of both vulnerability and viability. In some respects sanctions have more potential effectiveness than before because of the greater vulnerability of target states. In other respects it is more problematic to tap that efficacy. Thus the paradox, and thus the dilemmas for U.S. policy.

Summary

As with the other main issue areas of U.S. foreign policy, the post–Cold War international political economy poses complex policy choices amid dynamic patterns of change. Globalization has many aspects, and as stressed at the outset of this chapter is not inherently or exclusively a positive or negative force. Two things are certain, however. One is that globalization has made foreign economic and social policy issues more salient than in the past: we now hear much less "low politics" denigration of foreign economic policy issues compared to political-military ones. The other is that achieving foreign economic and social policy objectives is more complex and difficult now than when the United States enjoyed greater international economic dominance.

In some respects, despite all the changes, the international political economy has stayed remarkably stable. In trade, international finance, and development the three principal multilateral institutions continue to play central roles. Liberal norms and rules of open markets and nondiscrimination continue to define the game. Over the course of the 1990s many countries have adopted a capitalist economic system in full or in part. Communist command economies, African socialism, Latin American nationalist statism, and other alternative economic models largely were discredited and abandoned. It didn't seem to matter who the leader or what the country was, the speech was likely to be rich in rhetoric about free markets, free enterprise, and the other virtues of capitalism.

Yet by the latter years of the decade people came to realize that what we are seeing is not just the triumph but also the testing of capitalism on a world scale. More and more questions have been raised and doubts expressed about capitalism's flaws and failures. Some of the problems have involved corruption, as in Russia with the millions siphoned off by the "klepto-capitalists," and in East Asia, where "crony capitalism" had run rampant. Some involved the failure of capitalism to produce its promised "rising tide that lifts all boats." Not only has inequality among countries grown worse, but equity gaps within many countries also widened, in both the developed and the developing worlds. Capitalism is not about to be abandoned, but there is an increasing desire to search for modifications, adaptations, and possibly alternatives.

For U.S. policy this poses challenges in each of the three main economic policy areas: trade, international finance, and social stewardship. Free and fair trade is seen as ever more crucial to U.S. prosperity. This needs to be achieved, though, in the dual context of the WTO at the international level, and increasingly contentious domestic trade politics. In international finance and international development, questions are being raised about the classical free market-ism the United States espouses as its overall strategy and international political economy ideology. Where is the balance to be struck between markets' virtues and their imperfections and instabilities? What are the lessons of the 1990s financial crises that will help U.S. policy, the IMF, and others do a better job at financial crisis prevention and management? Even when global growth was going strong, its rising tide did not lift all boats: poverty deepened for billions of people. We know quite a bit about what doesn't work for development but still too little about what does, especially for sustainable development and responsible stewardship of the human condition and the global environment.

As for economic sanctions, they pose difficult policy choices between different components of the U.S. national interest. They also involve tough questions of efficacy, especially in light of the net negative costs they can have when they fail.

All told, the questions, issues, and policy choices posed by efforts to promote U.S. interests in prosperity are yet another area in which the new era and the new century present both challenges and opportunities for U.S. foreign policy.

Notes

1. J. David Richardson and Karin Rindal, *Why Exports Matter: More!* (Washington, D.C.: Institute of International Economics and the Manufacturing Institute, 1996), 1.
2. Roger C. Altman, "The Nuke of the 1990s," *New York Times Magazine*, March 1, 1998, 34.

[3]Ethan B. Kapstein, "Workers and the World Economy," *Foreign Affairs* 75:3 (May/June 1996), 16.

[4]Frederick W. Mayer, *Interpreting NAFTA: The Science and Art of Political Analysis* (New York: Columbia University Press, 1998).

[5]Bruce Stokes, "Team Players," *National Journal*, January 7, 1995, 18.

[6]Michael Hirsh and Karen Breslau, "Closing the Deal Diplomacy: In Clinton's Foreign Policy, the Business of America Is Business," *Newsweek*, March 6, 1995, 34.

[7]Stokes, "Team Players," 10–11.

[8]I. M. Destler, *American Trade Politics,* 2d ed. (Washington, D.C.: Institute of International Economics, 1992), 142–43.

[9]Stephen D. Cohen, "General Agreement on Tariffs and Trade," in Bruce W. Jentleson and Thomas G. Paterson, eds., *Encyclopedia of U.S. Foreign Relations* (New York: Oxford University Press, 1997), Vol. 2, 207.

[10]Edward Luttwak, "From Geo-Politics to Geo-Economics," *National Interest* 20 (Summer 1990), 17, 20.

[11]Luttwak, "From Geo-Politics to Geo-Economics," 19.

[12]John E. Rielly, ed., *American Public Opinion and U.S. Foreign Policy, 1994* (Chicago: Chicago Council on Foreign Relations, 1995), 21.

[13]Samuel P. Huntington, "America's Changing Strategic Interests," *Survival* 33:1 (January/February 1991), 8–10.

[14]Karin Lissakers, quoted in John M. Berry and Clay Chandler, "Fast Currency Trades Feed Fears of a Crisis," *Washington Post*, April 17, 1995, A13.

[15]Jean-Paul Fitoussi, quoted in Roger Cohen, "Redrawing the Free Market," *New York Times*, November 14, 1998, A17, A19.

[16]Joan E. Spero and Jeffrey A. Hart, *The Politics of International Economic Relations* (New York: St. Martin's, 1997), 44.

[17]Rockefeller Brothers Fund, *Global Interdependence and the Need for Social Stewardship* (New York: Rockefeller Brothers Fund, 1997), 9–10.

[18]World Bank, *Human Development 1996* (New York: Oxford University Press, 1996), Table 5.

[19]Alene Gelbard, Carl Haub, and Mary M. Kent, *World Population beyond Six Billion* (Washington, D.C.: Population Reference Bureau, 1999).

[20]Laurie Garrett, *The Coming Plague: Newly Emerging Diseases in a World Out of Balance* (New York: Penguin, 1994).

[21]Steven Kull and I. M. Destler, *Misreading the Public: The Myth of a New Isolationism* (Washington, D.C.: Brookings Institution Press, 1999), 113–33.

[22]Michael W. Foley, "Southern Mexico: Counterinsurgency and Electoral Politics," special report (Washington, D.C.: U.S. Institute of Peace Press, 1999); Michael Renner, "Chiapas: An Uprising Born of Despair," *WorldWatch*, January/February 1997, 12–24.

[23]Spero and Hart, *Politics of International Economic Relations*, 233.

[24]Thomas L. Friedman, "Don't Mess with Moody's," *New York Times*, February 22, 1995, A19.

[25]Spero and Hart, *Politics of International Economic Relations*, 219.

[26]Secretary-General Kofi Annan, "Markets for a Better World," speech at the World Economic Forum, Davos, Switzerland, January 1998, U.N. Press Release SG/SM/6448.

[27]Al Gore, *Earth in the Balance* (Boston: Houghton Mifflin, 1992).

[28]Claudette Antoine Werleigh, "The Use of Sanctions in Haiti: Assessing the Economic Realities," in *Economic Sanctions: Panacea or Peacebuilding in the Post–Cold War World?* ed. David Cortright and George Lopez (Boulder, Colo.: Westview, 1995), 169.

[29]Eric Hoskins, "The Humanitarian Impact of Economic Sanctions and War in Iraq," in *Political Gain and Civilian Pain: Humanitarian Impact of Economic Sanctions,* ed. Thomas G. Weiss, David Cortright, George A. Lopez, and Larry Minear (Lanham, Md.: Rowman and Littlefield, 1997).

[30]Bruce W. Jentleson, "Economic Sanctions and Post–Cold War Conflicts: Challenges for Theory and Policy," paper prepared for the Committee on International Conflict Resolution, Commission on Behavioral Sciences, National Research Council, National Academy of Sciences, 1999; Richard N. Haass, ed., *Economic Sanctions and American Diplomacy* (Washington, D.C.: Brookings Institution Press, 1998); Cortright and Lopez, eds. *Economic Sanctions.*

[31]David A. Baldwin, *Economic Statecraft* (Princeton: Princeton University Press, 1985), 57.

[32]Robert A. Pape, "Why Economic Sanctions Do Not Work," *International Security,* 22:2 (Fall 1997), 90–136.

[33]Baldwin, *Economic Statecraft,* 144.

10 *Principles: The Coming of a Democratic Century?*

Introduction: The Democratic Idealist Paradigm and the Post–Cold War Era

How captivating was the drama, how exhilarating the joy, how inspiring the sense of hope of those amazing days that marked the beginning of the 1990s. The Berlin Wall, that starkest symbol of the Cold War, crumbled as young Berliners from East and West danced on it. Nelson Mandela, imprisoned for almost thirty years by the apartheid governments of South Africa, was set free, and four years later became president of post-apartheid South Africa. Nicaragua, a country that had endured a decade of civil war and had a long history of U.S. intervention and occupation, held its first free elections ever. A coup attempt in the Soviet Union was put down by the Russian people led by a defiant Boris Yeltsin standing on a tank.

In the context of these and other such events, the Democratic Idealist paradigm seemed triumphant (see Dynamics of Choice, p. 363). It long had held that *right* should be given priority over *might*—and now, here we were witnessing "the end of history," as Francis Fukuyama termed it, not just the end of the Cold War but "the universalization of Western liberal democracy as the final form of human government." Fukuyama wasn't claiming that all conflict was over, or that there wouldn't be a few "isolated true believers." But he did see the Big Issues of world affairs as having been settled once and for all. "The triumph of the West, of the Western *idea,* is evident . . . in the total exhaustion of viable systematic alternatives to Western liberalism."[1] And first the Bush administration and then the Clinton administration minced few words in hailing the U.S. role in turning the tide of history.

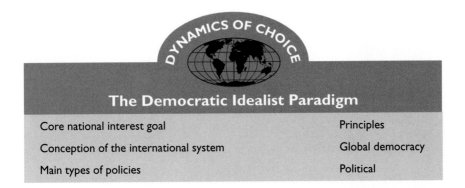

DYNAMICS OF CHOICE

The Democratic Idealist Paradigm

Core national interest goal	Principles
Conception of the international system	Global democracy
Main types of policies	Political

Moreover, the global spread of democracy was said to mean a safer and more peaceful world because, although democracies fought wars against non-democracies, democracies did not fight against each other. This was the other main Democratic Idealist proposition, that *right* ultimately makes for *might*, now manifested as the "democratic peace" theory. If the Clinton administration could be said to have had an operating paradigm, this was it—"democracies do not attack each other," President Clinton declared, so therefore "ultimately the best strategy to insure our security and to build a durable peace is to support the advance of democracy elsewhere."[2]

As the 1990s went on, however, we also witnessed horrors and inhumanity on scales that many had hoped were part of the past. Terms like "ethnic cleansing" had to be added to our vocabulary. Genocides were committed with horrific frequency. Terror tore societies apart. Human rights were further

Onlookers cheer as a man takes a sledgehammer to the Berlin Wall, the destruction of which symbolized the end of the Cold War. (*AP/Wide World Photos*)

Nelson Mandela raises his fist in triumph as he celebrates his release after twenty-seven years of imprisonment in South Africa. (*AP/Wide World Photos*)

trampled. It seemed, as Samuel Huntington responded to Fukuyama, that "so long as human beings exist, there is no exit from the traumas of history."[3] Huntington's own "clash of civilizations" theory, in which "the great divisions among humankind" with their deep cultural and historical roots were "the battle lines of the future," offered a much bleaker view.[4] Still others spoke of "the coming anarchy," global chaos, failed states, and the like.[5]

Consequently, on the eve of what was being foreseen as the "Democratic Century," the record was much more mixed, the policy choices facing the United States more complicated, and the global future of democracy more uncertain than it seemed in those heady days of 1989–91.

A Rwandan boy passes the bodies of those killed in the violent clashes between the Hutu and Tutsi ethnic groups. (*Betty Press/Woodfin Camp/PNI*)

A woman is dragged away by police officers while attempting to deliver a protest letter to the delegates of the Fifteenth Communist Party Congress in Beijing, China. *(AP/Wide World Photos)*

In this chapter we first want to take stock of *the status and prospects of global democracy and human rights,* assessing both the progress that has been made and the problems that have been encountered in regions and countries of particular concern to U.S. foreign policy. The next section examines the *democratic peace debate,* and the contending arguments and relative evidence about the extent to which principles and peace have the posited complementarity.

We then assess the *policy strategies for promoting democracy and protecting human rights,* linking these to some of the literature on democratization and political development, and focusing on U.S. policy along with some discussion of the U.N., other international actors, and nongovernmental organizations. The chapter's final section considers the *principles-power relationship* through the concept of "soft power," and how it roots American foreign policy in American domestic policy.

Global Democracy and Human Rights: Status and Prospects

As we survey the status of democracy and human rights in the world, we need to take into account the successes, the limits and setbacks, and the uncertainties that remain.

1990s Democratic Success Stories

Looking at the overall global democracy scorecard in Table 10.1, we can see how widespread democracy has become. Of 191 countries and other territories, 141 are ranked as democracies (74 percent). This is a much higher number and much higher percentage than a decade ago. Today's figures include 37 countries that have made a transition to democracy since 1989 (marked in Table 10.1 in **bold**), and only 7 countries that slipped from democracy to non-democracy (marked in *italics* in Table 10.1).

Among the new democracies is much of the former Soviet bloc. Nine of these countries—the Czech Republic, Estonia, Hungary, Latvia, Lithuania, Poland, Romania, Slovakia, and Slovenia—make it into the "free" category; Russia and ten others—Albania, Armenia, Azerbaijan, Bosnia-Herzegovina, Croatia, Georgia, Kyrgyzstan, Macedonia, Moldova, and Ukraine—to "partly free"; Belarus, Kazakhstan, Tajikistan, Turkmenistan, Uzbekistan, and Yugoslavia are noncommunist but still not free.

Also included as democracies are all the countries of Latin America except Cuba. This, too, is a major historical shift. Panama, Nicaragua, and Haiti are the three Latin American countries that have become democracies since 1989. Going back just a few more years, such other countries as El Salvador, Honduras, Argentina, Chile, Brazil, Ecuador, Paraguay, and Peru also were not democracies. Indeed almost every Latin American country has had a military coup at least once in the twentieth century. Now, though, there are some signs that Latin American militaries have become more accepting of the principles of civilian control and the illegitimacy of the military playing an active role in politics. A scene at the second Conference of Defense Ministers of the Americas held in Argentina in 1996 was illustrative: "The civilian cabinet ministers in their business suits were in the front row. Almost all of the generals with their epaulets and medals and gold trim were relegated to the back—a vivid reminder that the balance of power has clearly shifted to the civilians."[6]

In Africa the most remarkable case is South Africa. The apartheid system had ensured the white minority's total control of the government and the economy, and had condemned the black majority to oppression, injustice, and poverty—indeed, later revelations pointed to torture and assassination plots against black leaders ordered by government officials. Yet by 1994 Nelson Mandela, a former political prisoner, had been elected president of South Africa. Black majority rule was established, with protections for white minority rights. And although the transition to democracy is far from over, and not everything has gone perfectly, it is not hard to imagine a more violent and undemocratic path that South Africa could have taken to this point.

TABLE 10.1   The Status of Global Democracy

Democracies (141)

(a) Free (88)

Andorra	El Salvador	**Malawi**	Saint Lucia
Argentina	**Estonia**	Mali	Saint Vincent &
Australia	Finland	Malta	the Grenadines
Austria	France	Marshall Islands	San Marino
Bahamas	Germany	Mauritius	**Sao Tome &**
Barbados	Greece	Micronesia	**Principe**
Belgium	Grenada	Monaco	**Slovakia**
Belize	Guyana	**Mongolia**	**Slovenia**
Benin	Honduras	Namibia	Solomon Islands
Bolivia	Hungary	Nauru	South Africa
Botswana	Iceland	Netherlands	Spain
Bulgaria	India	New Zealand	Sweden
Canada	Ireland	Nicaragua	Switzerland
Cape Verde	Israel	Norway	Taiwan
Chile	Italy	**Palau**	Thailand
Costa Rica	Jamaica	**Panama**	Trinidad & Tobago
Cyprus	Japan	Papua New	Tuvalu
Czech Republic	Kiribati	Guinea	United Kingdom
Denmark	Korea, South	Philippines	United States
Dominica	**Latvia**	Poland	Uruguay
Dominican	Liechtenstein	Portugal	Vanuatu
Republic	**Lithuania**	**Romania**	Venezuela
Ecuador	Luxembourg	Saint Kitts-Nevis	Western Samoa

(b) Partly free (53)

Albania	**Croatia**	**Kyrgyzstan**	**Russia**
Antigua &	**Eritrea**	**Lesotho**	Senegal
Barbuda	**Ethiopia**	Liberia	**Seychelles**
Armenia	Fiji	**Macedonia**	Sierra Leone
Azerbaijan	**Gabon**	Madagascar	Singapore
Bangladesh	**Georgia**	Malaysia	Sri Lanka
Bosnia &	Ghana	Mexico	Suriname
Herzegovina	Guatemala	**Moldova**	Tanzania
Brazil	**Guinea Bissau**	Morocco	Turkey
Burkina Faso	**Haiti**	**Mozambique**	Tonga
Central African	Indonesia	Nepal	Uganda
Republic	**Iran**	Nigeria	**Ukraine**
Colombia	Jordan	Paraguay	Zambia
Comoros	Kuwait	Peru	Zimbabwe

(*Continued on page 368*)

Table 10.1   The Status of Global Democracy   *(Continued)*

Nondemocracies (not free) (50)

Afghanistan	Congo (Demo-	Laos	*Swaziland*
Algeria	cratic Republic	Lebanon	Syria
Angola	of)	Libya	Tajikistan
Bahrain	Cuba	Maldives	Togo
Belarus	Djibouti	Mauritania	*Tunisia*
Bhutan	Egypt	Myanmar (Burma)	Turkmenistan
Brunei	Equatorial Guinea	Niger	United Arab
Burundi	*Gambia*	Oman	Emirates
Cambodia	Guinea	*Pakistan*	Uzbekistan
Cameroon	Iraq	Qatar	Vietnam
Chad	*Ivory Coast*	Rwanda	Yemen
China	Kazakhstan	Saudi Arabia	*Yugoslavia*
Congo (Republic	Kenya	Somalia	
of)	Korea, North	Sudan	

Note: Bold indicates post-1989 democracy. Italics indicate shift from democracy to non-democracy since 1989. The data are from surveys done by Freedom House, a New York–based organization. The basic distinction between democracies and nondemocracies is based on formal structures and processes; democracies have political systems that are civilian, constitutional, multiparty, and subject to competitive elections. The free/partly-free distinction is based on two additional criteria: the actual performance of the system (e.g., how strong is the constitution, just how free were the elections, does the elected government hold real power or is power vested in economic elites, the military or other unaccountable groups, how widespread is political corruption?) and respect for or repression of civil liberties (such as freedom of the press, freedom of speech, freedom of religion, freedom from ethnic violence). Although this is not a universally accepted scale, it is the same one that the U.S. Agency for International Development (AID) uses to assess its democracy-promotion programs.
Sources: Freedom House, *Freedom in the World: The Annual Survey of Political Rights and Civil Liberties, 1998–99* (New Brunswick, N.J.: Transaction Publishers, 1999), and author's updates.

Limits and Setbacks

There are quite a few cases and countries, though, on the other side of the scale. In terms of regions, the major concerns for democratization are with Africa and the Middle East.

Almost half of the countries in Africa are still nondemocracies. Many have been torn by civil wars and genocidal killings—e.g., Angola, Liberia, Somalia, Rwanda, Burundi, Congo (the former Zaire), and others. There is no doubt that some of Africa's problems are the legacies of the Cold War, when the United States readily supported dictators friendly to its cause, and the Soviet Union supported various Afro-Marxist-Leninist regimes. The European colonial powers (France, Britain, and Belgium, especially) also bear a substantial share of responsibility for their disregard of tribal and ethnic divisions in drawing country boundaries as they were withdrawing from their colonial empires. But to acknowledge the degree of Western responsibility is not to dismiss the responsibility of Africa's own leaders, whose rivalries, repression, and corruption have taken their toll on their own people.[7]

The very low percentage (about 25 percent) of Arab-Muslim countries that are even partly free democracies seems at least somewhat consistent with Huntington's "clash of civilizations" analysis. "Western ideas of individualism, liberalism, constitutionalism, human rights, equality, liberty, the rule of law, democracy, free markets, the separation of church and state, often have little resonance in Islamic societies," Huntington contends.[8] Saudi Arabia and most of the other Persian Gulf Arab states are monarchies or sheikdoms. Others, such as Syria, Libya, and Iraq, are dictatorships. Egypt has elections, but not free ones, and Egyptian President Hosni Mubarak has been in power for close to two decades. Of Arab countries, only Morocco, Jordan, Lebanon, and Kuwait get a partly free rating.[9]

The relation of Islamic fundamentalism to human rights and democratization is particularly controversial. "Democracy is irrelevant to Islam and Islam is superior to democracy," is how one noted scholar assesses the political dogma common to Islamic fundamentalist leaders. "Their notion of the 'rule of law' refers to the unalterable law of Islam," hardly a basis for social tolerance or political pluralism.[10] In a number of instances where militants have come to power, domestic repression has been of totalitarian reach, seeking to regulate virtually all aspects of society and individual conduct in accordance with fundamentalist interpretations of the Koran. An "ends-justify-the-means" logic is often used to justify terrorism, assassinations, and other political violence. Others argue that the extremist aspects of Islamic fundamentalism need to be seen as reactions to the repressiveness of the old orders and to the threats that modernization and Westernization pose to traditional religious teachings and culture. The ways in which Islamism contributes to social and economic reform also are stressed, such as through social welfare programs run through local mosques and other religious organizations.

The overall global human rights situation also is an area in which the limits of progress are quite evident. Some sense of the scope and horror of the persecution and killing that continue around the world is conveyed in one of

Amnesty International's recent annual global human rights reports (see Perspectives on p. 371). Thousands of people have been killed without legal due process (extrajudicial executions). Thousands of others were subjected to torture, detained without trial, or held as political prisoners or prisoners of conscience. More than 140,000 people have "disappeared," presumably at the hands of governments and for political reasons. The items listed in the box are just excerpts from a report that runs over three hundred pages.

Uncertainties: Challenges of Democratic Consolidation and Institutionalization

The only certainty about the future of global democracy and human rights is uncertainty. The problems and setbacks that feed pessimism have to be kept in perspective—after all, who believed that the early 1990s successes were possible even just a few years before they occurred? The lesson that endures despite the fading euphoria is that positive political change is always possible. This is a main reason why theories like Huntington's clash of civilizations are too deterministic, as if states, their leaders, and their people can only play out the civilizational script as already inscribed over the centuries, and cannot shape their societies, their political systems, and their values in an evolving way.

Yet so, too, does there need to be a tempering of Fukuyama's end-of-history optimism on the other side. It takes nothing away from the successes achieved thus far to acknowledge that to declare democracy is not the same as to consolidate and institutionalize it. History is replete with cases of democratic revolutions that failed—the 1917 February Revolution in czarist Russia, for example, which gave way to Lenin and the Bolsheviks, and the 1920s and 1930s Weimar Republic in Germany, which elected as chancellor one Adolf Hitler.

Democracy can be said to be consolidated and institutionalized when governing regimes can change, but the political system itself remains stable. The political change that does occur must be within the bounds of a constitutional order and peaceful, with little or limited political violence. This is the challenge facing so many of the newly democratic countries. Of particular concern in this regard is Russia. What has been achieved in that country should not be underestimated. Very few people anywhere predicted that Russia would have had such a peaceful transition from a communist to a democratic political system. A bicameral representative legislature was put in place, and the Duma (the lower house of the legislature) in particular was given a major role in governing. Russia's new constitution has held up despite a number of crises.

PERSPECTIVES
PERSPECTIVES
PERSPECTIVES

THE STATUS OF GLOBAL HUMAN RIGHTS

Extrajudicial executions
Thousands of extrajudicial executions or possible extrajudicial executions were reported in 63 countries, including Bahrain, Burundi, Colombia, India, Russia, and Rwanda.

Disappearances
The fate of more than 140,000 people in 49 countries who disappeared in recent years remains unknown. Many of those, in countries including Burundi, Rwanda, Colombia, Iraq, Sri Lanka, and Turkey, may have subsequently been killed.

Torture or ill treatment
At least 10,000 detainees were subjected to torture or ill treatment, including rape, in 114 countries, including Yugoslavia, Indonesia (including East Timor), Iran, Mexico, and Sudan. More than 4,500 people died as a result of torture in custody or inhuman prison conditions in 54 countries including Egypt, Kenya, Myanmar (Burma), and Turkey.

Prisoners of conscience
Prisoners of conscience or possible prisoners of conscience were held in 85 countries, including Bosnia & Herzegovina, China, Kenya, Peru, and Tunisia.

Unfair trials
A reported 27 countries, including China, Colombia, Nigeria, Saudi Arabia, and Yugoslavia, imprisoned people after unfair trials.

Detention without charge or trial
Forty-three countries, including Azerbaijan, India, Israel (and the occupied territories), areas under the jurisdiction of the Palestinian Authority, Paraguay, and Rwanda, held a total of more than 46,000 people without charging them with any crime.

Human-rights abuses by armed opposition groups
Armed opposition groups committed abuses, including torture, hostage-taking, and deliberate and arbitrary killings, in 41 countries, including Afghanistan, Algeria, Colombia, Sierra Leone, and the United Kingdom.

Source: Amnesty International, *1997 Annual Report* (New York: Amnesty International, 1997).

Free elections have been held at the local, provincial, and national level, including in 2000 the election of Vladimir Putin as the new president succeeding Boris Yeltsin—the first democratic succession in Russian history.

Still Russia's road to democracy has been anything but straight and smooth. Back in October 1993 President Yeltsin resorted to a tank attack on the Russian parliament to break a deadlock. In other instances as well, concerns about his commitment to democracy have been raised, as in early 1996 when Sergei Kovalev, whom Yeltsin had appointed chair of the Russian human rights commission, was so disillusioned that he resigned and wrote an open letter to Yeltsin: "The main things the country expected from you were the will to make changes and honesty . . . [but] you have consistently taken decisions which—instead of strengthening the rule of law in a democratic society—have revived the blunt and inhuman might of a state machine that stands above justice, law and the individual. . . . [I]f democracy is fated to someday exist in Russia (and I believe it will), it will exist not because of you, but in spite of you."[11] In the years following Yeltsin's 1996 re-election, his debilitating ill health and mounting incapacity to govern effectively made him increasingly unpopular. Putin began his presidency with impressive popularity, but also amidst some doubts about his commitment to sustaining democracy. Broader questions also remain as to whether if political and economic conditions do not get better the Russian people may turn to a "strongman" leader, whether military or ultranationalist or some other antidemocrat.

As a broader issue, although communism has been defeated, the question remains of whether other competing ideologies and political models may emerge. In their fundamentals, socialism and communism were efforts to address the problem of social, political, and economic inequality. Although these particular remedies largely failed, the core problem of inequality remains— indeed, as we saw in Chapter 9, income gaps and disparities in wealth have been growing wider in many societies around the world. If democracy and capitalism do not more effectively deal with these fundamental problems, it stands to reason that other ideologies will be articulated and other political models advanced with at least the promise of doing so.

This possibility may bear especially on Latin America, where, as assessed by one prominent analyst, "severe deficiencies mark political life—weak capacity and performance of government institutions, widespread corruption, irregular and often arbitrary rule of law, poorly developed patterns of representation and participation, and large numbers of marginalized citizens."[12] Underlying this analysis is the fact that Latin America is the region with the greatest inequalities in the distribution of wealth among social classes. Although there has been some growth of middle classes, Latin American economies still tend to be dominated by wealthy elites with large impoverished masses of urban poor and rural *campesinos* (peasants). In Mexico, for example, the richest 10 percent of the population controls 41 percent of the country's wealth, while the share of the bottom half of the population is only 16 percent, an even wider gap than in the 1980s; as of the mid-1990s, according to U.N. and World Bank figures, the number of Mexicans living in extreme poverty had increased from 17 million to 22 million. In a number of Latin American countries the possibility of popular unrest pulling the military out of the barracks and back into politics cannot be dismissed; in the early 1960s, for example, a democratizing wave then gaining force was swept away by a string of military coups.

Latin America is also plagued by its infamous drug cartels. In Colombia the drug cartels have assassinated government officials who sought to crack down on them, including supreme court justices and a popular presidential candidate; their leaders even continue to run their businesses from jail (see Perspectives on p. 374). Mexico and Panama are among the other Latin American countries that must cope with the reality that "narco-democracies" cannot remain democracies for very long.

Asia also has tremendous uncertainties. In China prodemocratization and human rights pressures continue against Communist Party rule. In late 1998 the Chinese government seemed to have taken a positive step in finally signing an important global human rights treaty, but only weeks later it unleashed another major crackdown against political dissidents. Three leading activists who were trying to set up an opposition political party were sentenced to lengthy prison terms. Another of China's numerous democratization and human rights issues is the problem of Tibet and its struggle for religious freedom and cultural autonomy.

Earlier in the 1990s in other parts of East Asia a great deal of attention was being paid to ideas about "the Asian way," a political approach that, while still somewhat democratic, puts more emphasis on the importance of the collectivity over the individual and justifies some limitations on freedom in the name of authority and social order.[13] In contrast to Fukuyama, proponents of the Asian way question whether democracy, or at least the American version of it, really is the best system. And in contrast to Huntington, they question whether Asian culture and political traditions are such a bad model—indeed, they argue that the United States, with all its societal problems, could benefit from emulating the Asian way. Some, though, see all this as rationalization for

PERSPECTIVES
PERSPECTIVES
PERSPECTIVES

"COLOMBIA SAYS DRUG BARONS THREATEN, BRIBE CONGRESS FROM JAIL"

BOGOTA, Colombia, Dec. 18 — The Colombian Congress wound up one of its most controversial sessions today amid growing evidence that jailed leaders of the Cali cocaine cartel continue to use bribes and threats to seek legislation favoring their interests. . . .

The revelations stirred national and international outrage. Facing U.S. economic sanctions and a public outcry over the vote, President Ernesto Samper led a successful government lobbying effort to revive the bill in a conference committee. It was passed on Monday.

"It would have been better if the Congress had voted to pass the bill out of conviction and not pressure, but they passed it," said Enrique Santos Calderon, a political analyst. "For the first time, business groups, the [Roman Catholic] church, the international community and media all reacted against the national disgrace, and it was too much pressure even for the cartels."

But the cartels may not remain passive in the face of defeat. On Monday and Tuesday, two car bombs were set off—one in Cali and one in the northern city of Monteria—killing five people. Car bombs have long been a favorite instrument of terror of the drug cartels, and police blamed them for the attacks.

"It is a reminder from them of what can happen," said Santos, one of the Colombians willing to talk openly about the attacks. "They are showing they can still react." . . .

Although Colombians are accustomed to the interference of the drug barons, the brazenness of their recent efforts caused alarm and, for the first time, brought public acknowledgment from the government that traffickers continue to operate from prison cells.

Chief prosecutor [former General Alfonso] Valdivieso, in an interview, called the cartel's ability to reach beyond prison walls "terrifying."

"We will have to make greater efforts to keep the prisons from being a mockery, a place of privilege where the criminals can continue to carry out crimes," he said.

(*Continued on page 375*)

("Drug Barons Threaten, Bribe" *Continued from page 374*)

In one taped telephone conversation released by police, Miguel Rodriguez asks his attorney how things are going in Congress. "The atmosphere is positive, but we are lacking oxygen," the lawyer replied, referring to money. Rep. Ingrid Betancourt has said traffickers were offering $25,000 a vote....

Source: Douglas Farah, "Colombia Says Drug Barons Threaten, Bribe from Jail," *Washington Post*, December 19, 1996, p. A36. © 1996, The Washington Post. Reprinted with permission.

leaders who want to perpetuate their own power. In Malaysia in 1998, for example, Prime Minister Mahathir bin Mohamad, a leading proponent of the Asian way, arrested his own deputy prime minister on contrived sexual-perversion charges in order to remove him as a potential challenger. In Singapore, the government bans household satellite TV dishes, which are hard to regulate, but allows cable television, whose channels can be regulated through licensing. The growth and accessibility of the Internet, which opens up enormous free flows of information, is presenting an even greater problem for such authoritarian societies.

In the Middle East, Iran poses some of the most significant and intriguing uncertainties. The 1978–79 Islamic fundamentalist revolution led by Ayatollah Khomeini that overthrew the shah established a theocratic state. Elections had been held in the years that followed and a president and parliament have existed, but the principal governing authority has rested with the religious "supreme leader"—Khomeini until his death in 1989, and thereafter Ayatollah Khamenei, his successor. Then in 1997, in a surprise result, the presidential election was won by Mohammad Khatami, a more moderate proreform *mullah* (religious leader) over the candidate favored by the theocrats. Khatami's victory came about largely because of strong support among women and youth (the voting age is sixteen) and other groups within Iranian society favoring liberalization. Tensions between the moderates and the fundamentalists grew even more intense. Elections in early 2000 produced a strong reformist majority in the *majlis* (parliament), setting off a fundamentalist backlash including the shutting down of newspapers and a wave of political killings. Whether Khatami and his allies succeed in bringing reform within the structure of the Islamic republic or the conservative fundamentalists succeed in quashing such efforts will tell a great deal about the compatibility of Islamic fundamentalism and democracy.

Note also needs to be made of South Africa. For amid the peacefulness of its post-apartheid transition and other aspects of its democratic success, there also have been some worrying signs. Crime rates in South Africa are extremely high: an average of 53.4 murders per 100,000 people in the late 1990s, compared to an international average of 5.5; an estimated 500 crime syndicates operating in the country; a crime-solving rate of only 23 percent; and only 3.6 percent of perpetrators imprisoned. And even before the global recession hit, in 1997–98 South Africa's per capita gross domestic product (GDP) grew only 2 percent, well below the rate needed to even come close to meeting expectations for economic progress and narrowing of the racial inequality gap.

Serious questions thus remain about the future of democracy and human rights around the world. There is reason for optimism, but also some basis for pessimism and much uncertainty. It is very important to take a long-term view of developments in this area. In the United States' own history it took 11 years after declaring independence to develop a workable constitution (the first version, the Articles of Confederation, failed). It took 89 years for slavery to be abolished. It took 144 years until women gained the right to vote. It was 188 years until full constitutional protections were guaranteed to all citizens. Thus we cannot expect full and uninterrupted democratization in only a decade among the world's nascent democracies.

Principles and Peace: The Democratic Peace Debate

According to the theory of the democratic peace, the United States should support the spread of democracy not just because it is the right thing to do, but also because history demonstrates that democracies do not fight wars against fellow democracies; thus it is in the U.S. interest to support democratization in order to reduce the risks of war. The theory does not claim that democracies don't go to war at all. They have, and they do—against non-democracies. But they don't, and they won't, it is argued, against other democracies. This is the tenet of the democratic peace paradigm that right makes for might, that the world is a safer and a better place to the extent that democracy spreads. For American foreign policy, the promotion of democracy thus has the added value of serving objectives of peace as well as of principles.

Is this theory valid? Let's examine the main arguments and evidence first from proponents and then from critics of the theory.

The Democratic Peace Theory

Proponents of the democratic peace theory make the sweeping claim that "the absence of war between democratic states comes as close to anything we have to an empirical law in international relations."[14] The empirical evidence as they present it indeed is impressive:

- Democracies have not fought any wars against each other in the entire period of world history since 1815. This encompasses 71 interstate wars involving nearly 270 participants.
- Since the end of World War II democracies have been only one-eighth as likely as nondemocracies to threaten to use military force against another democracy, and only one-tenth as likely to even use limited force against each other.
- Democracies have fought numerous wars against nondemocracies, however, including World War I, World War II, and numerous wars during the Cold War.[15]

The central tenets of the democratic peace paradigm and their logic and philosophical basis, although very often associated with President Woodrow Wilson in the history of U.S. foreign policy, can be traced all the way back to the eighteenth-century European political philosopher Immanuel Kant and his book *Perpetual Peace*. The basic argument has three components: the constraints imposed by democratic political systems, the internationalization of demo-cratic norms, and the bonds built by trade.

DOMESTIC POLITICAL CONSTRAINTS   We already have seen how, historically, going to war has been one of the recurring great debates in American politics. Kant, who was writing before there even was a United States of America with its own constitution and foreign policy, made his argument with reference to democracies generally. If "the consent of the citizenry is required in order to decide that war should be declared," he wrote, "nothing is more natural than that they would be very cautious in commencing such a poor game. . . . But, on the other hand, in a constitution which is not republican, and under which the subjects are not citizens, a declaration of war is the easiest thing to decide upon, because war does not require of the ruler . . . the least sacrifice of the pleasure of his table, the chase, his country houses, his court functions and the like."[16] Kant also stressed, though, that these constraints were less likely vis-à-vis nondemocracies, toward which mass publics were more prone to being aroused by crusade-like appeals. Democracies' willingness to go to war against nondemocracies and their unwillingness to go to war against each other thus follow the same domestic political logic.

INTERNATIONALIZATION OF DEMOCRATIC NORMS   All democracies, no matter what their particular representative structure, must practice compromise and consensus-building in their domestic politics and policy. Their watchwords need to be tolerance and trust, and the essence of a successful democratic system is managing if not resolving conflicts and tensions within society in lawful and peaceful ways. As Michael Doyle, whose articles were among the first to advance the democratic peace thesis, states, democracies, "which rest on consent, presume foreign republics to also be consensual, just, and therefore deserving of accommodation."[17] Nondemocracies, in contrast, as another author puts it, "are viewed *prima facie* as unreasonable, unpredictable."[18] There is a rational logic here, not just ideology. It makes sense not to go to war against a country that you are confident won't move quickly to war against you. But going to war may become the rational choice if you fear the other may seek to strike pre-emptively or by surprise.

BONDS OF TRADE   The combination of this spirit of political commonality and the common tendency of democracies to have free-market economic systems also leads them to develop trade and other economic relations with one another. "The 'spirit of commerce,'" in Kant's term, in turn becomes another factor inhibiting war. The same idea also is found in the work of such other eminent political philosophers as Montesequieu, who wrote of "the natural effect" of trade as being "to bring about peace," and John Stuart Mill, who went even further in seeing the expansion of international trade in the mid-nineteenth century as "rapidly rendering war obsolete."[19] The basic ideas are that as trade develops there becomes more to lose from going to war, and in any event that war would be against people who are no longer strangers. This is said to be especially true today, given how international interdependence now encompasses not just trade but investment, finance, and many other economic interconnections.

What has made the democratic peace paradigm especially significant is that the Clinton administration has based much of its foreign policy on it. President Clinton's statement cited earlier that "democracies do not attack each other," and that therefore "the best strategy to insure our security and to build a durable peace is to support the advance of democracy elsewhere," was from his 1994 State of the Union address. Clinton's advisers coined the term "enlargement," playing off the old Cold War "containment," to refer to the spread of global democracy and the U.S. interests thus served. As laid out in a major Clinton administration policy statement, "all of America's strategic interests—from promoting prosperity at home to checking global threats abroad before they threaten our territory—are served by enlarging the community of democratic and free-market nations. Thus, working with new democratic states to help preserve them as democracies committed to free markets and respect for human rights is a key part of our national security strategy."[20] Ensuring the success of democracy was thus posed as a pragmatic and not just an idealistic goal, serving peace as well as principles.

Critiques and Caveats

Three main arguments have been made by those who question the democratic peace theory.

SPURIOUS RELATIONSHIP?   Some scholars question whether there really is a strong relationship between states' forms of government and the likelihood of their going to war against each other. These critics contend that on two counts the claim for this causal link is "spurious," meaning not valid because of methodological problems. One is a definitional point about how both "democracy" and "war" are defined by democratic peace theorists, and the resulting criteria for including or excluding cases. These critics examined the empirical data going back to 1815 and cited a number of cases in which they say democratic peace proponents inaccurately excluded some conflicts that involved democracies vs. democracies, or miscategorized countries that fought wars as nondemocracies when they should be considered democracies.[21] Among the historical examples cited are the American Civil War and Finland's siding with the Axis powers in World War II. Applying the theory to the contemporary context is problematic: so many of today's wars are ethnic conflicts, civil wars, and other intrastate conflicts, yet the democratic peace theory principally addresses classical interstate wars.

A second methodological criticism is that democratic peace theorists confuse correlation with causality, mistakenly emphasizing the nature of the domestic political system as the cause of peaceful relations rather than a Realist calculation that cooperation served national interests better than conflict. For example, with regard to the claim that the United States, Western Europe, and

Japan didn't fight wars with each other from 1945–91 because they are democracies, critics argue that the more important factor was these countries' shared security interests based on the Cold War and the common threat from the Soviet Union. There also are a number of historical cases of "near-miss" crises in which democracies almost did go to war against each other, but didn't for reasons that had more to do with assessments of their interests than with the other side's being a democracy. These include two crises between the United States and Great Britain in the nineteenth century, as well as some others.[22]

The dynamics of democracy, producing as they sometimes do openings for demagoguery and enemy-bashing, also can exacerbate tensions. During the Cold War in the United States wariness about being branded "soft on communism" fed involvement in Vietnam and elsewhere. In Russia in the 1990s the Duma (the elected lower house of the legislature) has been a bastion of aggressive nationalism. In India in 1998 the Hindu nationalist Bharatiya Janata Party went ahead with nuclear tests as one of its first actions on coming to power, and virtually all other political parties in the country were reluctant for domestic political reasons to oppose the tests. In Pakistan the political pressure on Prime Minister Nawaz Sharif and his party to counter with nuclear tests of its own was irresistible.

TRADE AND PEACE?   A second point raises doubts about how much trade actually inhibits war. On the eve of World War I, Sir Norman Angell, the foremost heir to the Kant-Montesquieu-Mill tradition, diagnosed war as "a failure of understanding" that could be corrected by the kind of mutual familiarity and interchange bred by international commerce. Yet the fact that Germany was Britain's second leading trade partner didn't stop the two countries from going to war. There are other historical cases as well in which high levels of economic interdependence did not prevent war. Moreover, high levels of trade surely do not prevent other political and diplomatic conflicts. U.S.-European and U.S.-Japanese relations provide numerous examples.

AGGRESSIVE TENDENCIES OF DEMOCRATIZING STATES   Third, and more in the way of a qualifying caveat than straight criticism, is that even if one accepts that mature democracies may not fight with each other, states that are still undergoing democratization and are not yet stable democracies may actually be even *more* aggressive and warlike than stable nondemocracies. These transition periods are notoriously unstable, as elites and other groups compete for political influence, and as the general public struggles with the

10.4

economic difficulties of transitions, the disorientation of political change, and an uncertain future. They thus are quite susceptible to "belligerent nationalism" as a rallying cry and diversion from domestic problems. As political scientists Edward Mansfield and Jack Snyder put it, "elite groups left over from the ruling circles of the old regime, many of whom have a particular interest in war and empire, vie for power and survival with each other and with new elites representing rising democratic forces. Both old and new elites use all the resources they can muster to mobilize mass allies, often through nationalistic appeals, to defend their positions and to stake out new ones. However, like the sorcerer's apprentice, these elites typically find that their mass allies, once mobilized, are difficult to control. When this happens, war can result from nationalist prestige strategies that hard-pressed leaders use to stay astride their unmanageable political coalitions."[23]

If the critics are right, then the Clinton policy of enlargement is problematic. At minimum U.S. policy needs to be more attentive to the risks of aggressive foreign policy fallout during democratic transitions in cases like Russia's. Or it may be that the whole focus on political ideology is misdirected, that democracy is neither a necessary nor a sufficient condition for peaceful relations, and focusing on it detracts from power-based considerations like the balance of power, deterrence, and the convergence or divergence of interests.

Policy Strategies for Promoting Democracy and Protecting Human Rights

The array of actors involved in promoting democratization may be broader than in any other area of foreign policy. The box on p. 382 provides an illustrative listing, in four main categories.

U.S. Government

The lead U.S. agency for democracy promotion is the Agency for International Development (AID). Throughout the 1990s AID has broadened its "development" mission to increasingly include political as well as economic development. AID runs some programs directly, and also provides funding to nongovernmental organizations (NGOs). The National Endowment for Democracy receives funds from Congress and AID and channels them principally to four NGOs (see the discussion of NGOs below).

KEY ACTORS IN THE PROMOTION OF DEMOCRACY (PARTIAL LIST)

U.S. government
Agency for International Development (AID)
National Endowment for Democracy (NED)
U.S. Department of State, Bureau of Democracy, Human Rights, and Labor
U.S. Departments of Defense, Justice, Education, Commerce
U.S. Congress
State governments

International organizations
U.N. Commission on Human Rights
U.N. Electoral Assistance Units
International Court of Justice
International Institute for Democracy and Electoral Assistance
Organization for Security and Cooperation in Europe (OSCE)
Organization of American States (OAS)
Organization of African Unity (OAU)

Other governments
European Union (EU)
Swedish International Development Authority
Norwegian Agency for Development

Nongovernmental organizations (NGOs)
National Democratic Institute for International Affairs
International Republican Institute
Free Trade Union Institute
Center for International Private Enterprise
Foundation for a Civil Society
German political party *stiftungs*
Westminster Foundation for Democracy (United Kingdom)
International Center for Human Rights and Democratic Development
   (Canada)
Ford, Asia, Soros Foundations
American Bar Association, Central and East European Law Initiative
Amnesty International
Human Rights Watch

The State Department is involved principally through its Bureau of Democracy, Human Rights, and Labor. It also manages programs such as the Fulbright scholarships and other educational and cultural-exchange programs. Additional roles are played by almost every Cabinet department: the Pentagon works on civil-military relations, the Justice Department helps develop the rule of law, the Education Department conducts literacy training, the Commerce Department promotes free enterprise. The U.S. Congress also is involved, with its numerous legislative-exchange programs for legislators and their staffs from newly democratizing countries. Local governments participate too, through programs like "Sister Cities," linking people at the grassroots level across the United States to other cities around the world.* Some also take other initiatives, as did Dayton, Ohio, the city where the accords ending the Bosnian war were negotiated in 1995, in developing its own city-to-city contacts with Sarajevo, the capital of Bosnia (see Perspectives, p. 384).

International Organizations

The United Nations is involved in promoting democracy in a number of ways. The first time the U.N. was given a role in monitoring elections and helping build democratic political institutions was in 1989 in Namibia, a territory in Africa previously under U.N. trusteeship. Since then the U.N.'s electoral assistance and observer missions have been sent to numerous states. Its Commission on Human Rights provides a forum for human rights issues to be raised. The International Court of Justice, based in The Hague in the Netherlands, exercises some capacity to enforce international law. The U.N. High Commissioner for Refugees (UNHCR) seeks to provide protection and relief for populations displaced by war, repression, or natural disasters.

The Organization for Security and Cooperation in Europe (OSCE) has been the most active of regional multilateral organizations. It has sent election observers, conflict resolution teams, and other missions to a number of member countries. The Organization of American States (OAS), which has tolerated if not condoned military coups in the past, amended its charter in 1992 to suspend member states where democratic governments are overthrown. The Organization for African Unity (OAU) also has taken some of its own democratization initiatives. And the International Institute for Democracy and

---

*Davis, California, for example, is a sister city with three foreign cities: Uman, Ukraine; Rutillo Grande, El Salvador; and Qufu, China.

PERSPECTIVES
PERSPECTIVES
PERSPECTIVES

"DAYTON KEEPS FORGING NEW BOSNIAN LINKS"

SARAJEVO, Dec. 11 — Jan Vargo and Martha Lampe, two middle-aged women from Dayton, Ohio, never thought they would find themselves sitting in a snow-covered trench in the hills overlooking Sarajevo. The real-estate agent and owner of a string of child care centers had never given much thought to the war in Bosnia. "All the names were so strange and I couldn't figure out who were the good guys and who were the bad guys," said Lampe.

But after their Midwestern industrial city was chosen as the site for the Bosnian Peace Talks last year, Vargo and Lampe, like many Daytonians, began to show concern for the fate of the country. This week, they joined a group of 35 Daytonians who visited the Bosnian capital and found themselves taking a tour of the city's former front line with a demobilized soldier in the Bosnian army.

The travelers from Dayton—who included the mayor, the editor of the Dayton Daily News, several City Council members, an 81-year-old retired minister and an 18-year-old student—were part of a cultural exchange organized by the Friendship Force, a nonprofit organization in Atlanta. . . .

For Sarajevans who hosted the delegation members in their homes, the visiting Daytonians provided a sense of normalcy to people who have been accustomed to a steady stream of foreign peacekeepers, diplomats, aid workers and journalists. "It was so comforting to have someone come and stay with me," said Nada Bojanic, 54, of Sarajevo. "It was one of the best things to happen to me for a long time—just to make acquaintances with the outside world." . . .

Chris Sanders, 67, a volunteer with the Dayton Art Institute, met with Sarajevo museum curators and said she plans to help raise money for them. Jan Rudd, 62, a volunteer at Dayton's women's health clinic, met with women's organizations here and plans to organize links with women's groups in Dayton. Andrew Bosworth, the deputy director of international programs at the University of Dayton, met with Sarajevo University officials and local high school officials in an effort to organize

(*Continued on page 385*)

(**"Dayton Keeps Forging"**   *Continued from page 384*)
student exchanges. And Mike Turner, Dayton's 36-year-old mayor, put together a Dayton-Balkans business directory and is planning to return in March with a delegation of Dayton business executives. He said he also hopes to make Sarajevo Dayton's sister city.

Source: Stacy Sullivan, "Dayton Keeps Forging New Bosnian Links," *Washington Post*, December 12, 1996, p. A47.

Electoral Assistance (International IDEA) was set up in 1995 by fourteen governments including India, South Africa, Spain, the Scandinavian countries, and others.

Other Governments

The European Union (EU) long has made democracy a precondition for membership. This created an incentive for countries like Greece, Spain, and Portugal to democratize in the 1970s and 1980s, and does so today for the former communist countries seeking EU membership. The EU also has programs similar to the AID ones to provide direct democracy assistance. A number of countries also run their own bilateral democracy programs. The Scandinavian countries are widely regarded as world leaders in this area.

NGOs

NGOs often receive government or U.N. funding, but maintain significant independence in their democracy programs. In the United States, based on a model adapted from Germany, where each major political party has run international democracy-promotion programs since the 1950s, the four NGOs that get most of the National Endowment for Democracy funding are the Democratic Party's National Democratic Institute for International Affairs, the Republican Party's International Republican Institute, the AFL-CIO's Free Trade Union Institute, and the U.S. Chamber of Commerce's Center for International Private Enterprise. Another major U.S.-based NGO is the Foundation for a Civil Society. Britain has the Westminster Foundation for Democracy, Canada its International Center for Human Rights and Democratic Development.

Other NGOs active in building and supporting democracy include private nonprofit foundations such as the Ford, Soros, and Asia Foundations; professional associations such as the American Bar Association and its Central and Eastern Europe Law Initiative (ABA-CEELI); and groups with their own global networks of offices such as Amnesty International and Human Rights Watch.

Along with this identification of the "who" is the question of "how." To be sure, there is no single, one-size-fits-all strategy for democracy promotion. The foreign policy challenge for the United States as well as other international actors is to determine the right fit and right mix for different countries with different sets of problems, and to pursue those strategies with the right combination of international actors.

This generally involves five main objectives: facilitating free and fair elections; helping build strong and accountable political institutions; strengthening the rule of law; protecting human rights; and helping cultivate a robust civil society.

Facilitating Free and Fair Elections

International electoral assistance and monitoring often provides the most reliable assurance that elections in newly democratizing countries will be free and fair. The mere presence of American and other international observers can deter electoral fraud or detect attempted fraud. One major example is the 1986 presidential election in the Philippines. Then-dictator Ferdinand Marcos tried to steal the election in order to keep himself in power. But a bipartisan U.S. congressional observer team was there as witness to the fraud. Marcos initially was able to convince President Reagan back in Washington that there was "fraud on both sides." But when Reagan made this statement, Senator Richard Lugar, a Republican and head of the U.S. observer team, was in a position to state that "the President was misinformed." Senator Lugar was able to come to his own conclusion in part because, since 1983, when Marcos had assassinated opposition leader Benigno Aquino, some U.S. aid to the Philippines had been channeled to Catholic Church and human rights groups for purchasing computers and other equipment that gave them the technical capacity to independently count the votes. Marcos ended up having no choice but to concede the election to Corazon Aquino, wife of the assassinated opposition leader, and to flee the country.[24]

Another example is the February 1990 election in Nicaragua, the first free election in that country's history. An election-observer team, headed by former president Jimmy Carter and including a number of Latin American former presidents, monitored the voting processes. As the election returns were coming in, and it became clear that Sandinista President Daniel Ortega was going to lose to challenger Violeta Chamorro, word spread in Managua that Ortega and the Sandinistas might not accept the results. Because of both his pro–human rights record as U.S. president and the conflict resolution and humanitarian assistance work he had been doing as an ex-president, Jimmy Carter had a great deal of credibility with both sides in the Nicaraguan election and more generally in the eyes of the world. Carter shuttled between Ortega's headquarters and Chamorro's, and told Ortega in no uncertain terms that he would be declaring the elections as having been free and fair, and would oppose any move not to abide by their results. Ortega felt that he had little choice but to back off and accept the results. A crisis was averted, and Nicaragua started on the path to democracy.

On the other hand there have been a number of less successful cases. In Belarus and Armenia, two former Soviet republics, fraud occurred despite the presence of OSCE election-observer teams. The OSCE responded by not certifying the fairness of the elections, and OSCE member countries did impose some sanctions and penalties, but the results stood nevertheless. In Cambodia U.N. observers helped ensure the fairness of elections, but power struggles continued, civil war resumed, and coups were launched.

Critical forms of electoral assistance also need to be provided prior to the actual election day. *Voter education programs* help prepare populaces that may rarely or never have had a genuinely free and fair election to participate effectively. In Bangladesh, for example, AID support for voter-education programs run by NGOs helped ensure a 74 percent turnout in the 1996 parliamentary elections, the largest in Bangladesh's history (U.S. turnout in midterm congressional elections is about 34 percent). Special targeted efforts increased the voting rate of women, only 45 percent in 1991, to 80 percent.[25]

Political parties need to be built, either to fill the void or to replace old, undemocratic parties. Effective parties are essential for channeling and coalescing groups and individuals within society in ways that help make for organized and peaceful political processes. Helping countries create and strengthen democratic political parties involves everything from training in membership recruitment to fund-raising, public-opinion polling, message development, candidate selection systems, grassroots organizing, and, yes, even making campaign commercials. This is an area in which the National

Endowment for Democracy and its Democratic and Republican Party partners are very involved, as are the German party-based democracy-promotion *stiftungs.*

Building Strong and Accountable Political Institutions

Although democratic revolutions often are personality driven, with people mobilizing around a charismatic leader, long-term stable democracy requires strong and accountable *political institutions.* The democratization literature stresses three main sets of reasons why political institutionalization is important.[26] The first concerns maintenance of political stability. Political systems that have built strong political institutions are less dependent on and less vulnerable to the fate or whims of a particular governing regime. The stronger the political institutions, the better they can withstand the ups and downs of a governing regime's popularity, and the better they can stand up to any extra-constitutional challenges that a leader or regime may attempt, particularly those that would use or threaten force and violence for political change. This is particularly important vis-à-vis the military, as democracies with strong democratic institutions are better able to resist coups and maintain civilian control of the military.

The second set of reasons concerns representativeness. Political systems with strong political institutions are more likely to convey a sense of genuine choice, competition, and accountability. People need to feel that the system has integrity irrespective of whether their favored candidates win an election. This means believing in the fairness of the electoral process and feeling assured that civil liberties and minority rights will be guaranteed. Strong institutions help ensure a level of confidence in the rules of the game.

Third is effective governance. The instability that comes with weak institutions makes the steadiness and follow-through that governing requires very difficult to achieve. In contrast, well-institutionalized democracies are more capable of governing effectively because, as democracy scholar Larry Diamond writes, "they have more effective and stable structures for representing interests and because they are more likely to produce working legislative majorities or coalitions that can adopt and sustain policies."[27]

A main area for democratic institution-building is strengthening *legislatures.* To fulfill their representative functions legislatures must also develop other professional and institutional capacities to carry out such tasks as designing committee systems, developing the legal and technical expertise for drafting legislation, computerizing legislative operations, communicating and servicing constituencies, and building up research and library support systems. The U.S. Congress has developed a number of training and exchange programs with legislatures in newly democratizing countries, as have the parliaments and assemblies of a number of west European countries.

Another key area is *civil-military relations*. This is where the Pentagon has been playing an important role. A main example is the NATO Partnership for Peace (PFP) program, which has had the objective not only of fostering military cooperation but also the inculcation by Western NATO militaries in their ex-communist counterparts of the principles of civilian control of the military. Related to this are various training and education programs for military officers, as at the George C. Marshall Center for Security Studies, linked to NATO and based in Germany, with what Defense Secretary William J. Perry characterized in setting it up as a "democratic defense management" curriculum.[28]

Local government programs are the focus of a number of AID initiatives. An official AID document stressed the reasons for this focus: "Decentralization shifts responsibility for decision-making to the leadership and the citizens most directly affected. Fiscal decentralization helps improve local finances, enabling local officials to better provide for their constituencies. Improvements in service delivery build public confidence in democratic processes. Accordingly, they reinforce citizen participation."[29] Among the programs cited were aid to a fishermen's association in the Philippines seeking to ban commercial trawlers from local waters, the creation of a national mayors's association in Bulgaria, and a petition drive in Mozambique to help small farmers get titles to their lands.

Another main need has been for *anti-corruption initiatives*. It is hard enough to convince a long-suffering people that the benefits of democratization will take time, that they must hang in there and make individual sacrifices for the collective good. But if those who govern and their friends and associates are enriching themselves, the disillusionment and anger among the people are not hard to understand. In Russia, for example, corruption has been so endemic that economic privatization was dubbed *prikhvatizatsiya* (literally, "grabification"). There are few things that can more quickly and widely delegitimize a new government than corruption. One NGO called Transparency International was formed for the express purpose of fighting corruption. Each year it issues a list ranking countries by their levels of corruption.

In this regard and in many others, the accountability provided by a *free press* is crucial. Yet this also tends to be an area in which democratizing countries have limited experience and are in need of outside assistance. The

Vienna-based International Press Institute (IPI) has played an important role in this. With membership of about 2,000 leading editors, publishers, broadcasting executives, and journalists in more than eighty countries, IPI runs training programs and conferences for journalists from ex-communist and other newly democratizing countries. It also publishes a monthly magazine and an annual report monitoring press freedom.[30] Journalists also need protection against repression and assassinations targeted against them. In 1996, according to the New York–based Committee to Protect Journalists, 27 journalists were killed and a record-setting 185 in 24 different countries were jailed. Turkey was the worst offender, followed by Ethiopia, China, Kuwait, Nigeria, and Burma.

Strengthening the Rule of Law

The "rule of law" means that citizens are protected by a strong constitution and other legal guarantees against both arbitrary acts by the state and lawless acts by other citizens. A wide range of programs and initiatives are needed in this regard. They include assistance in the very drafting of a constitution, as well as in writing other legal codes. Courts may lack the most basic infrastructures of trained judicial reporters, computers for compiling jury lists, "bench books" for how to conduct jury trials, and the like. Law schools often need to have their curriculums overhauled. Police forces need to be trained. Special initiatives may be needed to help women, minorities, and the disadvantaged. Broad education programs on the very principle of the rule of law as the basis for justice need to be undertaken.

The American Bar Association's Central and East European Law Initiative (CEELI) is a good example. The ABA is the principal association of lawyers in the United States. Through CEELI it has been seeking to provide legal expertise to countries emerging from communism on constitutional law, judicial restructuring, criminal law, commercial law, environmental law, gender-related issues, and other legal areas. CEELI also has created partnerships linking law schools in the region with American law schools. The box on p. 391 lists some of the CEELI programs in Russia as illustrations. Note how these cover quite a range of topics, including how trials by jury are supposed to work, advocacy training for defense lawyers, a resource manual for commercial law, consumer rights protection, legal ethics, sexual harassment, domestic violence, criminal legal procedures such as pre-trial detention and plea bargaining, natural resource management, and bankruptcy law.

CEELI PROGRAMS IN RUSSIA

Legal profession reform and continuing legal education
1993: Workshop for lawyers of the Moscow Regional Collegium of Advocates to publicize and discuss Russia's new jury trial legislation
1995: Jury trial workshops for defense attorneys, including interactive training techniques and videotaping and critiquing of each attorney's performance
1997: Launch of program for commercial-law training
1997: Grants for programs on consumer-rights protection

Legal education
1993: Established law faculty training program to bring law professors to U.S.
1996: Established legal specialist program to assist Russian law schools in developing clinical, legal writing, and other innovative programs

Women's legal issues
1995: Workshop on sexual harassment, domestic violence, and women's rights law.
1997: Assistance for parliamentary hearing on "International Cooperation on the Trafficking in Women and Children"
1998: Grants for pro bono representation of women who are victims of sexual violence

Judicial reform
1993: Provided computers and other equipment for compiling jury lists and organizing trials to courts in nine regions in which jury trials were being started
1997: Workshop on judicial independence

Criminal law reform
1996: Workshops on such topics as pre-trial detention, plea bargaining, search and seizure, discovery, and investigating and prosecuting organized crime.

Source: Web site of the American Bar Association, http://www.abanet.org/ceeli, accessed on November 15, 1998.

Another challenge is reckoning with the past, or what is often called *transitional justice*.[31] Many newly democratizing societies are emerging from pasts that can only be characterized as horrific: El Salvador, with its decade of civil war, right-wing "death squads," and guerrilla violence; Cambodia, where the Khmer Rouge left hundreds of thousands dead in the "killing fields"; South Africa, with generations of discrimination, oppression, and killings under the apartheid system; Chile and Argentina, now freed from the torture, arbitrary arrests, and *desaparecidos* (the disappeared ones) under military dictatorships; Hungary, where property-rights claims must be adjudicated against confiscations not only made in the communist era but going back to the Nazi occupation.

The transitional-justice dilemma pulls between retribution and moving on. Many countries have granted amnesties for past political crimes as part of a reconciliation process. In South Africa the government of Nelson Mandela set up a process stressing amnesty in return for truth about the past. The South African "truth commission" heard startling and disturbing revelations from former high-level government officials admitting their roles in assassinations, attacks on unarmed protestors, and other heinous acts. Truth was being revealed, and overall it seemed that in the South African case it was contributing to national healing. In Guatemala, however, where the 1996 Law of National Reconciliation ending more than thirty years of civil war included a sweeping amnesty, some critics derided it as a "piñata of forgiving, of forgetting the human toll of the war they share responsibility for inciting."[32] And the human toll continued—in April 1998 a Roman Catholic bishop was bludgeoned to death in Guatemala City two days after having issued a scathing report on human rights abuses by the army, the government, and paramilitary units.

An interesting and precedent-challenging case arose in 1998–99 over charges of human rights violations by former Chilean dictator General Augusto Pinochet. Pinochet's rule, which lasted from 1973 to 1990, was notorious for brutal human rights violations. Part of the transitional justice agreement made in 1990 when democratic rule was restored in Chile was amnesty for Pinochet; in fact, he was made a senator for life. But it wasn't only Chileans who were killed, tortured, and abducted under Pinochet; some foreigners were as well. When Pinochet traveled to London in October 1998 for medical attention at a British hospital, a judge in Spain invoked international law to demand that he be extradited to Spain to face trial for the killing of Spanish citizens then residing in Chile.

The issue posed by this case was whether a violator of human rights like Pinochet could be tried by the courts of a country other than his own and on grounds inconsistent with the laws of his own country, based on charges of harm done to the other country's citizens. This situation made his case very different from cases involving the International Criminal Court or other international courts. Chilean government officials argued that others should not interfere, that this was their business, part of their effort "to re-establish peace in a country where friends and former enemies can coexist." Samuel Pisar, a distinguished French international lawyer and himself a survivor of the Nazi death camps, hailed Pinochet's arrest as manifesting the "almost universal clamor today that those who commit crimes against humanity must be pursued to the ends of the world, wherever and whenever they can be found, and brought to justice."[33] The British courts ended up ruling that the case could be brought, that there was a new legal reality called "universal jurisdiction" that in certain cases gave international treaties precedence over claims based on national sovereignty and the "sovereign immunity" of heads of state.

The Pinochet case presented a dilemma for the Clinton administration. It was pressured by the current Chilean government, a democratic one based on the post-Pinochet constitution and electoral system, not to support Spain and leave this as an internal Chilean matter. It also was pressured by human rights groups to support extradition, both to set an international precedent that could be applied to other dictators and as partial contrition for the support the Nixon administration gave to the original 1973 coup.

It will take time to realize the full significance of the Pinochet case, for U.S. foreign policy and for international relations generally. There is no doubt that it will have important precedents for human rights, and the related question of how far the balance may tip between universality and sovereignty (an issue we also discussed in Chapter 7).

Protecting Human Rights

At the Source on p. 394 lists the major internationally recognized human rights as delineated in one or more of three principal documents signed under the auspices of the United Nations: the 1948 Universal Declaration of Human Rights; the 1966 International Covenant on Economic, Social, and Cultural Rights; and the 1966 International Covenant on Civil and Political Rights.

There are a number of means by which the United States tries to use its leverage in bilateral relations with governments that violate human rights: these include diplomatic démarches, public denunciations, economic sanctions, and other political measures. The United States also is the only country

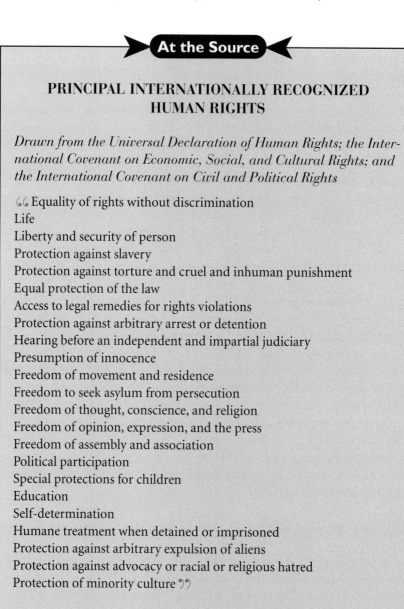

> ▶ **At the Source** ◀
>
> # PRINCIPAL INTERNATIONALLY RECOGNIZED HUMAN RIGHTS
>
> *Drawn from the Universal Declaration of Human Rights; the International Covenant on Economic, Social, and Cultural Rights; and the International Covenant on Civil and Political Rights*
>
> 66 Equality of rights without discrimination
> Life
> Liberty and security of person
> Protection against slavery
> Protection against torture and cruel and inhuman punishment
> Equal protection of the law
> Access to legal remedies for rights violations
> Protection against arbitrary arrest or detention
> Hearing before an independent and impartial judiciary
> Presumption of innocence
> Freedom of movement and residence
> Freedom to seek asylum from persecution
> Freedom of thought, conscience, and religion
> Freedom of opinion, expression, and the press
> Freedom of assembly and association
> Political participation
> Special protections for children
> Education
> Self-determination
> Humane treatment when detained or imprisoned
> Protection against arbitrary expulsion of aliens
> Protection against advocacy or racial or religious hatred
> Protection of minority culture 99
>
> Source: Jack Donnelly, "State Sovereignty and International Intervention: The Case of Human Rights," in Gene M. Lyons and Michael Mastanduno, eds, *Beyond Westphalia? State Sovereignty and International Intervention* (Baltimore: Johns Hopkins University Press, 1995), 117.

to issue its own country-by-country human rights reports. The practice was started in the late 1970s during the Carter administration and is now required by a law passed by Congress. Among the countries that came in for the most criticism in recent reports were the following:

China: "All public dissent against the party and government was effectively silenced by intimidation, exile, the imposition of prison terms, administrative detention or house arrest."

Nigeria: "Security forces committed extrajudicial killings, tortured and beat suspects and detainees; prison conditions remained life-threatening; and security officials continued to harass human rights and democracy activists."

Russia: "While the President and the Government have supported human rights and democratic practice in their statements and policy initiatives, they have not institutionalized the rule of law required to protect them. . . . There were no confirmed killings by agents of the Government. However, an undetermined number, up to several thousand, detainees and prison inmates died after beatings by security officials or due to harsh conditions in detention."

Haiti: "In practice the judiciary is weak and corrupt. . . . Arbitrary arrests, the clogged judicial dockets, lengthy pretrial detention, poor prison conditions, illegal searches and vigilante activity—including killings—also contributed to widespread human rights violations."

Saudi Arabia: "The government commits and tolerates serious human rights abuses. There is no mechanism for citizens to change their government, and citizens do not have this right."

Cuba: "Remains a totalitarian anachronism, where human rights deteriorated . . . and suppression of dissent worsened."[34]

"Human rights are and will remain a key element in our foreign policy," Secretary of State Madeleine Albright proclaimed during her first month in office. "That commitment matters to me, for I am a beneficiary of it," she added, with reference to her own childhood experiences as a Czech exile first from the Nazis and then the communists.[35] However, the Clinton human rights record has been inconsistent. In a number of cases the State Department human rights reports have been tough, but the policy has not been. This failure to follow through arguably is worse than if the report had never been issued, or at least not trumpeted. "How useful is a well done report if it has little or no impact on U.S. policy?" the Washington director of Human Rights Watch Asia asked, with China particularly in mind.[36]

Another example of inconsistency is in U.S. relations with Turkey, where power considerations have superceded principles. Turkey is a member of NATO, has been an important U.S. ally against Iraq, and has great geopolitical value to U.S. strategic interests, given its location at the crossroads of Eurasia and the Middle East. But about 20 percent of its population is Kurdish, and since about 1984 Kurdish separatists have been fighting a civil war with the Turkish government. On the one hand the PKK, or Kurdish Workers' Party, is Marxist and itself has been brutal and antidemocratic in attacks on its own Kurdish opponents as well as on Turkish government officials. But the State Department human rights report stated that "despite some reform and the government's stated commitment to respect human rights, serious human rights abuses continued. . . . The country's human rights record is inadequate and needs to be brought in line."[37] Turkish violations include instances in which American weapons, including F-16 fighter aircraft ostensibly provided as defense against Iraq and other external enemies, were used in attacks on the Kurds.

The United Nations has numerous entities that deal with human rights, some of which are listed in the box on p. 382. The U.N. Commission on Human Rights, which drafted the Universal Declaration of Human Rights and other human rights covenants, is the main U.N. forum in which human rights issues are raised. Its Subcommission on the Prevention of Discrimination and the Protection of Minorities makes recommendations on and conducts investigations of issues dealing with the prevention of discrimination and the protection of ethnic, racial, and linguistic minorities. The UNHCR is responsible for protecting refugees fleeing persecution, conflict, and widespread human rights violations, and promoting just resolution of refugee crises.

The U.N. also convenes special conferences, as with the 1993 World Conference on Human Rights in Vienna, attended by 171 states. The declaration agreed to at this conference stated that "human rights and fundamental freedoms are the birthright of all human beings; their protection and promotion is the first responsibility of governments."[38] Two years later the U.N. World Conference on Women was held in Beijing, focusing particularly on women's rights. This conference's "platform for action" advocated changing laws and practices that discriminate against or oppress women.

In addition, since 1946 the standing International Court of Justice (ICJ) located in The Hague has been the principal judicial organ of the U.N. Although the ICJ is an important institution, the limits of its power mirror some of the limits on the U.N. generally with regard to human rights. Back in April 1993, when the Bosnian war was still raging, the ICJ ruled that Serbia should stop its ethnic cleansing. A few months later, though, on an appeal from Serbia, the ICJ had to acknowledge that the means of enforcing its ruling were beyond the scope of its jurisdiction. This was indicative of the normative tension in the U.N.'s authority between universality and sovereignty, as discussed in Chapter 7, and a problem that has carried over with the newly established International Criminal Court (ICC).

NGOs such as Amnesty International and Human Rights Watch play such an important role in human rights advocacy that they are often referred to as the "conscience" of governments. Unbound by tradeoffs with other foreign policy objectives and less inhibited by the formalities of traditional diplomacy, human rights NGOs can be more vocal and assertive than governments or multilateral organizations. Their impact often is quite substantial both in terms of influencing official policy and initiating their own direct efforts. Indeed Amnesty International won the Nobel Peace Prize in 1977. Since then, with the Internet and faxes and other advanced communications making it both more difficult for repressive governments to hide their human rights violations and easier for advocacy groups to communicate with their own global networks of activists, the NGO role in human rights advocacy has grown even more significant.

Cultivating Civil Society

A strong civic society is one that has lots of what Harvard scholar Robert Putnam calls "social capital"—a public-spiritedness and community involvement that goes beyond just voting. It entails other forms of civic engagement, a sense of "reciprocity and cooperation," and a shared ethic among citizens of being "helpful, respectful and trustful towards one another, even when they differ on matters of substance."[39] The statement of goals by Dialog, a community outreach NGO in Poland, well captures what is meant by civic society: "to encourage citizens to respond actively to problems that concern them; and, through such responses, to build—or rebuild—a civil society. A society in which ordinary citizens trust each other, organize voluntarily to achieve common ends, expect local government to respond to their needs, and participate generally in the public life of the community."[40]

In many newly democratizing societies decades of dictatorship and even longer historical traditions of authoritarianism have left little base on which to build such practices and values. Particularly in states so recently torn by ethnic cleansing, genocide, and other bitter and violent societal rending, conceptions of trust and common goals can seem altogether alien. Yet it is in these very cases that cultivation of the values and practices of civil society is all the more essential, for as the British political scientist Richard Rose states, "the construction of trustworthy political institutions is more likely to happen from the bottom up than the top down."[41] Elections won't work, political institutions won't be stable, and the rule of law won't become ensconced unless the basic civic values of nonviolent resolution of political differences, tolerance for societal differences, and commitment to some level of political engagement provide a societal foundation.

Thus while policies geared to helping develop civic society are much less dramatic than election monitoring, much less visible than legislative exchanges, and much less noticeable than human rights advocacy, they are no less essential over the long term. Illustrative programs and policies include the National Endowment for Democracy's funding for a new high school civics curriculum in Russia, training of newly elected village committee members on effective local governance in China, civic and voter education initiatives by youth NGOs in Slovakia, public-advocacy training and assistance for a local association of small farmers seeking formal titles to their land in Mozambique, and training community leaders to become conflict mediators in Colombia.

Two points need to be made in summary. First is that while our focus has been on U.S. and other international policies and strategies, ultimately the key to successful democratization and well-protected human rights lies with *the leaders and peoples themselves.* The example of Nelson Mandela in South Africa shines above all. Here was a man who was held as a political prisoner for 27 years but who did not do unto his old enemies as they had done to him. As president, Mandela displayed extraordinary statesmanship and ruled in a spirit of reconciliation, not retribution. No wonder Mandela won the Nobel Peace Prize, along with F. W. de Klerk, the last white president of South Africa, who led the move to bring apartheid down from within. Other cases are less historically dramatic but also involve leaders and groups opting for peaceful and democratic transitions over their own narrow self-interests. When the opposite choice is made, though, the effects are devastating. One of the main paths to ethnic conflict in recent years has been when leaders foment political violence, when they play to and play up the historical roots of hatreds, and seek to mobilize groups around these divisions rather than seek reconciliation.

Another important characteristic of leaders is their ability to make the often difficult transition from leader of a revolutionary movement to leader of a government. Revolutionary leaders need to inspire their people, lead them to the barricades with bold rhetoric and defiance, project a persona larger than life, and often keep political power highly concentrated in their own hands and a small inner circle. But governing requires creating nascent political institutions, delivering services, building an economy, accepting accountability, and opening up processes for greater access and representation. The differences between the skills and dispositions required by these two roles are one of the reasons why great revolutionary leaders often are less successful when it comes to governing. This has been an issue for Yasir Arafat and the Palestine Liberation Organization as the Israeli occupation of Gaza and the West Bank comes to an end: they are having to make the transition from revolutionaries and terrorists to government officials and political leaders in responding to the day-to-day problems of the Palestinian people. The same issue also has been raised about Boris Yeltsin, whose defiant leadership on top of the tanks facing down the August 1991 military coup was crucial, but who has shown substantial limitations as president.

The second point concerns U.S. policy and the budget and other resources that need to be put into democracy promotion and human rights protection if they are to stand any chance of succeeding. The AID budget for democracy promotion is less than $1 billion. Adding in the State Department's democracy-promotion budget, appropriations to the National Endowment for Democracy, and other democracy and human rights–related budget items, the figure still is less than $2 billion. U.S. expenditures on military aid are more than five times greater than this. The U.S. defense budget is more than one hundred times greater than the amounts spent on democracy and human rights. Effective policies are not just about spending money, of course. But given how much there is to be done and in how many different countries American foreign policy interests are at stake, the chances of success for any of the strategies we have discussed are diminished if adequate budgets and other resources are not provided.

The U.S. domestic politics of democratization and human rights has two aspects. In terms of public opinion, there is little pressure generally for major increases in spending or extensive involvements. One survey showed that only 29 percent of the American public believed that promoting democratization should be a "very important" goal for U.S. foreign policy.[42] Such views can change, though, when there is a major democratization crisis or a high-profile human rights violation. Even when that is not the case, this is another area in which NGOs play a substantial and increasing role, both in bringing pressure to bear in Washington and through direct international activism.

Principles and Power: Significance and Sources of Soft Power

Principles as Power: Soft Power's Significance

The term "soft power" captures how American principles encompass more than just idealism and altruism. *Soft power,* as defined by Professor Joseph Nye, is based less on coercion and traditional measures of power than on intangible assets such as cultural attraction, political values, and societal strengths that others admire.[43] This is not a strictly new phenomenon; historically the United States and other major powers always have tried to use their reputations and ideologies as sources of power. But it is more important in the post–Cold War world, when power has become "less fungible, less coercive and less tangible."[44] It is part of how "right" can make for "might," how principles can be a source of power.

In 1990, on becoming the president of postcommunist Czechoslovakia, Vaclav Havel quoted Thomas Jefferson as the inspiration for the ideals for which he stood, indeed for which he had gone to jail as a political prisoner during the communist years. American power certainly played a role in bringing down the Soviet empire, and the pursuit of greater prosperity and the attractiveness of capitalism over communism also were important factors. Yet here was the leader of the Czechoslovak "Velvet Revolution," a name reflecting the peacefulness with which its country's communism was brought down, stressing not these material factors but the principles for which the United States stood as the basis for his greatest gratitude.

Yet it was just a year earlier that Chinese students protesting for greater democracy built a replica of the Statue of Liberty in Tiananmen Square. This was quite extraordinary for a number of reasons, including that China is a country that tends to look within its own culture and history for models. It was this very sense of respect and admiration for American principles that made it all the more consequential when, in the wake of the Tiananmen Square massacre and mass arrests, the United States put priority on geopolitical (power) and economic (prosperity) considerations in its relations with the Chinese government. In not standing by the Chinese students, the United States was seen by many as not standing up for its own principles.

The crucial policy choice from a soft-power perspective is not so much whether the United States still can claim to be truer to democratic values than other major powers, but whether it lives up to the standards to which it lays claim for itself. It is one thing to pursue a power politics foreign policy if the state doing so makes limited claims to standing for some set of values greater than self-interest. But if such claims are made, then it is more problematic. This was part of the problem in the Cold War era with the "ABC" (anything but communism) rationale for U.S. support to a number of Third World countries that were pro-West but hardly democratic (e.g., Vietnam, Central America, Iran). Nor is China the only post–Cold War issue on which such concerns have arisen. Russia and Turkey also have been discussed in this chapter; others could be added based on the 1990s record, and others no doubt will be in the decade ahead. The soft-power concept provides important perspective for understanding this issue not just as Democratic Idealism but also in terms of how power may be less well served than often is claimed. The issue is not about purity, but about contradiction.

Domestic Policy as Foreign Policy: Sources of Soft Power

In 1957, when the segregationist governor of Arkansas was blocking integration of the public schools, one of the reasons President Eisenhower sent in the National Guard was concern about how the U.S. record of segregation would undermine the mantle of principles in foreign policy. It was harder to sustain the claim to stand for freedom in foreign policy if it was not being lived up to in the United States' own domestic policy.

The Realist scholar Hans Morgenthau emphasized this point. The Cold War struggle ultimately will not be determined by military strength or diplomatic maneuvering, he wrote in 1967 with particular reference to Vietnam, but "by the visible virtues and vices of their [the U.S. and Soviet] respective political, economic and social systems. . . . It is at this point that foreign policy and domestic politics merge. . . . The United States ought to again concentrate its efforts upon creating a society at home which can again serve as a model for other nations to emulate."[45]

Earlier we discussed "the Asian way" and some of the flaws in its arguments for more limited conceptions of democracy as better fits for Asia. However, these flaws notwithstanding, Asian way advocates make some provocative points about American domestic society. "In most Asian eyes," Kishore Mahbubani of Singapore writes, "the evidence of real social decay in the United States is clear and palpable": a 560 percent increase in violent crime since 1960, and a total of 10,567 people killed by handguns in just one year (1990) compared to just 87 in Japan; increases since 1960 of greater than

400 percent in out-of-wedlock births, and more than 200 percent in teenage suicides; a 50 percent increase in hunger since 1985; schools in which the main problems have changed, according to a survey of teachers, from rather innocuous acts such as talking out of turn, chewing gum in class, and making noise to assault, robbery, rape, drug abuse, alcohol abuse, and pregnancy.[46]

Blame is aimed at both liberals and conservatives—liberals for being too permissive and relativistic and not giving due weight to discipline, tradition, and authority; conservatives for giving individual rights and freedom too blanket a priority over social cohesion and the public good. The American media and the absolutist value given to freedom of the press also are said to be part of the problem. The American media are depicted as having become overly aggressive, too muckraking, and too sensationalist, and emanating a self-righteous self-image that leads them "to undermine public confidence in virtually every public institution, while leaving their own powers neither checked nor balanced by any countervailing institution." Overall, and quite provocatively, the question is posed as to whether "in working so hard to increase the scope of individual freedom within their society, Americans have progressively cut down the thick web of human relations and obligations that have produced social harmony in traditional societies. . . . Is there *too much freedom* in American society?"[emphasis added][47]

One doesn't have to accept the defense of the Asian model to acknowledge some validity in the critique of the state of democracy in the United States. Nor are Asians the only ones to question the American model. To be sure, some of the critiques involve little more than ideological America-bashing. But some of the points raised also are made by critics within the United States. For a nation that allows its social problems to mount—its educational system to decline, its once-great cities to decay, its crime rate to shoot up, its race relations to fester—risks having its claim to moral leadership increasingly questioned around the world.

Summary

Will the twenty-first century be a democratic one? This is the question with which we began this chapter. The reasons why the answer still is uncertain should now be clear.

The falls of communism, apartheid, military dictatorships, and other forms of repression during the 1990s constituted historic progress in the spread of democracy and human rights around the world. Yet there were limits and setbacks to this progress, especially in regions like Africa and the Middle East, and a long list of human rights violations in all too many countries. The long-term trend depends on whether the political, social, economic, and other challenges to democratic consolidation and institutionalization are met.

This trend is of importance to the United States for a number of reasons. Democracy and individual freedom are the essence of the principles to which American foreign policy has long laid claim. They also further the U.S. interest in peace. The relationship posited by the democratic peace theory is a strong one, albeit not as simple or unequivocal as often portrayed.

Policies for promoting democracy and protecting human rights thus require serious and extensive attention. Key roles are played by a number of other international actors and by NGOs, but as partners with and complements to, not substitutes for, the United States. These policy strategies are varied; all require ongoing commitments. They pose a number of difficult policy choices, for devising effective strategies and for providing sufficient funding and other resources. They also pose many situations in which tradeoffs have to be made with other major U.S. foreign policy goals. This has come up repeatedly in our discussion, in this chapter and throughout the book, with power-principles, peace-principles, and prosperity-principles dilemmas. Yet the complementarities are more frequent and more significant than often recognized. This is one of the points of the democratic peace theory. It also is fundamental to the concept of soft power and other analyses that stress the normative and behavioral bases of American power.

The ancient Athenians, often credited with one of the earliest democracies, chose as their patron the goddess Athena. Athena herself was said to have sprung forth from the head of Zeus, the god of gods. Democracy, however, cannot just spring forth. It must be built, painstakingly, continuously, by those who want it for their own political systems and by those whose foreign policy is served by its global spread.

Notes

[1] Francis Fukuyama, "The End of History?" *The National Interest* 16 (Summer 1989), 3–4.

[2] Bill Clinton, "State of the Union Address," *New York Times,* January 26, 1994, A17.

[3] Samuel P. Huntington, "No Exit—The Errors of Endism," *The National Interest* 17 (Fall 1989), 10.

[4] Samuel P. Huntington, "The Clash of Civilizations?" *Foreign Affairs* 72:3 (Summer 1993), 22.

[5] Robert D. Kaplan, "The Coming Anarchy?" *Atlantic Monthly* 273 (February 1994), 44–46; Chester A. Crocker and Fen Osler Hampson with Pamela Aall, eds., *Managing Global Chaos:*

Sources of and Responses to International Conflict (Washington, D.C.: U.S. Institute of Peace Press, 1996); I. William Zartman, ed., *Collapsed States: The Disintegration and Restoration of Legitimate Authority* (Boulder, Colo.: Westview, 1995).

[6]Gabriel Escobar, "A Nod to Civilian Ascendancy," *Washington Post,* October 14, 1996, A23.

[7]See, for example, Donald Rothchild, *Managing Ethnic Conflict in Africa: Pressures and Incentives for Cooperation* (Washington, D.C.: Brookings Institution Press, 1997); David R. Smock, ed., *Making War and Waging Peace: Foreign Intervention in Africa* (Washington, D.C.: U.S. Institute of Peace Press, 1993).

[8]Huntington, "The Clash of Civilizations?" 40.

[9]On Arab democratization more generally, see John L. Esposito and John O. Voll, *Islam and Democracy* (New York: Oxford University Press, 1996); Yehudah Mirsky and Matt Ahrens, eds., *Democracy in the Middle East: Defining the Challenge* (Washington, D.C.: Washington Institute for Near East Policy, 1993); Saad Eddin Ibrahim, "The Troubled Triangle: Populism, Islam and Civil Society in the Arab World," *International Political Science Review,* 19 (October 1998), pp. 357–72; Augustus Richard Norton and Farhad Kazemi, eds., *Civil Society in the Middle East* (Leiden: Brill, 1994–95).

[10]Martin Kramer, "Where Islam and Democracy Part Ways," in Mirsky and Ahrens, eds., *Democracy in the Middle East,* 32, 34.

[11]Sergei Kovalev, "The Case against Yeltsin," letter of resignation as Chairman of the Russian Human Rights Commission, excerpted in *Washington Post,* January 29, 1996, A19.

[12]Thomas Carothers, "Democracy without Illusion," *Foreign Affairs* 76:1 (January/February 1997), 89.

[13]Kishore Mahbubani, "The United States: 'Go East, Young Man,'" *Washington Quarterly* 17:2 (Spring 1994), 5–23.

[14]Jack S. Levy, "Domestic Politics and War," in *The Origin and Prevention of Major Wars,* ed. Robert I. Rotberg and Theodore K. Rabb (Cambridge, U.K.: Cambridge University Press, 1989), p. 88.

[15]See, for example, Bruce Russett, *Grasping the Democratic Peace* (Princeton: Princeton University Press, 1993); John Owen, "How Liberalism Produces Democratic Peace," *International Security* 19:2 (Fall 1994), 87–125; Melvin Small and J. David Singer, "The War Proneness of Democratic Regimes," *Jerusalem Journal of International Relations* 1 (Summer 1976), 50—69.

[16]Immanuel Kant, "Perpetual Peace," cited in Michael W. Doyle, "Kant, Liberal Legacies, and Foreign Affairs," in *Debating the Democratic Peace,* ed. Michael E. Brown et al. (Cambridge, Mass.: MIT Press, 1997), 24–25.

[17]Doyle, "Kant, Liberal Legacies, and Foreign Affairs," 49.

[18]Owen, "How Liberalism Produces Democratic Peace," 96.

[19]Cited in Bruce W. Jentleson, "The Political Basis for Trade in U.S.-Soviet Relations," *Millennium: Journal of International Studies* 15 (Spring 1986), 27.

[20]"A National Security Strategy of Engagement and Enlargement," reprinted in *America's Strategic Choices,* ed. Michael E. Brown et al. (Cambridge, Mass.: MIT Press, 1997), 319.

[21]David E. Spiro, "The Insignificance of the Liberal Peace," *International Security* 19:2 (Fall 1994) 50–86.

[22]Henry S. Farber and Joanne Gowa, "Politics and Peace," *International Security* 20:2 (Fall 1995), 123–46; Christopher Layne, "Kant or Cant: The Myth of the Democratic Peace," *International Security* 19:2 (Fall 1994) 5–49.

[23]Edward D. Mansfield and Jack Snyder, "Democratization and the Danger of War," *International Security* 20:1 (Summer 1995), 7.

[24]Bruce W. Jentleson, "Discrepant Responses to Falling Dictators: Presidential Belief Systems and the Mediating Effects of the Senior Advisory Process," *Political Psychology* 11 (June 1990), 377–80.

[25]U.S. Agency for International Development (AID), *Agency Performance Report 1997,* available at http://www.info.usaid.gov/democracy/, accessed September 29, 1998, 37–39.

[26]Larry Diamond, *Promoting Democracy in the 1990s: Actors and Instruments, Issues and Imperatives* (Washington, D.C.: Carnegie Commission for Preventing Deadly Conflict, 1995), 40–48.

[27]Diamond, "Promoting Democracy in the 1990s," 41.

[28]William J. Perry, "Defense in an Age of Hope," *Foreign Affairs* 79:6 (November/December 1996), 69–70.

[29]AID, *Agency Performance Report 1997,* 42.

[30]Adam Feinstein, "Fighting for Press Freedom," *Journal of Democracy* 6 (January 1995), 159–68.

[31]Neil J. Kritz, ed., *Transitional Justice: How Emerging Democracies Reckon with Former Regimes* (Washington, D.C.: U.S. Institute of Peace Press, 1995).

[32]Francisco Goldman, "In Guatemala, All Is Forgotten," *New York Times,* December 23, 1996, A13.

[33]Genaro Arriagada, "Beyond Justice," *Washington Post,* October 25, 1998, C7; Charles Trueheart, "Pinochet Case Signifies Cries for Retribution," *Washington Post,* October 25, 1998, A21.

[34]U.S. Department of State, *Country Reports on Human Rights Practices for 1997,* available at http://www.state.gov/www/global/human_rights/1997_hrp_report/, accessed November 14, 1998.

[35]Norman Kempster, "Albright Promises to Make Human Rights a Priority," *Los Angeles Times,* January 31, 1997, A6; Thomas Lippman, "State Dept. Human Rights Report Chastises Several U.S. Allies," *Washington Post,* January 31, 1997, A16.

[36]Lippman, "State Dept. Human Rights Report Chastises Several U.S. Allies."

[37]U.S. Department of State, *Country Reports on Human Rights Practices for 1997,* report on Turkey.

[38]United Nations, World Conference on Human Rights, June 14–25, 1993, *Report,* A/CONF.157/24 (Part I).

[39]Robert D. Putnam, *Making Democracy Work: Civic Traditions in Modern Italy* (Princeton: Princeton University Press, 1993), 176. This section draws on an outstanding paper written by Sarah Schroeder, one of my students in Fall 1996, "How Should the United States Support Democracy Consolidation in Haiti? The Relationship between Civil Society and Political Institutions."

[40]Cited in Diamond, *Promoting Democracy in the 1990s,* 56–57.

[41]Richard Rose, "Rethinking Civil Society: Postcommunism and the Problem of Trust," *Journal of Democracy* 5 (July 1994), 29.

[42]John E. Rielly, ed., *American Public Opinion and U.S. Foreign Policy 1999* (Chicago: Chicago Council on Foreign Relations, 1999), 16.

[43]Joseph S. Nye, Jr., *Bound to Lead: The Changing Nature of American Power* (New York: Basic Books, 1990).

[44]Nye, *Bound to Lead,* 188.

[45]Hans J. Morgenthau, cited in Michael J. Smith, "Ethics and Intervention," *Ethics and International Affairs* 1989 (no. 3), 8.

[46]Mahbubani, "Go East, Young Man," 6 and *passim.*

[47]Mahbubani, "Go East, Young Man," 7, 9.

Index